Economic Sanctions Reconsidered

Second Edition

To George P. Shultz
Retired controller of "light switch diplomacy"

This second edition of *Economic Sanctions Reconsidered* is published in two volumes. This volume, *Economic Sanctions Reconsidered: History and Current Policy*, describes the methodology, principal findings, and policy conclusions of the study and presents 11 recent and important cases. The companion volume, *Economic Sanctions Reconsidered: Supplemental Case Histories*, contains 105 additional case studies of economic sanctions episodes.

Gary Clyde Hufbauer, Jeffrey J. Schott, and Kimberly Ann Elliott

Economic Sanctions Reconsidered

HISTORY AND CURRENT POLICY

Second Edition

Institute for International Economics
Washington, DC   1990

Gary Clyde Hufbauer is a Visiting Fellow at the Institute for International Economics and Marcus Wallenberg Professor of International Financial Diplomacy at Georgetown University. He was formerly Deputy Director of the International Law Institute at Georgetown University, Deputy Assistant Secretary for International Trade and Investment Policy of the US Treasury, and Director of the International Tax Staff at the Treasury. He has authored and edited numerous studies on international trade, investment, and tax issues, including *Europe 1992: An American Perspective, Trade Protection in the United States: 31 Case Studies, Trade Policy for Troubled Industries,* and *Subsidies in International Trade.*

Jeffrey J. Schott is a Research Fellow at the Institute for International Economics. He was formerly a Senior Associate at the Carnegie Endowment for International Peace and an International Economist at the US Treasury. His published works include *Completing the Uruguay Round: A Results-Oriented Approach to the GATT Trade Negotiations, Free Trade Areas and U.S. Trade Policy, The Canada–United States Free Trade Agreement: The Global Impact,* and *Auction Quotas and United States Trade Policy.*

Kimberly Ann Elliott is a Research Associate at the Institute for International Economics. She is the coauthor of *Trade Protection in the United States: 31 Case Studies* and *Auction Quotas and United States Trade Policy.*

INSTITUTE FOR INTERNATIONAL ECONOMICS
11 Dupont Circle, NW
Washington, DC 20036
(202) 328-9000   Telex: 261271 IIE UR   FAX: (202) 328-5432

C. Fred Bergsten, *Director*
Linda Griffin Kean, *Director of Publications*

The Institute for International Economics was created by, and receives substantial support from, the German Marshall Fund of the United States.

The views expressed in this publication are those of the authors. This publication is part of the overall program of the Institute, as endorsed by its Board of Directors, but does not necessarily reflect the views of individual members of the Board or the Advisory Committee.

Printed in the United States of America 92 91 90 5 4 3 2 1

Library of Congress Cataloging in Publication Data
Hufbauer, Gary Clyde.
    Economic sanctions reconsidered / Gary Clyde Hufbauer, Jeffrey J. Schott, Kimberly Ann Elliott.
    "November 1990."
    Economic Sanctions Reconsidered: History and Current Policy issued also separately
    Includes bibliographical references and index.
    Contents: 1. History and current policy – 2. Supplemental case histories.
    ISBN 0-881132-105-2
    1. Economic sanctions.   2. Economic sanction—Case studies.
I. Schott, Jeffrey J., 1949–.   II. Elliott, Kimberly Ann, 1960–.
III. Institute for International Economics (U.S.) IV. Title.
HF1413.5.H84b   1990
382′ .3–dc20   90-5390 **CIP**
ISBN paper (this volume): 0-88132-136-2   ISBN cloth (this volume): 0-88132-140-0
ISBN paper (two-volume set): 0-88132-105-2   ISBN cloth (two-volume set): 0-88132-115-X

PREFACE

This book presents a comprehensive analysis of the use of economic sanctions for foreign policy purposes since World War I. It does so by reviewing 116 cases in which sanctions have been employed, mostly by the United States, but by a number of other countries as well. The authors attempt to judge the effects of these efforts by scoring them against a consistent set of criteria. They then draw policy conclusions from the historical record in an effort to inform the debate on whether and how to use sanctions in the future, and indeed whether they might be expected to work in several crucial current cases.

In October 1983, the Institute published a summary of the major analytical conclusions and policy recommendations of the original version of this study, entitled *Economic Sanctions in Pursuit of Foreign Policy Goals*. That presentation, in our POLICY ANALYSES IN INTERNATIONAL ECONOMICS series, briefly summarized much of the technical analysis underlying the findings and the conclusions of the research. In mid-1985 we released the detailed case studies, the complete methodology used, and all of the underlying data. The volume quickly became widely viewed as the definitive work on the subject.

We are now releasing a revised version of the study that appraises the several major cases that have ensued since that time (including Iraq, Panama, and the additional South African sanctions), takes into account critiques of the initial study, and updates the conclusions and policy recommendations in light of the events of the last five years. In particular, the new edition addresses the question of whether sanctions may have "a new lease on life" in light of the apparent end of the Cold War. The study and its supporting documentation have now become so large that we are releasing it in two volumes in the hope that this will be more convenient for our readers. The first volume, *Economic Sanctions Reconsidered: History and Current Policy*, contains the analysis and policy recommendations and 11 important recent cases, while the second volume, *Economic Sanctions Reconsidered: Supplemental Case Histories*, contains the other 105 case studies.

The Institute for International Economics is a private nonprofit research institution for the study and discussion of international economic policy. Its purpose is to analyze important issues in that area, and to develop and communicate practical new approaches for dealing with them. The Institute is completely nonpartisan.

The Institute was created by a generous commitment of funds from the German Marshall Fund of the United States in 1981, and now receives about 15 percent of its support from that source. Major institutional grants are also being received from the Ford Foundation, the William and Flora Hewlett Foundation, the Alfred P. Sloan Foundation, and the C. V. Starr Foundation. A number of other foundations and private corporations are contributing to the increasing diversification of the Institute's financial resources. About 15 percent of the Institute's resources in our latest fiscal year came from outside the United States, including about 4 percent from Japan.

The Board of Directors bears overall responsibility for the Institute and gives general guidance and approval to its research program—including identification of topics that are likely to become important to policymakers over the medium run (generally one to three years) and which thus should be addressed by the Institute. The Director, working closely with the staff and outside Advisory Committee, is responsible for the development of particular projects and makes the final decision to publish an individual study.

The Institute hopes that its studies and other activities will contribute to building a stronger foundation for international economic policy around the world. We invite readers to let us know how they think we can best accomplish this objective.

C. FRED BERGSTEN
Director
November 1990

Acknowledgments

The authors are grateful to C. Fred Bergsten for reviewing the entire manuscript and offering numerous insightful comments. We would also like to thank Lee Remick and Joanne van Rooij for assistance in researching the cases, Mike Treadway for his thoughtful editing of the manuscript, Donna Baker for typing it, and Linda Griffin Kean, Sharada Gilkey, Tammy Randolph, and Vilma Gordon for sheparding the volumes through the publication process.

Contents of
Economic Sanctions Reconsidered

HISTORY AND CURRENT POLICY

Tables

Figure

Contents of
Economic Sanctions Reconsidered

SUPPLEMENTAL CASE HISTORIES

Economic Sanctions Reconsidered

Second Edition

1

INTRODUCTION

T
wo controversial actions by the United States in the early 1980s—President Jimmy Carter's grain embargo against the Soviet Union and President Ronald Reagan's attempt to block the Soviet-European gas pipeline project—rekindled a smoldering debate over the use of economic sanctions in pursuit of foreign policy goals. The debate continues to rage today, as policymakers in the United States and elsewhere decide how to respond to the Tiananmen Square massacre in China, the continuation of apartheid in South Africa, and most recently the Iraqi invasion and annexation of Kuwait. Advocates of sanctions regard them as an important weapon in the foreign policy arsenal. Skeptics question whether sanctions are an effective stand-alone instrument of foreign policy and whether the costs to the users of sanctions are worth the benefits derived.

To put these issues in perspective, we have delved into the rich history of the use of sanctions in the twentieth century in order to identify circumstances in which economic sanctions can succeed in attaining foreign policy goals. Our study concentrates on three central questions: What factors—both political and economic—usually result in a positive contribution of sanctions to the achievement of foreign policy goals? What are the costs of sanctions to both target and sender[1] countries, and to what extent do they influence policy

---

[1] We use the term "sender" to denote the country whose foreign policy goals are being pursued at least in part through the threat or imposition of economic sanctions. A synonymous term often found in the literature is "sanctioner."

decisions? And what lessons can be drawn from this experience to guide policymakers on the use of sanctions in the future?

A Case Study Approach

Much has been written about the use of economic sanctions in the conduct of foreign policy, and most of the literature takes the form of studies of individual sanctions episodes. In this study we attempt to extract propositions of general validity from that literature. The starting point for our analysis is the list in table 1.1 (at the end of this chapter) of 116 cases of economic sanctions, from the economic blockade of Germany in World War I through the US–UN embargo of Iraq in 1990. Abstracts of 11 important cases make up the bulk of this volume, while the companion volume, *Economic Sanctions Reconsidered: Supplemental Case Histories,* contains the other 105 cases. The abstracts summarize the key events in each case, the goals of the sender, the response of the target, the actions of third countries, and the economic costs to both target and sender. Each abstract concludes with overall assessments of the episode by scholars of the case and our own summary evaluation.

Because each abstract cites sources for all the data presented, we have minimized source notes in the analytical chapters. A bibliography of general references follows chapter 5. Moreover, because our abstracts summarize each episode, and because detailed narratives can be found in the literature, we deliberately refrain from extensive descriptions of the events of individual episodes in our analysis.

The cases listed in table 1.1 plainly do not include all instances since World War I of economic leverage applied by one sovereign state to try to change the conduct of another. To focus our analysis strictly on the use of sanctions to achieve foreign policy goals, we have taken care both to distinguish economic sanctions from other economic instruments and to separate foreign policy goals from other goals at home and abroad. The boundaries we have set may be described in the following way.

We define economic sanctions to mean the deliberate, government-inspired withdrawal, or threat of withdrawal, of customary trade or financial relations. "Customary" does not mean "contractual"; it simply means levels of trade and financial activity that would probably have occurred in the absence of sanctions. We generally exclude cases in which positive economic incentives (e.g., new aid or credits) are used to achieve foreign policy goals. However, when such incentives are closely paired with economic sanctions in a "carrot-and-stick" approach, they are covered in our abstracts and analysis.

We define foreign policy goals to encompass changes expressly and purportedly sought by the sender state in the political behavior of the target state. We rely on the public statements of officials of the sender country, supplemented by the assessment of historians of the episode, for identification of the foreign policy goals sought in each case.

We exclude from foreign policy goals the normal realm of economic objectives sought in banking, commercial, and tax negotiations between sovereign states. It may seem a violation of this rule that many of our cases deal with attempts to settle expropriation disputes. However, many expropriation episodes harbor political disputes that go beyond the compensation issues, and those are the episodes we seek to include in our analysis.

Sanctions also serve important domestic political purposes in addition to sometimes changing the behavior of foreign states. As David Lloyd George, then a leader of the British political opposition, remarked of the celebrated League of Nations sanctions against Italy in 1935, "They came too late to save Abyssinia, but they are just in the nick of time to save the Government" (Rowland 1975, 723). The same is true today. What president—or Kremlin leader for that matter—has not been obsessed with the need to demonstrate leadership, to take initiatives to shape world affairs, or at least to react forcefully to adverse developments? And what president—or Kremlin leader—is eager to go to war to make his point? The desire to be seen acting forcefully, but not to precipitate bloodshed, can easily overshadow specific foreign policy goals.

Indeed, one suspects that in some cases domestic political goals were the motivating force behind the imposition of sanctions. Such measures often succeed in galvanizing public support for the sender government, either by inflaming patriotic fever (as illustrated by US sanctions against Japan just prior to World War II) or by quenching the public thirst for action (as illustrated by US sanctions against Libyan leader Moammar Gadhafi's adventurism in northern Africa and elsewhere, and later against Manuel Noriega for many months prior to the actual invasion of Panama). It is quite clear that US, European, and British Commonwealth sanctions against South Africa, as well as US, EC, and Japanese sanctions against China in the wake of the Tiananmen Square massacre, were principally designed to assuage domestic constituencies, to make a moral and historical statement, and to send a warning to future offenders of the international order, whatever their immediate effect on the target country.

For a democratic nation these are appropriate goals. However, because of limitations on our resources, we have left to others the arduous task of unearthing the domestic side of the story: Have economic sanctions in fact been effective in satisfying domestic political purposes? Has their use for such purposes been worth the associated political and economic costs, both international and domestic? These are important questions that are worthy of additional research.

In this study we make no attempt to evaluate the merits of the foreign policy goals pursued through the use of sanctions. We do have opinions on those goals, but we doubt that many readers are eager to discover the collective wisdom of Hufbauer, Schott, and Elliott on the merits, for example, of the US government destabilizing the Trujillo regime in the Dominican Republic in 1960–61, or of the Indian government altering Nepal's posture toward China in 1988–89. Similarly, we do not explore the fascinating international legal questions raised by the imposition of sanctions, in particular the definition and proper limitation of extraterritorial measures, whereby one nation attempts to extend its laws to persons and firms overseas. Much literature is devoted to these questions, and we could not usefully contribute to the legal debate (on these issues see, for example, Marcuss and Richard 1981, Rosenthal and Knighton 1982, Moyer and Mabry 1983, Marcuss and Mathias 1984, and especially Carter 1988).

Finally, table 1.1 probably omits many uses of sanctions imposed between powers of the second and third rank. These cases are often not well documented in the English language, and we did not have adequate resources to study source material in foreign languages. Also, we may have overlooked instances in which sanctions were imposed by major powers in comparative secrecy to achieve relatively modest goals. To the extent of these omissions, our generalizations do not adequately reflect the sanctions experience of the twentieth century.[2]

Historical Overview

Economic sanctions entered the diplomatic armory long before World War I. Indeed the technique was used in ancient Greece. The most celebrated occasion was Pericles's Megarian decree, enacted in 432 BC in response to the kidnapping of three Aspasian women. Thucydides accords the decree only minor notice in *The Peloponnesian War*; by contrast, Aristophanes in his comedy *The Acharnians* (lines 530–43), assigns the Megarian decree a major role in triggering the war:

> Then Pericles the Olympian in his wrath
> thundered, lightened, threw Hellas into confusion,
> passed laws that were written like drinking songs
> [decreeing] the Megarians shall not be on our land, in our market, on
> the sea or on the continent. . . .
> Then the Megarians, since they were starving little by little, begged
> the

---

2 Richard James Ellings (1983) has written a Ph.D. thesis in which he lists 107 instances of the use of economic sanctions since World War II. Our table 1.1 contains some cases not in his work; others in his list do not fit our definition of sanctions. In some instances, Ellings has broken down lengthy episodes into two or more cases.

Lacedaemonians to have the decree
arising from the three strumpets withdrawn.
But we were unwilling, though they asked us many times. Then
came the clash of the shields.
Someone will say it was not right. But say, then, what was.
Come, if a Lacedaemonian sailed out in a boat
and denounced and confiscated a Seriphian puppy,
would you have sat still? (quoted in Fornara 1975)

Despite the rich history of sanctions episodes from ancient Greece through the nineteenth century, we start our investigation with World War I both because earlier episodes are less well documented and because lessons from the distant past may seem less relevant to today's problems. However, by way of historical perspective, table 1.2 (at the end of this chapter) lists selected pre–World War I instances of economic sanctions.

Most of these episodes foreshadowed or accompanied warfare. Only after World War I was extensive attention given to the notion that economic sanctions might substitute for armed hostilities as a stand-alone policy. Even through World War II, the objectives sought with the use of sanctions retained a distinctively martial flavor. Sanctions were usually imposed to disrupt military adventures or to complement a broader war effort. Of the 11 cases we have identified in table 1.1 between 1914 and 1940, all but 2 are linked to military action. Four of the cases involved League of Nations attempts, through collective action, to settle disputes. These efforts had varied results: from success in inducing Greece to back down from its incursion into Bulgaria in 1925, to the celebrated failure to persuade Italy to withdraw from Abyssinia in the mid-1930s.

In the period following World War II, other foreign policy motives became increasingly common, but sanctions were still deployed on occasion to force a target country to withdraw its troops from border skirmishes, to abandon plans of territorial acquisition, or to desist from other military adventures. In most instances in the postwar period where economic pressure was brought to bear against the exercise of military power, the United States played the role of international policeman. For example, in 1948–49 the United States was able to coerce the Netherlands into backing away from its military efforts to forestall Indonesian independence; in 1956, the United States pressed the French and the British into withdrawing their troops from the Suez region; and in the early 1960s, the United States persuaded Egypt to withdraw from Yemen and the Congo by withholding development and PL 480 food aid.

More recent attempts have not been as successful. Turkish troops remain in Cyprus more than 15 years after their invasion and in spite of US economic pressure in the mid-1970s. The Carter grain embargo and boycott of the 1980 Moscow Olympics did not discourage the Soviet occupation of Afghanistan.

Indeed, aside from the 1956 Suez incident, major powers have never been able to deter the military adventures of other major powers simply through the use of economic sanctions.

Closely related to these military adventure cases are those episodes in which sanctions are imposed to impair the economic capability of the target country, thereby limiting its potential for military activity. This was an important rationale for the broad-based multilateral controls on strategic trade that the United States instituted against the Soviet Union and China in the late 1940s, and the same rationale was cited by US officials in defense of sanctions against the Soviet Union following the invasion of Afghanistan and the crisis in Poland in the early 1980s. It is doubtful whether these cases have yielded positive results, not least because it is difficult to hamper the military capabilities of a major power with marginal degrees of economic deprivation.

In this book we do not evaluate the narrowly defined national security issues that arise in cases where sanctions are deployed to deprive an adversary of access to goods and technologies with direct military applications. Although attempts to impair another country's military potential usually entail narrowly defined national security controls—identifying military hardware and so-called dual-use technologies that can be denied the adversary—the sender country often seeks to limit the foreign policy options of the target state as well. In our view, the COCOM and CHINCOM controls of the Cold War period[3] were aimed both at restricting strategic exports to the Soviet Union and China, to prevent them from making technological advances in weaponry, and at impairing the ability of the Soviet and Chinese economies to support an expanded military machine capable of advancing those countries' foreign policy objectives. The latter goal—to inhibit potential Soviet and Chinese foreign policy responses by limiting the national capability to support a military machine—is the reason why these cases are included in our analysis.

Sanctions have also been deployed in pursuit of a number of foreign policy goals other than those related to warfare and national security. Especially noteworthy is the frequent resort to sanctions in an effort to destabilize foreign governments, usually in the context of a foreign policy dispute

---

3 Case 48–5: *US and COCOM v. USSR and COMECON* (1948–) and Case 49–1: *US and CHINCOM v. China* (1949–70). COCOM, the Coordinating Committee for Multilateral Export Controls, is an informal group of NATO countries (minus Iceland, plus Japan) which attempts to limit the shipment of strategic goods, broadly and narrowly defined, to the Soviet Union. CHINCOM, a parallel but smaller group of countries controlling exports to China, was disbanded in 1958, at which time China came under COCOM controls. COMECON, the Council for Mutual Economic Assistance, was an organization established in 1949 to facilitate economic cooperation among the Soviet Union and its satellites. After the dismantling of the Berlin Wall in November 1989, COMECON and its military counterpart, the Warsaw Pact, have become increasingly irrelevant organizations.

involving other issues. Destabilization episodes have often found a super-power pitted against a smaller country. By our count the United States has engaged in destabilization efforts 15 times, often against other countries in the Western Hemisphere such as Cuba, the Dominican Republic, Nicaragua, Brazil, Chile, and Panama. Sanctions contributed at least modestly to the overthrow of Trujillo in 1961, of Brazilian dictator João Goulart in 1964, and of Chilean President Salvador Allende in 1973; sanctions played a minor role in the electoral defeat of the Sandinistas in Nicaragua in 1990. On the other hand, Cuba under Fidel Castro has not succumbed to three decades of US economic pressure, in large measure because Castro received compensating aid from the Soviet Union. Likewise, despite intense US economic sanctions, Noriega was able to retain power in Panama; it finally took US military intervention to dislodge him.

The Soviet Union has also picked on its neighbors, although less successfully. Every time the Soviets have used sanctions in an effort to topple a rebellious government within the socialist bloc—Yugoslavia in 1948, China in 1960, Albania in 1961—the effort failed; the only Soviet success came in the "Nightfrost Crisis" of 1958, when Finland was coerced into adopting a more pliant attitude toward Soviet policies. Finally, the United Kingdom also has participated in the destabilization game through the use of economic sanctions to topple hostile or repressive regimes in areas where the British once exercised colonial influence: Iran in 1951–53, Rhodesia in 1965–79, and Uganda in 1972–79.

Since the early 1960s, sanctions have been deployed in support of numerous other foreign policy goals, most of them relatively modest compared to the pursuit of war, peace, and political destabilization. For example, sanctions have been used on behalf of efforts to protect human rights, to halt nuclear proliferation, to settle expropriation claims, and to combat international terrorism. Here again, the United States has played the dominant role as guardian of its version of global morality. Following a series of congressionally inspired initiatives beginning in 1973, human rights became a *cause célèbre* of the Carter administration. In the early phase, country-specific riders were attached to military aid bills requiring the Nixon and Ford administrations to deny or reduce assistance to countries found to be abusing human rights. Later, President Carter adopted the congressional mandate as his own guiding light. Eventually many countries in Latin America and elsewhere became targets of US sanctions. In a more limited way, Presidents Reagan and Bush also used sanctions to defend human rights and support democracy in Suriname, Haiti, Burma, Somalia, and the Sudan.

Sanctions were also frequently used, by both the United States and Canada in the 1970s and 1980s, to enforce compliance with nuclear nonproliferation safeguards. In 1974, Canada acted to prevent Pakistan from acquiring a nuclear explosive capability and tried to control the reprocessing of spent fuel in both India and Pakistan to guard against its use in weapons production. The United States joined the Canadians in applying financial pressure on South Korea to forestall its purchase of a nuclear reprocessing plant. Subsequently, the United States imposed sanctions on shipments of nuclear fuel and technology to South Africa, Taiwan, Brazil, Argentina, India, and Pakistan in similar attempts to secure adequate multilateral surveillance of nuclear facilities. Australia used sanctions in an effort to deter French testing in the South Pacific. These assorted efforts were highly successful with respect to Korea and Taiwan (at least initially) but had little impact on India, Pakistan, or France.

Since World War II the United States has used sanctions nine times in its efforts to negotiate compensation for property expropriated by foreign governments. However, expropriation claims have become less urgent in recent years; the last recorded use of sanctions in an expropriation dispute was against Ethiopia (commencing in 1976). In almost all the expropriation cases, the United States hoped to go beyond the claims issue and resolve conflicting political philosophies. This was true the first time the United States (in conjunction with the United Kingdom) pressured Iran with economic sanctions—seeking the overthrow of the regime of Prime Minister Mohammad Mussadiq in the early 1950s—and was behind US efforts to undermine Castro in Cuba, Goulart in Brazil, and Allende in Chile.

Antiterrorism has been another of the more modest—but increasingly important—policy goals sought by the United States through the imposition of economic sanctions. A wave of international plane hijackings in the 1960s and 1970s, together with the massacre of Israeli athletes at the Munich Olympics in 1972, focused world attention on terrorism. The hijacking problem was greatly reduced through international hijacking agreements, including one signed in 1973 by the United States and Cuba. Lethal terrorist raids, often funded by oil-rich radical Islamic countries, have proven much harder to control. In 1980, following a congressional directive, the US State Department branded four countries—Libya, Syria, Iraq, and South Yemen—as international outlaws because of their support of terrorist activities. The United States soon thereafter imposed sanctions on Libya and Iraq in an attempt to limit their activity as suppliers of military equipment to terrorist groups. Iraq was removed from the terrorism list in 1982, despite congressional opposition, whereas sanctions against Libya were expanded to cover all trade and finance in early 1986. Since then, Cuba, North Korea, and Iran have been added to the list of target countries on account of their support for terrorism.

This brief historical review illustrates the important role that economic sanctions have played since World War I in the conduct of US foreign policy. Of the 116 cases documented in table 1.1, the United States, either alone or in concert with its allies, has deployed sanctions 77 times. Other significant users have been the United Kingdom (22 instances, often in cooperation with the League of Nations and later the United Nations), the Soviet Union (10 uses, usually against recalcitrant satellites), and the Arab League and its members (4 uses of its oil muscle).

This overview demonstrates that sanctions have been deployed quite frequently in the post–World War II era. Table 1.3 summarizes the record, presenting, first, the number of sanctions episodes initiated in each five-year period beginning with 1911–15; second, the total cost imposed on target countries every fifth year beginning with 1915 (expressed as an annualized figure in current US dollars); and third, for comparison, the value of total world exports (expressed in current US dollars). The table indicates that the incidence of new episodes has increased from less than 5 in the pre-1945 period to approximately 10 to 15 in the post-1960 period. The annual cost imposed on target countries was quite high in 1915, on account of World War I; it fell markedly thereafter, and has since risen from very low levels in the 1920s and 1930s to some $1.5 billion and higher in the post-1965 period. The aggregate cost of sanctions peaked in 1980, when costs totaling some $5.9 billion were imposed on target countries.[4]

Table 1.3 also shows that, although sanctions activity has grown, particularly in recent decades, it has expanded much more slowly than world trade, which grew almost two-hundred-fold between 1915 and 1990 (expressed in current dollars). Compared to total world trade flows, the cost imposed by sanctions on target countries represents barely a ripple in the world economy.

The Cyclical Popularity of Sanctions

Like other fashions, economic sanctions wax and wane in popularity. After World War I, great hopes were held out for the "economic weapon," with President Woodrow Wilson the leading advocate. Speaking in Indianapolis in 1919, Wilson said:

> A nation that is boycotted is a nation that is in sight of surrender.
> Apply this economic, peaceful, silent, deadly remedy and there
> will be no need for force. It is a terrible remedy. It does not cost
> a life outside the nation boycotted, but it brings a pressure upon
> the nation which, in my judgment, no modern nation could resist.
> (quoted in Padover 1942, 108)

The League of Nations enjoyed minor success with the use of sanctions against smaller powers in the 1920s and 1930s. But with the failure of the League's campaign against Italy, the reputation of the "economic weapon"

---

4 However, our estimate of the annualized cost to Iraq of the UN embargo is more than $20 billion, which swamps even the highest estimates in other cases.

correspondingly sank. Scholars were quick to point out that sanctions had not in fact been used decisively against Italy, but the public at large simply concluded that sanctions were not equal to the task.

The reputation of the "economic weapon" was somewhat rehabilitated by the contribution of the naval blockade of Europe and the Allies' preemptive buying of strategic materials to the ultimate defeat of Germany and Japan during World War II. Sanctions were used frequently and with some success in the late 1940s and 1950s, but they did not again attract public notice until the US campaign against Cuba and the UK–UN campaign against Rhodesia in the 1960s. Overoptimistic British pronouncements in the Rhodesian case and the considerable success of Cuba—with massive aid from the Soviet Union—in withstanding US economic pressure again fostered disillusion. Disillusion grew progressively more fashionable with the extensive American reliance on sanctions, and a series of conspicuous failures, in the 1970s and early 1980s.

Probably the bottom of the most recent wave of disfavor was reached in the late 1980s.[5] But we would suggest that the "economic weapon" will not regain full respectability until a few significant episodes are recorded in which sanctions are deployed judiciously and successfully. Perhaps the US–UN embargo of Iraq will be such a case. However, most of the recent, well-publicized cases do not qualify: sanctions were of marginal use in persuading the Sandinistas to allow elections in Nicaragua; although some progress has been made, so far sanctions have not significantly altered the hard reality of apartheid in South Africa; Noriega held out in Panama until US troops intervened; and sanctions did not deflect the Chinese leadership from its repressive policy following the massacre in Tiananmen Square.

Sender Countries and Their Motives

Sanctions are part and parcel of international diplomacy, a tool for coercing target governments into particular avenues of response. The use of sanctions presupposes the sender country's willingness to interfere in the decision-making process of another sovereign government.

Among the cases we have documented, the countries that impose sanctions are for the most part large nations that pursue an active foreign policy. To be sure, there are instances of neighborhood fights: Indonesia versus Malaysia in the mid–1960s; Spain versus the United Kingdom over Gibraltar from the 1950s until 1984; India versus Nepal over the latter's rapprochement with China in 1989–90. But in the main, sanctions have been used by big powers, precisely because they are big and can seek to influence events on a global

---

5 A leading scholar, David A. Baldwin (1985), has written a book that seeks to rehabilitate the use of economic diplomacy as a tool of statecraft.

scale. Instances of the collective use of sanctions—the League of Nations against Italy in 1935–36, the United Nations against Rhodesia from 1965 to 1979, the Allies against Germany and Japan in World War II, the United Nations against Iraq in 1990—are in fact usually episodes of major powers enlisting their smaller allies.

"Demonstration of resolve" has often supplied the driving force behind the imposition of sanctions. This is particularly true for the United States, which frequently has deployed sanctions to assert its leadership in world affairs. US presidents seemingly feel compelled to dramatize their opposition to foreign misdeeds, even when the likelihood of changing the target country's behavior seems remote. In these cases sanctions often are imposed because the cost of inaction—in terms of lost confidence at home and abroad in the ability or willingness of the United States to act—is seen as greater than the cost of the sanctions. Indeed, the international community often expects such action from the United States, to demonstrate moral outrage and to reassure the alliance that America will stand by its international commitments. The impact of such moral and psychological factors on the decision to impose sanctions should not be underestimated, even if it is hard to document.

"Deterrence"—the notion that a sender country can discourage future objectionable policies by increasing the associated costs—is another frequently cited reason for sanctions. In many cases, such as the US sanctions against the Soviet Union over Afghanistan in 1980–81, it is difficult, if not impossible, to determine whether sanctions were an effective deterrent against future misdeeds. Under President Mikhail Gorbachev, the Soviet Union has dramatically changed its internal and external policies, but it is hard to credit even the combined effect of all US sanctions with more than a marginal role in this transformation.

Finally, sanctions are sometimes used as a surrogate for other measures. A diplomatic slap on the wrist may not hit where it hurts, but more extreme measures, such as covert action or military measures, may be excessive. Sanctions provide a popular middle road: they add teeth to international diplomacy, even when the bark is worse than the bite.

In a sense, the imposition of sanctions conveys a triple signal: to the target country it says the sender does not condone your actions; to allies it says that words will be supported with deeds; to domestic audiences it says the sender's government will act to safeguard the nation's vital interests.

The parallels between the motives for sanctions and the three basic purposes of criminal law—to punish, to deter, and to rehabilitate—are unmistakable. Countries that impose sanctions, like states that incarcerate criminals, may find their hopes of rehabilitation unrealized, but they may be quite satisfied with whatever punishment and deterrence are accomplished.

Nevertheless, in judging the success of sanctions, we confine our examination to changes in the policies and capabilities of the target country.

Limitations on the Use of Sanctions

Sanctions often do not succeed in changing the behavior of foreign countries. One reason for failure is plain: the sanctions imposed may simply be inadequate to the task. The goals may be too elusive, the means too gentle, or cooperation from other countries, when needed, too tepid.

A second reason for failure is that sanctions may create their own antidotes. In particular, economic sanctions may unify the target country both in support of its government and in search of commercial alternatives. This outcome is evident in a number of episodes; for example, a nationalistic reaction seems to have blunted the League's actions against Italy in 1935–36, Soviet sanctions against Yugoslavia in 1948–55, US measures against Indonesia in 1963–66, UN actions against Rhodesia in 1965–79, and US sanctions against Nicaragua in the 1980s. Benito Mussolini expressed Italy's nationalistic defiance of the League's sanctions in 1935 with these words: "To sanctions of an economic character we will reply with our discipline, with our sobriety, and with our spirit of sacrifice" (quoted in Renwick 1981, 18).[6]

A third reason why economic pressure may fail is that sanctions may prompt powerful or wealthy allies of the target country to assume the role of "black knight"; their support can largely offset whatever deprivation results from the sanctions themselves. In the period since World War II, offsetting compensation has occurred most conspicuously in episodes where the big powers were caught up in ideological conflict over the policies of a smaller nation: examples include the US sanctions against Cuba and later Nicaragua and Soviet sanctions against Yugoslavia and Albania. However, with the Kremlin's new approach to world affairs, it is entirely possible that "black knight" diplomacy will become a relic of the Cold War. The Soviet Union refused to buttress Daniel Ortega when the Sandinista government looked shaky in 1989, it made no effort to rescue Noriega, and it has joined in the US condemnation of Iraq. Another example of countervailing support, with different historical origins, is the Arab League campaign against Israel, a campaign that has helped ensure a continuing flow of public and private assistance to Israel from the United States and Western Europe.

A fourth possible reason for failure is that economic sanctions may alienate allies abroad and business interests at home. When a sender's allies do not share its goals, they may, in the first instance, ask exasperating questions about the probability of a successful outcome; in the second instance, they

---

6 Manuel Noriega used comparable rhetoric when the United States imposed sanctions on Panama in the late 1980s.

may refuse to take the stern measures requested against the target country, thereby making the sender's own initiatives seem all the more futile; finally, they may revolt and enforce national antisanctions laws, such as the US antiboycott provisions and the British Protection of Trading Interests Act, to counteract the impact of others' sanctions on their own foreign policy and economic interests. The protective legal barrier is a relatively new development, but one that has spread to a number of countries—France, Denmark, Australia, and others—where firms have been victimized by the errant aim of a sender state.

The backlash from the sender's allies may be exacerbated if attempts are made to enforce the sanctions on an extraterritorial basis, as the United States did in the 1981–82 Soviet-European pipeline case. The Europeans refused to cooperate with the United States and halt the pipeline project; indeed, they wondered who the real target of the sanctions was: the country subject to sanctions (the Soviet Union), or their own firms, whose trade was being hit by the measures. The internecine feud that ensued between the United States and Europe undercut the economic and psychological force of the sanctions, rendering the action ineffective.

Business firms at home may also experience severe losses when sanctions interrupt trade and financial contacts. Besides the immediate loss of sales, they may lose their reputation for reliability. Outcries from US business against both the grain embargo and the pipeline sanctions arose as much from the fear of future competitive weakness as "unreliable suppliers" as from the immediate sacrifice of grain, pipelaying equipment, and gas turbine sales to the Soviet Union. After the first flush of patriotic enthusiasm, such complaints can undermine a sanctions initiative.

These pitfalls are well known to most policy officials, and they can hardly escape the briefing memoranda prepared for world leaders considering sanctions. Why then are sanctions so frequently used? In the first place, as the results of this study show, sanctions have not been, on balance, nearly so unsuccessful as the episodes directed against the Soviet Union in the 1970s and 1980s would suggest. In the second place, world leaders often find the most obvious alternatives to economic sanctions unsatisfactory—military action would be too massive, and diplomatic protest too meager. Sanctions can provide a satisfying theatrical display, yet avoid the high costs of war. This is not to say that sanctions are costless. Our purpose in this study is precisely to suggest conditions in which sanctions are most likely to achieve a positive benefit at a bearable cost.

Plan of the Book

In chapter 2, we examine the components of a sanctions episode. In a simple and crude way, we attempt to quantify a number of dimensions. We explain our definition of success, our scheme for distinguishing objectives, our scale of international cooperation, and our measurement of economic costs. In chapter 3, we assess sanctions episodes in terms of their political variables. In chapter 4, we summarize the economic variables in a sanctions episode and relate the economic costs to the measure of success achieved. In chapter 5, we derive general lessons from the cases studied and offer a list of nine commandments that sender countries might follow to improve their prospects for achieving foreign policy goals. We also take a close look at recent US experience and consider what the end of the Cold War may mean for the future of sanctions. Appendix A explains how we calculate economic costs to the target country. Finally, the case abstracts in appendix B of this volume and the supplementary volume give details on each of the 116 cases we examined.

References

Baldwin, David A. 1985. *Economic Statecraft: Theory and Practice*. Princeton: Princeton University Press.

Carter, Barry E. 1988. *International Economic Sanctions: Improving the Haphazard U.S. Legal Regime*. Cambridge and New York: Cambridge University Press.

Ellings, Richard James. 1983. "Strategic Embargoes, Economic Sanctions, and the Structure of World Politics: Lessons from American Foreign Policy." Ph.D. diss., University of Washington.

Fornara, Charles. 1975. "Plutarch and the Megarian decree." 24 *Yale Classical Studies* 213–28

Marcuss, Stanley J., and D. Stephen Mathias. 1984. "U.S. Foreign Policy Export Controls: Do They Pass Muster Under International Law?" 2 *International Tax and Business Lawyer* (Winter): 1–28.

Marcuss, Stanley J., and Eric L. Richard. 1981. "Extraterritorial Jurisdiction in United States Trade Law: The Need for a Consistent Theory." 20 *Columbia Journal of Transnational Law* 439–83.

Moyer, Homer E., Jr., and Linda A. Mabry. 1983. "Export Controls as Instruments of Foreign Policy: The History, Legal Issues, and Policy Lessons of Three Recent Cases." 15 *Law and Policy in International Business* 1–171.

Padover, Saul K., ed. 1942. *Wilson's Ideals*. Washington: American Council on Public Affairs.

Renwick, Robin. 1981. *Economic Sanctions*. Harvard Studies in International Affairs 45. Cambridge: Harvard University Center for International Affairs.

Rosenthal, Douglas E., and William M. Knighton. 1983. *National Laws and International Commerce: The Problem of Extraterritoriality*. Chatham House Papers no. 17. London: Routledge & Kegan Paul for the Royal Institute of International Affairs.

Rowland, Peter. 1975. *David Lloyd George: A Biography*. New York: Macmillan.

Table 1.1 Chronological summary of economic sanctions for foreign policy goals, 1914–90

Case number	Principal sender	Target country	Active years	Goals of sender country
14–1	United Kingdom	Germany	1914–18	Military victory
17–1	United States	Japan	1917	(1) Contain Japanese influence in Asia; (2) Persuade Japan to divert shipping to Atlantic
18–1	United Kingdom	Russia	1918–20	(1) Renew support for Allies in World War I; (2) Destabilize Bolshevik regime
21–1	League of Nations	Yugoslavia	1921	Block Yugoslav attempts to wrest territory from Albania; retain 1913 borders
25–1	League of Nations	Greece	1925	Withdraw from occupation of Bulgarian border territory
32–1	League of Nations	Paraguay and Bolivia	1932–35	Settle the Chaco War
33–1	United Kingdom	USSR	1933	Release two British citizens
35–1	United Kingdom and League of Nations	Italy	1935–36	Withdraw Italian troops from Abyssinia
38–1	United Kingdom and United States	Mexico	1938–47	Settle expropriation claims

Case	Sender	Target	Period	Goal
39–1	Alliance Powers	Germany, later Japan	1939–45	Military victory
40–1	United States	Japan	1940–41	Withdraw from Southeast Asia
44–1	United States	Argentina	1944–47	(1) Remove Nazi influence; (2) Destabilize Perón government
46–1	Arab League	Israel	1946–	Create a homeland for Palestinians
48–1	United States	Netherlands	1948–49	Recognize Republic of Indonesia
48–2	India	Hyderabad	1948	Assimilate Hyderabad into India
48–3	USSR	United States, United Kingdom, and France	1948–49	(1) Prevent formation of a West German government; (2) Assimilate West Berlin into East Germany
48–4	USSR	Yugoslavia	1948–55	(1) Rejoin Soviet camp; (2) Destabilize Tito government
48–5	United States and COCOM	USSR and COMECON	1948–	(1) Deny strategic materials; (2) Impair Soviet military potential
49–1	United States and CHINCOM	China	1949–70	(1) Retaliation for Communist takeover and subsequent assistance to North Korea; (2) Deny strategic and other materials
50–1	United States and United Nations	North Korea	1950–	Withdraw attack on South Korea

Case number	Principal sender	Target country	Active years	Goals of sender country
51–1	United Kingdom and United States	Iran	1951–53	(1) Reverse the nationalization of oil facilities; (2) Destabilize Mussadiq government
54–1	USSR	Australia	1954	Repatriate a Soviet defector
54–2	India	Portugal	1954–61	Assimilate Goa into India
54–3	Spain	United Kingdom	1954–84	Gain sovereignty over Gibraltar
54–4	United States and South Vietnam	North Vietnam	1954–	(1) Impede military effectiveness of North Vietnam; (2) Retribution for aggression in South Vietnam
56–1	United States	Israel	1956–83 (intermittent episodes)	(1) Withdraw from Sinai; (2) Implement UN Resolution 242; (3) Push Palestinian autonomy talks
56–2	United Kingdom, United States, and France	Egypt	1956	(1) Ensure free passage through Suez Canal; (2) Compensate for nationalization
56–3	United States	United Kingdom and France	1956	Withdraw from Suez
56–4	United States	Laos	1956–62	(1) Destabilize Prince Souvanna Phouma government; (2) Destabilize General Phoumi government; (3) Prevent Communist takeover

57–1	Indonesia	Netherlands	1957–62	Control of West Irian
57–2	France	Tunisia	1957–63	Halt support for Algerian rebels
58–1	USSR	Finland	1958–59	Maintain pro–USSR policies
60–1	United States	Dominican Republic	1960–62	(1) Cease subversion in Venezuela; (2) Destabilize Trujillo government
60–2	USSR	China	1960–70	(1) Retaliation for break with Soviet policy; (2) Impair Chinese economic and military potential
60–3	United States	Cuba	1960–	(1) Settle expropriation claims; (2) Destabilize Castro government; (3) Discourage Cuba from foreign military adventures
61–1	United States	Ceylon	1961–65	Settle expropriation claims
61–2	USSR	Albania	1961–65	(1) Retaliation for alliance with China; (2) Destabilize Hoxha government
61–3	Western Allies	German Democratic Republic	1961–62	Berlin Wall
62–1	United States	Brazil	1962–64	(1) Settle expropriation claims; (2) Destabilize Goulart government
62–2	United Nations	South Africa	1962–	(1) End apartheid; (2) Grant independence to Namibia

Case number	Principal sender	Target country	Active years	Goals of sender country
62–3	USSR	Romania	1962–63	Limit economic independence
63–1	United States	United Arab Republic	1963–65	(1) Cease military activity in Yemen and Congo; (2) Moderate anti–US rhetoric
63–2	Indonesia	Malaysia	1963–66	Promote "Crush Malaysia" campaign
63–3	United States	Indonesia	1963–66	(1) Cease "Crush Malaysia" campaign; (2) Destabilize Sukarno government
63–4	United States	South Vietnam	1963	(1) Ease repression; (2) Remove Nhu; (3) Destabilize Diem
63–5	United Nations and Organization for African Unity	Portugal	1963–74	Free African colonies
64–1	France	Tunisia	1964–66	Settle expropriation claims
65–1	United States	Chile	1965–66	Roll back copper price
65–2	United States	India	1965–67	Alter policy to favor agriculture
65–3	United Kingdom and United Nations	Rhodesia	1965–79	Majority rule by black Africans
65–4	United States	Arab League	1965–	Stop US firms from implementing Arab boycott of Israel

67–1	Nigeria	Biafra	1967–70	End civil war
68–1	United States	Peru	1968	Forgo aircraft purchases from France
68–2	United States	Peru	1968–74	Settle expropriation claims
70–1	United States	Chile	1970–73	(1) Settle expropriation claims; (2) Destabilize Allende government
71–1	United States	India and Pakistan	1971	Cease fighting in East Pakistan (Bangladesh)
S–1	United States	Countries supporting international terrorism	1972–	Overview
72–1	United Kingdom and United States	Uganda	1972–79	(1) Retaliation for expelling Asians; (2) Improve human rights; (3) Destabilize Amin government
S–2	United States	Countries violating human rights	1973–	Overview
73–1	Arab League	United States and Netherlands	1973–74	(1) Retaliation for supporting Israel in October war; (2) Restore pre-1967 Israeli borders
73–2	United States	South Korea	1973–77	Improve human rights
73–3	United States	Chile	1973–	Improve human rights

Case number	Principal sender	Target country	Active years	Goals of sender country
S–3	United States and Canada	Countries pursuing nuclear weapons option	1974–	Overview
74–1	United States	Turkey	1974–78	Withdraw Turkish troops from Cyprus
74–2	Canada	India	1974–76	(1) Deter further nuclear explosions; (2) Apply stricter nuclear safeguards
74–3	Canada	Pakistan	1974–76	(1) Apply stricter safeguards to nuclear power plant; (2) Forgo nuclear reprocessing
75–1	United States and Canada	South Korea	1975–76	Forgo nuclear reprocessing
75–2	United States	USSR	1975–	Liberalize Jewish emigration
75–3	United States	Eastern Europe	1975–	Liberalize Jewish emigration
75–4	United States	South Africa	1975–82	(1) Adhere to nuclear safeguards; (2) Avert explosion of nuclear device
75–5	United States	Kampuchea	1975–79	(1) Improve human rights; (2) Deter Vietnamese expansionism

76–1	United States	Uruguay	1976–81	Improve human rights
76–2	United States	Taiwan	1976–77	Forgo nuclear reprocessing
76–3	United States	Ethiopia	1976–	(1) Settle expropriation claims; (2) Improve human rights
77–1	United States	Paraguay	1977–81	Improve human rights
77–2	United States	Guatemala	1977–86	Improve human rights
77–3	United States	Argentina	1977–83	Improve human rights
77–4	Canada	Japan and European Community	1977–78	Strengthen nuclear safeguards
77–5	United States	Nicaragua	1977–79	(1) Destabilize Somoza government; (2) Improve human rights
77–6	United States	El Salvador	1977–81	Improve human rights
77–7	United States	Brazil	1977–84	Improve human rights
78–1	China	Albania	1978–83	Retaliation for anti-Chinese rhetoric
78–2	United States	Brazil	1978–81	Adhere to nuclear safeguards
78–3	United States	Argentina	1978–82	Adhere to nuclear safeguards
78–4	United States	India	1978–82	Adhere to nuclear safeguards
78–5	United States	USSR	1978–80	Liberalize treatment of dissidents (e.g., Shcharansky)

Case number	Principal sender	Target country	Active years	Goals of sender country
78–6	Arab League	Egypt	1978–83	Withdraw from Camp David process
78–7	China	Vietnam	1978–88	Withdraw troops from Kampuchea
78–8	United States	Libya	1978–	(1) Terminate support of international terrorism; (2) Destabilize Gadhafi government
79–1	United States	Iran	1979–81	(1) Release hostages; (2) Settle expropriation claims
79–2	United States	Pakistan	1979–	Adhere to nuclear safeguards
79–3	Arab League	Canada	1979	Retaliation for planned move of Canadian embassy in Israel from Tel Aviv to Jerusalem
79–4	United States	Bolivia	1979–82	(1) Improve human rights; (2) Deter drug trafficking
80–1	United States	USSR	1980–81	(1) Withdraw Soviet troops from Afghanistan; (2) Impair Soviet military potential
80–2	United States	Iraq	1980–	(1) Terminate support of international terrorism; (2) Renounce chemical and nuclear weapons

Code	Sender	Target	Years	Objective
81–1	United States	Nicaragua	1981–90	(1) End support for El Salvador rebels; (2) Destabilize Sandinista government
81–2	United States	Poland	1981–87	(1) Lift martial law; (2) Free dissidents; (3) Resume talks with Solidarity
81–3	United States	USSR	1981–82	(1) Lift martial law in Poland; (2) Cancel USSR–Europe pipeline project; (3) Impair Soviet economic and military potential
81–4	European Community	Turkey	1981–82	Restore democracy
82–1	United Kingdom	Argentina	1982	Withdraw troops from Falkland Islands
82–2	Netherlands and United States	Suriname	1982–88	(1) Improve human rights; (2) Limit alliance with Cuba and Libya
82–3	South Africa	Lesotho	1982–86	(1) Return refugees suspected of antistate activities; (2) Destabilize Chief Jonathan
83–1	Australia	France	1983–86	Stop nuclear testing in the South Pacific
83–2	United States	USSR	1983	Retaliation for downing of Korean airliner

Case number	Principal sender	Target country	Active years	Goals of sender country
83–3	United States	Zimbabwe	1983–88	(1) Temper opposition in United Nations to US foreign policy; (2) Resume food shipments to Matabeleland; (3) Apologize for anti-US rhetoric
83–4	United States and Organization of Eastern Caribbean States	Grenada	1983	Destabilize Bishop-Austin regime
84–1	United States	Iran	1984–	(1) End war with Iraq; (2) Halt attacks on Gulf shipping
85–1	United States	South Africa	1985–	End apartheid
86–1	United States	Syria	1986–	End support of terrorism
86–2	United States	Angola	1986–	Expel Cuban troops
87–1	United States	Panama	1987–90	Destabilize Noriega
87–2	United States	Haiti	1987–90	(1) Improve human rights; (2) Restore democracy; (3) Stop drug smuggling
87–3	United States	El Salvador	1987–88	Reverse amnesty decision
88–1	Japan, West Germany, and United States	Burma	1988–	(1) Improve human rights; (2) Restore democracy

88–2	United States and United Kingdom	Somalia	1988–	(1) Improve human rights; (2) End civil war
89–1	India	Nepal	1989–90	Reduce ties with China
89–2	United States	China	1989–	Retaliation for Tiananmen Square
89–3	United States	Sudan	1989–	(1) Improve human rights; (2) Restore democracy
90–1	United States and United Nations	Iraq	1990–	(1) Withdraw from Kuwait; (2) Restore legitimate government; (3) Release hostages

Table 1.2 Selected pre–World War I episodes of economic sanctions for foreign policy goals

Sender country	Target country	Active years	Background and objectives	Resolution	Source
Athens	Megara	circa 432 BC	Pericles issued the Megarian decree limiting entry of Megara's products into Athenian markets in retaliation for Megara's attempted expropriation of territory and the kidnapping of three women.	The decree contributed to the Peloponnesian War between Athens and Sparta.	de Ste. Croix 252–60; Fornara 222–26
American colonies	Britain	1765	England passed the Stamp Act as a revenue measure; colonies boycotted English goods.	Britain repealed the Stamp Act in 1766.	Renwick 5
American colonies	Britain	1767–70	England passed Townshend Acts to cover salaries of judges and officials; colonies boycotted English goods.	Britain repealed the Townshend Acts except on tea; the tea tax gave pretext for the Boston Tea Party of 1774 and calling of the Continental Congress.	Renwick 5

Britain and France	France and Britain	Napoleonic Wars: 1793–1815	British goal: contain French expansion and eventually defeat Napoleon. French goal: deprive Britain of grain through the Continental System, and eventually defeat England.	"The experience of economic warfare during this period is inconclusive as to its possible effects when applied with more systematic organization." One result of sanctions was French development of sugar beet cultivation, anticipating development of substitutes in later war.	Jack 1–42
United States	Britain	1812–14	United States embargoed British goods in response to British Naval Acts limiting US trade with France. The total embargo, which evolved out of the Non-Intercourse Acts of 1809, followed an ineffective embargo imposed from 1807 to 1809.	The acts were revoked, but the United States, not knowing of the revocation, declared war two days later. The War of 1812 ensued.	Knorr 101–02
Britain and France	Russia	Crimean War: 1853–56	Britain and France blockaded the mouth of the Danube River so that the Russian army could not receive supplies by sea.	Russia was defeated and the partition of Turkey prevented.	Oppenheim 514

Sender country	Target country	Active years	Background and objectives	Resolution	Source
US North	Confederate states	Civil War: 1861–65	"In seapower, railroads, material wealth and industrial capacity to produce iron and munitions, the North was vastly superior to the South. This disparity became even more pronounced as the ever tightening blockade gradually cut off the Confederacy from foreign imports."	The South lost. Leckie: "Attrition and blockade had scuttled the Confederate capacity. . . ."	Leckie 513; Matloff 192
France	Germany	Franco-Prussian War: 1870–71	France declared war on Germany to prevent emergence of a unified German state. France blockaded the German coast and even blockaded three of its own ports that had been occupied by the Germans.	The German army prevailed despite supply problems.	Oppenheim 515
France	China	Indochina War: 1883–85	At war with China over the Vietnamese territory of Annam, France declared rice to be contraband because of its importance to the Chinese population.	China ceded to France control over the Annamese territory.	Oppenheim 554

United States	Spain	Spanish-American War 1898	Matloff: "To the extent the United States had a strategy for conduct of the war against Spain in the Caribbean, it consisted of maintaining a naval blockade of Cuba while native insurgent forces carried on a harassing campaign against Spanish troops on the island." A companion blockade of the Philippines was intended to deny Spain revenues from that colony.	The United States obtained independence for Cuba and, after occupying the Philippines and Puerto Rico, forced Spain to cede those territories and Guam to the United States for $20 million.	Matloff 324–26; Leckie 566
Britain	Dutch South Africa	Boer War: 1899–1902	The British denied articles of contraband to the Boers.	The Boers were eventually overwhelmed and South Africa was added to the British Empire.	Jack 73
Russia	Japan	Russo-Japanese War: 1904–05	Russia declared rice, all types of fuel, and cotton as contraband.	Following military defeat, Russia ceded portions of its own territory to Japan and recognized Korea as within Japan's sphere of influence.	Oppenheim 454
Italy	Turkey	1911–12	Italy used a limited blockade as part of its campaign to acquire Libya.	Italy acquired Libya from the Ottoman Empire.	Dupuy 926

Sources:
Dupuy, R. Ernest, and Trevor N. Dupuy. 1970. *The Encyclopedia of Military History.* New York: Harper & Row.
De Ste. Croix, G. E. M. 1972. *The Origins of the Peloponnesian War.* London: Duckworth.
Fornara, Charles. 1975. "Plutarch and the Megarian decree." 24 *Yale Classical Studies* 213–28.
Jack, D. T. 1941. *Studies in Economic Warfare.* New York: Chemical Publishing Co.
Knorr, Klaus. 1977. "International Economic Leverage and Its Uses." In *Economic Issues and National Security*, eds. Klaus Knorr and Frank N. Traeger. Lawrence, Kansas: Regents Press.
Leckie, Robert. 1968. *The Wars of America.* New York: Harper & Row.
Matloff, Maurice, ed. 1969. *American Military History.* Washington: GPO.
Oppenheim, L. 1921. "War & Neutrality." In *International Law: A Treatise*, ed. Ronald F. Roxburgh. Vol. 2, 3d ed. London: Longmans, Green.
Renwick, Robin. 1981. *Economic Sanctions.* Harvard Studies in International Affairs, no. 45. Cambridge, MA: Harvard University Center for International Affairs.

Table 1.3 Sanctions episodes initiated, aggregate cost of sanctions to target countries, and world exports, 1915–90

Year	Number of episodes initiated in past five years[a]	Aggregate annual cost each fifth year[b] (billions of dollars)	Total world exports[c] (billions of dollars)
1915	1	0.84	15[d]
1920	2	—	n.a.
1925	2	—	25[e]
1930	0	—	30
1935	3	0.09	n.a.
1940	3	0.78	25[f]
1945	1	0.03	50
1950	8	1.00	55
1955	5	1.20	85
1960	10	1.72	115
1965	16	2.19	165
1970	4	1.82	285
1975	13	2.36	795
1980	24	5.90	1,870
1985	13	2.57	1,810
1990	10	1.64	2,695[g]

n.a. = not available.

a. The counts are based on table 1.1; the figure for 1975, for example, represents cases initiated in 1971–75. The 1990 figures exclude US and UN v. Iraq because the costs in that case, an estimated $21.6 billion, are aberrant and would distort the data.

b. The figures represent the net annualized cost (after offsets) to target countries of outstanding cases, based on abstracts of 115 cases summarized in tables 4.1 through 4.5. All figures are in current dollars, rounded to the nearest $10 million.

c. Based on Yates for 1915 to 1940; *Yearbook of International Trade Statistics* for 1945; *International Financial Statistics* for 1950 to 1990. All figures are in current dollars, rounded to the nearest $5 billion.

d. Extrapolated from 1913 data ($21.0 billion).

e. Extrapolated from average of 1926–29 data ($31.8 billion).

f. Extrapolated from 1938 data ($22.7 billion).

g. 1988

Sources: Tables 1.1 and 4.3 through 4.7; P. Lamartine Yates, *Forty Years of Foreign Trade* (London: George Allen & Unwin, 1959); United Nations, *Yearbook of International Trade Statistics,* various issues; International Monetary Fund, *International Financial Statistics,* various issues.

2

ANATOMY OF A SANCTIONS EPISODE

The case abstracts in this and the supplemental volume provide the data base for our analysis of the effectiveness of economic sanctions. The narrative portion of each abstract sets out what happened and—in the views of actual participants and case historians—why it happened. Each abstract also contains statistical information on the economy of the target country and on economic relations between the target and sender countries. This information underlies our evaluation of motives and outcomes.

This chapter describes our definitions and methods. It may be skipped by readers who are eager to turn to the results.

Senders and Targets

We use the term "sender" to designate the country (or international organization) that is the principal author of the sanctions episode. More than one country may be engaged in the campaign, but usually a single country takes the lead and brings others along. The leader may enlist support through bilateral consultations or, less frequently, through an international organization—the League of Nations, the United Nations, or the Organization of American States, for example. In a few instances, two countries, or a country and an international organization, may share leadership, and in these cases both are listed as sender countries in table 1.1. Our abstracts concentrate on the motives and actions of the sender country, with separate mention made of the supporting cast.

We use the term "target" to designate the country that is the immediate object of the episode. On occasion, sanctions may be aimed at two or more countries—for example, the COCOM sanctions directed against the Soviet Union and its East European allies (Case 48–5). The lessons of a sanctions episode can also (and importantly) be intended for other countries that might be silently contemplating objectionable policies similar to those of the target—for example, engaging in terrorism, imprisoning political opponents, undertaking a nuclear weapons program, or embarking on a military adventure. However, our abstracts and analysis necessarily concentrate on the response of the immediate targets. It is always difficult to know when a good thrashing of one wrongdoer deters bystanders from committing similar misdeeds.

Types of Sanctions

There are three main ways in which a sender country tries to inflict costs on its target: by limiting exports, by restricting imports, and by impeding finance, including the reduction of aid. Most of the cases we have studied involve some combination of trade and financial sanctions. If only one or the other is imposed, financial sanctions are somewhat more likely to be chosen.

Trade sanctions engender costs to the target country in terms of lost export markets, denial of critical imports, lower prices received for embargoed exports, and higher prices paid for substitute imports. In a third of the cases studied, both export and import controls have been employed. In instances where only one or the other is invoked, export controls are almost always preferred to restrictions on imports. Exports have been restricted in such highly publicized cases as the Arab oil embargo of 1973–74 (Case 73–1), President Jimmy Carter's cutoff of grain shipments to the Soviet Union (Case 80–1), and the Western response to the Chinese massacre in Tiananmen Square (Case 89–2). One of the few examples of the use of import controls alone was the Soviet embargo on wool imports from Australia in 1954 in an unsuccessful attempt to force the return of a defected Soviet diplomat (Case 54–1).

Why have import controls been used less often? There seem to be two explanations: First, target countries usually can find alternative markets or arrange triangular purchase arrangements to circumvent the sender country's import controls. Indeed, for many products—especially bulk commodities such as oil and grains—it is hard to verify the origin of goods entering customs. Second, some important sender countries have only limited, if any, legal authority to impose import controls for foreign policy reasons. The

United States, for example, can only impose broad import limitations pursuant to a presidential declaration under section 232 of the Trade Expansion Act of 1962 or under the International Emergency Economic Powers Act (IEEPA).[1] A 1985 provision gives the president authority to ban imports from countries that support or harbor terrorists or terrorist organizations.[2] To date, the United States has invoked this provision only once: against Iran in 1987 (Case 84–1).

Prior to 1985 the United States only rarely imposed import sanctions, since a finding of a national security threat or other national emergency was necessary to do so. The most notable cases were against Iran in 1979–80 (Case 79–1), and against Libya (Case 78–8) pursuant to a 1975 national security finding under section 232 involving oil imports. In both cases, limited export and import controls ultimately were replaced with comprehensive trade and financial sanctions using authority under IEEPA. Presidents Reagan and Bush also invoked IEEPA in imposing comprehensive embargoes against Nicaragua in 1985 (Case 81–1) and Iraq in 1990 (Case 90–1), and extensive financial sanctions against Manuel Noriega in Panama in 1988–89 (Case 87–1).

Target countries are often hurt through the interruption of commercial and official finance. Financial sanctions were used alone or in combination with trade controls in 86 of our 116 cases. The interruption of commercial finance will usually require the target country to pay a higher interest rate to alternative creditors. The same happens when official finance is turned off. In addition, when a poor country is the target, the grant component of official financing may provide further leverage. The United States, for example, manipulated food and economic aid in the 1960s to great effect against the United Arab Republic (Case 63–1), India (Case 65–2), and Chile (in Cases 65–1 and 70–1). In the 1970s the United States used a carrot-and-stick approach with military aid, possibly improving the human rights situation in Brazil (Case 77–7), but failing to move Turkey out of Cyprus (Case 74–1). More recently, financial sanctions were delivered against Nicaragua and Panama, but in neither case did they provide a knockout punch.

The ultimate form of financial and trade control is a freeze of the target country's foreign assets, such as bank accounts held in the sender country. A

---

1 A major issue in the Export Administration Act debate of 1983–84 was whether to grant the president authority to control imports as a means of achieving foreign policy goals in "nonemergency" situations. Curiously, the Reagan administration did not want this additional authority, fearing that the forces of protection would champion its misuse. In chapter 5 of his authoritative study, Carter (1988) stresses the anomaly of narrow authority for import controls.

2 Section 505 of the International Security and Development Cooperation Act of 1985. In addition, section 504 of the statute provides specific authority to restrict Libyan imports. See Carter (1988, 111).

freeze not only stops financial flows; it also impedes trade. The US freeze of Iranian assets in late 1979 played a role in the eventual resolution of the hostage crisis, the UK freeze of Argentine assets (Case 82–1) made a modest contribution to the British victory in the Falklands in 1982. However, the US freeze of Panamanian assets failed to destabilize the Noriega regime.

Another key goal of an assets freeze is to deny an invading country the full fruits of its aggression. Such measures were used against Japan for that purpose just before and during World War II (Case 40–1). More recently, in the 1990 Middle East crisis the United States and its allies froze Kuwait's assets to prevent Saddam Hussein from plundering them.

Foreign Policy Goals

We have found it useful to classify the case histories in this study into five categories, according to the major foreign policy objective sought by the sender country:

☐ Change target-country policies in a relatively modest way (modest in the scale of national goals, but often of burning importance to participants in the episode); this type of goal is illustrated by the human rights, terrorism, and nuclear nonproliferation cases.

☐ Destabilize the target government (including, as an ancillary goal, changing the target country's policies); this category is illustrated by the US campaigns against Fidel Castro (Case 60–3) and Manuel Noriega (Case 87–1), and the Soviet campaign against Marshal Tito (Case 48–4).

☐ Disrupt a minor military adventure, as illustrated by the UK sanctions against Argentina over the Falkland Islands.

☐ Impair the military potential of the target country, as illustrated by the sanctions imposed during World Wars I and II (Cases 14–1 and 39–1) and the COCOM sanctions against the Soviet Union and its allies.

☐ Change target-country policies in a major way (including the surrender of territory), as illustrated by the UN campaign against South Africa over apartheid and control of Namibia (Case 62–2) and the Indian sanctions designed to reverse Nepal's pro-China line (Case 89–1).

An episode may have more than one objective. Such cases are classified according to the most difficult objective, except in a few instances where two objectives are judged to be equally important; in those few instances the cases are cross-listed. For example, in the US campaign against Cuba, the principal objective shifted from settlement of expropriation claims, to destabilization, to an attempt to disrupt military adventurism. Destabilization usually presupposes a lesser goal, in the Cuban instance settlement of the expropriation dispute. Hence, we submerge the expropriation dispute within the destabilization category. However, we cross-list this case as a disruption of military adventure case as well as a destabilization episode because both objectives seemed equally important—and equally elusive.

Other examples of multiple policy goals are Case 44–1: *US v. Argentina* and Case 63–1 involving US sanctions against the United Arab Republic. In the Argentine case, the United States was initially preoccupied with ending the love affair between Argentina and fascism; later, senior US officials began to view President Juan Perón as an outright exponent of fascism and therefore a target for removal from office. We have listed this case solely as a destabilization episode, although it had another important goal, namely, ridding Argentina of fascist tendencies. In the UAR case, the United States wanted to convince President Gamal Abdel Nasser both to moderate his anti-American rhetoric and to cease military operations in Yemen and the Congo. Since the two goals were equally important, but quite different, this case has been listed both as a disruption of military adventure case and as a modest policy goal case.

Attempts to impair the military power of an adversary usually encompass an explicit or implicit goal—however elusive—of destabilizing the target country's government. Hence, we do not list these cases under the destabilization heading. Where appropriate, however, these cases are cross-listed under the category of disruption of military adventure when the conflict is less than a major war. An example is Case 49–1: *US and CHINCOM v. China.*

To summarize, even though the goals of destabilization and impairment of military potential usually encompass other policy disputes, the cases are not cross-listed under those other headings. However, if a case also entails disruption of a military adventure, it is listed under that heading as well.

Sender countries do not always announce their goals with clarity. Indeed, obfuscation is the rule in destabilization cases. The Soviet Union never directly said it wished to overthrow either Tito or Albanian President Enver Hoxha (Case 61–2); the United States was equally circumspect in its public statements about Castro, Allende, and the Sandinistas. Moreover, goals may change during the course of an episode. Here, as elsewhere in this study, we must rely on newspaper accounts and other secondary sources in assigning episodes to categories.

Overview of the Variables

Whether to impose sanctions—and if so, how—is influenced by a whole host of factors, both domestic and international, which constrain the actions a sender country can take in pursuit of its foreign policy goals. For example, conflicting pressures within the sender government often lead to an indecisive response, which neither emits the desired political signal nor imposes arduous costs on the target country.

The classic example of confused signals was the League of Nations sanctions against Italy in 1935–36 (Case 35–1). The major powers in the League (the United Kingdom and France) were torn between their desire to stop the Italian advance in Abyssinia and their fear of upsetting the political balance in Europe. With an eye on upcoming national elections, British leaders in particular wanted to keep the peace in Europe; thus, even while the League Council was considering sanctions, attempts were being made to appease the Italians by ceding some territory in Abyssinia.

Clearly, there are a number of underlying elements that may influence the outcome of a sanctions episode. The factors that influenced a specific episode are described in the abstract of each case. Here we have divided these factors, somewhat artificially, into two clusters: a group of "political" variables and a group of "economic" variables. The political variables that we have scored (by no means an exhaustive list) include:

☐ Companion policies used by the sender country, namely, covert maneuvers (identified by a J in the case abstracts and in the tables in chapter 3), quasi-military activity (identified by a Q), and regular military activity (identified by an R)

☐ The number of years economic sanctions were in force

☐ The extent of international cooperation in imposing sanctions, scaled from 1 (no cooperation) to 4 (significant cooperation)

☐ The presence of international assistance to the target country (indicated by an A)

☐ The political stability and economic health of the target country, scaled from 1 (a distressed country) to 3 (a strong and stable country)

☐ The warmth of prior relations (i.e., before the sanctions episode) between sender and target countries, scaled from 1 (antagonistic) to 3 (cordial).

The economic variables that we have scored (again not an exhaustive list) include:

☐ The cost imposed on the target country, expressed in absolute terms, in per capita terms, and as a percentage of its gross national product (GNP)

☐ Commercial relations between sender and target countries, measured by the flow of two-way trade between them expressed as a percentage of the target country's total two-way trade

☐ The relative economic size of the countries, measured by the ratio of their GNPs

☐ The type of sanctions used, namely, an interruption of exports from the sender country (identified by an X), an interruption of imports to the sender country (identified by an M), or an interruption of finance (identified by an F)

☐ The cost to the sender country, expressed as an index scaled from 1 (net gain to sender) to 4 (major loss to sender).

In this chapter, we describe our approach to distilling and quantifying "success," and then discuss each of the underlying political and economic variables. In chapter 3 we discuss the connection between success and the political variables. In chapter 4 we examine the relationship between success and the economic variables. Finally, in chapter 5 we summarize our findings and draw policy conclusions.

The Success of an Episode

The "success" of an economic sanctions episode—as viewed from the perspective of the sender country—has two parts: the extent to which the policy outcome sought by the sender country was in fact achieved, and the contribution made by the sanctions (as opposed to other factors, such as military action) to a positive outcome.

Policy outcomes are judged against the foreign policy goals of the sender country. As noted earlier, *domestic* political motives may overshadow concerns about changing foreign behavior. Unfortunately, the literature on individual economic sanctions episodes seldom evaluates the role of domestic political objectives, nor does it indicate whether they were satisfied. We have not attempted to fill those important gaps in our study. Instead we confine our examination to changes in the policies, capabilities, or government of the target country. However, casual observation indicates that, for example, sanctions against South Africa have been enormously satisfying to domestic political constituencies in Europe, the United States, and Canada. The same was true of British sanctions against Argentina in the context of the Falklands dispute, and of US sanctions against China following the Tiananmen Square massacre.

Our conclusions regarding both the achievement of the foreign policy goals and the contribution of sanctions to the outcome of particular episodes are heavily influenced by the qualitative conclusions reached by previous scholars of the episodes, as summarized in the abstracts. We recognize that such assessments entail a good deal of subjective evaluation. Indeed, since foreign policy objectives often come in multiple parts, since objectives evolve over time, and since the contribution of sanctions to the policy outcome is often murky, judgment plays an important role in assigning a single number to each element of the success equation. However, by relying on the consensus views of other analysts, we believe we have minimized the bias resulting from our personal views. This method of critical assessment works better, of course, when the case has been examined by two or more scholars. Fortunately, the major cases usually have been studied by several.

We have devised a simple index system, scaled from 1 to 4, to score each element. Our index system is described as follows:

Policy Result

(1) Failed outcome; illustrated by the Soviet attempt to destabilize Tito in the period 1948–55 (Case 48–4)

(2) Unclear but possibly positive outcome; illustrated by the Arab League's long campaign against Israel (Case 46–1), which to some extent has isolated Israel in the international community

(3) Positive outcome, that is to say, a somewhat successful result; illustrated by US efforts to prevent a communist takeover of the Laotian government during the period 1956–62 (Case 56–4)

(4) Successful outcome; illustrated by the joint efforts of the United Kingdom and the United States to overthrow Idi Amin in Uganda in the late 1970s (Case 72–1).

Sanctions Contribution

(1) Zero or negative contribution; illustrated by the US campaign against Noriega in Panama in 1988–89 (Case 87–1)

(2) Minor contribution; illustrated by the Soviet withdrawal of assistance from China in the 1960s (Case 60–2)

(3) Modest contribution; illustrated by the withdrawal of Dutch and American economic aid to Suriname between 1982 and 1988 (Case 82–2)

(4) Significant contribution; illustrated by the US success in destabilizing the government of Rafael Trujillo in the Dominican Republic in 1960–61 (Case 60–1).

By multiplication, the two elements are combined into a "success score" that ranges in value from 1 to 16. We characterize a score of 9 or higher as a "successful" outcome. Success does not mean that the target country was vanquished by the denial of economic contacts, or even necessarily that the sanctions decisively influenced the outcome. Success is defined against more modest standards. A score of 9 means that sanctions made a modest contribution to the goal sought by the sender country and that the goal was in part realized; a score of 16 means that sanctions made a significant contribution to a successful outcome. By contrast, a score of 1 indicates that the sender country clearly failed to achieve its goals or may even have left the sender country worse off than before the measures were imposed.

Companion Policy Measures

"War is nothing but the continuation of politics with the admixture of other means."[3] The same could be said of economic sanctions. Indeed, sanctions frequently serve as a junior weapon in a battery of diplomatic artillery aimed at the antagonistic state. Leaving aside the normal means of diplomatic protest—recalling an ambassador, canceling a cultural mission—we distinguish three types of companion policies: covert action, quasi-military action, and regular military action.

Covert action, mounted by the intelligence forces, often accompanies the imposition of economic sanctions when the destabilization of a target government is sought. In destabilization cases and in other episodes where major policy changes are sought, the sender state may also invoke quasi-military force—for example, massing troops at the border or stationing war vessels off the coast. Finally, sanctions may precede or accompany actual armed hostility.

Duration of Sanctions

The life of a sanctions episode is not often defined with the precision of a college matriculation and graduation. In the early phases, the sender country may take pains to conceal and even deny that it is imposing sanctions. This seems to have been the case when the United States first began its campaigns against Chile in 1970 and against Nicaragua in 1981. In other cases, the whole episode may pass with hardly an official word, as in the US actions against the United Kingdom and France in the Suez episode of 1956 (Case 56–3). In still other cases, the ending may be misty rather than sharp, as in the Soviet campaigns against Albania and China.

Our approach in dating episodes is to start the episode with the first recorded sanctions threat from official sources or the first recorded sanctions event, whichever comes earlier. We treat the episode as ended when the sender or the target country changes its policies in a significant way, or when the campaign simply withers away. Because the exact dates of onset and termination of sanctions episodes are often indistinct, we have arbitrarily decided to round the length of sanctions episodes to the nearest whole year, disregarding the beginning and the ending month, with a minimum of one year. For example, an episode that began in January 1981 and ended in November 1983 would be counted as lasting two years (1983 minus 1981 equals 2).

---

3 Carl von Clausewitz, *Vom Kriege* (1832), cited in *The Oxford Dictionary of Quotation*, 3d ed. (Oxford: Oxford University Press, 1979, 152).

International Cooperation

In high-profile cases, such as the two world wars, the League of Nations foray against Italy, the series of US sanctions against the Soviet Union, and the 1990 sanctions against Iraq, much emphasis has been placed on achieving international cooperation in order to deny the target country access to the supplies or markets of its principal trading partners. In fact, the degree of cooperation realized has usually disappointed the lead country. Even in World Wars I and II, when the Allies ultimately achieved a high degree of cooperation, Germany was able to draw on supplies from Eastern Europe and adjacent neutral powers. The following statement, taken not from a lament of President Reagan's advisers at the Versailles or the Williamsburg summit, but from a commentary on World War I, describes the problem:

> ... all attempts in this direction [of a permanent inter-Allied organization] had been wrecked by the contradictory nature of the commercial interests of the Allied nations, which were only kept in touch with one another by means of intermittent conferences. ... (Guichard 1930, 67)

Although a complete economic blockade is seldom achieved, there are substantial differences from episode to episode in the degree of cooperation realized. We have used an index scaled from 1 to 4 to grade the extent of cooperation:

(1) No cooperation: a single sender country imposes sanctions, and usually seeks no cooperation; illustrated by the US campaign against Brazil to destabilize President João Goulart (Case 62–1)

(2) Minor cooperation: the sender country enlists verbal support and possibly token restraints from other countries; illustrated by the US sanctions imposed on the Soviet Union in part for its support of repressive measures in Poland (Case 81–3)

(3) Modest cooperation: the sender country obtains meaningful restraints— but limited in time and coverage—from some but not all the important trading partners of the target country; illustrated by the US sanctions against Castro's Cuba and against Iran during the hostage crisis

(4) Significant cooperation: the important trading partners make a major effort to limit trade, although leakages may still exist through neutral countries; illustrated by the two world wars, the early years of COCOM, and the recent US and UN sanctions against Iraq.

The many efforts and the inevitable failures in building watertight economic barriers have led, we think, to an overemphasis on the role played by cooperation in determining the success or failure of a sanctions episode.

Proponents of economic sanctions often engage in a wishful, "if only" form of argument:[4] "if only" the United States would stop all commerce with South Africa; "if only" the Japanese would restrict their financial ties to China.

From the standpoint of the sender country, it is almost axiomatic that more cooperation is better than less. But other variables are also at play. A critical variable is the nature of the objective. The inspiring words of Robert Browning seem written for sender countries: "A man's reach should exceed his grasp, or what's a heaven for?" The pursuit of more ambitious objectives accompanied by much fanfare often goes hand in hand with efforts to enlist international cooperation. After all, other countries are not likely to rally in support of modest goals, and the grasp of ambitious objectives usually remains beyond the reach of sender countries, even when assisted by a large measure of international cooperation.

International Assistance to the Target Country

The mirror image of international cooperation with the sender country is the support the target country receives from its neighbors and allies. Target countries are seldom cut off from alternative markets or financing sources when sanctions are imposed; trade and financial channels usually remain open, even though at a higher cost. For this reason, we do not count evasive and covert trade as "assistance." Such transactions are part and parcel of every episode. Rather we are concerned with overt economic or military aid to the target country in response to the imposition of sanctions.

If a target country can rely on its friends to compensate for the burdens imposed by sanctions, the impact can be reduced. Indeed, in several Cold War cases, target countries have turned sanctions to their economic advantage, coaxing opponents of the sender country to provide new or additional funds in order to "make a stand" against the policy excesses of the rival power. The United States and its allies came to the rescue of Yugoslavia in the early postwar period when Tito was threatened by Josef Stalin. The Soviets in similar fashion joined forces with Colonel Haile-Mariam Mengistu in war-torn Ethiopia to deflect US attempts to foster human rights and gain compensation for expropriated property (Case 76–3). In both cases, the amount of aid provided to the target more than offset the economic impact of the sanctions. In addition, there have been many episodes—such as the Soviet efforts against Albania and the US efforts against Nicaragua—where assistance from a major foreign power provided welcome moral support to the target.

---

4 As an example of the "if only" argument in the Rhodesian context, see Brown-John (1975, 378).

We do not attempt to scale the degree of international assistance. Instead we simply identify those cases where significant assistance was given to the target country.

Economic Health and Political Stability

The economic and political atmosphere in the target country is critical to the outcome of a sanctions episode. An analogy with rainmaking is appropriate. If storm clouds are overhead, rain may fall without anyone's help. If moisture-laden clouds are in the sky, chemical seeding may bring forth rain. But if the skies are clear and dry, no amount of human assistance will produce rain. Similarly, sanctions may be redundant, productive, or useless in pursuing foreign policy goals, depending on the economic health and political stability of the target country.

It is no simple matter to summarize the complex of events that describe a country's economy and politics at a point in time. Our task is made more difficult because we wish to know what the target country's health and stability would have been in the absence of sanctions over a period of time; that is, we want to separate the underlying conditions in the target country from the effect of the sanctions themselves. Consider, for example, the problem of assessing health and stability in the context of a successful destabilization case. At the beginning of the episode, the target country might be experiencing significant problems; shortly before its downfall, the target government might well have reached a crisis stage quite apart from the pressure imposed as a result of sanctions. We have heroically put these difficulties to one side in devising an index to describe the overall political and economic health of the target country, throughout the period of the sanctions episode and in the hypothetical absence of sanctions:

(1) Distress: a country with acute economic problems, exemplified by high unemployment and rampant inflation, coupled with political turmoil bordering on chaos; illustrated by Chile at the time of Allende and by Uganda in the later years of the Amin regime

(2) Significant problems: a country with severe economic problems, such as a foreign-exchange crisis, coupled with substantial internal dissent; illustrated by Ceylon under S.W.R.D. Bandaranaike (Case 61–1)

(3) Strong and stable: a country with the government in firm control (even though dissent may be present) and an economy experiencing only the normal range of inflation, unemployment, and similar ills; illustrated by India during the nuclear nonproliferation campaigns of the 1970s (Cases 74–2 and 78–4) and China at the time of the Tiananmen Square massacre.

Prior Relations Between Sender and Target

Sanctions are imposed against friends and foes alike. Against belligerent countries, forceful sanctions may be needed to coerce the target government into yielding, especially since the domestic political consequences of backing down can be damaging. On the other hand, a friendly country will often consider the importance of its overall relations with the sender country before fashioning a response to economic sanctions. Such considerations led South Korea and Taiwan to accede to mild US pressure and to forgo construction of nuclear reprocessing plants in the mid-1970s (Cases 75–1 and 76–2). With friends, subtle sanctions may succeed.

To reflect the role of prior relations in determining the outcome of a sanctions episode, we have constructed an index by which to classify the cases according to the state of political relations between the sender and target countries before the imposition of sanctions:

(1) Antagonistic: the sender and target countries are in opposing camps; illustrated by most East-West cases, US–Japan relations prior to World War II, and Arab-Israeli relations

(2) Neutral: the sender country does not have strong ties to the target, but there is a workable relationship without antagonism; illustrated by relations between Spain and the United Kingdom despite centuries of dispute over Gibraltar (Case 54–3), and US relations with Haiti prior to the 1987 sanctions (Case 87–2)

(3) Cordial: the sender and target countries are close friends and allies; illustrated by ties between the Arab League and Egypt prior to the Camp David accords (Case 78–6), US relations with the United Kingdom and France before the Suez crisis of 1956, and Indian relations with Nepal before the 1989 dispute.

Estimating the Costs

Sanctions are designed to penalize the target country for its unwanted behavior. In theory, the target country will weigh the costs imposed by the sanctions against the benefits derived from continuing its policies—the higher the net cost, the more likely it is that the target country will alter its policies. The absolute cost exacted on a target country is not the best measure of the potential impact, however: a cost of $100 million means more to Chile, for example, than to the Soviet Union. We have therefore related our estimated cost figures to the GNP of the target country. Our methodology for estimating the cost to the target country is explained in detail in appendix A.

We have not attempted to calculate the actual costs of sanctions to sender countries, nor have we attempted to measure the political costs visited on the sender as a result of flexing its economic muscle. Instead, we have drawn from the case abstracts a rough sense of the trade or financial loss incurred by the sender from the imposition of sanctions, and we have related this loss to the sender country's total external trade. Illustrations of our approach are provided in chapter 4. The following index reflects our judgment as to the relative cost to the sender country:

(1) Net gain to sender: usually cases where aid is withheld; illustrated by the US suspension of aid to Turkey in 1974

(2) Little effect on sender: cases where a trivial dislocation occurs; illustrated by the US export controls on nuclear fuel shipments to Taiwan in 1976

(3) Modest loss to sender: some trade is lost, but neither the size nor the concentration of the loss is substantial; illustrated by the League of Nations campaign against Italy in 1935–36

(4) Major loss to sender: large volumes of trade are adversely affected; illustrated by the two world wars and the recent US–UN sanctions against Iraq.

Country Size and Trade Linkages

Quite apart from the magnitude of costs that the sender imposes on the target, the outcome of a sanctions episode may be influenced by the relative size of the two countries and the trade links between them. The imposition of even minor sanctions carries the implicit threat of more drastic action. Whether that threat looms large or small depends very much on relative country sizes and trade flows. Hence, we include among our economic variables a ratio between sender-country and target-country GNP levels, and figures on trade between target and sender expressed as a percentage of the target country's total trade.

References

Brown-John, C. Lloyd. 1975. *Multilateral Sanctions in International Law: A Comparative Analysis*. New York: Praeger.

Carter, Barry E. 1988. *International Economic Sanctions: Improving the Haphazard U.S. Legal Regime*. Cambridge: Cambridge University Press.

Guichard, Louis. 1930. *The Naval Blockade, 1914–1918*. New York: Appleton.

3

POLITICAL VARIABLES

I n evaluating the success of economic sanctions, the first step is to distinguish between the types of foreign policy objectives sought in different sanctions episodes. The nature of the objective may be the most important political variable of all: sanctions cannot stop a military assault as easily as they can free a political prisoner. Accordingly, our discussion is organized around five major groups of objectives, namely, modest changes in policy, destabilization of the target government, disruption of military adventures, impairment of military potential, and other major policy changes. As mentioned in chapter 2, in classifying cases where more than one goal was sought, the more ambitious goal takes precedence, except in a few cases where both goals are deemed of equal weight. Thus, destabilization cases usually involve, as ancillary goals, the search for modest or even major policy changes.

Six political variables are considered in this chapter: the presence of companion policies (e.g., covert action); the extent of international cooperation with the sender; the presence of international assistance to the target; the duration of sanctions; the health and stability of the target country; and prior relations between sender and target.

Modest Changes in Policy

Sanctions have been frequently threatened or deployed in pursuit of relatively modest changes in the policies of target countries. Modest changes are not trivial changes. Changes that we have labeled modest may have seemed overwhelmingly important at the time of the confrontation to the target or the sender country. But in the grander scale of events, the settlement of an expropriation dispute or a limited improvement in respect for human rights does not compare with stopping a military adventure or destabilizing a government.

Illustrative of these episodes is Case 75–1 in which financial sanctions dissuaded South Korea from procuring a nuclear reprocessing plant from France. The objective was quite specific, and the sender states had a great deal of leverage due to Korea's "sensitivity . . . to a slight hardening in Canadian and American financial terms [for nuclear transactions]" (Wohlstetter 1976–77, 168).

The United States has been particularly active in the pursuit of modest policy goals, accounting for 41 of the 51 cases listed in table 3.1 (the United States was a co-sender in 5 of the 41 cases). This lopsided US weight may partly reflect our omission of contests between second- and third-rank powers over modest policy goals.

Of the 51 modest change cases listed in table 3.1, there are some 23 in which we scored the outcome as positive (score of 3) or successful (score of 4). (Tables 3.1 through 3.5 appear at the end of this chapter.) In 25 of the 51 cases, we conclude that sanctions made a contribution to the outcome ranging from modest (3) to significant (4). The combined result is that in 17 of the 51 cases we obtain a success score of 9 or higher. Thus, by our analysis, in one-third of the modest policy change cases, the sender country made some progress in achieving its goals through the use of economic sanctions. This, we think, is a significant finding. However, even these results should be further qualified: the success rate since 1973 is dramatically lower than that before 1973.

In their quest for modest policy changes, sender countries usually do not employ covert force, nor do they engage in quasi-military measures or regular military action. Rather, in this group of cases, sanctions tend to stand alone as the policy instrument.

Because of the narrow scope of objectives sought in this category, supporters seldom rally to help the target country counter the sanctions. The threat is usually small in political terms; both the sender and the target country treat the policy dispute as a bilateral affair.

For the same reasons, international cooperation with the sender is generally minor or nonexistent. Indeed, it is usually not sought. In part, the reason is that the sanctions in these cases were often imposed against friendly or neutral countries. In only 8 of the 51 cases (16 percent) were sanctions directed against hostile target countries. A look at table 3.1 reveals that there is little correlation between the extent of international cooperation and the contribution of sanctions to the policy outcome.

In the 17 cases for which the success score was 9 or higher, the average sanctions period was 2.8 years. In the 34 cases with success scores of 8 or lower, the average sanctions period was 5.2 years, and in 6 of these unsuccessful cases sanctions have been in effect for 10 years or more. Shorter is better.

The average score for the economic health and political stability of the target country in successful cases was 2.1 (in terms of our index, which assigns a maximum score of 3). The health and stability score in less successful episodes was also 2.1. Obviously, this indicator gives no guidance in distinguishing between failure and success among this set of cases.

Destabilizing a Government

Destabilization episodes usually spring from conflicts over other issues. In some instances, the underlying dispute involves modest changes in target-country policies, for example, to compensate for expropriation (as in Case 62–1: *US v. Brazil*), to renounce terrorism (Case 78–8: *US v. Libya*), to better safeguard human rights (Case 77–5: *US v. Nicaragua*), or to cease drug-dealing (Case 87–1: *US v. Panama*). In other instances, destabilization is sought because the target government has adopted a hostile attitude in its overall relations with the sender country.

This category of cases has a decided Cold War flavor—for example, in episodes involving Yugoslavia, Finland, and Albania, the Soviet Union found its smaller allies wandering from the socialist sphere, whereas in cases involving Cuba, Brazil, Chile, and Nicaragua (under the Sandinistas), the United States found its Western Hemisphere neighbors stealing away from the capitalist camp. Over half the cases involved attempts to overthrow the regimes of former friends. Correspondingly, when relations between sender and target were cordial before the episode, the chances of success were greater.

Table 3.2 summarizes 21 destabilization cases. Our research suggests that sanctions, coupled with other policies, are surprisingly successful in destabilizing governments. In over half the cases, the success score is 9 or greater; in one of the remaining cases (Case 78–8) the outcome remains in doubt. This high success rate contrasts sharply with the skepticism expressed in the literature, and compares positively with the results of sanctions used for other foreign policy goals.

It must be emphasized that economic sanctions unassisted by companion measures seldom achieve destabilization. Covert action and quasi-military operations regularly play a role in destabilization cases; indeed, companion policies were present in all but five of the episodes. On the other hand, international cooperation is not an important ingredient of successful destabilization episodes: in two cases the Soviet Union was supported by its East European allies, and the United States enjoyed some international cooperation in its efforts to isolate Cuba, but in each instance the target country received considerable material and moral support from an opposing major power. That support compensated for the impact of the sanctions on the target country and led to low success scores.

In the 11 cases with a success score of 9 or higher, the average sanctions period was 3.8 years; in the 10 other cases the average sanctions period was 7.4 years. Thus, sanctions that have an early impact are the most effective. If an episode drags on, it probably indicates that the target government was more resistant to erosion.

The average index of economic health and political stability for target governments that succumbed to destabilization was only 1.4. By contrast, the average index for target regimes that resisted destabilization is 1.9. It is prosaic but true: governments in distress are more easily destabilized.

In cases where another goal underlies or accompanies that of destabilization, we have generally listed the case only in the destabilization group. After all, a destabilization attempt presupposes policy disputes as well as personality differences. We make an exception, however, when the sender country seeks both to destabilize a government and to disrupt a military adventure; such cases are cross-listed under both headings.

Disrupting Military Adventures

At the end of World War I the classic rationale offered for economic sanctions was to persuade hostile countries to abandon their military adventures. Lord Curzon, a member of the war cabinet of British Prime Minister David Lloyd George, suggested in 1918 that the sure application of sanctions might have averted the outbreak of a lesser conflict than World War I:

> [Sanctions] did not, it is true, succeed in preventing the war; they have not, at any rate at present curtailed its duration, but I should like to put it this way. I doubt very much whether, if Germany had anticipated when she plunged into war the consequences, commercial, financial, and otherwise, which would be entailed upon her by two, three, or four years of war, she would not have been eager to plunge in as she was. Remember this. Though possibly we have not done all we desired, we have done a great deal, and we could have done a great deal more if our hands had not been tied by certain difficulties. It is naturally a delicate matter for me to allude to this. A good many of them have been removed by the

entry of the United States of America into the war, but we have always the task of handling with great and necessary delicacy the neutral states, and this difficulty still remains with us. (Mitrany 1925, 36)

Apparently influenced by advocates such as Lord Curzon and President Wilson, British and American policy officials came increasingly to use sanctions as an explicit substitute for military action or as a key component of an overall effort to disrupt unwelcome military adventures.

Table 3.3 identifies 18 military adventure cases. We define a military adventure as an action on a less grand scale than, for example, the Napoleonic Wars or the two world wars. The classic instance of the use of sanctions in such circumstances is Case 35–1: *UK and League of Nations v. Italy*; others include Case 40–1: *US v. Japan,* and Case 60–3: *US v. Cuba.* There are few ambiguous cases in this group: when sanctions succeeded, they did so decisively; when they failed, they flopped. In 6 of these cases, a success score of 9 or higher was reached; in another 12 cases, sanctions failed to deter the target country's martial ambitions.

The presence of companion measures—covert interference and military and quasi-military action—was not decisive in distinguishing between success and failure cases. In only one episode, Case 82–1: *UK v. Argentina,* were companion policies used to good effect. In six other instances, companion policies did not materially advance the desired outcome.

International cooperation has been of marginal significance in this group of cases. The average degree of cooperation in the 6 success cases, as measured by our index, is 2.3 (where 4 is the maximum); the average in the 12 failure cases was 2.2. In the success episodes, the sanctions period on average lasted 1.2 years. In the failure episodes, the average sanctions period was 4.4 years.

Target countries that engage in military adventures are usually not in acute distress. At most they have significant internal problems—for example, malfunctioning economies in Egypt in the mid-1960s and in Turkey in 1974. However, our data indicate that the weaker the condition of the target country, the more likely it is that sanctions will succeed: the average health and stability index for target countries was 2.0 in success cases and 2.3 in failure cases.

An additional feature that helps distinguish between success and failure episodes in this group of cases is the prior relations index. Success more often (but not invariably) resulted when the target country was either an ally, or at least neutral and on friendly terms with the sender country, prior to the episode: Case 25–1: *League of Nations v. Greece,* Case 48–1: *US v. Netherlands,* Case 56–3: *US v. UK and France,* and Case 63–1: *US v. United Arab Republic.* By contrast, in cases where a background of hostility preceded the use of sanctions, success proved elusive: Case 40–1: *US v. Japan,* Case 49–1: *US and*

CHINCOM v. China, and Case 80–1: *US v. USSR.* The average prior relations index for target countries was 2.3 in success cases and 2.1 in failure cases.

Impairing Military Potential

The immediate purpose of practically every economic sanctions episode is to diminish the potential power of the target country. Nevertheless, we can distinguish between the imposition of short-term economic measures to achieve defined political goals and the conduct of a long-term campaign to weaken a major adversary. Table 3.4 lists 10 episodes in which weakening the target's economy became an end in its own right. These episodes usually involve contests between major powers, often in wartime or in the shadow of war.

In neither World War I nor II, nor in the Korean War, did the Allies believe that sanctions would decisively contribute to the outcome. Instead, they hoped and expected that economic denial would marginally limit the adversary's military capabilities. Economic sanctions became a minor adjunct to a major war effort, and "trading with the enemy" was labeled an offense in its own right, quite apart from calculations of cost and benefit. These features distinguish the impairment episodes from the disruption of military adventure cases. Similarly, for nearly four decades (until 1990), the United States sought to constrain the Soviet military machine by denying it technological sustenance, initially through COCOM and later, in the 1980s, through additional measures associated with the Afghanistan invasion and the Polish crisis.

Apart from the two world wars, we assign these episodes low success scores. With the exception of North Korea and North Vietnam, the target countries were economically healthy and politically stable. Economic difficulties and political separatism in the Soviet Union were suppressed until the late 1980s. With the exception of North Korea, North Vietnam, and Israel, the targets were major powers. It is unreasonable to expect that sanctions that disrupt a modest amount of trade or finance can significantly detract from the economic strength of a major power.

It is not surprising that the two successes in this category were associated with major wars. But even in wartime, as subsequent studies of defeated Germany showed, it was hard to find key economic links whose destruction—whether by sanctions or by bombing—would cripple the war machine. Instead, the contribution of sanctions was one of attrition. Similarly, if COCOM played any role in the economic troubles of the Soviet Union, it was small. Internal mismanagement and the inherent contradictions of Marxism were far greater factors.

Other Major Policy Changes

Under this heading we put cases that are not already covered by the destabilization and military impairment groupings. Examples include Case 62–2: *UN v. South Africa* and Case 85–1: *US v. South Africa,* both of which had the objective of ending the South African policy of apartheid and its control of neighboring Namibia; Case 73–1: *Arab League v. US and Netherlands,* over the target countries' support of Israel; and Case 89–1: *India v. Nepal,* over Nepal's relations with China.

As table 3.5 shows, in only 5 of the 20 cases was a success score of 9 or better reached. Two of these cases involved civil wars: India's forced assimilation of Hyderabad (Case 48–2) and Nigeria's defeat of Biafra (Case 67–1). In these two cases, the success of sanctions was clear-cut. A borderline success case was the Arab League boycott: the sudden rise in the price of oil in 1973–74 from $2.59 per barrel to $11.65 per barrel gave the Organization of Petroleum Exporting Countries (OPEC) instant and spectacular wealth. In our judgment, the sanctions were not a significant cause of the price leap. However, the threat to withhold oil from diplomatic adversaries contributed to a shift in West European and Japanese policies on the Palestinian question. Accordingly, we conclude that sanctions made a positive contribution to the diplomatic achievements of the OPEC group. Other borderline success cases are Case 81–2: *US v. Poland,* in which US sanctions contributed to political liberalization, and Case 89–1, in which India reversed the brief pro-China line of the Nepalese government.

To mention just a few of the failures, there is little evidence that the Arab League boycott has moved Israel on the question of establishing a Palestinian homeland, or that sanctions helped Indonesia prevent the consolidation of neighboring territory into the nation of Malaysia. Success in abolishing apartheid in South Africa has remained elusive, although the freeing of Nelson Mandela was an important step toward the larger goal. It is noteworthy that the target countries in this group generally enjoy high levels of economic health and political stability, and that the failure cases on average lasted 8.7 years.

References

Mitrany, D. 1925. *The Problem of International Sanctions.* London: Oxford University Press.

Wohlstetter, Albert. 1976–77. "Spreading the Bomb Without Quite Breaking the Rules." 25 *Foreign Policy* (Winter): 88–96, 145–79.

Table 3.1 Cases involving modest changes in target-country policies: political variables

Case[a]	Sender and target	Policy result[b] (index)	Sanctions contribution[c] (index)	Success score[d] (index)	Companion policies[e]	International cooperation with sender[f] (index)	International assistance to target[g]	Sanctions period[h] (years)	Health and stability[i] (index)	Prior relations[j] (index)
33–1	UK v. USSR	4	3	12	—	1	—	1	2	1
38–1	UK, US v. Mexico	3	3	9	—	2	—	9	3	2
54–1	USSR v. Australia	1	1	1	—	1	—	1	3	1
56–2	US, UK, France v. Egypt	3	3	9	R	2	—	1	2	2
61–1	US v. Ceylon	4	4	16	—	1	A	4	2	2
62–3	USSR v. Romania	1	1	1	—	4	—	1	3	3
63–1	US v. United Arab Republic[k]	4	4	16	—	1	—	2	2	2
64–1	France v. Tunisia	3	3	9	—	1	—	2	2	3
65–1	US v. Chile	3	4	12	—	1	—	1	2	2
65–2	US v. India	4	4	16	—	1	—	2	2	2
68–1	US v. Peru	1	1	1	—	1	—	1	2	2
68–2	US v. Peru	3	4	12	—	1	—	6	2	2
73–2	US v. South Korea	2	2	4	—	1	—	4	2	3
73–3	US v. Chile	3	2	6	—	1	—	17+	1	2
74–2	Canada v. India	2	2	4	—	2	—	2	3	2
74–3	Canada v. Pakistan	2	2	4	—	2	—	2	2	2
75–1	US, Canada v. South Korea	4	4	16	—	2	—	1	3	3
75–2	US v. USSR	3	2	6	—	1	—	15+	3	1
75–3	US v. Eastern Europe	4	2	8	—	1	—	15+	3	1
75–4	US v. South Africa	2	2	4	—	2	—	7	3	2
76–1	US v. Uruguay	3	2	6	—	1	—	5	2	2
76–2	US v. Taiwan	4	4	16	—	1	—	1	3	3

Case		C1	C2	C3	C4	C5	C6	C7	C8	C9
76–3	US v. Ethiopia	2	1	14+	A	2	—	6	3	2
77–1	US v. Paraguay	2	3	4	—	1	—	6	3	2
77–2	US v. Guatemala	2	2	9	A	1	—	6	2	3
77–3	US v. Argentina	2	2	6	—	1	—	6	2	3
77–4	Canada v. Japan, EC	3	3	1	—	1	—	9	3	3
77–6	US v. El Salvador	2	1	4	—	1	—	6	3	3
77–7	US v. Brazil	2	2	7	—	1	—	9	3	3
78–1	China v. Albania	3	3	5	—	1	—	1	1	1
78–2	US v. Brazil	2	2	3	—	2	—	4	2	2
78–3	US v. Argentina	2	2	4	—	2	—	4	2	2
78–4	US v. India	2	3	4	—	2	—	4	2	2
78–5	US v. USSR	1	3	2	—	3	—	1	1	1
79–1	US v. Iran	3	1	2	A	2	Q	12	3	4
79–2	US v. Pakistan	2	2	11+	—	3	—	1	1	1
79–3	Arab League v. Canada	2	3	1	A	2	—	12	3	4
79–4	US v. Bolivia	2	1	3	—	3	—	6	3	2
80–2	US v. Iraq	2	2	10+	A	2	—	4	2	2
82–2	Netherlands, US v. Suriname	3	1	6	—	3	J	9	3	3
83–1	Australia v. France	3	3	3	—	1	—	1	1	1
83–2	US v. USSR	1	3	1	—	4	—	1	1	1
83–3	US v. Zimbabwe	2	2	5	—	1	—	4	2	2
84–1	US v. Iran	1	2	6+	—	2	Q	6	3	2
86–1	US v. Syria	1	2	4+	—	2	—	6	3	2
87–2	US v. Haiti	2	1	3	—	2	—	6	3	2
87–3	US v. El Salvador	3	1	1	—	3	—	16	4	4
88–1	Japan, West Germany, US v. Burma	2	1	2+	—	3	—	6	3	2
88–2	US, UK v. Somalia	3	1	2+	—	2	—	4	2	2
89–2	US v. China	3	3	1+	—	3	—	1	1	1
89–3	US v. Sudan	3	1	1+	—	2	—	1	1	1

a. The *case* numbers are those in table 1.1.

b. The *policy result*, on an index scale of 1 to 4, indicates the extent to which the outcome sought by the sender country was achieved. Key: 1 = failed outcome; 2 = unclear but possibly positive outcome; 3 = positive outcome; 4 = successful outcome.

c. The *sanctions contribution*, on an index scale of 1 to 4, indicates the extent to which the sanctions contributed to a positive result. Key: 1 = zero or negative contribution; 2 = minor contribution; 3 = modest contribution; 4 = significant contribution.

d. The *success score* is an index on a scale of 1 to 16, found by multiplying the policy result index by the sanctions contribution index.

e. Types of *companion policies* are covert action (J), quasi-military operations (Q), and regular military action (R).

f. The extent of *international cooperation with sender*, on an index scale of 1 to 4, indicates the degree of assistance received by the principal sender country in applying sanctions. Key: 1 = no cooperation; 2 = minor cooperation; 3 = modest cooperation; 4 = significant cooperation.

g. *International assistance to target*, indicated by an A, is judged to exist when another country (usually a major power) extends significant economic or military assistance to the target country. The mere transshipment of goods subject to sanction is not counted here as assistance.

h. The *sanctions period* is the time (rounded to the nearest year) from the first official threat or event to the conclusion. The minimum period is one year. A "+" indicates that the sanction is still in effect as this book goes to press.

i. *Health and stability* is an index, scaled from 1 to 3, that represents the target country's overall economic health and political stability (abstracting from sanctions) during the sanctions episode. Key: 1 = distressed country; 2 = country with significant problems; 3 = strong and stable country.

j. *Prior relations* is an index, scaled from 1 to 3, that measures the degree of warmth, prior to the sanctions episode, in overall relations between target and sender country. Key: 1 = antagonistic; 2 = neutral; 3 = cordial.

k. This case is also listed in table 3.3.

Table 3.2 Cases involving destabilization of target-country governments: political variables

Case[a]	Sender and target	Policy result[b] (index)	Sanctions contribution[c] (index)	Success score[d] (index)	Companion policies[e]	International cooperation with sender[f] (index)	International assistance to target[g]	Sanctions period[h] (years)	Health and stability[i] (index)	Prior relations[j] (index)
18–1	UK v. Russia	1	1	1	Q,R	4	—	2	1	1
44–1	US v. Argentina	2	2	4	—	2	—	3	2	2
48–4	USSR v. Yugoslavia	1	1	1	Q	4	A	7	2	3
51–1	UK, US v. Iran	4	3	12	J	2	—	2	2	3
56–4	US v. Laos	3	3	9	J	2	—	6	1	3
58–1	USSR v. Finland	4	4	16	—	1	—	1	2	3
60–1	US v. Dominican Republic	4	4	16	Q,J	3	—	2	1	3
60–3	US v. Cuba[k]	1	1	1	Q,J	3	A	30+	2	3
61–2	USSR v. Albania	1	1	1	J	4	A	4	2	3
62–1	US v. Brazil	4	3	12	J	1	—	2	1	2
63–3	US v. Indonesia[k]	4	2	8	—	1	—	3	2	2
63–4	US v. South Vietnam	4	3	12	J	1	—	1	1	3
65–3	UK, UN v. Rhodesia	4	3	12	Q	4	A	14	2	3
70–1	US v. Chile	4	3	12	J	1	—	3	1	2
72–1	UK, US v. Uganda	4	3	12	—	2	—	7	1	2
77–5	US v. Nicaragua	4	3	12	—	1	—	2	1	3
78–8	US v. Libya	2	2	4	Q,J	1	—	12+	3	1
81–1	US v. Nicaragua	4	2	8	Q,J	1	A	9	2	2
82–3	South Africa v. Lesotho	4	4	16	Q	1	—	2	2	3
83–4	US, OECS v. Grenada	4	2	8	R	3	—	1	1	2
87–1	US v. Panama	4	1	4	Q,J,R	1	A	3	2	3

a.–j. See table 3.1.

k. These cases are also listed in table 3.3.

Table 3.3　Cases involving disruption of military adventures (other than major wars): political variables

Case[a]	Sender and target	Policy result[b] (index)	Sanctions contribution[c] (index)	Success score[d] (index)	Companion policies[e]	International cooperation with sender[f] (index)	International assistance to target[g]	Sanctions period[h] (years)	Health and stability[i] (index)	Prior relations[j] (index)
21–1	League v. Yugoslavia	4	4	16	—	4	—	1	2	2
25–1	League v. Greece	4	4	16	—	4	—	1	2	2
32–1	League v. Paraguay, Bolivia	3	2	6	—	3	—	3	2	2
35–1	UK, League v. Italy	1	1	1	—	4	A	1	3	2
40–1	US v. Japan	1	1	1	—	2	—	1	3	1
48–1	US v. Netherlands	4	4	16	—	1	—	1	2	3
49–1	US, CHINCOM, v. China[k]	1	1	1	R,Q	3	A	4[l]	3	1
56–3	US v. UK, France	4	3	12	—	1	—	1	3	3
57–2	France v. Tunisia	1	1	1	R	1	A	6	2	3
60–3	US v. Cuba[m]	1	1	1	J,Q	3	A	15+[n]	2	3
63–1	US v. United Arab Republic[o]	4	4	16	—	1	—	2	2	2
63–3	US v. Indonesia[m]	4	2	8	—	1	—	3	2	2
71–1	US v. India, Pakistan	2	1	2	Q	1	—	1	2	2
74–1	US v. Turkey	1	1	1	—	1	—	4	2	3
75–5	US v. Kampuchea	1	1	1	—	1	—	4	1	2
78–7	China v. Vietnam	3	1	3	R	3	A	10	2	3
80–1	US v. USSR (Afghanistan)[k]	1	1	1	J	3	—	1	3	3
82–1	UK v. Argentina	4	3	12	R	3	—	1	1	2

a.–j. See table 3.1.

k. These cases are also listed in table 3.4.

l. For this case, the length of the episode is linked to the Korean war period only.

m. These cases are also listed in table 3.2

n. For this case, the length of the episode is linked to the deployment of Cuban troops in foreign countries (e.g., Angola).

o. This case is also listed in table 3.1.

Table 3.4 Cases involving impairment of military potential (including major wars): political variables

Case[a] Sender and target	Policy result[b] (index)	Sanctions contribution[c] (index)	Success score[d] (index)	Companion policies[e]	International cooperation with sender[f] (index)	International assistance to target[g]	Sanctions period[h] (years)	Health and stability[i] (index)	Prior relations[j] (index)
14–1 UK v. Germany	4	3	12	R	4	A	4	3	1
39–1 Alliance Powers v. Germany, Japan	4	3	12	R	4	A	6	3	1
46–1 Arab League v. Israel	2	2	4	R	3	A	44+	3	1
48–5 US, COCOM v. USSR, COMECON	3	2	6	—	4	A	42+	3	1
49–1 US, CHINCOM v. China[k]	1	1	1	R,Q	3	A	21	3	1
50–1 US, UN v. North Korea	2	1	2	R	4	A	40+	2	1
54–4 US, South Vietnam v. North Vietnam	1	1	1	R	2	A	36+	2	1
60–2 USSR v. China	2	2	4	Q	3	—	10	3	3
80–1 US v. USSR (Afghanistan)[k]	1	1	1	J	3	—	1	3	1
81–3 US v. USSR (Poland)	1	1	1	—	2	—	1	3	1

a.–j. See table 3.3.

k. These cases are also listed in table 3.1.

Table 3.5 Cases involving other major changes in target-country policies (including surrender of territory): political variables

Case[a]	Sender and target	Policy result[b] (index)	Sanctions contribution[c] (index)	Success score[d] (index)	Companion policies[e]	International cooperation with sender[f] (index)	International assistance to target[g]	Sanctions period[h] (years)	Health and stability[i] (index)	Prior relations[j] (index)
17–1	US v. Japan	2	2	4	—	1	—	1	3	2
48–2	India v. Hyderabad	4	3	12	R	1	—	1	2	3
48–3	USSR v. US, UK, France	1	1	1	Q	1	A	1	3	1
54–2	India v. Portugal	4	2	8	R	1	—	7	3	2
54–3	Spain v. UK	2	3	6	—	1	—	30	3	2
56–1	US v. Israel (intermittent episodes)	2	1	2	—	1	—	4	3	3
57–1	Indonesia v. Netherlands	4	2	8	R	2	—	5	3	2
61–3	Western Allies v. German Democratic Republic	1	1	1	Q	3	A	1	3	1
62–2	UN v. South Africa	2	3	6	—	3	—	28+	3	2
63–2	Indonesia v. Malaysia	1	1	1	Q	1	—	3	2	2
63–5	UN, Organization of African Unity v. Portugal	4	2	8	—	3	—	11	2	2
65–4	US v. Arab League	2	3	6	R	2	—	25+	3	2
67–1	Nigeria v. Biafra	4	3	12	R	1	—	3	1	3
73–1	Arab League v. US, Netherlands	3	3	9	—	3	A	1	3	2
78–6	Arab League v. Egypt	1	1	1	—	3	A	5	2	3
81–2	US v. Poland	3	3	9	—	3	A	6	1	2
81–4	EC v. Turkey	2	3	6	—	2	—	1	2	3
85–1	US v. South Africa	2	3	6	—	4	—	5+	2	2
86–2	US v. Angola	2	1	2	J	1	—	4+	2	1
89–1	India v. Nepal	3	3	9	—	1	—	1	2	3
90–1	US, UN v. Iraq[k]	—	—	—	Q	4	—	1+	2	2

a.–j. See table 3.1.
k. As this book goes to press, it is still too early to score this case; other variables are as of the moment the book goes to press.

4

![black bar]

ECONOMIC VARIABLES

The data for the economic variables in the sanctions episodes we studied are summarized in tables 4.3 through 4.7 at the end of this chapter. As in chapter 3, we have grouped the cases according to the principal foreign policy objective in each case. However, in this chapter we organize the discussion according to the economic variables.

Size of Sender and Target Countries

The economy of the sender country is usually very much larger than that of the target country. In most cases, the sender's GNP is over 10 times greater than the target's GNP, and in over half the ratio is greater than 50. When the goal is destabilization of the target country, the GNP ratio exceeds 100 over 70 percent of the time. These figures reflect, on the one hand, the prominence of the United States, the United Kingdom, and the Soviet Union as senders and, on the other hand, the small size of the countries they usually try to influence with economic sanctions.

In many instances, when the GNP ratio is under 10, sanctions founder. Several cases that entail major policy changes belong to this category of failures. These cases either involve big-power confrontations or sender countries that are not major powers. Examples are the series of US–USSR confrontations and Canadian attempts to advance nuclear nonproliferation policies in the mid-1970s. In several instances, however, sanctions were successful even though the GNP ratio was less than 10: the two world wars; US efforts against the United Kingdom and France during the Suez crisis (Case 56–3); the Arab oil embargo against the United States and the Netherlands (Case 73–1; in this case, the GNP ratio was less than 1); and the British sanctions against Argentina during the Falklands war (Case 82–1). But in most of these instances military victory was critical to the success of the episode.

Another aspect of these cases should be noted. The two cases in which sanctions were not accompanied by military conflict involved a strategic commodity: oil. During the Suez crisis, the United States threatened to provoke a sterling crisis in the United Kingdom by denying it access to its reserves with the International Monetary Fund (IMF), as well as dollar credits that it needed to replenish its oil reserves. More directly, in the 1973 oil embargo case, the Arab countries' control of vast oil supplies gave them leverage far out of proportion to the size of their economies as measured by their GNP. By the same token, a target country's control of a strategic commodity may increase its counterleverage out of proportion to the size of its economy. For example, even though the US economy is 54 times larger than South Africa's, US policymakers have been hesitant in their application of sanctions, partly out of concern that South Africa would retaliate by withholding exports of key metals and minerals.

Trade Linkages

Since sender countries are generally very large countries, it is not surprising that the target's import and export trade with the sender usually accounts for over 10 percent of the target's total trade. In the cases we have scored as successes, the sender country accounts, on average, for over a quarter of the target country's total trade. Even when the sender country interrupts only a small portion of that trade, the interruption carries an important message to the target country: change your policies or risk a larger disturbance.

The trade ratios in cases involving modest policy goals vary greatly. Some cases were successful when only a small amount of bilateral trade was involved: for example, in Case 61–1 the United States accounted for only 9 percent of Ceylon's exports and 3 percent of its imports. Yet many other cases were unsuccessful even when a high proportion of trade was at stake: such was the case in the confrontation between the United States and Guatemala over human rights (Case 77–2); over one-third of Guatemala's total trade was with the United States. In general, however, higher trade linkages are more closely associated with success episodes (average trade linkage of 25 percent) than with failure episodes (average trade linkage of 15 percent).

Because of the usually close geographic proximity of senders and targets in destabilization cases, their trade linkages are generally strong. One exception is Case 72–1: *UK and US v. Uganda,* over the atrocities of the Idi Amin regime. But in almost every case in this group, the sender takes more than 10 percent of the exports, and supplies over 10 percent of the imports, of the target country. Within this group, the extent of linkage appears somewhat greater for success cases (average of 38 percent) than for failure cases (average of 27 percent).

Trade linkage does not appear to distinguish between success and failure in episodes involving the disruption of military adventure or the impairment of military potential (these cases are listed in tables 4.5 and 4.6). However, in cases involving other major policy changes, listed in table 4.7, the trade linkage was decidedly higher in success episodes than in failures. Some successful cases involve high trade dependencies (Case 25–1: *League of Nations v. Greece*; Case 63–1: *US v. United Arab Republic*; Case 81–4: *EC v. Turkey*), whereas other successes occur when the bilateral trade relations are small (for example, Case 82–1; in this case, however, the financial ties between the United Kingdom and Argentina were much stronger than the trade ties). Conversely, high levels of bilateral trade do not ensure success, as is evident in the UN sanctions against South Africa from 1962 on (Case 62–2) and Soviet measures against China in the 1960s (Case 60–2).

Type of Sanction

Success may depend, to some extent, on whether the sanctions hit a sensitive sector in the target country's economy. A $100 million cost may have quite different effects—at home and abroad—depending on whether it is imposed by way of export sanctions, import sanctions, or financial sanctions. Officials in the US State Department and other foreign ministries spend long hours tailoring their creations because they believe that the cut of a sanction matters a great deal.

Trade Sanctions

When trade weapons are deployed, sender countries more frequently use export than import controls. One reason is that sender countries are more likely to enjoy a dominant market position as suppliers of exports than as purchasers of imports. Hence, for a given interruption of trade, sender countries may inflict greater pain by stopping exports than by stopping imports. The dominant position of the United States as a manufacturer of military hardware and high-technology equipment has particularly influenced US tactics. In addition, there are certain products or technologies—for example, nuclear materials and technologies—that sender countries may simply wish to deny to certain targets because the "toys" are too dangerous. However, global economic development and the rapid diffusion of technologies mean that unilateral export controls generally provide less leverage today than in the period shortly after World War II.

A second reason for the emphasis on export controls, and one peculiar to the United States, is that the Congress has given the president much greater flexibility to restrain exports than to slow imports. Exports may be stopped readily through the mechanisms of the Export Administration Act, whereas imports can be slowed only by invoking the more cumbersome International Emergency Economic Powers Act, the national security section (section 232) of the Trade Expansion Act of 1962, or preexisting quota legislation (such as sugar or textile quotas).

As Carter (1988) has noted, Congress was prepared, in revising the Export Administration Act in 1985, to expand the president's authority to control imports for foreign policy reasons. However, President Ronald Reagan did not want this new authority for fear it would be later misused for protectionist purposes. Reagan's concerns were in a sense borne out by the nature of import controls later imposed by Congress against South African goods (Case 85–1): these controls were applied selectively to textiles and apparel, iron and steel, agricultural products, and a few other items.

However, it is worth pointing out that export controls often result in a concentrated burden on individual companies in the sender country, whereas import controls usually spread the burden more widely. This is one argument for devising statutes that make it equally easy (or equally hard) for the executive branch to impose import controls as to impose export controls.[1]

Financial Sanctions

Financial sanctions were used alone, without trade controls, in 32 of our 116 cases. Export and/or import sanctions, unaccompanied by financial measures, were used in only 24 instances. Financial sanctions in combination with trade controls were deployed in 55 of our 116 cases,[2] and in 34 of these 55 cases all three types of sanctions were imposed. The United States, which was a sender in 77 cases overall, has played an even more dominant role in the use of financial sanctions, employing them in 90 percent of the cases in which they were used without accompanying trade controls (see tables 4.3 to 4.7). Indeed, as the comparative data in table 4.1 reveal, the United States was not only the

---

1 Article XXI of the General Agreement on Tariffs and Trade (GATT) enables a country to take "any action which it considers necessary for its national security interests. . . . " Notwithstanding this provision, Nicaragua challenged US sanctions on sugar imports as inconsistent with the GATT (Case 81–1). A GATT panel determined that these import controls, imposed for foreign policy purposes, do not fall within the purview of Article XXI.

2 In the remaining five cases, sanctions were threatened but not imposed.

dominant user overall of economic sanctions in the post–World War II era, but also a far more frequent user of financial sanctions than the European Community or Japan.

The most common type of financial sanction is the interruption of official development assistance. Although Export-Import Bank financing, multilateral development bank loans,[3] and other forms of official and private credit have been linked to political goals from time to time, the majority of cases involve the manipulation of bilateral economic and military assistance to developing countries.

The ultimate financial sanction is a freeze of financial assets held by the target country in the sender country. An assets freeze not only stops financial flows but also impedes trade. The legal and political consequences of an assets freeze are severe, because it entails blocking access by the target country to its own property. For this reason, foreign assets have only been frozen in times of great hostility. In fact, all 13 cases occurred either during or just prior to a period of military conflict or were accompanied by some degree of military force. In all of these cases, financial sanctions were also supplemented with trade controls, often in the form of a complete embargo.

In our judgment, only 3 of 12 assets freeze cases had a positive or successful outcome to which sanctions contributed modestly (the remaining episode, Case 90–1: *US and UN v. Iraq,* remains undecided as this book goes to press).[4] The assets freezes imposed by the United States against Iran in 1979 (Case 79–1) and by the United Kingdom against Argentina in 1982 clearly contributed to the resolution of those conflicts by inhibiting the ability of the target countries to purchase weapons and ammunition (in the Iranian case, Tehran was inhibited in pursuing its war against Iraq). Economic sanctions, including an assets freeze, also contributed to Egyptian President Gamal Abdel Nasser's willingness to negotiate a compromise solution for governing the Suez Canal

---

3 The charters of the IMF, World Bank, and other international financial institutions (IFIs) prohibit them from using their funds for political purposes. The US Congress has from time to time passed amendments to appropriations bills requiring the US representatives to these institutions to vote no or to abstain from votes on loans to various countries. However, such US actions usually had no effect since the United States no longer has veto power in the IFIs, and other members either have not shared US goals or its willingness to politicize those institutions. Nevertheless, suspension of multilateral loans does appear as a sanction in some cases, usually those involving expropriation or nationalization, which is deemed an inappropriate economic policy by the IFIs.

4 Baldwin (1985), among other observers, would rate episodes a success if they signalled that military action was imminent. By this standard, we would concede that many of the episodes were a "success". By our standard, however, the following cases were failures: Case 40–1: *US v. Japan*; Case 44–1: *US v. Argentina*; Case 50–1: *US and UN v. North Korea*; Case 54–4: *US and South Vietnam v. North Vietnam*; Case 60–3: *US v. Cuba*; Case 75–5: *US v. Kampuchea*; and Case 57–1: *Indonesia v. Netherlands* in 1957. Case 87–1: *US v. Panama* had a "successful" outcome, but the sanctions were a nonsignificant factor.

Table 4.1 Comparison of US, EC, and Japanese sanctions in recent and continuing episodes[a]

Target	Period	United States			European Community[b]			Japan		
		Export	Import	Financial	Export	Import	Financial	Export	Import	Financial
COMECON	Since 1948	X			X			X		
North Korea	Since 1950	X	X	X						
Vietnam	Since 1957	X	X	X						
Cuba	Since 1960	X	X	X						
South Africa	Since 1962	X	X	X	X	X	X	X	X	X
Angola	Since 1974		X	X						
Cambodia	Since 1975	X	X	X	X		X			
Libya[c]	Since 1978	X	X	X	X			X		
Iran[d]	1979–81	X		X	X					
Pakistan	Since 1979			X	X					
Bolivia	1979–82	X		X						
USSR	1980–81	X								
Iraq	Since 1980	X								
Nicaragua	1981–90	X	X	X						
Poland	1981–87	X	X	X			X			X
USSR	1981–82	X		X			X			
Suriname[f]	1982–88			X						
USSR	1983		X			X			X	
Zimbabwe	1983–88			X						
Grenada	1983	X	X	X						

Iran[g]	Since 1984	X	X			X	
Panama	1987–90	X	X	X			
El Salvador	1987–88		X	X			
Haiti	1987–90			X			X
China	Since 1989	X	X	X	X	X	X
Iraq	Since 1990	X	X	X	X	X	X

a. An X indicates the use of this type of sanction. For continuing episodes, an X is only used if the measure is currently in force.

b. Sanctions by the European Community includes both those by the EC as a political entity and those by any of its member states.

c. The EC has limited arms shipments to Libya.

d. EC and Japanese restraints on trade with Iran were mild.

e. France cooperated in restricting nuclear technology.

f. In the EC, only the Netherlands imposed financial sanctions.

g. France banned Iranian oil imports.

Sources: Hufbauer (1990).

after he had nationalized it in the summer of 1956 (Case 56–2). In general, however, even the freezing of assets made a limited contribution to cases involving the pursuit of major objectives, and in these cases sanctions were usually a small supplement to the use of military force.

Comparing Financial and Trade Sanctions

The economic and political effects of trade and financial sanctions differ in several ways. Trade controls are usually selective, affecting one or a few goods: for example, Soviet imports of wool from Australia in 1954 (boycotted in the context of an espionage scandal; Case 54–1) or US exports of nuclear technology to various developing countries in the 1970s. In such cases, the trade may only be diverted rather than cut off. Whether import prices paid by (or export prices received by) the target country increase (or decrease) after the sanctions are applied depends on the market in question. Often the price effects are very modest.

In contrast, alternative financing may be harder to find and is likely to carry a higher price (i.e., a higher interest rate) and require greater credit security because of the uncertainties sanctions create. Official development assistance may be irreplaceable. In addition, financial sanctions, especially involving trade finance, may interrupt a wide range of trade flows even without the imposition of explicit trade sanctions.

The economic effects of financial sanctions also may tilt the political balance more sharply in the sender country's favor. The pain from trade sanctions, especially export controls, usually is diffused through the target country's population. Financial sanctions, on the other hand, are more likely to hit the pet projects or personal pockets of government officials who are in a position to influence policy. On the sender's side of the equation, an interruption of official aid or credit is unlikely to create the same political backlash from business firms and allies abroad as an interruption of private trade.

Comparing episodes of financial sanctions with trade sanctions reveals other factors that may contribute to leverage. All but 3 of the 32 cases in which financial sanctions were used alone feature the United States as a sender; it was a co-sender with the Netherlands in one of these (Case 82–2, against Suriname), and with Japan and Germany in another (Case 88–1, against Burma). Only two episodes did not involve the manipulation of economic, food, or military assistance: Case 56–3 (the Suez crisis) and Case 86–2: *US v. Angola*. The 24 trade cases in which trade controls alone were imposed (import controls 3 times, export controls 16 times, and the two together 5 times) present a rather different picture. The United States was the principal sender in only half the cases and was a target in two. The Soviet Union, which is represented in none of the financial-only cases, was a sender in two cases in which only trade sanctions were used and a target in six.

The different cast of characters and the predominance of aid manipulation in the financial sanctions episodes creates significant differences in relevant economic and political variables:

☐ The cost to the sender of financial sanctions was, on average, negligible

☐ The economic and political health and stability of the target were typically very weak

☐ Relations between sender and target were relatively close prior to the imposition of sanctions

☐ The incidence of international cooperation with the sender country was relatively low—usually because it was not needed

☐ The economic costs of sanctions as a percentage of target-country GNP were nearly twice as high when finance was interrupted as when trade alone was interrupted.

If one views financial sanctions in their overall context, it is perhaps not surprising that a successful outcome was scored in 13 of the 32 financial-only cases (41 percent). By contrast, a successful outcome was scored in only 6 of the 24 trade-only cases (25 percent) and in 18 of the 55 combined trade-finance cases (33 percent).

The Cost of Sanctions

Sanctions are supposed to impose economic penalties in order to coerce the target country to alter its policies; if the sanctions impose no costs, they are unlikely to change foreign behavior. In short, the level of costs importantly determines the success or failure of a sanctions episode.

Costs to Targets

Economists have constructed fairly elaborate theoretical models to suggest how the conditions of supply and demand for the sanctioned commodity might affect the level of costs incurred by the sender and imposed on the target, and how the balance of costs might affect the outcome of a sanctions episode. Unfortunately, the more elaborate the model, the less likely that it is tarnished by economic data. In fact, few studies go beyond anecdotal accounts of the costs that economic sanctions impose on target countries. We have therefore developed a very simple analytical construct to guide our own rudimentary efforts to estimate the costs imposed on the target country. Our methodology is detailed in appendix A.

To calculate the cost of sanctions to the target country in each episode, we have estimated the initial deprivation of markets, supplies, or finance, expressed on an annualized basis in current US dollars. To calculate the welfare loss to the target's economy, we then used our own judgment to estimate the "sanctions multiplier" that should be applied in the context of the particular episode. Some types of sanctions affect the target country more than others for a given interruption of trade or finance. The welfare loss caused by reductions in aid may be 100 percent of the value of the aid; on the other hand, trade controls may cause less harm than the value of the shipments affected because of the availability of other markets or substitution of other goods.

We recognize that the third law of physics—for every action there is a reaction—seems to play a role in the course of a sanctions episode. The impact of sanctions on the target country may be partially or totally offset by the helping hand of another major power. There are several instances in which the target has actually become better off, in economic terms, as a result of the sanctions. Soviet attempts to pressure Yugoslavia in 1948 (Case 48–4) failed miserably from Moscow's perspective, but yielded Marshal Tito an abundant harvest of Western aid and trade credits. In a similar fashion, American efforts to sway Ethiopian policy on human rights and compensation issues (Case 76–3) helped push Colonel Haile-Mariam Mengistu into the waiting and generous arms of the Soviets. In our cost estimates we attempt to reflect these offsetting benefits.

A brief survey of three cases may help illustrate our calculations of economic costs.

Case 35–1: UK and League of Nations v. Italy (1935–36: Abyssinia)

In a belated attempt to coerce Italy into withdrawing its troops from Abyssinia, the League agreed in late 1935 to a limited trade embargo and to restrictions on loans and credits to Italy. The sanctions did not include key commodities such as oil, nor were they universally applied by League and non-League members (the most important nonmember, the United States, did not apply sanctions). Nonetheless, trade was sharply reduced from the presanction period. Financial conditions in Italy were also affected by the sanctions (and the cost of the war): the lira was devalued by 25 percent in November 1935, and Italy was forced to sell about $94 million in gold between November 1935 and June 1936 to bolster its dwindling reserves.

The sanctions caused a decline in both exports and imports. During the six months when sanctions were in effect, exports dropped by $56 million and imports by $72 million from the previous year's levels. Yet in analyzing this period, M. J. Bonn noted that "[s]tocks on hand, the practice of economies, the development of substitutes, and the purchase of goods with gold, foreign securities, emigrants' remittances and tourists' disbursements kept the country going without too severe a strain" (Bonn 1937, 360). The elasticity of substitution was undoubtedly high. Accordingly, we estimated the welfare loss to the Italian economy at 30 percent of the value of interrupted trade, or $34 million and $43 million, respectively, for exports and imports, when calculated on an annualized basis. In addition, we estimated that Italy incurred a financial loss of $9 million because of forced gold sales, which we estimated to have been made at a 10 percent discount. In sum, we estimate that the sanctions led to an $86 million loss in welfare to the Italian economy, equal to 1.7 percent of GNP.

Case 48–4: USSR v. Yugoslavia (1948–55: Nationalism)

Soviet leader Josef Stalin used economic pressure and threats of military intervention in an attempt to force Marshal Tito's Yugoslavia back into the Soviet fold. Almost all economic ties between Yugoslavia and the Soviet bloc were suspended by mid-1949. The sanctions led Yugoslavia to expand its trade and to seek military and economic aid from the West. Total trade flows were not reduced, but there was a dramatic shift in the direction of trade: in 1948, over 50 percent of Yugoslav trade was with the Soviet Union and Eastern Europe; by 1954, over 80 percent of trade was with the United States and Western Europe.

Yugoslavia claimed it lost $400 million between 1948 and 1954 as a result of the Soviet sanctions. Our calculations are in the same ball park. We took the amount of Soviet credits offered to Yugoslavia at the end of the sanctions episode—$289 million in 1955—as a surrogate for the reduction in aid from the COMECON countries. Spreading the credits over a six-year period and estimating the welfare loss at 75 percent of the value of the aid yields an annualized cost of $36 million. The suspension of debt payments by COMECON countries also cost the Yugoslavs about $300 million over the period 1948–54, which, when valued at 70 percent of the lost revenues, led to a further loss of $35 million per year. The confrontation with the Soviet bloc also caused a sharp increase in military expenditures, which accounted for 22 percent of national income during 1950–54 (Farrell 1956, 27–30). The increase in the military budget was directly attributable to the heightened tensions caused by the Soviet sanctions; accordingly, we also took account of increases in the Yugoslav military budget over the sanctions period. Annual military expenditures in 1950–54 ran about $162 million above the 1948 level; we estimated the annual welfare loss at 25 percent of the additional expenditures, or $40.5 million a year.

These various costs amounted to 3.6 percent of Yugoslav GNP in 1952. However, the costs were more than offset by compensating aid flows from the United States and Europe and loans from the World Bank. From 1950 to 1954, Yugoslavia received about $1 billion in military and economic aid from the West. Clearly, such funds would not have been forthcoming in the absence of a breach in the Soviet bloc. We estimated Yugoslavia's welfare gain as 75 percent of the transfers, or $187.5 million a year. As a result, there was an annual net welfare *gain* to the Yugoslav economy during this period of $76 million, equal to 2.5 percent of GNP.

Case 60–1: US v. Dominican Republic (1960–62: Trujillo)

The notorious abuses of Rafael Trujillo prompted the United States in 1960 to impose a limited trade embargo to destabilize the Trujillo regime. The embargo covered arms, petroleum products, trucks, and spare parts. In addition, the United States imposed a special entry fee of 2 cents a pound for sugar imported from the Dominican Republic in excess of the established quota. Although nominally multilateral, for all practical purposes the sanctions were imposed only by the United States.

The most costly measure was the US sugar fee. It has been estimated elsewhere (Brown-John 1975, 229) that this fee cost the Dominican Republic about $12.5 million per year. Imports of the sanctioned petroleum products fell by 25 percent, but limited product coverage and alternative sourcing in Europe softened the impact on the Dominican economy. Accordingly, we estimated the annual welfare loss due to the petroleum embargo at 30 percent of the trade affected by the sanctions, or only $0.7 million on an annual basis. Imports of trucks, buses, and parts were so small that the losses caused by the sanctions had a negligible impact. Nonetheless, in total the sanctions put the squeeze on an already shaky economy and contributed both to a drop in per capita GNP from $293 in 1960 to $267 in 1961 and to a decline of $28 million in gold and foreign-exchange reserves. We estimated that the drop in reserves resulted in a welfare loss of $2.8 million (10 percent of the actual decline). Overall, then, the sanctions cost the Dominican Republic some $16 million, equal to 1.9 percent of GNP in 1960.

As these three examples show, we tried to err on the side of overestimating the economic impact of sanctions on target countries. Nevertheless, we uncovered few cases in which sanctions inflicted a heavy cost relative to national income. Very seldom did the costs of sanctions (expressed on an annualized basis) reach even 1 percent of the target country's GNP. Of course, government officials fight very hard for policy changes that might change GNP by 1 percent, and elections are won or lost, and coups are staged, with the expenditure of far less money. Still, the numbers seem small.[5]

Why don't sanctions impose a heavier cost on the target country? The most important reason is that sender countries encounter great difficulty in

---

5 The outlier on this variable is Iraq; we estimate that the UN embargo is costing the Iraqi economy nearly half its 1988 level of output.

extending the scope of sanctions to cover a broad range of economic activity and a large number of trading partners. Even when allied governments embark on a joint sanctions effort, the obstacles are formidable. Sanctions create powerful incentives for evasion. It could be said that a sieve leaks like a sanction. Ingenious new trading relationships, devised by domestic and third-country firms, flower because it is difficult to trace the origin and destination of traded goods. In the 1980s, Iran and Argentina obtained spare military parts, and Libya marketed its oil in Europe (albeit at some cost and delay) thanks to triangular trade arrangements. Moreover, transshipments can be routed through friendly (or at least not antagonistic) countries: for many years, the lifeline for Rhodesia was its continuing trade with South Africa, Zambia, and Mozambique.

The US–UN sanctions against Iraq will provide a most interesting test case. Almost all countries have joined in the embargo, making it the most watertight array of trade and financial restrictions since World War II. But how much Iraqi and Kuwaiti oil will be surreptitiously sold via Iran? To what extent will civilian supplies and war material leak back across the frontiers with Jordan, Turkey, and Iran? Will the exception, in both the US and the UN resolutions, allowing for "humanitarian" food shipments, prove to be Saddam's lifeline?

Despite the many leakages, sanctions do impose a cost. And when the costs exceed 1 percent of GNP, sanctions often succeed. Destabilization episodes stand out as cases where the sender country is generally willing and able to turn the screws hard. In more than two-thirds of the destabilization cases, the cost of sanctions equaled or exceeded 1 percent of GNP. By contrast, when a sender seeks modest policy goals, it seldom inflicts heavy costs: in only 20 percent of the cases listed in table 4.3 did the costs exceed 1 percent of GNP. Yet even sanctions that exert a modest impact relative to GNP can contribute to the successful achievement of foreign policy goals. The fear of deprivation can be just as important as deprivation itself. Moreover, policy decisions often turn on amounts that are quite small in GNP terms.

Costs to Senders

Foreign policy measures generally entail domestic costs, and sanctions episodes are no exception. Domestic firms pay an immediate price when trade, aid, or financial flows are disrupted. Moreover, sanctions increase the long-term uncertainty, and therefore the cost, of doing business abroad. All trading partners of the sender country, not just the target country, may be prompted to diversify their sources of supply and seek alternative partners for joint ventures and technologies not developed in the sender country. In cases involving a large number of economically significant countries or a strategic commodity, as with the US–UN embargo of Iraq and the 1973 Arab oil embargo of the United States and the Netherlands, sanctions may even have broader macroeconomic effects.

There is a limited exception to the general rule that sanctions entail costs for the sender country. If the sender seeks to coerce the target by cutting aid or official credits, the sender may enjoy an immediate economic gain due to a reduction in budget expenditures.[6] But even in these instances, the corollary loss of trade contacts may entail an economic burden, in the form of lost sales and jobs, on the sender country.

It is often said that the sender country in a sanctions episode should seek to maximize its political gains and to minimize its economic costs. Sometimes this advice is translated into the recommendation that the sender country should seek to maximize the ratio of costs inflicted to costs incurred. At best, these precepts are honored in the abstract. The domestic costs of a sanctions episode are rarely calculated—and almost never in advance—for two basic reasons.

First, it is just plain hard to quantify the costs to the sender country. Too many intangible factors are at play. If the green eyeshade staff of the Office of Management and Budget were ever asked to calculate the costs of imposing sanctions, they would be aghast. Hard data rarely exist. And many costs appear only years later in the form of lost sales opportunities for domestic firms branded with the tag of "unreliable supplier."

The second reason for not making advance calculations is that, for large countries, the overall impact on the sender's economy may be regarded as trivial. In most of the cases we have examined, the cost to the target is less than 1 percent of its GNP. The costs borne by the sender country, as a percentage of its GNP, usually will be very much less, since as a rule the sender has by far the larger economy. From the lofty perspective of the White House or 10 Downing Street, the costs may seem entirely affordable.

However, the US grain embargo and pipeline sanctions cases of the early 1980s (Cases 80–1 and 81–3) focused attention on the very different perspective of the individual firm. Sanctions are paid for by the industries whose trade is most deeply affected. In contrast, most other foreign and defense policies are financed out of general treasury revenues.

Sanctions can amount to a discriminatory, sector-specific, and therefore unfair tax to finance foreign policy. In many instances, sanctions restrict the

---

6 In the US Foreign Assistance Act of 1989, numerous provisions were inserted conditioning aid on the actions of foreign countries: section 511 (human rights); section 512 (which singles out Angola, Cambodia, Cuba, Iraq, Libya, Vietnam, South Yemen, Iran, and Syria for general bad behavior); section 513 (military coups); section 518 (the Brooke amendment, on countries in default); section 527 (monitoring the UN voting records of aid recipients); section 539 (refugee resettlement); and sections 563 and 564 (terrorism).

sale of goods that are available from competitors in foreign countries, or require the cancellation of existing contracts, or both. The impact of sanctions may fall most heavily on those few firms that suffer lost sales and damaged reputations. This sort of lopsided burdensharing can quickly arouse political opposition to the goals of the sender government.

Reflecting these concerns, the US Export Administration Act of 1979 contained safeguards to guard against its overzealous use and the consequent damage to US export interests.[7] However, the grain embargo and pipeline cases quickly revealed these safeguards to be ineffective. The Export Administration Act was therefore eventually extended as the Export Administration Amendments Act of 1985 (1985 EAAA), which put additional limits on presidential power. The most important new limitations are a time limit on agricultural embargoes, a provision limiting the president's power to impose controls on exports subject to existing contracts, and stricter criteria for the imposition of controls, taking the availability of foreign substitutes into account.

Congress, in the 1985 EAAA, inserted a sunset provision that permitted the president to enact a 60-day embargo on agricultural goods, which could be extended for one year if Congress endorsed the sanctions by joint resolution. Otherwise, after 60 days the export controls would expire. However, the president is given unfettered discretion, in section 2406(g)(3)(B)(ii) of the legislation, to block all agricultural exports as part of a generalized export embargo.

The 1985 amendments also protect existing contracts for export or reexport: section 108(1) provides that the president can break those contracts only when a "breach of peace" threatens the strategic interests of the United States and he has conferred with Congress. The contract sanctity issue cuts in two directions. On the one hand, sanctions are more likely to be effective when they are imposed abruptly and with maximum force. This argues for canceling existing contracts in spite of the inevitable domestic dissatisfaction. On the other hand, if existing contracts are honored, domestic costs will be reduced, but the initial impact on the target country will be lessened, providing time for the target country to adjust and to attract compensating foreign assistance. The "breach of peace" threshold represents Congress's attempt to resolve this dilemma.

Finally, the 1985 EAAA requires the president to dismantle national security and foreign policy controls when the goods in question are available from foreign sources. Section 2405(h)(3) of the act states that if the secretary

---

7 This discussion of the Export Administration Act is drawn from Hufbauer (1990).

of commerce "affirmatively determines that a good or technology . . . is available in sufficient quantity and comparable quality from sources outside the United States . . . so that denial of an export license would be ineffective [in accomplishing the purpose of the controls] . . . then he must provide an export license." Unlike national security export controls, whose success depends on the prohibition of access to controlled goods (a modern form of contraband), the success of foreign policy sanctions does not entirely depend on restricting access to goods from other countries. However, the availability of goods from other sources lessens the impact of the sanctions, raises the level of international cooperation required to implement the sanctions, and increases the domestic political costs of maintaining the controls. It is clearly preferable to impose sanctions on goods not readily obtainable in foreign markets.

It may be useful to illustrate our construction of the cost-to-sender index through a review of two cases.

Case 73–2: US v. South Korea (1973–77: Human Rights)

Sanctions generally impose small costs on domestic economic interests—and generate little or no domestic political opposition—when they involve the closing of the bilateral aid spigot. This is clearly illustrated by US actions in support of human rights in South Korea following President Park Chung Hee's declaration of martial law in 1972. The average US citizen did not feel the pinch from the substantial cutback in economic aid (mostly PL 480 food aid) and military aid to South Korea; indeed, the US government "profited" from the reduced expenditures, although the reduction of a few hundred million dollars in aid transfers had little impact on the budget deficits that were incurred during this period.

From 1974 to 1978, average US economic and military aid to South Korea declined by over $450 million from the average level for the period 1970–73. Although the cutbacks in PL 480 and military aid led to some increased costs for the United States (for example, in terms of storage and other incidental expenses for grain), the short-run impact on the US budget was minimal (about 1 percent of the deficit) but favorable. In this case, then, the cost to the sender was negative: the United States was actually slightly better off, in economic terms, as a result of the sanctions. This result illustrates those cases that we accorded a cost-to-sender index number of 1.

Case 80–1: US v. USSR (1980–81: Afghanistan)

Much has been written about the economic impact of the post-Afghanistan grain embargo on the US farm sector. When the Carter administration imposed the embargo in January 1980, it estimated that US farm income would be reduced by $2.0 billion to $2.25 billion as a result of a cut of 17 million tons in grain shipped to the Soviet Union. Measures were introduced to soften the blow on the US farmer, including purchases for the grain reserve and increases in loan, release, and call prices. These measures added an additional $2 billion to $3 billion to the federal deficit during fiscal years 1980 and 1981.[8] The purchases for the grain reserve, which sopped up about $2.4 billion in grain that would have been dumped on the market, alone cost the US taxpayer (according to estimates of the General Accounting Office) over $600 million in direct budgetary expenditures, including costs incurred in the purchase, storage, and resale of the grain.

The extent to which the embargo imposed a welfare loss on the US farm sector as a whole is more difficult to measure. The Congressional Research Service noted that it took nine months for wheat, corn, and soybean prices to recover from the initial shock of the embargo (Congressional Research Service 1981, 45–46); at the same time, farm income plummeted, although how much of the fall was due to the embargo and how much to other factors (for example, high interest rates) is hard to quantify. In any event, US farmers lost a significant share of the Soviet market. Even though the US share of the world market actually grew by 2 percent in the 1980–81 marketing year over preembargo levels (US Congress 1983), these lost sales to the Soviet Union probably imposed a welfare loss to US farmers through their effect on prices and stunted trade opportunities.

The grain embargo was accompanied by export controls on high-technology products and superphosphoric acid, affecting close to $500 million in prospective US exports. Using the same methodology that we employed to calculate the cost to the target country, we estimate the welfare loss to US producers, after accounting for substitution and price effects, at about 30 percent of the value of trade affected by the sanctions. This translates into a $150 million loss for producers of superphosphoric acid and high-technology products and at least $600 million for producers of farm goods. In sum, the sanctions against the Soviet Union—by this admittedly rough estimate—did inflict significant costs on US economic interests. In GNP terms, the costs to the United States were negligible, yet the sanctions did result in substantial trade diversion and important losses for specific sectors of the US economy. These losses in turn created political problems for the Carter administration.

We have not based our cost-to-sender index on costs as a percentage of GNP; instead we only consider whether there has been a modest or substantial level of trade diversion that might be expected to create, as it did in this case, domestic political opposition to the sanctions. By this standard, the Afghanistan case was given an index number of 3 to reflect the significant cost to the sender.

---

8 *Weekly Compilation of Presidential Documents*, 28 January 1980, 105ff.

In over 40 percent of the cases involving modest policy goals, listed in table 4.3, the sender country enjoyed a net gain (usually quite small) as a result of withholding aid and official credits. The only episode in the modest policy goals category in which significant trade diversion occurred, with consequent losses to the affected firms in the sender country, was the case involving US efforts to release hostages held by Iran (Case 79–1).

The successful destabilization cases listed in table 4.4, except for the Rhodesian episode (Case 65–3), generally cost the sender country rather little. The average cost-to-sender index for the successful cases was 1.5. In contrast, the average for failed cases was 2.3, and some of these episodes were rather expensive to the sender. US traders have long since adjusted to the Cuban embargo, but the initial measures entailed losses of some consequence for particular US industries. In the Libyan case (Case 78–8), some US oil companies were placed in a disadvantaged position. Exxon, for example, sold its Libyan assets for substantially less than their book value.

In the successful cases involving disruption of military adventures, listed in table 4.5, the average cost to the sender was again relatively low: the average index is just 1.7. For disruption cases with failed outcomes, the cost-to-sender index was 1.9. Here again the data suggest that failed episodes were generally more costly to the sender—a finding that will come as no surprise to the farmers affected by the Carter grain embargo.

When countries resort to sanctions in order to impair the military potential of target countries, or to pursue other major policy changes, not only are they distinctly unsuccessful (except when the sanctions are accompanied by actual warfare) but they also invariably are forced to accept a significant economic burden.[9] In the success cases, the costs to the sender were understandably great in the two world war cases and in Case 67–1: *Nigeria v. Biafra*. On the other hand, India prevailed over Hyderabad (Case 48–2) at relatively little cost, and the Arab countries clearly gained from their mid-1970s oil embargo. However, this sample is too small to yield clear trends.

The average cost-to-sender index in the impairment of military potential cases that failed was 3.0; the average cost-to-sender index in the failures among the other major policy change cases was 2.3. Although small in GNP terms, the annualized cost figures in these cases probably run in the hundreds of millions of dollars, and those losses are usually concentrated on relatively few firms.

To summarize: higher failure rates are associated with greater costs borne by the sender country. On the one hand, failed cases may entail intrinsically

---

9 Case 90–1: *US and UN v. Iraq* is excluded from these averages, but it is clear that the cost-to-sender index in that case will be 4 because of the significant rise in oil prices due to the embargo.

tougher objectives, and the sender government may be willing to expend greater effort in achieving its goals; on the other hand, as costs mount, pressures may arise within the sender country to abandon the attempt, thereby contributing to the failure of the episode.

Table 4.2   Rough estimate of the impact of US sanctions on US exports, 1987 (millions of dollars)

Target	Actual US exports to target	Actual OECD exports to target	Hypothetical US exports to target[a]	Estimated impact of sanctions[b]
COMECON[c]	2,189	37,988	6,838	4,649
North Korea	0	452	99	99
Vietnam	23	312	69	46
Cuba	1	882	432	431
South Africa	1,295	9,553	1,624	329
Angola	94	759	129	35
Cambodia	0	7	1	1
Libya	0	3,410	341	341
Iran	54	6,075	911	857
Nicaragua	3	210	103	100
Panama[d]	634	4,108	743	109
Total	4,293	63,756	11,290	6,997

a. For COMECON, hypothetical US exports are estimated by assuming that the United States would have, in the absence of sanctions, maintained its share of OECD exports to Europe (excluding intra–EC trade), namely, 18 percent. For North Korea, Vietnam, and Cambodia, it is assumed that the United States would have maintained its 22 percent share of OECD exports to the non–OECD Far East. For Libya, it is assumed that the United States would have maintained its 10 percent share of OECD exports to Africa. For South Africa and Angola, it is assumed that the United States would have maintained its 17 percent share of OECD to South Africa in 1985. For Iran, it is assumed that the United States would have maintained its 15 percent share of OECD exports to the Mideast. For Cuba and Nicaragua, it its assumed that the United States would have maintained its 49 percent share of OECD exports to non–OECD America. For Panama, see note d.

b. This estimate is calculated as the difference between the hypothetical and the actual US exports to the target country.

c. Data for COMECON also include the residual effect of repeated US sanctions directed against the Soviet Union.

d. No export sanctions were imposed against Panama; however, financial sanctions severely curtailed economic activity in Panama. The actual export figure is for 1988 (after sanctions took their toll), whereas the hypothetical figure is for 1987 (before economic chaos set in).

Sources: Organization for Economic Cooperation and Development, Foreign Trade by Commodities, Exports, vols. I and II, Paris 1989.

One rough-and-ready attempt to measure US exports lost on account of economic sanctions is reproduced in table 4.2. For the year 1987, it is calculated that US exports were reduced by about $7.0 billion as a result of economic sanctions then in effect; most of the loss (some $4.6 billion) was attributable to COCOM controls (then in full force). Significant US export losses were also incurred in Cuba, South Africa, Libya, and Iran.

The costs of economic sanctions are not confined to the economic realm. A failed episode can impose heavy political costs on the sender country, particularly if the episode precipitates a public outcry. US sanctions against the Soviet Union over the Yamal pipeline project and Soviet support of repression in Poland (Case 81–3) badly disturbed the NATO alliance. The Reagan administration was derided by its domestic political opponents for the failure of its sanctions policies against Nicaragua and Panama (Cases 81–1 and 87–1). Earlier celebrated episodes in which failure exacted large political costs for the governments of the sender countries include Case 35–1: *UK and League of Nations v. Italy* and Case 40–1: *US v. Japan* (1940–41).

Even successful sanctions episodes can impose political costs on the sender country. Examples include the US response to the Franco-British Suez invasion (Case 56–3), which left a bitter taste in Europe for many years; the destabilization campaign and eventual overthrow of Salvador Allende (Case 70–1: *US v. Chile*), which gave the United States a reputation for being willing to use the CIA to accomplish "dirty tricks"; and Case 77–4: *Canada v. Japan and EC*, in which Canadian insistence on nuclear safeguards (prompted by the "peaceful" Indian nuclear explosion) irked Canada's trading partners and allies.

We have not attempted to systematically assess the political cost of each episode to the sender country. All diplomacy has its political costs; some episodes are dear and others are cheap. The political costs of economic sanctions may be lower or higher than the political costs of achieving the same diplomatic ends by different means. We leave these matters for other scholars to explore.[10]

---

10 Baldwin (1985) addresses these questions.

References

Baldwin, David A. 1985. *Economic Statecraft: Theory and Practice*. Princeton: Princeton University Press.

Bonn, M.J. 1937. "How Sanctions Failed." 15 *Foreign Affairs* (January): 350–61.

Brown-John, C. Lloyd. 1975. *Multilateral Sanctions in International Law: A Comparative Analysis*. New York: Praeger.

Congressional Research Service. 1981. *An Assessment of the Afghanistan Sanctions: Implications for Trade and Diplomacy in the 1980s*. Washington: GPO.

Farrell, R. Barry. 1956. *Yugoslavia and the Soviet Union 1948–1956*. Hamden, CT: Shoe String Press.

Hufbauer, Gary Clyde. 1990. *The Impact of U.S. Economic Sanctions and Controls on U.S. Firms*. A Report to the National Foreign Trade Council. Washington (April).

US Congress. Office of Technology Assessment. 1983. *Technology and East-West Trade: An Update*. Washington.

Table 4.3 Cases involving modest changes in target-country policies: economic variables

Case[a]	Sender and target	Success score[b] (index)	Cost to target[c] (millions of dollars)	Cost as percentage of GNP[d]	Cost per capita (dollars)	Trade linkage[e] (percentages)	GNP ratio: sender to target[f]	Type of sanction[g]	Cost to sender[h] (index)
33–1	UK v. USSR	12	4	negl.	negl.	13	1	M	2
38–1	UK, US v. Mexico	9	2	0.2	0.11	70	75	M,F	2
54–1	USSR v. Australia	1	50	0.5	5.56	3	18	M	2
56–2	US, UK, France v. Egypt	9	138	3.4	5.87	23	160	X,F	2
61–1	US v. Ceylon	16	8.7	0.6	0.86	6	375	F	1
62–3	USSR v. Romania	1	—	—	—	41	24	—	2
63–1	US v. United Arab Republic[1]	16	54	1.4	1.93	15	153	F	1
64–1	France v. Tunisia	9	12	1.5	2.67	48	106	M,F	2
65–1	US v. Chile	12	0.5	negl.	0.06	37	98	M,F	2
65–2	US v. India	16	41	negl.	0.08	24	13	F	1
68–1	US v. Peru	1	33	0.7	2.60	10	186	F	1
68–2	US v. Peru	12	35	0.7	2.72	10	186	F	1
73–2	US v. South Korea	4	333	1.8	9.60	29	78	F	1
73–3	US v. Chile	6	54	0.6	5.29	18	187	F	1
74–2	Canada v. India	4	33	negl.	0.06	2	2	X,F	2
74–3	Canada v. Pakistan	4	13	0.1	0.18	2	14	X	2
75–1	US, Canada v. South Korea	16	—	—	—	32	87	—	2
75–2	US v. USSR	6	102	negl.	0.40	4	2	M,F	2
75–3	US v. Eastern Europe	8	37	negl.	0.51	1	5	M,F	1
75–4	US v. South Africa	4	2	negl.	0.08	12	43	X	2
76–1	US v. Uruguay	6	10	0.3	3.57	10	452	X,F	1

76–2	US v. Taiwan	16	17	0.1	1.01	32	100	X	2
76–3	US v. Ethiopia	6	(160)	(5.5)	(5.67)	22	592	M,F	1
77–1	US v. Paraguay	6	2	0.1	0.71	13	959	F	1
77–2	US v. Guatemala	6	21	0.4	3.17	37	355	F	1
77–3	US v. Argentina	6	62	0.1	2.38	13	38	X,F	2
77–4	Canada v. Japan, EC	9	115	negl.	0.31	2	0.1	X	2
77–6	US v. El Salvador	6	13	0.5	3.02	32	685	F	1
77–7	US v. Brazil	9	94	0.1	0.84	19	12	F	1
78–1	China v. Albania	1	43	3.3	16.54	34	249	X,M,F	2
78–2	US v. Brazil	4	5	negl.	0.04	22	11	X	2
78–3	US v. Argentina	4	0.2	negl.	negl.	14	34	X	2
78–4	US v. India	4	12	negl.	0.02	13	18	X	2
78–5	US v. USSR	1	51	negl.	0.19	3	2	X	2
79–1	US v. Iran	12	3,349	3.8	90.51	13	28	X,M,F	3
79–2	US v. Pakistan	1	34	0.2	0.43	10	114	F	1
79–3	Arab League v. Canada	12	7	negl.	0.30	2	1	X,M,F	2
79–4	US v. Bolivia	6	48	1.7	8.73	22	562	F	1
80–2	US v. Iraq	4	22	0.1	1.71	5	69	X	2
82–2	Netherlands, US v. Suriname	9	80	7.8	202.53	37	2,565	F	1
83–1	Australia v. France	1	negl.	negl.	negl.	negl.	0.3	X	2
83–2	US v. USSR	1	negl.	negl.	negl.	2	2	M	2
83–3	US v. Zimbabwe	4	27	0.4	3.55	7	462	F	1
84–1	US v. Iran	6	130	negl.	2.83	3	25	X,M,F	2
86–1	US v. Syria	6	4	negl.	0.39	3	189	X,F	2
87–2	US v. Haiti	6	56	2.9	10.37	74	2,383	F	1

Case[a]	Sender and target	Success score[b] (index)	Cost to target[c] (millions of dollars)	Cost as percentage of GNP[d]	Cost per capita (dollars)	Trade Linkage[e] (percentages)	GNP ratio: sender to target[f]	Type of sanction[g]	Cost to sender[h] (index)
87–3	US v. El Salvador	16	—	—	—	42	1,006	F	1
88–1	Japan, West Germany, US v. Burma	6	234	2.1	5.85	22	803	F	1
88–2	US, UK v. Somalia	4	49	2.0	6.90	10	1,429	F	1
89–2	US v. China	1	322	0.1	0.29	10	13	X,F	2
89–3	US v. Sudan	1	91	0.1	3.96	7	408	F	1

Negl. = negligible; — indicates none, because sanctions did not go beyond threat stage.

a. The *case numbers* are those in table 1.1.

b. The *success score* is an index on a scale of 1 to 16, found by multiplying the policy result index by the sanctions contribution index (see tables 3.1 through 3.5).

c. The *cost to target* is expressed in millions of current US dollars, as estimated in the case abstracts. Parentheses indicate a gain to the target country.

d. The *cost as percentage of GNP* is the cost of sanctions to the target country as a percentage of its GNP. Parenthesis indicate a gain.

e. The *trade linkage* equals the average of presanction target-country exports to the sender country (as a percentage of total target-country exports) and imports from the sender country (as a percentage of total target-country imports).

f. The *GNP ratio* is the ratio of the sender country's GNP to the target country's GNP.

g. *Types of sanction* include the interruption of commercial finance, aid, and other official finance (F), the interruption of exports from the sender country to the target country (X), and the interruption of imports by the sender country from the target country (M).

h. The *cost to sender* is an index number scaled from 1 to 4. Key: 1 = net gain to sender; 2 = little effect on sender; 3 = modest welfare loss to sender; 4 = major loss to sender.

i. This case is also listed in table 4.5.

Table 4.4 Cases involving destabilization of target-country governments: economic variables

Case[a]	Sender and target	Success score[b] (index)	Cost to target[c] (millions of dollars)	Cost as percentage of GNP[d]	Cost per capita (dollars)	Trade linkage[e] (percentages)	GNP ratio: sender to target[f]	Type of sanction[g]	Cost to sender[h] (index)
18–1	UK v. Russia	1	446	4.1	2.49	19	1	X,M,F	3
44–1	US v. Argentina	4	29	0.8	1.82	19	58	X,F	2
48–4	USSR v. Yugoslavia	1	(76)	(2.5)	(4.47)	13	52	X,M,F	1
51–1	UK, US v. Iran	12	186	14.3	11.14	42	235	X,M,F	1
56–4	US v. Laos	9	5	4.2	2.08	2	4,372	F	1
58–1	USSR v. Finland	16	45	1.1	10.23	19	58	X,M,F	2
60–1	US v. Dominican Republic	16	16	1.9	5.52	56	596	X,M,F	2
60–3	US v. Cuba[i]	1	114	4.4	16.76	47	173	X,M,F	3
61–2	USSR v. Albania	1	3	0.6	1.76	51	494	X,M,F	2
62–1	US v. Brazil	12	110	0.6	1.49	49	30	F	1
63–3	US v. Indonesia[i]	8	110	2.0	1.05	25	145	F	1
63–4	UK, UN v. South Vietnam	12	9	0.3	0.59	20	206	F	1
65–3	UK, UN v. Rhodesia	12	130	13.0	28.89	69	1,388	X,M,F	3
70–1	US v. Chile	12	163	1.5	17.16	17	102	F	1
72–1	UK, US v. Uganda	12	36	2.6	3.44	22	860	X,M,F	2
77–5	US v. Nicaragua	12	22	1.0	9.48	27	913	X,F	1
78–8	US v. Libya	4	246	1.3	90.74	20	118	X,M,F	3
81–1	US v. Nicaragua	8	45	3.2	16.67	33	1,727	X,M,F	3
82–3	South Africa v. Lesotho	16	27	5.1	19.29	100	103	X,M	2
83–4	US, OECS v. Grenada	8	negl.	negl.	negl.	1	32,900	X,M,F	2
87–1	US v. Panama	4	319	6.0	138.70	50	854	M,F	3

negl. = negligible

a.–h. See table 4.3

i. These cases are also listed in table 4.5.

Table 4.5 Cases involving disruption of military adventures (other than major wars): economic variables

Case[a]	Sender and target	Success score[b] (index)	Cost to target[c] (millions of dollars)	Cost as percentage of GNP[d]	Cost per capita (dollars)	Trade linkage[e] (percentages)	GNP ratio:[f] sender to target	Type of sanction[g]	Cost to sender[h] (index)
21–1	League v. Yugoslavia	16	—	—	—	27	37	—	2
25–1	League v. Greece	16	—	—	—	36	56	—	2
32–1	League v. Paraguay, Bolivia	6	4	3.0	1.03	74	224	X	2
35–1	UK, League v. Italy	1	86	1.7	1.98	16	6	X,M,F	3
40–1	US v. Japan	1	88	0.9	1.21	31	11	X,F	3
48–1	US v. Netherlands	16	14	0.2	1.43	9	45		1
49–1	US, CHINCOM v. China[i]	1	106	0.5	0.20	38	13	X,M,F	3
56–3	US v. UK, France	12	167	0.3	3.25	10	7	F	2
57–2	France v. Tunisia	1	7	0.9	1.75	66	76	F	1
60–3	US v. Cuba[j]	1	114	4.4	16.76	47	173	X,M,F	3
63–1	US v. United Arab Republic[k]	16	54	1.4	1.93	15	153	F	1
63–3	US v. Indonesia[j]	8	110	2.0	1.05	25	145	F	1
71–1	US v. India, Pakistan	2	117	0.2	0.18	19	16	X,F	1
74–1	US v. Turkey	1	77	0.2	1.92	12	42	F	1
75–5	US v. Kampuchea	1	42	6.8	6.27	negl.	2,523	X,M,F	1
78–7	China v. Vietnam	3	254	3.5	5.20	12	41	F	1
80–1	US v. USSR (Afghanistan)[i]	1	525	negl.	2.00	4	2	X	3
82–1	UK v. Argentina	12	979	0.6	34.84	5	3	X,M,F	2

a.–h. See table 4.3.

i. These cases are also listed in table 4.6.

j. These cases are also listed in table 4.4.

k. This case is also listed in table 4.3.

Table 4.6 Cases involving impairment of military potential (including major wars): economic variables

Case[a]	Sender and target	Success score[b] (index)	Cost to target[c] (millions of dollars)	Cost as percentage of GNP[d]	Cost per capita (dollars)	Trade linkage[e] (percentages)	GNP ratio:[f] sender to target	Type of sanction[g]	Cost to sender[h] (index)
14–1	UK v. Germany	12	843	7.1	12.58	9	1	X,M,F	4
39–1	Alliance Powers v. Germany, Japan	12	688	1.6	5.00	15	2	X,M,F	4
46–1	Arab League v. Israel	4	258	4.1	123.00	3	2	X,M,F	4
48–5	US, COCOM v. USSR, COMECON	6	706	0.2	2.28	24	3	X	3
49–1	US, CHINCOM v. China[i]	1	106	0.5	0.20	38	13	X,M,F	3
50–1	US, UN v. North Korea	2	8	1.2	0.83	20	378	X,M,F	2
54–4	US, South Vietnam v. North Vietnam	1	129	3.1	3.96	1	358	X,M,F	2
60–2	USSR v. China	4	287	0.5	0.42	46	4	X,M,F	4
80–1	US v. USSR (Afghanistan)[i]	1	525	negl.	2.00	4	2	X	3
81–3	US v. USSR (Poland)	1	480	negl.	1.79	2	2	X	3

a.–h. See table 4.

i. These cases are also listed in table 4.5.

Table 4.7　Cases involving other major changes in target-country policies (including surrender of territory): economic variables

Case[a]	Sender and target	Success score[b] (index)	Cost to target[c] (millions of dollars)	Cost as percentage of GNP[d]	Cost per capita (dollars)	Trade linkage[e] (percentages)	GNP ratio:[f] sender to target	Type of sanction[g]	Cost to sender[h] (index)
17–1	UK v. Japan	4	23	0.8	0.44	21	13	X	2
48–2	India v. Hyderbad	12	18	2.0	1.10	99	22	X,F	2
48–3	USSR v. US, UK, France	1	258	0.1	1.05	1	0.4	X,M	3
54–2	India v. Portugal	8	negl.	negl.	negl.	negl.	13	X,M,F	2
54–3	Spain v. UK	6	5	negl.	0.10	1	0.2	X,M	2
56–1	US v. Israel (intermittent episodes)	2	16	0.1	4.13	22	218	X,F	2
57–1	Indonesia v. Netherlands	8	69	0.7	6.27	3	0.2	X,M,F	2
61–3	Western Allies v. German Democratic Republic	1	—	—	—	12	40	—	2
62–2	UN v. South Africa	6	273	2.8	15.08	77	130	X,F	3
63–2	Indonesia v. Malaysia	1	29	1.0	3.14	7	2	X,M	4
63–5	UN, Organization of African Unity v. Portugal	8	11	0.3	1.25	15	10	X,M,F	2
65–4	US v. Arab League	6	8	negl.	0.06	10	31	X,F	2
67–1	Nigeria v. Biafra	12	220	15.2	14.67	50	3	X,M,F	3
73–1	Arab League v. US, Netherlands	9	5,697	0.4	25.55	3	0.04	X	1
78–6	Arab League v. Egypt	1	(77)	(0.4)	(1.88)	4	16	X,M,F	3
81–2	US v. Poland	9	246	0.1	6.83	4	17	X,M,F	2
81–4	EC v. Turkey	6	300	0.5	6.47	34	40	F	1
85–1	US v. South Africa	6	550	0.8	17.19	12	54	X,M,F	2
86–2	US v. Angola	2	4	negl.	0.44	25	437	X,M	2
89–1	India v. Nepal	9	132	4.6	7.25	28	94	X,M	2
90–1	US, UN v. Iraq[i]	—	21,600	48.0	1,255.81	100	242	X,M,F	4

a.–h. See table 4.

i. As this book goes to press, it is still too early to score this case; other variables are as of the time the book goes to press.

5

CONCLUSIONS AND RECOMMENDATIONS

A number of lessons can be abstracted from the sanctions episodes of the past 75 years. In this concluding chapter we first assess the overall effectiveness of sanctions as a tool of foreign policy, based on the experience of 115[1] cases, and group the lessons learned into a list of suggestions for increasing the prospects for success. We then explore the implications of recent US experience, and of the end of the Cold War, for the future use of economic sanctions. We conclude with a list of do's and don'ts—nine commandments—to guide governments in the use of economic sanctions.[2]

The purposes of a sanctions campaign must be clearly identified before its effectiveness can be assessed. Sender countries usually pursue more than one goal and may use sanctions as a warning shot against future misdeeds, by the target country or others. We have chosen to focus on the effectiveness of sanctions in coercing the identified target country to conform to the sender's demands in the episode at hand.

---

1 We have referred to all 116 cases of sanctions in other parts of the book where we had enough information to include the UN embargo of Iraq. As we went to press, the outcome of that case was not known, and thus we could not assign a success score under our methodology. Although this case is referred to where appropriate, it is omitted from the 115 cases on which our calculations and the tables in this chapter are based.

2 Those readers familiar with the first edition of this study will note that we have dropped the multiple regression analysis. The regression was rudimentary and, although it largely confirmed the conclusions derived from our simple statistical analysis, it provided few additional insights.

As one sanctions scholar has observed, "Compellant purposes of sanctions are the most difficult to achieve. . ." (Leyton-Brown 1987, 304). However, sanctions also may be intended to demonstrate resolve both at home and abroad, to express outrage, to punish, or to deter. Many of the cases we have judged to be failures would be considered successes if measured against other criteria. Moreover, the design of a sanction intended for symbolic or signaling purposes may not be appropriate for a sanction meant for coercion. Nonetheless, we believe that a careful analysis of the factors contributing to the success of coercive sanctions is important and can provide insights to guide the use of sanctions in other circumstances as well.[3]

Before moving to the results, a word of caution. Forecasting the outcome of statecraft, like forecasting the stock market, is a hazardous business. As one might expect from a diverse collection of 115 cases, the statistical results are not always clear-cut. Idiosyncratic influences are often at play. Human personalities and plain luck may well determine the outcome of a sanctions episode. Much depends on the kaleidoscope of contemporaneous world events and other factors not captured by our variables. Hence our summary assessments and nine commandments must be read as general indicators, not infallible guideposts, in the fine art of statecraft.

Are Sanctions Effective?

In designing foreign policy strategy, policymakers need to take a close look at both the cost and the effectiveness of sanctions. Although it is not true that sanctions "never work," they are of limited utility in achieving foreign policy goals that depend on compelling the target country to take actions it stoutly resists. Still, in some instances, particularly situations involving small target countries and relatively modest policy goals, sanctions have helped alter foreign behavior. Table 5.1 summarizes the scorecard.

By our standards, successful cases are those with an overall success score of 9 or higher; failed cases are those with a score of 8 or lower (the success score is arrived at by multiplying the assigned policy result score by the sanctions contribution score, where 4 is the maximum result for each; see tables 3.1 to 3.5). We must emphasize that a score of 9 does not mean that economic sanctions achieved a foreign policy triumph. It means only that sanctions made a modest contribution to a goal that was partly realized, often at some

---

3 David Baldwin (1985) has argued the case for a broader definition of success in evaluating the utility of "economic statecraft." Margaret Doxey (1987, 144) has emphasized the importance of identifying whether a goal is coercive or symbolic and of designing the sanction accordingly. Michael Malloy (1990) has taken a different tack, arguing that the effectiveness of sanctions should be judged against the immediate "instrumental" goal (denying goods, markets, or finance) and not confused with the effectiveness of the overall foreign policy that sanctions serve.

political cost to the sender country. Nor does a score of 8 indicate dismal failure. In fact, in all of the cases assigned a score of 8 and about a third of those scored as 6, the sender's objective was at least partially achieved but sanctions played only a minor role in the outcome.

Sanctions have been successful—by our definition—in 34 percent of the cases overall. However, the success rate importantly depends on the type of policy or governmental change sought. Episodes involving destabilization succeeded in half the cases, usually against target countries that were small and shaky. Cases involving modest goals and attempts to disrupt minor military adventures were successful about a third of the time. Efforts to impair a foreign adversary's military potential, or otherwise to change its policies in a major way, succeeded only infrequently.

Of course, some sanctions fail because they were never intended to succeed, in the sense of producing a real change in the target's behavior. As one analyst has noted, when sanctions have been used primarily for domestic political or other rhetorical purposes, " 'effective' sanctions [in an instrumental sense] were not a primary policy goal, and such sanctions were not imposed" (Malloy 1990, 626). This is clearly demonstrated by the Bush administration's sanctions against China after the massacre in Tiananmen Square.

Table 5.1 Success by type of policy goal

Policy goal	Success cases	Failure cases	Success ratio (percentage of total)
Modest policy change	17	34	33
Destabilization	11	10	52
Disruption of military adventures	6	12	33
Military impairment	2	8	20
Other major policy changes	5	15	25
All cases[a]	41	79	34

a. Five cases are classified under two different policy goals: 49-1: *US v. China;* 60-3: *US v. Cuba;* 63-1: *US v. United Arab Republic;* 63-3: *US v. Indonesia;* and 80-1: *US v. USSR (Afghanistan).* Since all but one of these cases are failures, double-counting them adds a small negative bias to the success ratio.

Sanctions may also be imposed timidly, and hence ineffectively, if conflicting goals are not weeded out. For example, the Reagan administration attempted in 1988 to impose sanctions that would force Manuel Noriega out of power without permanently damaging the Panamanian economy. Sanctions were imposed incrementally and then gradually weakened by a number of exemptions intended to support the second goal. In the end, the sanctions proved inadequate to remove Noriega, and military force had to be applied.

Nine Commandments

It is clear that sanctions sometimes bear fruit, but only when planted in the right soil and nurtured in the proper way. We therefore offer nine propositions for the statesman who would act as a careful gardener. These recommendations are intended to maximize the chances of success when sanctions are deployed to coerce changes in the policies of a target country. Not all of the commandments may be appropriate in every situation, nor are they necessarily optimal toward achieving other types of goals. However, we would caution that, if a particular case requires that the commandments be modified or ignored, success is likely to prove even more elusive than if they had been followed. Since sanctions entail both political and economic costs, which are sometimes substantial, we believe this conclusion should not be taken lightly.

I. "Don't Bite Off More Than You Can Chew."

Policymakers often have inflated expectations of what sanctions can accomplish. This is especially true of the United States today and was true of the United Kingdom in an earlier era. At most there is a weak correlation between economic deprivation and political willingness to change. The *economic* impact of sanctions may be pronounced, both on the sender and on the target, but other factors in the situation often overshadow the impact of sanctions in determining the *political* outcome.

Sanctions are seldom effective in impairing the military potential of an important power, or in bringing about major changes in the policies of the target country.[4] Of the 30 cases involving these high policy goals,[5] success was achieved in 7, or only 23 percent of the time. Excluding the two world wars and the two civil wars (Case 48–2: *India v. Hyderabad* and Case 67–1: *Nigeria v. Biafra*), we have found only three cases in which economic coercion was effective in changing a major policy of the target country.

In Case 73–1: *Arab League v. US and Netherlands,* the Arab oil embargo helped accomplish two of its four objectives: it caused a significant shift, namely, a more pro-Arab slant, in European and Japanese policies toward the Palestinian question, and it supported OPEC's decision to boost the world price of oil, to its members' enormous economic benefit. But the embargo failed to get Israel to retreat behind its pre-1967 frontiers, and it failed to persuade the United States to abandon its pro-Israel policy stance. The sanctions were an important factor in the attainment of results that, on

---

4 See Chapter 3 for definition of "major changes in the policies of the target country."

5 We use the term "high policy goals" to refer only to episodes involving military impairment and other major policy change. Some authors have used the same phrase to refer to cases involving destabilization and disruption of military adventure as well.

balance, must be deemed at least marginally successful from the Arab viewpoint. In Case 81–2: *US v. Poland,* sanctions exacerbated a deteriorating economic situation and encouraged the gradual softening of the Communist government's crackdown on the Solidarity union movement. In the third case, India's trade embargo against landlocked Nepal (Case 89–1) contributed to the political unrest that forced King Birenda to recognize long-banned opposition parties and ultimately allowed a more pro-Indian government to take power. In the other cases where impairment was sought and attempts were made to change major policies of target countries, sanctions have been ineffective.

To justify even a remote hope for success in military impairment and major change cases, sender countries should form a near monopoly over trading relations with the target country. This obvious precept, learned in the first and second world wars, was forgotten in the case of UN sanctions against South Africa (Case 62–2)[6] and turned on its head in the case of US sanctions to block construction of the Soviet-European gas pipeline. It was recalled and forcefully implemented in Case 90–1: *US and UN v. Iraq,* and as this book went to press the authors expected sanctions—backed by the threat of military action—to succeed in dislodging Iraq from Kuwait.

II. "More Is Not Necessarily Merrier."

In general, the greater the number of countries needed to implement sanctions, the less likely it is that they will be effective. The 1990 UN embargo against Iraq, which is unprecedented in its comprehensive coverage and almost universal participation, is the exception that proves the rule. Few, if any, cases provide the glue for common action by raising such dominating security concerns as the Iraqi threat to world oil supplies. In most instances, multilateral sanctions are not associated with success.

The idea that international cooperation is a necessary ingredient in all sanctions cases is misplaced. A country looks to its allies for help when its goals are ambitious; in cases involving more modest goals, such cooperation is not needed. These conclusions are borne out in table 5.2, which compares successful and failed cases based on the extent of international cooperation achieved (as measured by our international cooperation index, with its maximum score of 4). On average, the degree of international cooperation is

---

6 Sanctions, though imposed only on selected products by major trading partners, have contributed to the progress made in South Africa in 1989–90, and that case may yet move into the success column. However, as we went to press, the legal underpinnings of apartheid—the Group Areas Act and the Population Registration Act—were still in place, and large numbers of political prisoners were still being held. Although Nelson Mandela has credited sanctions for his release and for other reforms adopted by the South African government, he has also called for their continuance until the end of apartheid is more certain.

actually somewhat less in successful than in failed cases. The difference is most marked in episodes involving modest goals and destabilization, which tend to be pursued unilaterally from the outset.

Table 5.2 Success and international cooperation

| | Average international cooperation index[a] | |
Policy goal	Success cases	Failure cases
Modest policy changes	1.5	1.7
Destabilization	1.7	2.4
Disruption of military adventures	2.3	2.2
Military impairment	4.0	3.0
Other major policy changes	1.8	1.9
All cases	1.8	2.0

a. See text for definition of index.

To be sure, international cooperation may serve three useful functions: to increase the moral suasion of the sanction, to help isolate the target country from the global community psychologically as well as economically, and to preempt foreign backlash, thus minimizing corrosive friction within the alliance. However, pressing too hard to corral reluctant allies can have the perverse effect of undermining the economic impact of the sanctions, if multilateral agreement takes too long to achieve or requires watering down the sanctions imposed.

When a sender country has thought it necessary to seek cooperation from other countries, it was probably pursuing a sufficiently difficult objective that the prospects for ultimate success were not bright. Without significant cooperation from its allies, a sender country stands little chance of achieving success in cases involving high policy goals. However, international cooperation does not guarantee success even in these cases, as evidenced from the long history of US and COCOM strategic controls against the Soviet Union and COMECON, and by the Arab League's futile boycott of Israel.

These observations, together with our statistical analysis, suggest that overemphasis on international "cooperation," and especially attempts to force it with the heavy hand of extraterritorial controls, will seldom yield desirable results. Sanctions should be either deployed unilaterally, because the need for one's allies is slight, or designed in cooperation with one's allies in order to reduce backlash and evasion.

This last point is significant. Too many cooks *opposing* sanctions can spoil the sender's broth. Adversaries of the sender country may be prompted by a sanctions episode to assist the target. Such opposition has frequently occurred in episodes that either provoked or derived from East-West rivalry. Assistance extended by a "black knight" not only offsets the economic cost inflicted on the target country; it also bolsters the target government's standing at home and abroad.

Table 5.3 indicates that external assistance to the target country erodes the chances of sender-country success, particularly in cases where the policy goal is destabilization of the target government or disruption of a military adventure. With the end of the Cold War, however, black knights may in the future be less likely to appear on the sanctions scene to rescue target countries.

Table 5.3   Success and international assistance to target country

Policy goals	Incidence of international assistance (percentage of cases)	
	Success cases	Failure cases
Modest policy changes	12	12
Destabilization	9	80
Disruption of military adventures	0	42
Military impairment	100	62
Other major policy changes	40	20
All cases	17	28

III. "The Weakest Go to the Wall."

For our case sample as a whole, there seems to be a direct correlation between the political and economic health of the target country and its susceptibility to economic pressure. Table 5.4 reports the average health and stability index (with a maximum value of 3) for both successful and failed cases. The table clearly demonstrates that countries in distress or experiencing significant problems are far more likely to succumb to coercion by the sender country.

Table 5.4   Success and health and stability of target country

Policy goal	Average health and stability index[a]	
	Success cases	Failure cases
Modest policy changes	2.1	2.1
Destabilization	1.4	1.9
Disruption of military adventures	2.0	2.3
Military impairment	3.0	2.7
Other major policy changes	1.8	2.6
All cases	1.9	2.3

a. See text for definition of index.

When certain types of policy goals are at issue, the health and stability of the target country are usually an important determinant in the success of the episode. This is most true of the destabilization cases, where successes generally came against weak regimes. The average health and stability index was also lower in successful than in failed cases when disruption of military adventures and other major policy changes were at stake. In episodes involving modest policy goals and impairment of military potential, the results based on the health and stability of the target country are less clear-cut—in the former set of cases because a wide variety of countries have been targeted for modest reasons, and in the latter because countries only attempt military impairment when the target is strong enough to be a threat.

Table 5.5   The importance of size

| Policy goal | Average GNP ratio: sender to target | Percentage of cases where the GNP ratio is: | | | | | |
| | | 0 to 10 | | 11 to 100 | | 101 and over | |
		Success	Failure	Success	Failure	Success	Failure
Modest policy changes	213[a]	6	12	12	24	16	31
Destabilization	427[a]	0	5	10	10	43	33
Disruption of military adventures	62[a]	11	11	17	33	5	22
Military impairment	76	20	50	0	10	0	20
Other major policy changes	57	10	20	15	40	0	15
All cases	187	23	24	36	38	41	38

a. These averages exclude cases where the GNP ratio is over 2,000 (56-4: *US v. Laos;* 75-5: *US v. Kampuchea;* 82-2: *Netherlands and US v. Suriname;* 83-4: *US and OECS v. Grenada;* and 87-3: *US v. Haiti*) because their inclusion would unduly bias the results.

In the great majority of cases we have documented, the target country also has been much smaller than the sender country. Thus, whereas sanctions typically involve only a small proportion of the trade or financial flows of the sender country, they can significantly affect the external accounts of the target country. Table 5.5 shows that in cases involving modest goals the sender's economy is on average more than 200 times larger than the target's economy, and in cases involving destabilization the average ratio exceeds 400. For cases involving the disruption of military adventures, military impairment, and other major policy change, the results in table 5.5 indicate less of a size differential between sender and target. However, there is still a significant mismatch in economic clout: in 77 percent of the disruption of military adventure cases, 30 percent of the military impairment cases, and 60 percent of the other major change cases, the sender country's GNP was over 10 times the size of the target country's GNP.

Because senders' economies are almost always much bigger then their targets', relative size is not very helpful in predicting success in the majority of cases. Although few of our cases involved countries of nearly equal size, the sample does support the conclusion that size is usually a necessary, but is not a sufficient, condition for success.[7] The relative size of the target economy is less important than other factors that come into play, such as the extent of trade linkage, the economic impact of the sanctions, and the warmth of relations between sender and target prior to the imposition of sanctions.

IV. *"Attack Your Allies, Not Your Adversaries."*

Economic sanctions seem most effective when aimed against erstwhile friends and close trading partners. In contrast, sanctions directed against target countries that have long been adversaries of the sender country, or against targets that have little trade with the sender country, are generally less successful.

We quantified the warmth of preepisode relations between sender and target countries by means of an index scaled from 1 (antagonistic) to 3 (cordial). Table 5.6, which reports the average prior relations index in successful and failed cases, indicates that, for most types of sanctions, preepisode relations were warmer in successful than in failed cases.

Table 5.6   Success, prior relations, and trade linkage

Policy goal	Prior relations index[a]		Average trade linkage (percentage of total trade)[a]	
	Success cases	Failure cases	Success cases	Failure cases
Modest policy changes	2.4	2.0	25	15
Destabilization	2.7	2.2	38	27
Disruption of military adventures	2.3	2.1	16	28
Military impairment	1.0	1.2	12	17
Other major policy changes	2.6	2.0	36	16
All cases	2.4	2.0	28	19

a. See text for definitions.

---

7 Sanctions contributed to a positive outcome in only 2 of 19 cases in which the GNP ratio was under 10 and military conflict or control of oil reserves was not a factor (see chapter 4).

The higher compliance with sanctions by allies and trading partners reflects their willingness to bend on specific issues in deference to an overall relationship with the sender country. Such considerations may not be decisive in the calculus of an antagonistic target country, or a target country that has little economic contact with the sender. In addition, an ally will be a less likely candidate for offsetting assistance from black knights, and less willing to accept it if offered. Sanctions may succeed more often against friends than against foes, but a word of caution must be inserted: the preservation of political alliances and economic ties should be equally important to prospective senders as to intended targets.

Likewise, the trade linkage data, also reported in table 5.6, suggest that success is more often achieved when the target country conducts a significant portion of its trade with the sender. We measured trade linkage as the average of, first, the target country's imports from the sender, as a percentage of the target's total imports, and second, the target country's exports to the sender as a percentage of the target's total exports. In most episodes involving modest policy goals or destabilization attempts, the trade linkage exceeds 20 percent; further, the trade linkage in successful cases is generally higher than in failed cases. Cases involving disruption of military adventures also have trade linkages at the 20 percent level; in this category, however, failed cases exhibit a somewhat higher trade linkage than successes.

In the military impairment cases, the trade linkage is usually less than 20 percent. Although the trade linkage is perversely higher in failed cases in this group, the distinction between successful cases and failures is not significant—the only successes in this category are the sanctions applied during the two world wars. Similarly, in cases involving other major policy changes, the trade linkage is usually low, although in three of the five successful episodes the average trade linkage was over 50 percent. Taking all categories together, successful cases exhibit a higher average trade linkage (28 percent) than do failed cases (19 percent).

V. "If It Were Done, When 'Tis Done, Then 'Twere Well It Were Done Quickly."

A heavy, slow hand invites both evasion and the mobilization of domestic opinion in the target country. Sanctions imposed slowly or incrementally may simply strengthen the target government at home as it marshals the forces of nationalism. Moreover, such measures are likely to be undercut over time either by the sender's own firms or by foreign competitors. Sanctions generally are regarded as a short-term policy, with the anticipation that normal commercial relations will be reestablished after the resolution of the crisis. Thus, even though popular opinion in the sender country may welcome the introduction of sanctions, the longer an episode drags on, the more public support for sanctions dissipates.

The cases we have documented show a clear association, summarized in table 5.7, between the duration of sanctions and the waning prospects of success. The impact of sanctions may be less than expected either because the sanctions take too long to bite or because their bite loosens too soon. A critical question in the 1990 Iraq case is whether the UN coalition will have the patience to outwait Saddam Hussein and allow the sanctions time to reach full force.

Table 5.7 Success and the duration of sanctions

	Length of episode (years)	
Policy goal	Success cases	Failure cases[a]
Modest policy changes	2.8	5.2
Destabilization	3.8	7.4
Disruption of military adventures	1.2	4.4
Military impairment	5.0	24.4
Other major policy changes	1.8	2.6
All cases	2.9	8.0

a. The periods for the failure cases are biased on the low side because several cases are still ongoing.

However, it is not the passage of time alone that undermines economic sanctions. Other factors are correlated with the length of an episode. Episodes between erstwhile allies are generally short, to the point, and often successful. Further, the target country is more likely to receive assistance from another major power if the episode continues for a number of years. Finally, the greater the latent likelihood of success, the shorter the sanctions period necessary to achieve results.

In any event, the inverse relationship between success and the duration of sanctions argues against a strategy of "turning the screws" on a target country, slowly applying more and more economic pressure over time until the target succumbs. Time affords the target the opportunity to adjust: to find alternative suppliers, to build new alliances, and to mobilize domestic opinion in support of its policies.

VI. "In For a Penny, In For a Pound."

Cases that inflict heavy costs on the target country are generally successful. As shown in table 5.8, the average cost to the target for all successful cases was 2.4

percent of GNP; by contrast, failed episodes barely dented the economy of the target country, with costs averaging only 1 percent of GNP. Both averages reflect the heavy costs typically imposed in destabilization, military impairment, and other major policy change cases, which counterbalance the generally minor impact of sanctions in cases involving modest policy changes.

Table 5.8   Success and costs to the target country

Policy goal	Costs as percentage of GNP	
	Success cases	Failure cases
Modest policy changes	1.2	0.4
Destabilization	4.1	2.2
Disruption of military adventures	0.4	2.0
Military impairment	4.3	1.2
Other major policy changes	4.5	0.5
All cases	2.4	1.0

The seemingly perverse result in cases involving disruption of military adventures, where the average costs of failed cases are much higher than those for successes, reflects the experience of the early League of Nations sanctions against Yugoslavia and Greece. In these two episodes, the mere threat of sanctions succeeded in forcing the invading armies to withdraw, and therefore no costs were imposed on the target country.

The conclusion to be drawn from these findings is that if sanctions can be imposed in a comprehensive manner, the chances of success improve. Sanctions that bite are sanctions that work. However, there is a "black knight corollary" to this conclusion: sanctions that attract offsetting support from a major power may cost the target country little on a net basis and are less likely to succeed.

VII. "If You Need to Ask the Price, You Can't Afford the Yacht."

The more it costs a sender country to impose sanctions, the less likely it is that the sanctions will succeed. This conclusion finds support in table 5.9, which shows that the average cost-to-sender index (scored from 1 to 4, with 1 representing a net gain and 4 a major loss to the sender), is generally lower in successful than in failed cases. The exceptions are the two world wars. In most other instances, the cost to the sender country in successful episodes is insignificant, and often the short-term result is a net gain (usually where the sanction is in the form of a cutoff of aid).

Table 5.9 The price of success

Policy goals	Average cost to sender index[a]	
	Success cases	Failure cases
Modest policy changes	1.6	1.5
Destabilization	1.5	2.3
Disruption of military adventures	1.7	1.9
Military impairment	4.0	3.0
Other major policy changes	2.0	2.3
All cases	1.8	2.0

a. See text for definition of index.

The basic conclusion to be drawn from table 5.9 is clear: a country should shy away from deploying sanctions when the economic costs to itself are high. Countries that shoot themselves in the foot may not mortally wound their intended targets. Although we did not attempt to measure the political costs of sanctions episodes to sender countries, we believe this conclusion would apply with equal force to episodes that entail high political costs. The early-1980s Soviet gas pipeline case is a good example of how self-imposed economic and political costs can cause a sanctions campaign to backfire and undercut the sender's foreign policy objectives.

These results suggest that sender governments should design sanctions so as not to inflict unduly concentrated costs on particular domestic groups. One example of actions to avoid, in all but extreme situations, is the retroactive application of sanctions to cancel existing contracts. Such actions not only leave the affected firms high and dry, with unsold inventories and excess capacity, but they also sour those firms' chances of competing for future business. If the sender government believes that retroactive application is essential to the success of an episode, then it should compensate the affected domestic firms at least for the loss on unsold inventories.

The sanctions episodes that are least costly to the sender are often those that make use of financial leverage—manipulating aid flows, denying official credits, or, at the extreme, freezing assets—rather than trade controls. Denial of finance may also compound the cost to the target country by inhibiting its ability to engage in trade even without formal trade controls being imposed. Table 5.10 shows that financial sanctions have been used alone more often and more effectively than trade controls alone.

Table 5.10 Success by type of sanction

	Financial sanctions				Trade sanctions alone	
	Alone		With trade sanctions			
Policy goal	Success cases	Failure cases	Success cases	Failure cases	Success cases	Failure cases
Modest policy change	7	13	6	10	3	10
Destabilization	4	1	6	8	1	1
Disruption of military adventures	3	4	1	6	0	2
Military impairment	0	0	2	5	0	3
Other major policy changes	0	2	3	8	2	4
All cases[a]	14	20	18	38	6	19

a. These figures include five cases listed under two different policy goals (see table 5.1), but they exclude five cases in which sanctions never went beyond the threat stage.

When financial, export, and import controls are all used in a single episode, it is usually because the goal is ambitious. A major reason for the better track record of financial sanctions alone is that they typically involve relatively modest goals, sought through the reduction, suspension, or termination of economic or military assistance from richer nations (usually the United States) to smaller and poorer developing countries.

VIII. "Choose the Right Tool For the Job."

Economic sanctions are often deployed in conjunction with other measures directed against the target: covert action, quasi-military measures, or regular military operations. As table 5.11 shows, companion measures are used most frequently in episodes involving destabilization and impairment of military potential. By contrast, companion policies are seldom used in cases involving modest policy changes, and were used in fewer than half the disruption and major policy change cases.

Table 5.11 Success and companion policies

	Incidence of companion policies (percentage of cases)	
Policy goals	Success cases	Failure cases
Modest policy changes	18	3
Destabilization	73	80
Disruption of military adventures	17	50
Military impairment	100	75
Other major policy changes	40	40
All cases	39	34

The figures on success and failure in cases involving companion policies are somewhat misleading, since our methodology only recognizes success in cases where sanctions made a positive contribution to the policy outcome. In several cases counted as failures—for example, the US sanctions against the Sandinistas in Nicaragua (Case 81–1) and against Noriega in Panama (Case 87–1)—the sender country achieved its goal, but military or covert measures swamped the impact of the sanctions. It may also be unfair to say that sanctions "failed" in other cases—for example, the United States versus Grenada (Case 83–4)—where the military weapon was unsheathed before sanctions had been given a chance to work. Rather than buttressing a sanctions campaign, companion measures are frequently used when sanctions are perceived to be either wholly inadequate or simply too slow.

IX. "Look Before You Leap."

Sender governments should think through their means and objectives *before* taking a final decision to deploy sanctions. Leaders in the sender country should be confident that their goals are within their reach, that they can impose sufficient economic pain to command the attention of the target country, that their efforts will not prompt offsetting policies by other powers, and that the sanctions chosen will not impose insupportable costs on their domestic constituents and foreign allies. These conditions will arise only infrequently, and even then the odds of success are slim.

Sanctions imposed for symbolic purposes—for the benefit of allies or a domestic audience—should be just as carefully crafted. For example, although some analysts have argued that imposing a high cost on one's own economy sends a signal of seriousness, the intended signal may be quickly drowned out by a cacophony of protests from injured domestic parties. Efforts to extend sanctions extraterritorially may produce the same effect abroad.

Although economic sanctions may be the best or even the only option in some cases where it is necessary to "do something," not just any sanction will do—the sanction chosen must be appropriate to the circumstances. Senders usually have multiple goals and targets in mind when they impose sanctions, and coercion is not always at the top of the list. Prudence argues that one carefully analyze the unintended costs and consequences before choosing a particular measure. It makes sense to tailor sanctions carefully to the objective they are genuinely intended to achieve.

Recent Experience and Prospects For the Future

Success in the use of sanctions has proved more elusive in recent years than in earlier decades, primarily as a result of welcome changes in the world economy: a more open international system with new and emerging economic superpowers. The question for the 1990s is whether changes in the global political system (in particular the end of the Cold War) can reverse this trend.

If one splits the case sample roughly in half, into those initiated before 1973 and those begun after that date, a striking difference emerges: almost half the sanctions episodes in the pre-1973 period succeeded, whereas the success rate among the cases begun after 1973 was just under a quarter. Just as striking is the fact that the "other major goals" category is the only one to show an increase in its success rate (although in this category the number of cases dropped by nearly half); meanwhile the success rate for cases involving modest goals plummeted (table 5.12).

These general trends need to be qualified. First, seven cases is a small number on which to base conclusions about the use of sanctions for ambitious goals. Moreover, two of the three "major" victories involved unusual circumstances. As noted in chapter 4, control of strategic commodities can provide senders (and targets) with leverage out of proportion to their overall economic size. Oil was the critical factor in one case (Case 73–1: *Arab League v. US and Netherlands*), and control of major transit routes in and out of a mountainous, landlocked country provided unusual leverage in the other (Case 89–1: *India v. Nepal*). Whether the end of the Cold War will increase the prospects for multilateral sanctions, and hence for success in "high" policy goal cases, is explored below.

Table 5.12 Success by period

	Pre-1973		1973–89	
Policy goal	Success cases	Failure cases	Success cases	Failure cases
Modest policy changes	9	3	8	31
Destabilization	9	6	2	4
Disruption of military adventures	5	8	1	4
Military impairment	2	6	0	2
Other major policy changes	2	11	3	4
All cases[a]	27	34	14	45

a. These figures include five cases listed under two different policy goals (see table 5.1).

Second, the increasing use of sanctions despite their declining effectiveness can be attributed entirely to US experience. Other senders, including multilateral coalitions in which the United States played a relatively minor role, both reduced their reliance on sanctions and improved their record: from 10 successes in 28 attempts prior to 1973, to 6 of 13 since then. In contrast, after posting a better than .500 average in the earlier period, the United States has batted under .200 since 1973.

Declining Success and Declining Hegemony

Reflecting its roles as economic hegemon and political and military super-power, the United States in the decades following World War II attempted to impose its will on a wider variety of targets and sought a broader array of objectives than did any other country, including the Soviet Union (which generally confined its use of sanctions to trying to keep rebellious allies in line). The unique US role translated into less reliance on international cooperation and, on average, more distant relations and weaker trade linkages with its targets than was observed with other users of sanctions. This in turn has contributed to a lower average cost imposed on target countries, although the dominant role played by foreign aid in US sanctions has also meant that they imposed lower average costs on the US economy (table 5.13 summarizes the US experience with sanctions).

The sharp upswing in the use of US sanctions for modest goals began in the early 1970s, when détente with the Soviet Union briefly allowed the United States to turn its attention to other matters, such as human rights violations and nuclear proliferation. Because the targets of these policies were more likely to be found among the developing countries, they tended to be economically weaker and less stable than the average target in earlier years. Furthermore, détente together with economic problems at home made the Soviet Union less and less willing and able to play the black knight and provide offsetting assistance to target countries.

All of these factors should have boded well for US sanctions in the 1970s. However, the global economy had also changed, and although US goals were more modest and the targets usually even smaller and weaker than before, the United States found that it had less leverage. In the early years after World War II, the US economy was the reservoir for rebuilding war-devastated countries. It was also the major if not sole supplier of a variety of goods and services. Well into the 1960s, the United States remained the primary source of economic assistance for developing countries.

Table 5.13   The US experience with sanctions[a]

Sender	Number of cases	Incidence of companion policies (percentage of cases)	International cooperation with sender (index)	Target health and stability (index)	Prior relations (index)	Cost to target as percentage of GNP	Trade linkage (percentage)	Cost to sender (index)
United States								
Pre-1973[b]								
Successes	18	44	1.6	1.8	2.3	2.0	24	1.5
Failures	17	47	2.2	2.5	1.8	1.3	24	2.1
Since 1973								
Successes	8	25	1.7	1.6	2.7	1.6	25	1.6
Failures	38	21	1.8	2.1	1.9	0.7	15	1.7
Other[b]								
Successes	16	44	2.3	2.2	2.3	3.3	32	2.3
Failures	25	48	2.4	2.5	2.2	1.1	21	2.3

a. See text for explanation of variables.

b. Includes two cases that have been cross-listed under "United States" and "Other" (39-1: *Alliance Powers v. Germany and Japan*, and 61-3: *Western Allies v. German Democratic Republic*).

Since the 1960s, however, trade and financial patterns have grown far more diversified, new technology has spread more quickly, and the US foreign aid budget has virtually dried up for all but a few countries. Recovery in Europe and the emergence of Japan have created new, competitive economic superpowers, and economic development has reduced the pool of potentially vulnerable targets. These trends are starkly illustrated by the declining average trade linkage between the United States and its targets (from 24 percent prior to 1973 to only 17 percent since), the lower costs imposed on targets (1.7 percent of GNP v. 0.9 percent of GNP), and the fading utility of manipulating aid flows. For example, the success rate for financial sanctions used alone (these are usually cases involving reductions of aid to developing countries) declined from nearly 80 percent before 1973 to less than 20 percent since then.

The Soviet invasion of Afghanistan and the election of Ronald Reagan brought an intensification of the Cold War that restored an East-West flavor to sanctions campaigns. This change in emphasis manifested itself in several differences between the sanctions cases in the 1980s and those in the decade preceding. Only about half of the 1980s cases involved modest goals, down from three-quarters in the 1970s; the incidence of companion policies nearly tripled (although from a low level given the predominance of modest goals in the 1970s); and the average cost imposed on the target doubled. Perhaps in recognition of its declining leverage, the United States also tried to harness more international cooperation. Still, the costs imposed remained below pre-1970 levels, the average trade linkage remained low, the average cost borne by the US economy (although still small) increased, and the overall effectiveness of sanctions continued to decline.

As this study goes to press, the United States could boast of only three successes in the 1980s: convincing Poland to reduce its repressive policies early in the decade (eventually leading to free elections and a Solidarity-led government); forcing El Salvador to prosecute rebels accused of killing Americans in a San Salvador café (despite a Salvadoran court ruling that they were covered by El Salvador's political amnesty law); and, in cooperation with the Netherlands, encouraging Suriname to improve its human rights record and hold elections.

In three other cases, the United States achieved a successful outcome, but regular or quasi-military action either superseded the sanctions (Grenada and Panama) or was the overwhelming factor in the success of the policy (Nicaragua). In several other cases, including South Africa, sanctions have had an observable impact, but they have not yet achieved the desired changes in target behavior.

Whatever the outcome in South Africa and other episodes, one thing is clear: the outcome of the Iraq case will color world opinion on the utility of sanctions for years to come. Many parallels can be drawn between the 1935 League of Nations sanctions against Italy and the 1990 United Nations sanctions against Iraq. But the strongest parallel is the power of each episode to shape informed opinion. If sanctions succeed in prying Iraqi troops out of Kuwait, a new era of superpower cooperation in the use of economic weapons may dawn; if sanctions fail, or if military force is required, then conventional wisdom will long hold that even draconian economic measures against an isolated target are futile.

To return to the main story, the most obvious and important explanation of the sharp decline in the effectiveness of US sanctions is the relative decline of the US position in the world economy. However, the evidence from the cases suggests three other contributing causes. First, although the United States typically took smaller bites in the 1970s and 1980s, it did not always finish what it started. Although détente allowed cases involving modest goals to multiply, concerns about Soviet influence or strategic position still claimed first priority in the strategic planning of the US government and frequently undermined the pursuit of less central goals. For example, the United States has been reluctant to enforce sanctions vigorously against El Salvador, Guatemala, and others for fear of weakening these regimes and allowing leftist rebel victories, which would benefit the Soviet Union. It also backed off on sanctions against Pakistan's nuclear program following the Soviet invasion of Afghanistan.

There may also be a misclassification problem, which would help to explain the anomaly noted above of sanctions becoming less effective in achieving modest goals, but more effective in pursuit of major goals. Although the goals in several more recent cases may have been modest from the perspective of the United States—and indeed seemed so to us, relative to the surrender of territory or threats to sovereignty and independence—they were often of central importance to targeted regimes whose leaders believed that their survival depended on stifling domestic political opposition or keeping up with a regional rival thought to be pursuing a nuclear weapons option. To military leaders in Argentina, Brazil, El Salvador, Pakistan, and elsewhere it seemed better to forgo continued US economic or military assistance, or imports of nuclear technology from the United States—and to seek alternative suppliers—than to risk losing power and possibly their lives. However, reclassifying the human rights and nuclear proliferation cases under the "other major goal" heading only reshuffles success rates by goal—reducing it for major goals and raising it slightly for modest goals. It does not affect the overall conclusion.

A second and related trend is the growing assertiveness of Congress in foreign policy in the past 15 years. The Hickenlooper amendment to the Foreign Assistance Act of 1962 (originally sponsored by Senator Bourke B.

Hickenlooper [R–IA]), which prompted executive branch action in many of the expropriation disputes of the 1960s, was a rare example of congressionally mandated economic sanctions in the early postwar period. In the 1970s, however, Congress increasingly forced the president's hand and constrained his discretion in various foreign policy situations by passing legislation requiring the use of economic sanctions. The confused signals sent by administrations that were forced to implement legislatively mandated sanctions may have led target countries to believe, often correctly, that the sanctions would not be sustained.

Finally, whereas financial measures were part of the sanctions package in more than 90 percent of episodes prior to 1973, they were present in only two-thirds of the cases after that. In the antiterrorism and nuclear nonproliferation cases, denial of key hardware was typically as important as inducing a change in policy, and so selective export controls were the tool of choice. Because alternative suppliers of the sanctioned goods were usually available, both goals proved elusive.

The type of financial sanction used most frequently also changed. Economic aid was the dominant choice in the earlier period, whereas military assistance was prominent in the later period, especially in the human rights cases, where military governments were often the target. Again, in some cases alternative sources of arms and financial assistance were available. Even more important, however, these governments perceived internal dissent to be a greater threat to their longevity than US enmity and sanctions.

Sanctions After the Cold War

The inevitable decline of American postwar hegemony has substantially reduced the utility of unilateral US economic sanctions. Moreover, the US experience and increasing global economic interdependence have convinced most other countries—never as enamored of sanctions as the United States—that the use of economic leverage for foreign policy ends was largely anachronistic. The end of the Cold War raises two questions for the future of sanctions: Can the utility of unilateral US sanctions be restored? And does the UN embargo of Iraq presage a new approach to international diplomacy, with multilateral sanctions playing an important role?

The decline in superpower rivalry, combined with severe economic problems at home, means that the Soviet Union is far less likely to play the black knight to countries seeking assistance to offset the impact of US sanctions. Although Libya and occasionally sympathetic neighbors (South Africa for Rhodesia and Saudi Arabia for Pakistan) have played this role, the resources and commitment of potential new black knights are certain to pale beside those of the Soviet Union at the height of the Cold War.

However, even if black knights are fewer in the 1990s, the scope for unilateral US action will continue to diminish. Changes in the international economy in recent decades have reduced the number of targets likely to succumb to unilateral economic coercion, even if black knights go the way of dragons. Many potential targets have developed strong and diversified economies that will never again be as vulnerable as they once were. And even relatively weak economies are less vulnerable today as a result of the growth in world trade and the rapid dispersion of technology, which mean that most US exports can be replaced at little cost and alternatives even to the large US import market can usually be found.

Does this mean that the second commandment, regarding international cooperation, should be dropped? We think not, for two reasons. First, ambitious goals will still be more difficult to achieve than modest ones, regardless of the degree of cooperation. Second, Iraq notwithstanding, multilateral cooperation is likely to be as difficult to achieve in the future as it has been in the past.

For many, the embargo of Iraq has provided a vision of a post–Cold War world in which the United Nations, without the superpower rivalries that have hamstrung it in the past, would finally play the dispute-settlement role originally intended for it. Success in the Middle East could revive enthusiasm for Woodrow Wilson's vision of sanctions as an alternative to war, but that enthusiasm is likely to be short-lived for two reasons.

First, economic sanctions seldom if ever achieve the sort of outright victory that military action can, although they may achieve a compromise solution that is preferable to war. The UN embargo may succeed in getting Iraqi troops out of Kuwait, but it probably will not be sufficient to rid the world of Saddam Hussein or his military might.

Although the end of the Cold War opened the door for an unprecedented degree of international cooperation against Iraq, the real source of that near unanimity was the threat to global prosperity and political stability posed by Hussein's aggression. Had the invasion of Kuwait not placed Hussein in a position to control the second-largest oil reserves in the world, with his million-man army poised on the Saudi Arabian border, it is unlikely that the world would have united in condemning him. Even with the stakes so high, China was a reluctant participant in many of the UN actions against Iraq. China might well have blocked some or all of those actions, using its veto in the UN Security Council, if not for its desire to rehabilitate its own international image and see the sanctions imposed after the Tiananmen Square massacre lifted. Since, few situations pose the global risks of Iraq's invasion of Kuwait, the degree of cooperation achieved in this case is unlikely to be repeated.

A more relevant case study for the post–Cold War world may be South

Africa. There, despite 30 years of UN and various bilateral sanctions, a peaceful end to apartheid remains a dream, though a less distant one than in the early to mid-1980s. The five permanent members of the UN Security Council, as well as virtually all the members of the General Assembly, are united in their abhorrence of apartheid, but they differ widely on how to end it. For 15 years after the Sharpeville massacre, the United Nations could manage no more than to call on its members to voluntarily restrict arms sales to South Africa. Nearly 15 years and thousands of lives farther down the road, the arms embargo (mandatory since 1977) is still the only UN sanction in place.

Over the years, political and economic concerns other than ending apartheid have frequently dominated policy toward South Africa in important sender countries. In the 1980s, public campaigns against apartheid intensified in the United States, Europe, and elsewhere in response to increasing repression and violence in South Africa, but still sanctions were imposed reluctantly and selectively.

While condemning apartheid in the 1960s and 1970s, the United States soft-pedaled sanctions because of fears that the result would be increased Soviet influence in a region considered strategic. In the 1980s, even after the easing of Cold War tensions, the Reagan administration worried that South Africa would retaliate against sanctions by restricting the export of certain strategic minerals and metals for which the only alternative source was the Soviet Union. Congress eventually passed the Comprehensive Anti-Apartheid Act over a presidential veto in 1986, but even that legislation imposed only partial sanctions. Moreover, the choice of sanctions appeared to reflect commercial as well as foreign policy goals. Only US exports of petroleum products and weapons and munitions were barred, while US imports of such domestically sensitive import-competing products as textiles and apparel, iron and steel, and agricultural products were banned.

Sanctions against South Africa by most of Europe (outside of Scandinavia) and Japan have been even less resolute, as these countries have allowed economic interests to dominate their policy in this area. The United Kingdom has substantial investments in and trade with South Africa, and Prime Minister Margaret Thatcher, who appears to have a genuine ideological aversion to the use of economic sanctions, blocked significant measures by either the European Community or the Commonwealth, and led the fight for lifting sanctions after President Frederick W. de Klerk released Nelson Mandela from prison.

Because the screws were tightened slowly and only part of the way, we estimate that the post-1985 sanctions against South Africa cost it less than 1 percent of GNP. Moreover, the "sanctions" that appear to have had the greatest impact in this period—the freeze on new lending to and substantial capital outflows from South Africa—were imposed by skittish financial institutions, not by governments. Thus, even if a peaceful resolution is eventually achieved in South Africa, it seems likely at the end of 1990 that government-imposed economic sanctions will have played no more than a modest role in the outcome.

Do's and Don'ts

The end of the Cold War removes one significant obstacle to the use of economic sanctions as a tool of international diplomacy. However, it will not erase all the economic and political interests that divide countries, or even different governments within the same country over time. Nor does it make difficult objectives easy, or strong and stable targets more susceptible to economic pressure. This does not mean that the United Nations should eschew sanctions, but only that effective multilateral sanctions are likely to remain rare events.

The problems for individual sender countries are even more difficult. One byproduct of the evolution of the world economy since World War II has been a narrowing of the circumstances in which unilateral economic leverage may be effectively applied. Success increasingly depends on the subtlety, skill, and creativity with which sanctions are imposed—a test the United States has frequently failed. Still, the United States and others are unlikely to forgo attempts at economic coercion entirely. Bearing that in mind, we present our short list of "do's and don'ts" for the architects of a sanctions policy designed to change the policies of the target country:

(1) Don't bite off more than you can chew.

(2) Don't exaggerate the importance of international cooperation with your policies—it may not be necessary in small episodes—but don't underestimate the role of international assistance to your target.

(3) Do pick on the weak and helpless.

(4) Do pick on allies and trading partners, but remember, good friends are hard to come by and sad to lose.

(5) Do impose the maximum cost on your target, but. . .

(6) Don't pay too high a price for sanctions yourself.

(7) Do apply sanctions decisively and with resolution, but. . .

(8) Don't expect sanctions to work right away, and don't jump to covert maneuvers or military action too soon.

(9) Do plan carefully: economic sanctions may worsen a bad situation.

"FOREWARNED IS FOREARMED."

References

Baldwin, David A. 1985. *Economic Statecraft*. Princeton, NJ: Princeton University Press.

Doxey, Margaret P. 1987. *International Sanctions in Contemporary Perspective*. New York: St. Martin's Press.

Leyton-Brown, David, ed. 1987. *The Utility of International Economic Sanctions*. London: Croom Helm.

Malloy, Michael P. 1990. *Economic Sanctions and U.S. Trade*. Boston: Little, Brown and Company.

General Bibliography

Note: This bibliography lists only general reference works. A detailed bibliography accompanies the abstract of each episode.

Abbott, Kenneth W. 1981. "Linking Trade to Political Goals: Foreign Policy Export Controls in the 1970s and 1980s." 65 *Minnesota Law Review:* 739–889.

Adler-Karlsson, Gunnar. 1968. *Western Economic Warfare, 1947–1967: A Case Study in Foreign Economic Policy.* Stockholm: Almqvist and Wiksell.

Alting von Geusau, A. M. Frans, and Jacques Pelkmans. 1982. *National Economic Security: Perceptions, Threats and Policies.* Tilburg, the Netherlands: John F. Kennedy Institute.

Ayubi, Shaheen, Richard E. Bissell, Nana Amu-Brafih Korsah, and Laurie A. Lerner. 1982. *Economic Sanctions in U.S. Foreign Policy.* Philadelphia Policy Papers. Philadelphia: Foreign Policy Research Institute.

Baer, George W. 1967. *The Coming of the Italo-Ethiopian War.* Cambridge, MA: Harvard University Press.

Baldwin, David A. 1971. "The Power of Positive Sanctions." 24 *World Politics* (October):19–38.

———. 1984. "Economic Sanctions as Instruments of Foreign Policy." Paper presented at the meeting of the International Studies Association, Atlanta (March).

———. 1985. *Economic Statecraft.* Princeton, NJ: Princeton University Press.

Ball, George W. 1968. *The Discipline of Power: Essentials of a Modern World Structure.* Boston: Little, Brown.

Barber, James. 1979. "Economic Sanctions as a Policy Instrument." 55 *International Affairs* (July):367–84.

Bayard, Thomas O., Joseph Pelzman, and Jorge Perez-Lopez. 1983. "Stakes and Risks in Economic Sanctions." 6 *The World Economy* (March):73–87.

Becker, Abraham S. 1984. *Economic Leverage on the Soviet Union in the 1980s.* R-3127-USDP. Prepared for the Office of the Under Secretary of Defense for Policy. Santa Monica, CA: Rand (July).

Bienen, Henry, and Robert Gilpin. 1979. "Evaluation of the Use of Economic Sanctions to Promote Foreign Policy Objectives." Boeing Corp., unpublished (2 April).

Blechman, Barry M., and Stephen S. Kaplan. 1978. *Force Without War: U.S. Armed Forces as a Political Instrument.* Washington: Brookings Institution.

Brown-John, C. Lloyd. 1975. *Multilateral Sanctions in International Law: A Comparative Analysis.* New York: Praeger.

Carter, Barry E. 1988. *International Economic Sanctions: Improving the Haphazard U.S. Legal Regime.* Cambridge: Cambridge University Press.

"Conference on Extraterritoriality for the Businessman and the Practicing Lawyer." 1983. 15 *Law and Policy in International Business:* 1095–1221.

Daoudi, M. S., and M. S. Dajani. 1983. *Economic Sanctions: Ideals and Experience.* London: Routledge and Kegan Paul.

DeKieffer, Donald E., ed. 1983. "Incentives: Economic and Social." 15 *Case Western Reserve Journal of International Law* (Spring).

————. 1988. "Foreign Policy Trade Controls and the GATT." 22 *Journal of World Trade* (June): 73–80.

Doxey, Margaret P. 1980. *Economic Sanctions and International Enforcement*. 2d ed. New York: Oxford University Press for Royal Institute of International Affairs.

————. 1983. "International Sanctions in Theory and Practice." 15 *Case Western Reserve Journal of International Law* (Spring).

————. 1983. "International Sanctions: Trials of Strength or Tests of Weakness." 12 *Millenium* (May):79–87.

————. 1987. *International Sanctions in Contemporary Perspective*. New York: St. Martin's Press.

Finney, Lynne Dratler. 1983. "Development Assistance—A Tool of Foreign Policy." 15 *Case Western Reserve Journal of International Law* (Spring).

Freedman, Robert Owen. 1970. *Economic Warfare in the Communist Bloc: A Study of Soviet Economic Pressure Against Yugoslavia, Albania, and Communist China*. New York: Praeger.

Galtung, Johan. 1967. "On the Effects of International Economic Sanctions: With Examples from the Case of Rhodesia." 19 *World Politics* (April):378–416.

Guichard, Louis. 1930. *The Naval Blockade: 1914–1918*. New York: D. Appleton.

Highley, Albert E. 1938. *The First Sanctions Experiment: A Study of League Procedures*. Geneva: Geneva Research Centre (July).

Hirschman, Albert O. 1980. *National Power and the Structure of Foreign Trade*. Expanded edition. Berkeley: University of California Press.

Hufbauer, Gary Clyde. 1990. *The Impact of U.S. Economic Sanctions and Controls on U.S. Firms*. A Report to the National Foreign Trade Council. Washington: National Foreign Trade Council (April).

International Institute for Strategic Studies. 1982. *Strategic Survey 1982–83*. London: International Institute for Strategic Studies.

Jack, D. T. 1941. *Studies in Economic Warfare*. New York: Chemical Publishing.

Knorr, Klaus. 1977. "International Economic Leverage and Its Uses." In *Economic Issues and National Security*, ed. Klaus Knorr and Frank Traeger. Lawrence, KS: Regents Press.

————. 1975. *The Power of Nations: The Political Economy of International Relations*. New York: Basic Books.

Lenway, Stefanie Ann. 1988. "Between War and Commerce: Economic Sanctions as a Tool of Statecraft." 42 *International Organization* (Spring):397–426.

Leyton-Brown, David, ed. 1987. *The Utility of International Economic Sanctions*. London: Croom Helm.

Lillich, Richard B. 1975. "Economic Coercion and the International Legal Order." 51 *International Affairs* (July):358–71.

Lipton, Merle. 1988. *Sanctions and South Africa: The Dynamics of Economic Isolation*. Special Report no. 1119. London: The Economist Intelligence Unit.

Losman, Donald L. 1979. *International Economic Sanctions: The Cases of Cuba, Israel, and Rhodesia*. Albuquerque: University of New Mexico Press.

Malloy, Michael P. 1990. *Economic Sanctions and U.S. Trade*. Boston: Little, Brown.

Marcuss, Stanley J., and D. Stephen Mathias. 1984. "U.S. Foreign Policy Export Controls: Do They Pass Muster Under International Law?" 2 *International Tax and Business Lawyer* (Winter):1–28.

Marcuss, Stanley J., and Eric L. Richard. 1981. "Extraterritorial Jurisdiction in United States Trade Law: The Need for a Consistent Theory." 20 *Columbia Journal of Transnational Law:* 439–83.

Medlicott, W. N. 1952. *The Economic Blockade.* 2 vols. London: Longman, Green.

Mitrany, D. 1925. *The Problem of International Sanctions.* London: Oxford University Press.

Moyer, Homer E., Jr., and Linda A. Mabry. 1983. "Export Controls as Instruments of Foreign Policy: The History, Legal Issues, and Policy Lessons of Three Recent Cases." 15 *Law and Policy in International Business:* 1–171.

National Academy of Sciences. 1987. *Balancing the National Interest: U.S. National Security Export Controls and Global Economic Competition.* Report of the Panel on the Impact of National Security Controls on International Technology Transfer, Committee on Science, Engineering, and Public Policy. Washington: National Academy Press.

Nincic, Miroslav, and Peter Wallensteen, eds. 1983. *Dilemmas of Economic Coercion: Sanctions in World Politics.* New York: Praeger.

Olson, Richard Stuart. 1979. "Economic Coercion in World Politics: With a Focus on North-South Relations." 31 *World Politics* (July):471–94.

Perlow, Gary H. 1983. "Taking Peacetime Trade Sanctions to the Limit." 15 *Case Western Reserve Journal of International Law* (Spring).

Renwick, Robin. 1981. *Economic Sanctions.* Harvard Studies in International Affairs no. 45. Cambridge, MA: Harvard University Center for International Affairs.

Rosenthal, Douglas E., and William M. Knighton. 1983. *National Laws and International Commerce: The Problem of Extraterritoriality.* Chatham House Papers no. 17. London: Routledge & Kegan Paul for the Royal Institute of International Affairs.

Schreiber, Anna P. 1973. "Economic Coercion as an Instrument of Foreign Policy: U.S. Economic Measures Against Cuba and the Dominican Republic." 25 *World Politics* (April):387–413.

Shultz, George P. Speech delivered 14 October 1978. Reprinted in *Washington Post,* 29 August 1982.

US Congress. Office of Technology Assessment. 1983. *Technology and East-West Trade: An Update.* Washington.

US Department of Commerce, Bureau of Export Administration. 1990. *1990 Annual Foreign Policy Report to the Congress.* Washington (February).

US General Accounting Office. 1983. *Administration Knowledge of Economic Costs of Foreign Policy Export Controls.* Report to Senator Charles H. Percy. Washington.

US Library of Congress, Congressional Research Service. 1988. *U.S. Economic Sanctions Imposed Against Specific Foreign Countries: 1979 to the Present.* CRS Report for Congress 88–612 F, rvd. 9 September. Washington.

Wallensteen, Peter. 1968. "Characteristics of Economic Sanctions." 5 *Journal of Peace Research:* 248–67.

Walters, Francis P. 1952. *A History of the League of Nations.* 2 vols. London: Oxford University Press.

Weintraub, Sidney, ed. 1982. *Economic Coercion and U.S. Foreign Policy: Implications of Case Studies from the Johnson Administration.* Boulder, CO: Westview Press.

Wu, Yuan-Li. 1952. *Economic Warfare.* New York: Prentice Hall.

Appendix A

Estimating the Cost of Sanctions: Methodology

This appendix sets forth the basic analytical model we have used to guide our efforts to estimate the costs of sanctions to both target and sender countries. The following discussion focuses solely on the costs imposed on the target country, but parallel analysis also is relevant for the calculation of the welfare costs to the sender country.

Figure B.1 shows supply and demand curves for a hypothetical good or service (e.g., bank credit) exported from the sender country to the target country. The presanction equilibrium price P_1 and quantity Q_1 are shown by the intersection of the supply and demand schedules at point e_1. In the first instance, the sender and its allies deprive the target country of supplies of the good or service in the amount dQ. Since the sender country and its allies are ordinarily not the only suppliers of the good or service, overall supply availability does not decline by the full amount dQ. Instead, the supply curve facing the target country shifts from S_1 to S_2. This horizontal shift corresponds to the removal of the amount dQ from the pool of supplies available to the target country. Other suppliers, responding to the abandoned market and potentially higher prices, provide an additional quantity indicated by x to the target country. As a result, the net quantity supplied to the target country declines by the amount y. The postsanction equilibrium of price and quantity is at point e_2, and the postsanction price is P_2, which is higher than the initial price P_1 by the amount dP.

How much does the target country lose from this sequence of events? The answer to that question depends on the loss in consumer surplus, that is, the reduction in the gains that purchasers enjoy from engaging in market transactions. Consumer surplus is measured by the difference between the total amount actually paid for the quantity consumed (price times quantity) and the total amount that consumers would pay if the market could be segregated and each consumer were charged the maximum price he is willing to pay. Note that the concept of consumer surplus applies with equal force to spare parts, capital goods, and food. It therefore might better be called "purchaser surplus" than consumer surplus.

In figure B.1, the level of consumer surplus before the imposition of sanctions is shown by the triangular area bounded by P_1, P_3, and e_1. When sanctions are imposed, shifting the supply curve from S_1 to S_2, the trapezoidal area bounded by P_1, P_2, e_1, and e_2 is subtracted from the previous level of consumer surplus. This loss to consumers represents the cost that export sanctions impose on the target country. By inspection, it is intuitively obvious that the steeper the slope of the demand curve in the neighborhood of the initial equilibrium price (i.e., the more "essential" the item to the target country and the smaller the range of substitute products), and the steeper the slope of the supply curve (i.e., the smaller the range of available alternatives), the greater will be the deprivation experienced by the target country.

The loss of consumer surplus is customarily referred to as a "welfare loss." The area of the trapezoid representing lost consumer surplus approximately equals the rectangle denoted by $Q_1 dP$. Hence, as a first approximation, we may write:

(1) $Q_1 dP$ = welfare loss

With the use of some algebra, the change in price dP can be expressed in terms of the elasticity of supply E_s and the elasticity of demand E_d. The elasticity of supply is defined as the ratio between the percentage change in quantity supplied, to a rough approximation denoted as x/Q_1, and the percentage change in price, denoted as dP/P_1. Similarly, the elasticity of demand is defined as the ratio of the percentage change in quantity demanded, denoted as y/Q_1, and the percentage change in price, denoted as dP/P_1. These elasticities can be represented by the following equations:

(2) $(x/Q_1)/(dP/P_1) = E_s$.

(3) $(y/Q_1)/(dP/P_1) = E_d$.

As noted earlier, supply and demand curves that are more steeply sloped in the neighborhood of the initial equilibrium price are characterized by smaller elasticities of supply and demand.

We may note further that:

(4) $x + y = dQ$.

We thus have three equations, (2), (3), and (4), and three unknowns, x, y, and dP. By solving these three equations algebraically it can be shown that:

(5) $dP = [P_1 dQ]/[(E_d + E_s)(Q_1)]$.

Substituting this expression for dP in equation (1), we obtain the following result:

(6) $P_1 dQ/(Ed + Es)$ = welfare loss.

In equation (6), $P_1 dQ$ represents the face value of the reduction in supply from the sender and its allies, before the price paid by the target country rises and other suppliers partly fill the gap.

To summarize, in this simple construct, the welfare loss inflicted on the target country depends on the size of the initial deprivation, the elasticity of supply, and the elasticity of demand. Table B.1 gives some hypothetical values of demand and supply elasticities and the resulting values of the expression $1/(Es + Ed)$. This expression may be thought of as the "sanctions multiplier": the coefficient applied to the initial deprivation of supplies experienced by the target country in order to calculate the welfare loss.

By a similar analysis, it can be shown that equation (6) also describes the welfare loss imposed when the sender country closes its markets and the target country initially loses sales in the amount dQ. In this case, however, the welfare loss represents a reduction in producer surplus, not consumer surplus. That is to say, the welfare loss represents a burden on the producers in the target country—a deduction of part of the difference between the market price they actually receive for the product and the price they would receive if the market could be segregated and each producer were paid the lowest price he would be willing to accept.

Figure B.1 Illustration of welfare loss from the imposition of export sanctions

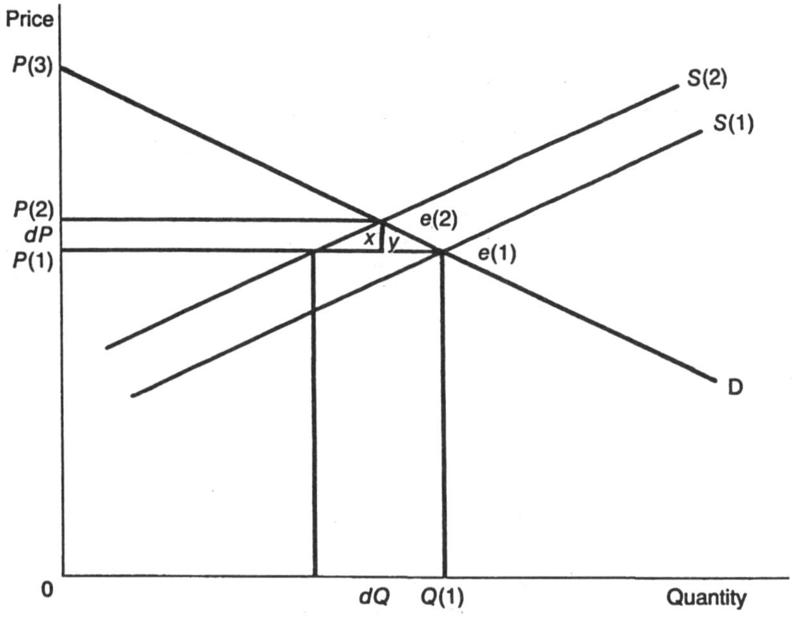

In order to calculate the cost of each sanctions episode to the target country, we first estimate the initial deprivation of markets or supplies, expressed on an annualized basis in current US dollars. We then use our own judgment to estimate the "sanctions multiplier" that should be applied in the particular episode. As a general proposition, we have tried to err on the side of overestimating the appropriate "sanctions multiplier." To illustrate, we apply a multiplier of near 1.00 to most reductions in aid, and a multiplier between 0.10 and 0.50 to most reductions in the supply or demand for goods. In a war context, we may apply a multiplier as high as 2.00. The estimates are generous because, in most contexts, the combined supply and demand elasticities would ordinarily exceed 5.0, simply because the target country is likely to be a small factor in world markets. A combined elasticity greater than 5 would correspond to a sanctions multiplier of less than 0.2.

Appendix B

Selected Case Histories

CASE 48-5

US and COCOM v. USSR and COMECON
(1948– : Technology Controls)

Chronology of Key Events

15 January 1948	US Department of Commerce requires licenses for all commercial shipments to Europe after 1 March 1948. (Adler-Karlsson 22)
Late March 1948	Congress inserts requirement in foreign aid bill that European recipients assure that goods US deems "strategic" will not be reexported to Eastern bloc. However, controls are laxly enforced: "The impression that is gained . . . is that at least up till October 1948, the enforcement of the US export regulations was more or less in a mess, with many loopholes to circumvent the existing laws." (Adler-Karlsson 25)
1948–49	US begins informally to enlist West European cooperation in coordinated embargo against Communist bloc. Efforts are stimulated by Berlin crisis, Communist leader Mao Zedong's triumph in China, explosion of first Soviet atomic bomb, break between Soviet leader Joseph Stalin and Marshal Tito followed by COMECON embargo against Yugoslavia. (US Congress 1979, 153)
28 February 1949	Congress enacts Export Control Act of 1949. (Woolcock 8)
22 November 1949	Under US leadership, Consultative Group (ministerial-level group, which rarely meets, intended to guide export control policy) and Coordinating Committee for Multilateral Export Controls (COCOM; designed as permanent, policy-implementing working group) are secretly formed, eventually include representatives of 16 NATO countries (entire NATO membership except Iceland) plus Japan. Under COCOM procedures, items on embargo list, exceptions to list must be agreed unanimously. Europeans are less enthusiastic about COCOM than US for several reasons: they historically have engaged in more East-West trade, are less convinced about balance of pain and benefit resulting from sanctions; they are less sure than US that technical problems can be resolved adequately; they place less emphasis on Soviet economic dependence as fulcrum of leverage; they resent pressure to restrict commercial ties. (Wolf 53; US Congress 1979, 153; Adler-Karlsson 6)
1 January 1950	COCOM begins operation with membership consisting of US, UK, France, Italy, Benelux countries. Later that year, Norway, Denmark, Canada, West Germany join. (US Congress 1979, 153)

September 1950	Congress passes Cannon amendment to 1951 Supplemental Appropriations Act forbidding US aid to any nation that exports "strategic" goods, as designated by US, to Communist bloc; however, legislation contains presidential waiver authority. (Adler-Karlsson 27)
January 1952	Congress passes Battle Act requiring nations to comply with US export regulations in order to receive aid. COCOM largely achieves this objective. (Adler-Karlsson 27)
1952	Portugal, Japan join COCOM. Most COCOM nations join in formation of China Committee (CHINCOM) to limit trade with China. (Adler-Karlsson 52)
1953	Greece, Turkey join COCOM. COCOM secrecy is loosened somewhat, although lists themselves are classified. Stalin's death, liberalization in USSR are followed by shortening of COCOM lists in period 1954–58. (US Congress 1979, 153)
August 1957	Eisenhower administration relaxes controls on trade with Poland following Wladyslaw Gomulka's rise to power there. (Garson 64)
1958	CHINCOM is abolished; controls on exports to China are folded into broader COCOM controls. Second major revision of COCOM lists is completed; "after 1958, almost all observers agree that the COCOM lists (as they still existed in 1967) mainly include goods which are conventionally understood as having a 'strategic importance'." US, however, unilaterally continues to maintain stricter embargo, based on old list. (Evans 12–13; Adler-Karlsson 8)
1963	US accepts view of European allies that "nonstrategic Western trade with the Soviet bloc, or the denial thereof, cannot affect basic Soviet military capability.... That capability is independently based on the Soviet's own advanced weapons-technology and military production." (Garson 14, citing Battle Act Report of 1963)
July 1964	COCOM controls are relaxed on trade with Romania because of its perceived desire for independence from USSR. (Garson 64)
September 1966	US administration spokesman: "[the US welcomes] increased trade in nonstrategic goods with Eastern European countries to weaken their ties with what was once a monolithic Soviet bloc." (Garson 64)
1969	Congress passes Export Administration Act that essentially switches US "from a policy of economic denial to a more narrow strategic embargo." Three reasons are cited for switch: National Security Adviser Henry A. Kissinger's aim of fostering "web of interdependence"; sense that "our policy of maintaining a broad trade embargo on USSR clearly had not significantly retarded Soviet economic growth or inhibited Soviet foreign policy"; allies' increasing refusal to cooperate in broad policy of denial. (Bingham 896)
1972	US begins normalization of relations with Beijing, drops "China differential" whereby restrictions imposed on exports to China are tighter than on those to Eastern Europe. (Meese 23)

1980	Following Soviet invasion of Afganistan, US tightens export licensing procedures for high technology products, adopts policy of not requesting "exceptions" for sale of items on COCOM's "dual-use" (i.e., items having both civilian, military uses) list to Soviet Union. Latter is significant change since US had requested more exceptions than any other member in 1970s. (Congressional Research Service 66)
July 1981	At Ottawa economic summit, Western leaders support US initiative for high-level review of COCOM controls. (Woolcock 3)
11 January 1982	NATO ministers agree to "reflect on longer term East-West economic relations, particularly energy, agricultural commodities and the export of technology" in order to "protect [NATO's] competitive position in the field of military and technological capabilities." (Woolcock 70)
21 January 1982	At US urging, COCOM holds meeting of deputy ministers (first at that high a level in 23 years); Reagan administration pushes for tighter controls on high-technology items, puts forward proposals to add 100 items to COCOM list, including robots, large dry docks (USSR is using Japanese dry dock to build aircraft carrier), computers, microprocessors. US also proposes "no exceptions" policy on computers. (Woolcock 68; *Wall Street Journal,* 19 January 1982, 33; *New York Times,* 20 January 1982, A8)
November 1982	UK, France, West Germany refuse to appoint permanent subcommittee of military experts to aid COCOM in decisions about military significance of certain dual-use items put forward by US at January meetings. *(Financial Times* [London], 13 November 1982, 2)
November 1982	Senate Subcommittee on Investigations charges Commerce Department with lax enforcement of export controls. Report states that Soviets have major program under way for acquiring Western technology by any means available. *(Washington Post,* 15 November 1982, A1).
December 1982	US, France agree on series of projects designed to strengthen Western control over trade with East. *(Washington Post,* 15 December 1982, A1)
March 1983	President Ronald Reagan approves National Security Decision Directive 75, which sets policy of using economic pressure to limit resources, foreign policy and military options open to USSR. *(Washington Post,* 21 March 1983, A3)
January 1984	It is reported that "Nearly 100 Soviet officials were expelled from Western countries last year, chiefly for attempted or successful industrial espionage." *(Financial Times,* 24 January 1984, 10)
12 July 1984	COCOM members agree to extend restrictions on large computers, some types of software, sophisticated telecommunications equipment. Restrictions on "many varieties of commonly available desktop computers" are removed. Pentagon official says, "There's a red line on the high end and more decontrol on the low end, which satisfies business interests all around." *(Washington Post,* 17 July 1984, A1)

| 12 July 1985 | Reagan signs Export Administration Act reauthorization bill, which includes provisions intended to streamline licensing process, reduce differences between US list of controlled items and those of other members of COCOM. *(International Trade Reporter,* 17 July 1985, 920; 24 July 1985, 952) |

| 16 December 1985 | Commerce Secretary Malcolm Baldrige outlines agreement to relax COCOM controls on export to China of items in 27 categories below "green line," which may now be shipped to China at each nation's discretion, without COCOM review. Previously, 70 percent to 80 percent of exceptions requests being filed concern sales to China. In 1984, US alone filed 3,122 applications for embargo exceptions, 89 percent of them for sales to China. *(Financial Times,* 10 January 1985, 4; *International Trade Reporter,* 23 October 1985, 1330; 1 January 1986, 11; *Facts on File* 821) |

| Summer 1986 | Spain joins COCOM. *(International Trade Reporter,* 20 August 1986, 1056) |

| January 1987 | National Academy of Science, National Academy of Engineering release report that conservatively estimates "direct, short-run economic costs" to US of its export controls system to be $9 billion, 188,000 jobs annually, with "associated GNP loss of $17 billion." Most of cost is from potential sales to Western countries of goods on low end of technology scale that are lost due to delays in licensing process and reexport requirements. Report concludes that administration's approach has resulted in "increasing friction between the United States and its closest allies and is an increasing cost to United States (and Western) economic vitality and innovative capacity." Report recommends ending Pentagon's de facto veto over high-technology exports, bringing US controls into conformity with those of other COCOM members. (National Academy 1987, App. D) |

| 22 October 1987 | Following attacks on US–owned and US–flagged tankers in the Persian Gulf, Reagan administration announces that it is suspending its review of controls on high-technology exports to China in retaliation for China's alleged sale of Silkworm missiles to Iran. China denies making sales, despite satellite photos apparently confirming them. *(Facts on File* 798) |

| 9 March 1988 | Following China's qualified support for proposed UN arms embargo against Iran, Reagan administration announces that it will resume its review of export control policy with view to relaxing controls on shipments to China. *(Facts on File* 172) |

| 23 August 1988 | Reagan signs Omnibus Trade and Competitiveness Act of 1988, which includes amendments to Export Administration Act requiring administration to remove certain items from control list, lift reexport requirements for most items destined for COCOM members, create new general license (not requiring prior approval for each shipment) for items below green line destined for COCOM members. (PL 100–418, Secs. 2414–16; Hirschhorn 390–92) |

31 March 1989	COCOM approves use of distribution licenses, which allow several shipments to be made under single license, for exports to China of goods below green line. Implementation of license is postponed indefinitely, however, following Chinese government's violent crackdown on prodemocracy demonstrators in Tiananmen Square in June (see Case 89–2 US v. China [1989– : Tiananmen Square]). *(Inside US Trade,* 7 April 1989, 1)
29 May 1989	President George Bush announces termination of "no exceptions" policy in COCOM imposed in response to Soviet invasion of Afghanistan. *(Washington Post,* 30 May 1989, A1)
25–26 October 1989	In wake of revolutionary changes in Eastern Europe, COCOM members agree to consider loosening export controls applied to Poland, Hungary. US maintains cautious position, reportedly is isolated on issue of how fast to lift controls on dual-use items. West Germany is most vociferous proponent of more rapid decontrol, in particular of machine tools, telecommunications equipment. *(Washington Post,* 27 October 1989, A27; *Financial Times,* 2 November 1989, 8; *International Trade Reporter,* 1 November 1989, 1408–09)
4 January 1990	Top Commerce Department official says that US plans to propose "license-free zone" for sales of most goods to COCOM members with adequate enforcement systems. Under plan, only "products incorporating the highest technology, such as supercomputers, would still require export licenses. . . ." *(Journal of Commerce,* 5 January 1990, 1A)
14–15 February 1990	Senior trade officials from COCOM countries meet in Paris, agree to finalize plans by summer for decontrolling exports of "32-bit microcomputers, high-tolerance machine tools, some kinds of telecommunications switching equipment and cables." COCOM members also agree to extend "green line" treatment to Eastern European countries with adequate enforcement systems; US blocks extension of more liberal treatment to USSR as desired by most European members. Administration officials announce they are initiating "strategic review" of export policies in light of changes in Eastern Europe, USSR. Hungary, Poland, Czechoslovakia indicate willingness to establish export control systems, including unannounced inspections by COCOM representatives, in order to qualify for loosened export controls. *(Financial Times,* 17 February 1990, 2; *Washington Post,* 17 February 1990, C1; *International Trade Reporter,* 14 March 1990, 361)
21 February 1990	In what he calls "major departure" from previous policy, Assistant Secretary of Defense for International Security Policy Stephen J. Hadley testifies that Defense Department supports administration's COCOM proposal to relax controls on computers, machine tools, certain telecommunications equipment: "A more restrictive approach than our allies will only disadvantage U.S. companies. That

is not only unfair, but it will lead to an erosion of the U.S. technology base in key areas." *(International Trade Reporter,* 28 February 1990, 288)

18 March 1990   East Germany holds its first democratic election in over 50 years. Alliance for Germany, led by East German counterpart of West German Christian Democratic Union, wins 48 percent of vote, 193 of 400 seats in parliament. In May, the two Germanys take first step toward full unification by signing treaty that provides for monetary union. *(Washington Post,* 19 March 1990, A1; 11 April 1990, A16; *Financial Times,* 19 May 1990, 1)

May 1990   In preparation for June COCOM meeting, Bush administration announces its willingness to lift restrictions on 30 categories of goods and technology, loosen controls on another 13 categories; changes would include "substantial" easing of controls on machine tools, computers, some telecommunications equipment, would leave restrictions on another 70 categories pending "total overhaul" of existing system of export controls. US also adopts position that would treat USSR in same fashion as China with respect to access to computers. Poland, Hungary, Czechoslovakia, once they have erected their promised export control systems, would receive even more favorable treatment. *(Financial Times,* 4 May 1990, 6; *Washington Post,* 24 May 1990, E1)

23 May 1990   West Germany announces that its COCOM allies have agreed to eliminate restrictions on most high-technology exports to East Germany. *(Washington Post,* 24 May 1990, E1)

Early June 1990   Despite opposition from US intelligence agencies concerned about possible compromise of their intelligence-gathering capabilities, Bush administration agrees to allow sales of sophisticated telecommunications equipment to Hungary, Poland, Czechoslovakia once they have established adequate export control systems. The other COCOM ministers formally agree to US proposals on 7 June in Paris. Commerce Secretary Robert A. Mosbacher says, "I am absolutely delighted. . . . We held Cocom together. We are supplying our Eastern European friends with the technology they need. And we are helping the competitiveness of Ameican companies." US also announces that it will lift restrictions on most exports to other COCOM members by beginning of July. Commerce Department officials estimate that 20,000 of 25,000 licenses issued for West-West transfers in 1989 would not have been necessary under new rules. Overall, relaxation of licensing for both East-West, West-West trade is estimated to affect $75 billion in US exports of computers, telecommunications, machine tools. *(Financial Times,* 4 May 1990, 6; *Washington Post,* 7 June 1990, E1; 8 June 1990, F1; 19 June 1990, D1)

Goals of Sender Countries

Klaus Knorr

"Thus, after World War II, the United States placed an embargo on the export of a wide range of 'strategic goods' to the Soviet Union. The object then was not to coerce Russia to do something or other, but to obstruct the growth of her military strength." (Knorr 1975, 5)

"Although motivations were mixed, ranging from a sheer desire to express righteous antagonism to the idea of waging comprehensive economic warfare against the Communist bloc, the main purpose came to be that of maintaining Soviet, and later Chinese, military inferiority, presumably in the interest of curbing their capacity for aggression. . . . The intent was to weaken, not coerce." (Knorr 1975, 142)

Gunnar Adler-Karlsson

"By the end of 1949 the control machinery was being used almost exclusively to keep out of the hands of Russia and her satellites items that might contribute to their military strength." (Adler-Karlsson 25)

Stephen Woolcock

In early 1970s US adopts linkage policy based on developing "web of constructive relationships," believing that increased trade and economic links—fostered by a carrot-and-stick approach using trade credits and sanctions—could contribute to improved East-West relations. (Woolcock 13)

Lawrence J. Brady, assistant secretary of commerce

"The basic US aim is for the West to maintain its 'qualitative' advantage over the Soviet Union. The United States wants to avoid a repeat of the 1970s when the Soviets narrowed their technology gap with the West, thanks largely to acquisitions—legally and illegally—of Western technology." (*Journal of Commerce*, 4 October 1982, 1A)

Lionel H. Olmer, under secretary of commerce for international trade

"Our national security export control system serves a . . . protective function by enabling the West to preserve its lead over the USSR in technology relevant to military purposes. The control system, though cumbersome and sometimes inefficient, is very much like a fisherman's net. Sometimes the holes in the net are opened more widely. Sometimes they are drawn more closely. We have an ongoing series of consultations with the Allies and US business over the spacing of these holes. But it would be extremely shortsighted to argue that the net should be taken away or that mutual security would be enhanced by an unimpeded flow of technology from West to East." (US Senate 1982, 12)

McGeorge Bundy

"When I first encountered this question of the definition of exports that would be helpful to the Soviet Union, it was in 1948 when I was a very junior person in the Economic Cooperation Administration, the Marshall Plan, and was assigned briefly to that issue. And one of the items that was proposed for embargo by the Defense Department was baseball bats. When we asked why that was, the answer was that baseball bats were issued to troops and were helpful to morale. . . . There is a recurrent tendency, I think, when there is tension between us and the Soviet Union for people to put quite a lot of pressure on. The general feeling in such times is that if the Defense Department says no, or indeed if some section of the Defense Department says no, we better be very careful." (US Senate 1980, 21)

Secretary of Commerce Robert A. Mosbacher

December 1989: "I think we should open the door to that degree it does not affect our national security. I think we will, particularly with the Eastern European countries, starting with Poland and Hungary, open the door to higher technology.... We're willing to do it with them because they have told us they will protect us and give us the opportunity to review what they're doing with the high-tech items.... The Soviet Union has several steps to take before we're ready to get into that same mode with them, and eventually they may be included, but not yet." *(Washington Post,* 18 December 1989, A11)

Response of Target Countries

Gunnar Adler-Karlsson

"Several politicians in both the East and the West also believe that Stalin *did* exploit [the embargo] to his own advantage. Not only did he try to sow the seeds of disunity inside the West by making the businessmen of each country believe that their competitors in the other Western nations could trade much less restricted by the embargo than themselves. More important may be that the embargo policy, being a very evident and forceful example of Western hostility, could be used by Stalin to push the bloc together in a harsh manner, blaming the harshness of a policy he anyway had intended to realize, on the Western embargo actions." (Adler-Karlsson 7)

"The Soviet response to the embargo policy had mainly two forms. On the one hand it sought to influence the West Europeans to keep the restrictions down as much as possible; on the other it had to find ways and means to circumvent those restrictions that did come into existence." (Adler-Karlsson 78)

Central Intelligence Agency

In 1982: "The combination of past Soviet acquisition practices and projected Soviet military needs indicates that the United States and its Allies are likely to experience serious counterintelligence and related industrial security and export control problems over the next five to ten years." (Central Intelligence Agency 12)

Attitude of Other Countries

Sweden, Switzerland, Iceland, Austria, Finland

These countries initially choose not to compromise their neutrality by joining COCOM. Sweden, Switzerland are seen as major alternative suppliers of items on COCOM list. Their relationship with COCOM is informal, their cooperation "unpredictable." In 1981–82, however, Sweden quietly negotiates unwritten accord with US upgrading its cooperation; in return for beefed-up enforcement, US agrees to treat Swedish importers like importers from COCOM countries. Although agreements are not publicized, Switzerland, Austria reportedly follow suit. (US Congress 1979, 153; *Financial Times,* 25 April 1985, 7; *Wall Street Journal,* 15 January 1987, 1)

West Germany, United Kingdom, France

"Originally all three countries ... adhered to COCOM because they believed it was in their own political and economic self-interest and because they were concerned about the Soviet threat. They were dependent on the US for their economic recovery and for their defense against the USSR." (Yergin 10)

"With the passage of time, all to some degree, have come to regard COCOM . . . as an American instrument for controlling and limiting European competition. The unpredictability of American policy and its repeated changes of direction regarding trade controls have made the Europeans doubly suspicious of American motives." (Yergin 3–5)

"The United States and [West Germany] converged in their view of trade in the 1950s and 1960s, but today [in 1980] they increasingly diverge over the politics of East-West trade. The FRG believes that East-West trade can be a stabilizing force, creating interdependencies that may serve to moderate Soviet behavior." (Yergin 26)

"[France] has never officially recognized COCOM's existence, has consistently maintained that security controls should be decided nationally and has led the opposition to any formal treaty establishing COCOM, as sought by the United States on various occasions." (Woolcock 61)

1989–90: "For West Germany and a number of other COCOM members, assisting Eastern Europe and the Soviet Union with reform now seems the surer path to security than the more vigilant U.S. approach. In private conversations, many European officials express the view that the security gains of consolidating reform in the Soviet and Eastern Europe outweigh any risk associated with relaxed technology transfer restrictions." (US House of Representatives 4)

Japan
In anticipation of March 1983 COCOM meetings, Japanese government announces "it basically cannot agree to the expanding of the COCOM restriction framework, going beyond the scope of military materials . . . the Japanese side fears that 'if restrictions are expanded in order to prevent the Soviet Union's acquisition of foreign currencies, it may even lead to the denial of East-West trade, as a whole, in the end,' and it intends to assert reversely that 'the development of East-West trade will increase the degree of the Soviet economy's dependence on the nations of the West, and this will reversely have big plus effects on security.' " *(Nihon Keizai,* 16 March 1983, 1)

Singapore
Singapore becomes first non–NATO country other than Japan to cooperate publicly with US on controlling technology diversion to Soviet bloc. According to Minister of Finance Dr. Tony Tan, "Singapore is prepared to cooperate not only with the US but also with the other members of CoCom and to discuss the possibility of arriving at a mutually acceptable arrangement." *(Financial Times,* 25 April 1985, 7)

Legal Notes

Office of Technology Assessment
The formulation of the framework of [COCOM] . . . is thus shrouded in secrecy. It is, in fact, doubtful whether any written understanding has ever existed; most likely a gentleman's agreement was undertaken, members agreeing to follow the licensing rules laid down by unanimous decisions among the group. "Because it is an informal and voluntary organization, COCOM has no power of enforcement. It is based neither on treaty nor executive agreement." (US Congress 1979, 153)

Economic Impact

Observed Economic Statistics

COCOM control lists have several parts: Munitions list, including all military items Atomic energy list, including sources of fissionable materials, nuclear reactors and their components Industrial/commercial list, composed of:

International List I: embargoed items

International List II: quantitatively controlled items

International List III: exchange of information and surveillance items.

Items on list I of industrial/commercial list cannot be exported to Communist-bloc nations unless exception is granted. List II items may be exported but only in specified quantities. Amounts above specified total require special exception. List III items may be sold but must be reported to COCOM, their end use tracked. "Most of the dual use items that pose the greatest problems for export controls are contained in List I. . . ." (US Congress 1979, 155)

In November 1949, COCOM embargo list has 86 items; total rises to 270 by November 1951 before dropping to 170 in August 1954, 118 in July 1958. It then rises again to 161 by August 1965, declines slowly through the 1970s. (US Congress 1979, 156)

"In 1987, the Department of Commerce, which has primary jurisdiction over export licensing, processed 104,320 validated licenses involving more than $80 billion worth of goods. Nearly 90 percent of these licenses involved West-West transactions." (Quigley 167)

On 27 September 1989, Commerce Department announces that number of export licenses approved for Soviet destinations has risen 80 percent since 1 June compared to same period in 1988, primarily because of President Bush's lifting of "no exceptions" policy adopted after Soviet invasion of Afghanistan. (*International Trade Reporter*, 4 October 1989, 1255)

Annual average of USSR imports of all goods from developed West: $676 million (1950–59); $2.7 billion (1960–70); $11.6 billion (1970–80). (Knorr 1975, 154; Portes 89)

Developed-country high-technology exports to Soviet Union, Eastern Europe, 1970–81 (millions of dollars except where noted)

Year	USSR	Eastern Europe	Total high-technology exports[a]	Total mfg. exports	High-technology exports as percentage of total mfg. exports
1970	403	414	817	4,971	16.4
1972	582	619	1,201	7,168	16.8
1974	1,036	1,223	2,259	15,978	14.1
1976	1,627	1,525	3,152	20,607	15.3
1977	2,003	1,741	3,744	21,306	17.6
1979	2,371	2,360	4,731	27,445	17.2
1980	2,330	2,194	4,524	29,252	15.5
1981	1,735	1,721	3,456	25,475	13.6

a. Annual average 1970–81: $2,985 million.
Source: US Department of Commerce 7, 13; US Congress Office of Technology Assessment 1983, 51.

OECD: exports of manufactured goods to Eastern Europe, Soviet Union, 1980–87
(millions of dollars)

Year	Exports
1980	29,729
1981	25,593
1982	25,255
1983	25,081
1984	22,771
1985	24,022
1986	28,234
1987	30,362

Source: Organization for Economic Cooperation and Development.

Calculated Economic Impact (annual cost to target country)

Reduction in high-technology exports, estimated to have accounted, in absence of controls, for additional 5-percentage-point share of total USSR, Eastern Europe imports of manufactured goods; welfare loss valued at 125 percent of difference between actual imports, potential high-technology imports.

1950–59	$69 million
1960–69	$280 million
1970–79	$1,015 million
1980–87	$1,649 million

Relative Magnitudes

Gross indicators of COMECON economies	
COMECON GNP (1950)[a]	$148 billion
COMECON population (1948–50)	245 million
COMECON GNP (1970)	$688 billion
COMECON population (1970)	346 million
Annual effect of sanctions (1950–69) related to gross indicators	
Percentage of GNP	0.1
Per capita	$0.71
Annual effect of sanctions (1970–87) related to gross indicators	
Percentage of GNP	0.2
Per capita	$3.85

COMECON trade with COCOM as percentage of total trade	
Exports (1948)	32
Imports (1948)	31
Exports (1970)	15
Imports (1970)	15
Ratio of COCOM GNP (1950: $447 billion) to COMECON GNP	3
Ratio of COCOM GNP (1970: $2,204 billion) to COMECON GNP	3

a. Based on USSR only.

Assessment

Stephen Woolcock

"Although it seems clear that Western technology has been of importance to the Soviet economy, it is impossible to say whether or not it is of such importance that the threat of denial would influence Soviet policy. Recent research . . . suggests that the impact of Western exports depends on the ability of the Soviet economy to absorb and thus reproduce Western technological know-how." (Woolcock 32)

Gunnar Adler-Karlsson

"It is today impossible to maintain the original embargo motives, that the American restrictions over East-West trade to an appreciable extent can slow down the growth of the Soviet economy or of the military sector of that economy." (Adler-Karlsson 8)

Rand Report for US Department of Defense

"[Export controls] 'would not halt Soviet economic or military development and will only slow it slightly. . . .' As export controls move away from areas in which the USA stands to make 'near-term military gains,' toward 'technologies that afford the Soviets longer term industrial gains. . . the benefits of export controls become more diffuse and uncertain, while the costs of trying to enforce them become progressively greater.' " (Woolcock 46)

Lionel H. Olmer, testifying at congressional hearing, March 1983

Because "very, very slow progress" has been made in harmonizing US, Western European, Japanese export controls, "American business is taking a hosing in a number of specific areas." (New York Times, 2 March 1983, D2)

Panel on the Impact of National Security Controls on International Technology Transfer

"The panel notes in conclusion that there is a need for national security export controls and that current statutory authority recognizes the necessity to accommodate both military security and economic vitality. But the recent performance of the U.S. government on this matter has not been satisfactory—and will be increasingly less so because of prevailing trends in international trade and technology diffusion—because it has tended to focus on tightening controls while giving little attention to their effectiveness and costs. . . . In the absence of appropriate corrective measures, these continuing problems will exact ever-higher tolls—on both Western economic vitality and innovative capacity and on the military security of the United States and its allies." (National Academy 1987, 177)

Kevin Quigley and William Long

"At a time when the dramatic transformations taking place in the East bloc are bringing an end to the Cold War, [an export] control regime that affects nearly one-third of all U.S. exports seems highly anachronistic. Not only is such a system out of touch politically with the new era in East-West relations that is emerging, but as a practical matter it is economically untenable in today's competitive global marketplace. . . . In short, the U.S. export-control system subordinates the country's economic competitiveness to military concerns at a time when economic concerns are growing in importance. Moreover, the system does not even succeed in safeguarding U.S. national security, because its extensive scope stifles the civilian technological advancement that is increasingly essential to maintaining a strong military." (Quigley and Long 165)

Authors' Summary

Overall assessment

☐ Policy result, scaled from 1 (failed) to 4 (success)   3

☐ Sanctions contribution, scaled from 1 (none) to 4 (significant)   2

☐ Success score (policy result *times* sanctions contribution),
scaled from 1 (outright failure) to 16 (significant success)   6

Political and economic variables

☐ Companion policies: J (covert), Q (quasi-military), or R (regular military)   —

☐ International cooperation with sender, scaled from 1 (none) to 4 (significant)   4

☐ International assistance to target: A (if present)   A

☐ Sanctions period (years)   42+

☐ Economic health and political stability of target, scaled from
1 (distressed) to 3 (strong)   3

☐ Presanction relations between sender and target, scaled from
1 (antagonistic) to 3 (cordial)   1

☐ Type of sanction: X (export), M (import), F (financial)   X

☐ Cost to sender, scaled from 1 (net gain) to 4 (major loss)   3

Comments

Our success scores do not address the utility of national security controls that seek to limit exports of technology and goods directly relevant to military uses. Rather, they assess the success of COCOM in using broader measures of economic denial to limit the resources available to the Soviet defense establishment and to maintain a technological edge in weaponry. Although quantitative estimates cannot be made, most observers believe that the COCOM controls had little impact on Soviet economic growth or defense spending. Any potential impact was undermined by intense, often successful Soviet effort to acquire restricted technology by covert means, as well as, in the 1980s, by the rapid dispersion of technology to an increasing number of non–COCOM developing countries. Although economic constraints have contributed in recent years to Soviet adoption of a more moderate foreign policy, most dramatically in the late 1980s in allowing Eastern Europe to "go its own way," we attribute those developments primarily to inefficiencies in the Soviet system itself rather than to external pressures.

Bibliography

Adler-Karlsson, Gunnar. 1968. *Western Economic Warfare, 1947–67: A Case Study in Foreign Economic Policy.* Stockholm: Almqvist and Wiksell.

Bingham, Jonathan B., and Victor C. Johnson. 1979. "A Rational Approach to Export Controls." 58 *Foreign Affairs* (Spring): 894–920.

Central Intelligence Agency. 1982. *Soviet Acquisition of Western Technology.* Washington.

Congressional Research Service, Library of Congress. 1981. *An Assessment of the Afganistan Sanctions: Implications for Trade and Diplomacy in the 1980s.* Prepared for House Committee on Foreign Affairs. 97 Congress, 1 session. Washington.

Drabek, Zdenek. 1983. "The Impact of Technological Differences on East-West Trade." 119 *Weltwirtschaftliches Archiv* 630–48.

Facts on File. 1985, 1987, 1988.

Garson, John R. 1971. "The American Trade Embargo Against China." In *China Trade Prospects and US Policy,* ed. Alexander Eckstein. New York: Praeger.

Hirschhorn, Eric L., and Joseph Tasker, Jr. 1989. "Export Controls: Toward a Rational System for Everyone except Toshiba, with All Deliberate Speed." 28 *Law and Policy in International Business* 369–401.

Knorr, Klaus. 1973. *Power and Wealth: The Political Economy of International Power.* New York: Basic Books.

———. 1975. *The Power of Nations: The Political Economy of International Relations.* New York: Basic Books.

Meese, Sally A. 1984. "Export Controls to China: An Emerging Trend for Dual-Use Exports." 7 *The International Trade Law Journal* (Fall): 20–37.

National Academy of Sciences, National Academy of Engineering, Institute of Medicine. 1987. *Balancing the National Interest: U.S. National Security Export Controls and Global Economic Competition.* Report of the Panel on the Impact of National Security Controls on International Technology Transfer, Committee on Science, Engineering, and Public Policy. Washington: National Academy Press.

Portes, Richard. 1983. *Deficits and Detente.* Background paper for report of international conference on balance of trade in COMECON countries. New York: Twentieth Century Fund.

Quigley, Kevin F.F., and William J. Long. 1989–90. "Export Controls: Moving Beyond Economic Containment." 7 *World Policy Journal* (Winter): 165–88.

US Congress. Office of Technology Assessment. 1979. *Technology and East-West Trade.* Washington.

———. 1983. *Technology and East-West Trade: An Update.* Washington.

US Department of Commerce. International Trade Administration. 1983. "Quantification of Western Exports of High Technology Products to Communist Countries." Washington.

US House of Representatives. Committee on Foreign Affairs, Subcommittee on International Economic Policy and Trade. 1990. Testimony by William J. Long. 101 Cong., 2 sess., 25 January. Washington.

US Senate. Committee on Banking, Housing, and Urban Affairs, Subcommittee on International Finance. 1980. *Hearings on Trade and Technology, Part 2, East-West Trade and Technology Transfer.* 96 Cong., 1 sess., 28 November 1979. Washington.

US Senate. Committee on Foreign Relations, Subcommittee on International Policy. 1982. *Hearings on Economic Relations with the Soviet Union.* Testimony by Lionel H. Olmer, under secretary of commerce for international trade. 97 Cong., 2 sess., 30 July. Washington.

Wickens, Justin H. 1984. *Technology Transfer Controls: Theory and Practice.* Paper prepared for Executive Seminar in National and International Affairs, Foreign Service Institute, 26 sess. Washington.

Wolf, Thomas. A. 1973. *US East-West Trade Policy.* Lexington, MA: Lexington Books.

Woolcock, Stephen. 1982. *Western Policies on East-West Trade.* Chatham House Papers no. 15. London: Royal Institute of International Affairs.

Yergin, Angela Stent. 1980. *East-West Technology Transfer: European Perspectives.* The Washington Papers no. 75. Beverly Hills, CA: Sage Publications.

CASE 78–8

US v. Libya

(1978– : Gadhafi)

Chronology of Key Events

See also Summary S–1 US v. Countries Supporting International Terrorism (1972– : Overview)

1978	US bans military equipment sales to Libya in retaliation for Libyan support of terrorist groups. *(New York Times,* 21 January 1982, A1)
2 March 1979	Deputy Assistant Secretary of State Morris Draper informs Congress that State Department, having received assurances that planes would be used only for national airline, has approved sale of three Boeing 747s, two 727s to Libya. *(New York Times,* 3 March 1979, A5)
29 September 1979	Revised Export Administration Act, with amendment on terrorism sponsored by Congresswoman Millicent Fenwick (R-NJ), is enacted. In accordance with amendment, State Department names Libya, Syria, Iraq, South Yemen as countries which, because of support for terrorism, may not receive certain US exports; export of some other goods is made contingent upon congressional approval. (Flores 564, 570)
18 March 1981	Secretary of State Alexander M. Haig, Jr., claims that Libya is running training camps for terrorists. *(Facts on File* 169)
6 May 1981	US closes Libyan diplomatic mission in Washington, citing *inter alia* its "support for international terrorism." *(New York Times,* 7 May 1981, A1)
August 1981	US Navy F-14s are fired upon by, shoot down two Libyan fighter jets over Gulf of Sidra, which Libya claims as territorial waters. *(New York Times,* 20 August 1981, A1)
28 October 1981	US imposes controls on exports of small aircraft, helicopters, aircraft parts, avionics to Libya to "limit Libyan capacity to support military adventures in neighboring countries." (General Accounting Office [GAO] 4)
November 1981	Exxon Corp. abandons its Libyan operations. *(Wall Street Journal,* 11 December 1981, 3)
6 December 1981	US defense attaché is murdered in Paris; some observers suspect Libyan involvement. (Schott 16; Flores 582)

7 December 1981	President Ronald Reagan claims US has evidence that Libyan leader Moammar Gadhafi has sent assassination teams to murder top US officials. *(Washington Post,* 11 December 1981, A28)
11 December 1981	Reagan administration calls on Americans residing in Libya (primarily 1,500 technicians) to leave "as soon as possible," citing "the danger which the Libyan regime poses to American citizens." US passports are declared invalid for travel to Libya. *(Washington Post,* 11 December 1981, A1; *Wall Street Journal,* 11 December 1981, 3)
12 December 1981	US oil firms agree to withdraw US personnel from Libya but announce they will be replaced with other foreign technicians. *(Washington Post,* 12 December 1981, A1)
21 January 1982	Libya is reported to have rebuilt 400 heavy-duty trucks (sold to Libya by Oshkosh Trucks) to carry tanks and for other military purposes, despite written guarantees in February 1978 that vehicles would be used solely for agricultural purposes. *(New York Times,* 21 January 1982, A1)
10 March 1982	Reagan embargoes crude oil imports from Libya, invoking section 232 of Trade Expansion Act of 1962, drawing on same national security finding made in case of Iranian oil in 1979. Presidential Proclamation 49072 states: "Libyan policy and action supported by revenues from the sale of oil imported into the United States are inimical to United States national security." In addition, US restricts exports of sophisticated oil, gas equipment, technology but does not impose retroactive controls or embargo export of items that are available abroad. (Schott 18, 39; *Wall Street Journal,* 9 November 1982, 39)
November 1982	US State Department warns oil companies (notably Charter Oil, Coastal Corp.) against selling refined products derived from Libyan crude in US. Central Intelligence Agency (CIA) mounts opposition to Libyan occupation of Chad, assists Libyan exiles. CIA Director William J. Casey says these activities might lead to "ultimate" removal of Gadhafi. *(Newsweek,* 8 November 1982, 55; *Wall Street Journal,* 9 November 1982, 39)
December 1982	US bars Boeing sale of 12 commercial jets to Libyan Arab Airlines for $600 million. *(New York Times,* 26 August 1983, A24)
August 1983	Libya sends troops into Chad in hope of overthrowing government of Hissen Habré. France, US support Habré. Reagan administration is divided over export license application for shipment of $40 million marine mooring system to Libya. *(New York Times,* 19 August 1983, A1, A6; 26 August 1983, A24)
5 December 1983	Reagan reportedly considers "State Department proposal to block exports of any US–made product that would contribute substantially to the development of Libya's economy." Proposed policy, arising out of Libyan request to purchase irrigation, oil-refining equipment, would effectively block "almost all major exports to Libya." Other elements of administration continue opposition to

restrictive approach on exports to Libya. *(Wall Street Journal, 5 December 1983, 3; New York Times, 16 December 1983, A18)*

18 March 1984
In response to alleged Libyan bombing of Omdurman, Sudan, US sends two AWACS surveillance planes to Egypt. *(Facts on File 197)*

3 October 1984
US charges Libya with complicity in laying of mines in Red Sea. *(Facts on File 807)*

3 November 1985
Washington Post reports that President Reagan has authorized covert operation to undermine Gadhafi regime, based on June 1984 CIA assessment that "no course of action short of stimulating Qaddafi's fall will bring any significant and enduring change in Libyan policies." *(Washington Post, 3 November 1985, A1)*

15 November 1985
US bars imports of refined petroleum products from Libya, which have increased following opening of Ras Lanuf petrochemical processing complex earlier in year. (GAO 1987, 18)

27 December 1985
Coordinated terrorist attacks at Rome, Vienna airports kill 19 people, wound 110; US soon after links Abu Nidal, head of a Palestinian faction, to murders, claims he has received "a considerable amount of financing and assistance" from Gadhafi. White House and State Department officials call on other governments to exert economic pressure on Libya to halt its support of terrorism. *(Washington Post, 31 December 1985, A1)*

7 January 1986
President Reagan invokes International Emergency Economic Powers Act to implement comprehensive trade, financial controls against Libya. Order bars most exports, imports of goods, technology, services (except for humanitarian purposes), all loans or credits to Libyan government, transactions "relating to travel by a United States citizen or permanent resident alien to Libya, or to activities by any such person within Libya." However, Treasury regulations permit reexport of US goods to Libya that are substantially transformed in a third country. Given unwillingness of Western allies to join in sanctions against Libya, Reagan sends personal letters to allied leaders asking them "not to undercut U.S. sanctions against Libya by replacing American oil companies and workers being ordered out of that country." Administration officials admit that they did not consult with allies before taking action. *(New York Times, 8 January 1986, A6; 9 January 1986, A1; 10 January 1986, A6; Wall Street Journal, 8 January 1986, 2; Washington Post, 8 January 1986, A1; 10 January 1986, A30; GAO 1987, 11)*

8 January 1986
President Reagan orders freeze of Libyan government assets in US, including hundreds of millions of dollars of deposits held in domestic, foreign branches of American banks, real property, other investments. Action is taken to preclude Libyan withdrawals, deter Libya from collecting on performance bonds placed by US companies doing business with Libya, guard against Libyan expropriation

of US assets. *(New York Times,* 9 January 1986, A1; *Wall Street Journal,* 9 January 1986, 25; *New York Times,* 11 January 1986, A4; Caras 675)

15 January 1986 Deputy Secretary of State John C. Whitehead begins visit to nine NATO countries to seek their support for US sanctions against Libya. *(Washington Post,* 14 January 1986, A11)

7 February 1986 US revises sanctions to allow oil companies to continue operations in Libya temporarily to avoid "abandonment of contracts or concessions [which] would result in a substantial economic windfall to Libya." Rule allows sale of Libyan crude at Libyan ports, but bars drilling for, extracting, distributing, or marketing Libyan oil. Profits from such sales are to be placed in escrow account. In addition, companies are expected to dispose of their Libyan holdings "as soon as practicable on fair and appropriate terms," but no deadline is set. *(New York Times,* 8 February 1986, 33; *Washington Post,* 8 February 1986, A18; GAO 1987, 16)

24–25 March 1986 US Sixth Fleet challenges Gadhafi's claim to territorial waters in Gulf of Sidra, crosses his "Line of Death." Action provokes Libyan attack during which two Libyan patrol boats are sunk, onshore antiaircraft missile site is destroyed. *(Washington Post,* 25 March 1986, A1; *New York Times,* 26 March 1986, A1)

5 April 1986 Terrorist bomb destroys West Berlin discotheque frequented by US servicemen, killing three persons, injuring over 150. US charges Libyan complicity on basis of intercepted Libyan diplomatic transmissions. Reagan states that "evidence is direct, it is precise, it is irrefutable," begins planning military retaliation. *(Washington Post,* 15 April 1986, A1; *New York Times,* 15 April 1986, A1)

14 April 1986 In hopes of forestalling US military response to West Berlin bombing, EC countries agree to reduce size of Libyan embassies, restrict movements of Libyan diplomats in Europe. *(New York Times,* 15 April 1986, A12)

15 April 1986 US bombers attack Gadhafi headquarters, military airfields, suspected terrorist training camps around Tripoli, Benghazi in retaliation for Libyan role in 5 April bombing, and to deter future terrorist acts against US installations. UK allows US to use British airfields for exercise, but France denies overflight rights for US planes. *(Washington Post,* 15 April 1986, A1, A23; *New York Times,* 15 April 1986, A1)

5 May 1986 Leaders of seven major industrial countries at economic summit in Tokyo cite Libya for its support of international terrorism, list a broad range of measures from which each of them could choose to act against countries supporting international terrorism. List includes, *inter alia,* arms embargoes, limits on diplomatic missions, improved extradition procedures for accused terrorists, closer cooperation among law enforcement agencies. *(Washington Post,* 6 May 1986, A1, A14)

5 May 1986	State Department officials announce that special exemptions for US oil companies in Libya will not be extended beyond 30 June. Companies note that US action will result in sale of their assets at "fire-sale" prices, but that such losses will be minor since Libyan operations are small share of their total business. *(New York Times, 6 May 1986, A14)*
13 May 1986	Libyan Arab Foreign Bank files suit in London seeking payment of funds blocked by Bankers Trust London under US asset freeze. (Weisburg 1006–11)
23 June 1986	Treasury amends regulations on Libya to bar reexport of goods incorporating US products from third countries destined for Libyan petroleum or petrochemical industry. (GAO 1987, 12)
30 June 1986	Treasury revokes special exemptions for US oil companies but authorizes them to enter into standstill agreements with Libyan authorities to maintain their ownership rights for three years while they renounce claims to current oil production, rights to future reserves found in Libya, obligations to pay current operating expenses. (GAO 1987, 16–17)
August 1986	OPEC officials report that France has begun boycotting imports of Libyan oil, refined products. In further attempt to destabilize Gadhafi, Reagan administration sponsors disinformation campaign on extent of Libyan opposition to Gadhafi regime. *(Wall Street Journal, 6 August 1986, 20; Schumacher 335)*
Fall 1987	On 2 September, High Court of Justice in London rules in favor of Libya, orders Bankers Trust London to transfer to Libyan Arab Foreign Bank $131 million, plus accrued interest, that has been blocked by US asset freeze. US Treasury authorizes payment on 9 October. (Weisburg 1011)
Late 1988	Reagan administration accuses Libya of producing chemical weapons at plant near Rabta, south of Tripoli. Although Libya claims that plant produces pharmaceuticals, production ceases for over a year. *(New York Times, 8 March 1990, A17)*
1989	Gadhafi reportedly cuts back funding to numerous rebel movements, asks them to close their offices in Libya. In interview in magazine *Al Mussawar*, Gadhafi admits to having supported terrorists in past, but "when we discovered that these groups were causing more harm than benefit to the Arab cause, we halted our aid to them completely and withdrew our support." Action parallels drop in Libyan foreign reserves to under $3 billion in first quarter of 1989. *(Washington Post, 5 September 1989, A15; New York Times, 26 October 1989, A8)*
25 January 1990	President George Bush extends Libyan sanctions for another year, stating that Libya continues to pose an "unusual and extraordinary threat" to US national security. *(Journal of Commerce, 26 January 1990, 5A)*

March 1990	Within days of US intelligence reports that chemical weapons production has resumed at Rabta, Gadhafi blames West German agents for alleged fire at plant that he claims caused extensive damage. US intelligence agencies later conclude that alleged fire was elaborate hoax, that Rabta plant is intact, capable of resuming production. *(New York Times,* 16 March 1990, A3; *Washington Post,* 19 June 1990, A17)
April 1990	Gadhafi intervenes with Abu Nidal to obtain release of two French hostages, one Belgian; Gadhafi receives "personal thanks" of French President François Mitterrand. *(Washington Post,* 27 May 1990, A35)
June 1990	Palestinian terrorist, captured with several heavily armed comrades off coast of Israel, claims that they were trained in Libya, transported in Libyan boats, accompanied by Libyan adviser. A few months later, Gadhafi expels radical Palestinian group responsible for attack. *(Washington Post,* 7 June 1990, A30; 5 November 1990, A19)

Goals of Sender Country

December 1981

Administration officials emphasize that anti-Gadhafi strategy is not response to assassination reports. Instead, they say strategy is linked "to a presidential decision, taken months ago, to devote major US efforts to the task of weakening the Qadhafi regime." On 11 December, Deputy Secretary of State William P. Clark states that administration has acted in response to Gadhafi's "well-known efforts over the course of many years to undermine US interests and those of our friends, as well as Libya's support for international terrorism." *(Wall Street Journal,* 11 December 1981, 3, 31; *Washington Post,* 11 December 1981, A28)

August 1983

Anonymous administration official: "American policy is for Libya to get out of Chad. . . . The Libyans should not be in Chad. We have to show the Libyans they cannot win in Chad . . . ." *(New York Times,* 19 August 1983, A6)

January 1986

Secretary of State George P. Shultz claims that "Libya provides 'safe haven' and 'financial support' to terrorists and has distributed arms and explosives from its diplomatic posts abroad." He characterizes US sanctions as "a statement to everybody about how we feel," notes that "the administration is prepared in the future to take 'effective' and 'necessary' actions to fight terrorism." *(Washington Post,* 10 January 1986, A30)

President Reagan cites conditions for lifting sanctions: "[Gadhafi] would have to reveal by action that he has severed those connections [Libya's financial support, provision of training camps for terrorists] and is no longer backing these terrorist groups." *(New York Times,* 12 January 1986, A12)

April 1986

President Reagan, following bombing raid on Tripoli, Benghazi: "We believe that this preemptive action against his terrorist installations will not only diminish Colonel Qaddafi's capacity to export terror, it will provide him with incentives and reasons to alter his criminal behavior." *(Washington Post,* 15 April 1986, A23)

Response of Target Country

11 December 1981

Libyan Oil Minister Abdessalem Mohammed Zagaar labels Reagan administration measures "an act of aggression," calls upon OPEC for assistance; OPEC rejects proposal for joint action. *(Washington Post,* 11 December 1981, A1; 12 December 1981, A1)

9 January 1986

After imposition of unilateral US sanctions, Gadhafi warns "that continued American hostility toward his country would lead to 'more cooperation' between Libya and the Soviet Union." He adds that he may reassess Libya's policy denying base rights to Soviet ships at Libyan ports: "We may have to tip the balance in the Mediterranean if we feel we are threatened by a superpower such as the Americans." *(New York Times,* 10 January 1986, A1; *Washington Post,* 10 January 1986, A1)

15 January 1986

Gadhafi in televised speech: "I declare that we shall train [Arab guerrillas] for terrorist and suicide missions and allocate trainers for them and place all the weapons needed for such missions at their disposal. I offer to the best of my ability to these volunteers, with the Palestinians at their head, my personal protection because Libya is a base for the liberation of Palestine." *(New York Times,* 16 January 1986, A8)

21 January 1986

Foreign Minister Ali Treki reports that Libya's relations with other Arab countries have improved since imposition of US sanctions, that asset freeze prompted many of them to move assets out of US. *(New York Times,* 22 January 1986, A4)

28 January 1986

In proposal conveyed to Italian Prime Minister Bettino Craxi, Gadhafi offers to stop supporting terrorism if US promises not to attack Libya. Italian officials interpret move as "trying to open channels to the U.S. and Italy in the hopes of ending the confrontation." *(New York Times,* 29 January 1986, A16)

Attitude of Other Countries

West Germany, France

On 12 December 1981, West German Foreign Minister Hans-Dietrich Genscher, French Foreign Minister Claude Cheysson, among other Europeans, urge Secretary of State Haig to treat Libya in more friendly fashion. According to one French diplomat, Haig in appeal for NATO support against Libya only "convinced himself." *(Washington Post,* 11 December 1981, A25; 12 December 1981, A18)

"France banned sales of new weapons systems to Libya after demonstrators burned down its embassy in 1980, although it still provides spare parts for the French-built Mirage fighter planes and other equipment used by the Libyan military." *(New York Times, 11 January 1986, A4)*

"[A]lthough France has also reacted with concern to Libyan moves in Africa, it has refused in part for economic reasons to treat Colonel Qaddafi as a pariah. It buys oil from Libya and argues that it is important to keep lines of communication open with the Libyans. In addition to this specific difference, President François Mitterrand of France has sought to distance his policy toward Chad from Washington's. But American officials in the White House, Pentagon and State Department all said today that American and French policy has been closely coordinated." *(New York Times, 19 August 1983, A6)*

In January 1986, West Germany rejects US call for sanctions, which it characterizes as "not a suitable instrument." Continuing German opposition to sanctions is also tied to presence of 1,500 German workers in Libya, "fear that the conflict may increasingly be thrust into the East-West arena." However, Chancellor Helmut Kohl notes that Germany "had in recent years scaled back its economic involvement [in Libya] and that Bonn did not export arms or nuclear technology to Libya." It is later revealed, however, that West German firms played "major" role in construction of chemical plant in Libya widely suspected of being used to produce chemical weapons. *(New York Times, 4 January 1986, 1; 10 January 1986, A6; 8 March 1990, A17; Washington Post, 4 January 1986, A15)*

United Kingdom

Following murder of London policewoman by machine gun fire from inside Libyan embassy in April 1984, UK breaks diplomatic relations with Libya, bans arms exports, restricts government export credit guarantees. *(Washington Post, 4 January 1986, A15; New York Times, 17 January 1986, A3)*

Sir Geoffrey Howe, British Foreign Secretary, indicates that UK will not join US economic sanctions, but "will continue to urge the European allies to isolate Libya diplomatically and militarily." *(New York Times, 17 January 1986, A3)*

Italy

In January 1986, Italy bars arms sales to Libya, takes steps "to prevent Italian companies from taking over business from Americans who withdraw because of the United States economic sanctions." It emphasizes, however, that further measures should only be taken jointly by all members of European Community. At same time, Italian leaders express concern "that Mr. Reagan's policies on Libya might harm the chances of a negotiated peace settlement in the Middle East." *(New York Times, 10 January 1986, A1, A6)*

Foreign Minister Giulio Andreotti notes "that since 1981 Italy has signed no new arms contracts with Libya and that any Italian weapons the Libyans are now receiving had been sold under pre-1981 contracts." *(Washington Post, 10 January 1986, A25)*

Belgium, Luxembourg

Private trade mission representing 14 companies goes ahead with its visit to Libya in late January 1986, noting that "if the Americans leave, many companies will be interested in replacing them." *(New York Times, 11 January 1986, A4)*

Canada

In response to US sanctions in January 1986, Canada suspends insurance coverage, subsidies for companies operating in Libya, bars new contracts to export advanced oil-drilling equipment to Libya, acts to "block any attempts by Libya to obtain technical assistance through Canada that was denied by the United States." No action is taken, however, against Canadians who seek to replace US workers forced to leave Libya. *(New York Times,* 11 January 1986, A5; *Washington Post,* 11 January 1986, A18)

Islamic Conference, Arab League

In January 1986, 45-member Islamic Conference unanimously passes resolution denouncing US sanctions, calls on its members "to take the necessary actions deemed appropriate to counter these oppressive American measures." However, conference fails to approve call for economic sanctions against US. *(New York Times,* 10 January 1986, A1; *Washington Post,* 11 January 1986, A18)

Arab League officials lobby European governments to oppose US request to join in sanctions against Libya. However, League itself only issues warning to US "against the dangers of an armed aggression against Libya." In addition, Saudi Arabia offers to offset economic impact of sanctions on Libyan economy. *(New York Times,* 22 January 1986, A4; *Washington Post,* 31 January 1986, A25)

Organization of Petroleum Exporting Countries

On 12 December 1981, OPEC ministers reject Libyan appeal for "joint action" against US. *(Washington Post,* 12 December 1982, A1)

Economic Impact

Observed Economic Statistics

Libya: trade with United States and total trade, 1980–88 (millions of dollars)

Year	US exports to Libya	US imports from Libya	Total Libyan exports	Total Libyan imports
1980	509	8,905	21,919	6,776
1981	813	5,476	15,575	8,382
1982	301	533	13,300	8,608
1983	191	1	12,116	7,730
1984	200	10	10,655	7,058
1985	311	47	10,897	5,488
1986	46	2	6,204	4,607
1987	—	—	6,878	5,142
1988	—	—	6,793	6,225

— = negligible.

Source: International Monetary Fund.

US sales of small aircraft, helicopters, aircraft parts, avionics to Libya in 1980 total $7.58 million. (GAO 19)

Mobil announces termination of Libyan operations; Mobil was producing 100,000 barrels (bbl) per day in 1980; 30,000–40,000 bbl per day in late 1982. *(Washington Post, 26 February 1982, A1; New York Times, 5 January 1983, D6)*

US oil imports from Libya pre-March 1982 are approximately 150,000 bbl per day because of recession (down from 700,000 bbl per day in 1981). US oil company assets in Libya at end of 1981 are valued at $600 million. (Schott 16–18)

Potential impact of December 1983 proposed change in policy toward exports to Libya is estimated at $150 million a year. *(Wall Street Journal, 5 December 1983, 3)*

Shrinking oil receipts put pressure on Libyan budget, since oil accounts for almost all of Libya's export earnings. Despite severe shortages of food, consumer goods in 1985, Gadhafi orders cut in 1986 budget for imports to leave more money for capital projects; military budget is estimated at $2 billion, or about 40 percent of projected oil income. *(New York Times, 29 January 1986, A16; New York Times, 2 May 1986, D1; Schumacher 340)*

Budget squeeze in 1985 forces cancellation of $4.2 billion Soviet nuclear power plant, more than $1 billion in housing, road projects, $700 million in military construction projects. (Schumacher 334, 337)

All but one US oil company temporarily suspend exports of Libyan crude following announcement of US sanctions in January 1986; however, level of production is reportedly maintained by European oil companies in Libya. Prior to sanctions US companies account for about one-third of Libyan production of 1.2 million bbl per day. Action is also related to plunge in spot oil prices from $25 per bbl to $17 per bbl in mid-January before rebound to about $20 per bbl. *(New York Times, 29 January 1986, A16; Washington Post, 30 January 1986, A1)*

US oil companies receive more than $150 million annually from sales of Libyan oil on the world market. *(New York Times, 31 January 1986, A1)*

Treasury estimates, on basis of cash flow analysis, value of US oil concessions, other assets in Libya at "more than $1 billion." However, Occidental Petroleum, largest US operator in Libya, reports that its Libyan assets of $120 million only amount to about 1 percent of its worldwide total. *(New York Times, 6 May 1986, A14)*

US asset freeze affects less than $1 billion in Libyan bank deposits, of which $250 million is at Libya's primary US clearing bank, Bankers Trust. (Weisburg 997, 1000)

In 1986, Libya is in arrears on $3 billion to $4 billion in loans from Western countries; Italy, Libya's largest creditor, has agreed in 1984 to oil barter arrangement to reduce Libyan debt. In addition, Libya owes about $4 billion to USSR for military equipment. *(Financial Times, 22 April 1986, 4)*

Calculated Economic Impact (annual cost to target country)

Period I:
Cutoff of US imports of 150,000 bbl per day of Libyan oil; with no reduction in overall Libyan exports,[a] cutoff forces Libya to discount price by estimated 10 percent (or $3.70 per bbl)—of which 5 percent is attributable to market forces, 5 percent to sanctions. $101 million

Reduction in nonoil US–Libyan trade as result of export, import controls; welfare loss estimated at 30 percent of face value of trade (including welfare cost of blocked US exports of sensitive oil, gas field technology).	10 million
Withdrawal of US citizens from Libya; estimated 10 percent increase in estimated $75,000 average annual salary to hire non–US oil field workers to replace about 750 US employees who leave.	6 million
Suspension of sale of Boeing jets to Libya; welfare loss estimated at 10 percent of value of trade.	60 million
Offset	
Sale of Exxon's Libyan assets to Libya for less than book value ($121 million v. $95 million settlement); welfare gain valued at 100 percent.	($26 million)
Total, 1981–85	$151 million
Period II:	
Reduction in US trade with Libya as result of embargo; welfare loss estimated at 30 percent of drop in trade from average annual value in 1983–85.	$253 million
Freeze of Libyan assets in US (estimated as $1 billion less $131 million ordered released by British court); welfare loss estimated as 10 percent of face value of assets frozen.	87 million
Total, 1986–90	$340 million
Average annual total, 1981–90	$245 million

a. During this period Libya sends crude to European refineries for processing, charges price tied to output of product (which yields substantially less than official price of Libyan crude). During 1982, Libya substantially increases crude sales (from 0.9 million bbl per day to 1.7 million bbl per day) through this unconventional method of discounting price of crude oil.

Relative Magnitudes

Gross indicators of Libyan economy	
Libyan GNP (1978)	$18.3 billion
Libyan population (1978)	2.7 million
Annual effect of sanctions related to gross indicators	
Percentage of GNP	1.3
Per capita	$90.74
Libyan trade with US as percentage of total trade	
Exports (1980)	34
Imports (1980)	6
Ratio of US GNP (1978: $2,164 billion) to Libyan GNP	118

Assessment

Washington Post

Anonymous Arab editor: "To you in the United States [Gadhafi] may be a villain, but to many Arabs, the more he is attacked, the more he comes out a hero, a man who can stand up to a superpower." *(Washington Post,* 9 December 1981, A11)

Jeffrey J. Schott

"It is safe to say that the world oil glut and the consequent fall in oil prices have hurt the Libyans more than the US trade sanctions. Any subsequent moderation in Qaddafi's policies was probably attributable more to financial constraints imposed by the market than by the United States." (Schott 18)

"The Exxon pullout probably would have occurred even without the political pressures that built up during 1981." (Schott 39)

General Accounting Office

As of May 1987, "the impact on the Libyan oil and petrochemical industry has been minimal. . . . The departure of U.S. oil companies from Libya has had little effect because the oil previously produced and sold by these companies is now produced and marketed by the Libyans, providing them with additional revenues. . . . [P]roduction levels of Libyan crude oil have remained about the same as they were before the imposition of the sanctions. . . . In addition, the extensive foreign availability of oil field equipment, supplies, and services allows Libya to meet its oil industry needs without having to rely on U.S. oil equipment and servicing companies." (GAO 1987, 2–3)

Geoffrey Kemp, former National Security Council staffer

"If the American goal is to topple the Qaddafi regime altogether, then sanctions won't do the job. But if the U.S. has the more modest goal of deterring Qaddafi from his most egregious actions, then sanctions might be successful . . . . Reducing Qaddafi's oil revenues wouldn't reform his character, but it would surely force him to cut back on development, arms purchases and funds for terrorists. The question, as always, is whether our European allies will cooperate." *(Washington Post,* 12 January 1986, D1)

Edward Schumacher

"Indeed, the April 1986 raid on Libya brought a lull in Arab-related terrorism. And the governments of Western Europe, scarcely supportive of the American show of force, nevertheless imposed sanctions, in part to placate the Americans. The sanctions prompted the departure of more than 600 Libyans from Western Europe, thus dismantling a logistical network for terror . . . . The lull in terrorism was short-lived." (Schumacher 329)

Washington Post

"Four years after U.S. warplanes bombed Gadhafi's house [in Tripoli] for his alleged support of terrorism, the Libyan leader seems eager to play the powerful penitent who can persuade Palestinian terrorist Abu Nidal to free hostages and can mediate between hard-liners in the Arab world. Gadhafi's drive for Western acceptance is fueled largely by a realization that he has lost the generous support—including military advisers and arms—that he once enjoyed from the Soviet bloc. . . . . But Gadhafi has not turned his back on revolutionary causes. . . . Rebels who espouse 'anti-imperialist' causes are still regular guests here. And recently two Libyan 'diplomats' were expelled from Ethiopia for allegedly planting bombs aimed at an Israeli envoy." *(Washington Post,* 27 May 1990, A35)

Authors' Summary

Overall assessment
☐ Policy result, scaled from 1 (failed) to 4 (success)   2

☐ Sanctions contribution, scaled from 1 (none) to 4 (significant)   2

☐ Success score (policy result *times* sanctions contribution), scaled from 1 (outright failure) to 16 (significant success)   4

Political and economic variables
☐ Companion policies: J (covert), Q (quasi-military), or R (regular military)   J, Q

☐ International cooperation with sender, scaled from 1 (none) to 4 (significant)   1

☐ International assistance to target: A (if present)   —

☐ Sanctions period (years)   12+

☐ Economic health and political stability of target, scaled from 1 (distressed) to 3 (strong)   3

☐ Presanction relations between sender and target, scaled from 1 (antagonistic) to 3 (cordial)   1

☐ Type of sanction: X (export), M (import), F (financial)   X, M, F

☐ Cost to sender, scaled from 1 (net gain) to 4 (major loss)   3

Bibliography

Bienen, Henry, and Robert Gilpin. 1979. "Evaluation of the Use of Economic Sanctions to Promote Foreign Policy Objectives." Boeing Corp., unpublished, 2 April. Seattle.

Caras, James. 1986. "Economic Sanctions: United States Sanctions against Libya." 27 *Harvard International Law Journal* (Spring): 672–78.

Flores, David A. 1981. "Export Controls and the US Effort to Combat International Terrorism." 13 *Law and Policy in International Business* 521–90.

General Accounting Office. 1983. *Administration Knowledge of Economic Costs of Foreign Policy Export Controls.* Report to Senator Charles H. Percy, 2 September. Washington.

———. 1987. *Libyan Trade Sanctions.* GAO/NSIAD-87-132BR. May. Washington.

International Monetary Fund. 1987, 1988. *Direction of Trade Statistics Yearbook.* Washington.

Schott, Jeffrey J. 1982. "Trade Sanctions and US Foreign Policy." Carnegie Endowment for International Peace, processed, 14 September. Washington.

Schumacher, Edward. 1986–87. "The United States and Libya." 65 *Foreign Affairs* (Winter): 329–48.

Weisburg, Henry. 1987. "Unilateral Economic Sanctions and the Risks of Extraterritorial Application: The Libyan Example." 19 *New York University Journal of International Law and Politics* 993–1011.

CASE 79–1

US v. Iran

(1979–81: Hostages)

Chronology of Key Events

16 January 1979	Shah Reza Mohammad Pahlavi flees Iran for Egypt; Ayatollah Ruhollah Khomeini, religious leader, announces from exile in Paris he will appoint provisional government to rule Iran. (Congressional Research Service [CRS] 12)
1 February 1979	Khomeini returns to Tehran; on 11 February, Prime Minister Shahpour Bakhtiar is succeeded by Mehdi Bazargan, Khomeini supporter. (CRS 12, 14–15)
14 February 1979	US embassy in Tehran is attacked, overrun; about 100 hostages are taken but released few hours later when Khomeini supporters disperse militants. (Rubin 369)
9 March 1979	*Middle East Economic Digest* reports large US oil companies, with US government support, have agreed to boycott Iranian oil on world market. (CRS 19)
22 October 1979	Shah arrives unannounced in New York City for medical treatment. On 3 November, Iranian Foreign Minister Ibrahim Yazdi formally protests US decision to admit shah. (CRS 34–35)
4 November 1979	Demonstrators overrun US embassy in Tehran, taking approximately 100 hostages, about 60 of whom are Americans. Demonstrators demand that US extradite shah. (CRS 35)
5 November 1979	Iran abrogates 1959 Cooperation Treaty with US, 1921 Friendship Treaty with USSR. Khomeini condones embassy takeover. (CRS 36)
6 November 1979	President Jimmy Carter sends Ramsey Clark, former attorney general, William Miller, Senate Intelligence Committee staff chief, to Iran to negotiate hostage release; Khomeini refuses to meet them. (CRS 36)
8 November 1979	US halts shipment of military spare parts to Iran. (CRS 38)
10 November 1979	Carter orders 50,000 Iranian students in US to report to immigration office with view to deporting those in violation of their visas. On 27 December 1979, US appeals court allows deportation of Iranian students found in violation. (CRS 38, 71)

12 November 1979	Invoking section 232 of Trade Expansion Act of 1962, and finding national emergency, Carter embargoes oil imports from Iran. Iran responds with oil export embargo against US. (CRS 38)
13 November 1979	US House of Representatives votes 379 to 0 to prohibit foreign aid, military assistance to Iran. (CRS 38)
14 November 1979	Invoking International Emergency Economic Powers Act, Carter freezes Iranian deposits in US banks and foreign subsidiaries, following announcement indicating that Iran might withdraw those assets. Tehran press announces closing of Iranian airspace, territorial waters to US aircraft, shipping. (CRS 39)
18 November 1979	Iran releases black and most women hostages. (CRS 40)
23 November 1979	Foreign Minister Abol Hassan Bani Sadr repudiates Iran's foreign debt. Iran estimates it at $15 billion, *Washington Post* at "closer to $7 billion." (CRS 42)
4 December 1979	UN Security Council resolution calls for release of hostages, peaceful settlement of US–Iranian differences, participation by Secretary General Kurt Waldheim in resolving dispute. (CRS 50)
15 December 1979	International Court of Justice orders release of hostages, restoration of US property. (CRS 61)
26 December 1979	USSR occupies Afghanistan. (*New York Times,* 27 December 1979, 1)
29 December 1979	US proposes in UN Security Council that Secretary General Waldheim return to Tehran for another attempt at mediation; US also proposes economic sanctions if agreement cannot be reached within one to two weeks. (CRS 73)
12 January 1980	Half an hour before a scheduled UN vote on sanctions, Iran submits written three-part proposal for releasing hostages. Vote is postponed to clarify details of proposal, which seems to involve UN investigation into "crimes" of the shah, UN endorsement of Iran's extradition request to Panama, return of shah's assets to Iran. (CRS 83)
13 January 1980	Iran fails to clarify its proposal; USSR vetoes US proposal for economic sanctions. US reiterates its determination to apply unilateral economic sanctions, seek allied support. (CRS 84)
29 January 1980	Six Americans are smuggled out of Iran by Canadian embassy officials. (Rubin 375)
7 February 1980	US State Department announces that additional economic sanctions will be held in abeyance while diplomatic negotiations at UN continue. (CRS 101)
7 April 1980	Carter escalates program of economic sanctions. He breaks diplomatic relations with Iran; imposes export embargo (excluding food, medicine); orders inventory of $8 billion in frozen assets and inventory of US financial claims against Iran to be paid out of those

assets; cancels all Iranian entry visas; closes Iranian embassy in Washington, five Iranian consulates; orders departure of all 35 remaining diplomats, 209 military students. Carter threatens to take "other actions" if hostages are not released promptly. (CRS 148)

17 April 1980	Carter announces further economic measures. He prohibits all financial transactions between US citizens and those of Iran; imposes import embargo; bans travel to Iran except for journalists; releases, for US purchase, impounded military equipment intended for use in Iran; asks Congress to pass legislation to permit use of frozen assets for claims, reparations. (CRS 158)
25–27 April 1980	Carter launches unsuccessful military attempt to rescue hostages; Secretary of State Cyrus R. Vance resigns; shah dies in Egypt. (CRS 168, 250)
22 September 1980	Iran-Iraq border dispute intensifies into full-scale war. (CRS 301)
2–20 November 1980	Iranian parliament (Majlis) issues conditions for release of hostages: US to pledge not to interfere in Iranian affairs in future; US to release frozen assets; US to lift economic sanctions; US to return shah's wealth to Iran. Carter responds that the conditions "appear to offer a positive basis" for resolution of crisis. On 10 November secret negotiations, led by Deputy Secretary of State Warren Christopher, commence in Algeria. On 20 November, Secretary of State Edmund S. Muskie says US has accepted conditions "in principle." (CRS 367, 391)
29 November 1980	Militants at US embassy in Tehran transfer responsibility for hostages to government. (CRS 398–99)
19 January 1981	Algeria announces commitments agreed to by US, Iran pertaining to release of hostages: declaration of noninterference in Iran by US; establishment of escrow account in Bank of England for transfer of frozen assets; agreement for settlement of claims; revocation of sanctions; release of hostages; blocking of transfer of shah's wealth, giving government of Iran access to US courts to sue for its return; prohibition on prosecution by hostages or their families of claims against Iran for seizure of embassy. (*New York Times*, 20 January 1981, 1; Carswell 254)
20 January 1981	Ronald Reagan is inaugurated as president; hostages are released in exchange for partial transfer of Iranian assets; on 18 February 1981, Reagan administration decides not to renounce accords. (Malawer 485)
2 July 1981	US Supreme Court in *Dames & Moore v. Regan* (453 US 654, 1981) upholds accords by denying right of US firm to make claims against Iranian assets except in context of arbitration agreement. (Malawer 477)
18 August 1981	US transfers Iranian funds to escrow account in The Hague, as authorized by accords. (Malawer 485)

April 1983   "Business contacts and commercial agreements between the United States and Iran, interrupted four years ago when Ayatollah Ruhollah Khomeini came to power, are slowly, haltingly resuming." (*Washington Post,* 10 April 1983, F1)

Goals of Sender Country

14 November 1979

"Although it was not universally understood, from the beginning the blocking had a dual purpose, the release of the hostages and the protection of the property claims of US individuals and corporations against Iran. The President's report to the Congress on [this day] explicitly stated those objectives." (Carswell 249)

28 November 1979

President Carter: "For the last 24 days our nation's concern has been focused on our fellow Americans being held hostage in Iran. We have welcomed some of them home to their families and their friends. But we will not rest nor deviate from our efforts until all have been freed from their imprisonment and their abuse. We hold the Government of Iran fully responsible for the well-being and the safe return of every single person." (Alexander 481)

22 January 1980

Carter says US is ready to help Iran meet Soviet threat from Afghanistan, establish new relationship following release of hostages. (CRS 90)

5 April 1980

White House press secretary Jody Powell states president's intent of applying political and economic sanctions if hostages are not transferred to government custody. (CRS 146)

20 October 1980

Carter says that if Iran will free hostages, the US will release frozen assets, lift economic sanctions, seek normal relations with Iran. (CRS 347)

Response of Target Country

5 November 1979

Khomeini, speaking immediately after embassy takeover: ". . . if they do not give up the criminals [the shah and Shahpour Bakhtiar, former prime minister, exiled in France] . . . then we shall do whatever is necessary. . . . " (CRS 36)

28 December 1979

Iranian Foreign Minister Sadegh Ghotzbadeh warns that increasing US economic pressure will result in quick trial of hostages. On 14 January 1980, Ghotzbadeh says Iran could hold hostages "more or less forever." (CRS 72, 84)

11 January 1980

Iranian Oil Minister Ali Akbar Moinfar says Iran will cut oil shipments to any nation supporting economic sanctions against Iran. He says Iran ships 1 million barrels per day to Western Europe, Japan. (CRS 82, 86)

15 February 1980

Director of Iran's central bank says US must release $6 billion in assets frozen by Carter in November 1979 before hostages will be freed. (CRS 106)

4 April 1980

Conservative clerical forces in Iran oppose any concessions to US, threaten total oil embargo—with help of Saudi Arabia, Bahrain, Kuwait, Iraq—against Western Europe, US if sanctions are imposed. (CRS 146)

8 April 1980

Iranian leaders almost welcome imposition of general economic sanctions, generally agreeing they will help rid Iran of American influence. Khomeini says sanctions are "good omen" because they signal US recognition of permanent loss of influence in Iran; students at embassy are pleased because sanctions will stop diplomatic efforts to have hostages released; Bani Sadr (now president) says Iran can handle effects of sanctions, says they allow Iran to "break free" of US; Revolutionary Council also "welcomes" action. Iran threatens again to halt oil shipments to any other nation supporting sanctions. (CRS 149)

19 April 1980

Iran imposes oil embargo against Portugal. (CRS 160)

24 April 1980

Foreign Minister Ghotzbadeh says it is "regrettable" that Europe has joined US sanctions but that Iran will never surrender to "force" and "pressure." (CRS 164)

13–14 June 1980

Bani Sadr says economic situation is worsening, and inflation, economic blockade, in conjunction with people's fears, could create "sick economy." Ghotzbadeh claims sanctions are not affecting Iran. (CRS 207, 208)

3 August 1980

Bani Sadr says that US economic sanctions have increased cost of Iran's imports by 20 percent to 25 percent, that Iran needs spare parts denied by sanctions, concedes that sanctions are hurting Iran. (CRS 256)

1 September 1980

Ettelaat (newspaper in Iran) says Majlis should take up hostage question as soon as possible because economic sanctions are causing "severe pressure" on Iran. (CRS 280)

2 September 1980

Iranian Oil Minister Moinfar says sanctions have failed, attributes drop in oil production to deliberate decision to conserve resources rather than lack of spare parts or foreign technicians. (CRS 281)

7 October 1980

Mansur Farhang, former Iranian representative to UN, currently aide to Bani Sadr, says it no longer is in Iran's interest to hold hostages. (CRS 327)

13 October 1980

New Iranian Prime Minister Mohammed Ali Rajai states it is in Iran's interest to solve hostage crisis but that US, for political reasons of its own, does not want it resolved. (CRS 336)

Legal Notes

US International Emergency Economic Powers Act of 1977, Sec. 203(a)(1)

"At the times and to the extent specified in section 202, the President may, under such regulations as he may prescribe by means of instructions, licenses, or otherwise—
(A) investigate, regulate, or prohibit—
(i) any transactions in foreign exchange
(ii) transfers of credit or payments between, by, through, or to any banking institution to the extent that such transfers or payments involve any interest of any foreign country or a national thereof
(iii) the importing or exporting of currency or securities; and
(B) investigate, regulate, direct and compel, nullify, void, prevent or prohibit, any acquisition, holding, withholding, use, transfer, withdrawal, transportation, importation or exportation of, or dealing in, or exercising any right, power, or privilege with respect to, or transactions involving, any property in which any foreign country or a national thereof has any interest; by any person, or with respect to any property, subject to the jurisdiction of the United States."

Attitude of Other Countries

Mexico

On 4 December 1979, President José López Portillo says US decision to freeze assets is "hasty," causes international monetary problem. (CRS 51)

Japan

On 14 December 1979, limits purchases of Iranian oil to 602,000 barrels per day, level prior to hostage takeover. Foreign Minister Saburo Okita says Japan has been forced to buy Iranian oil on spot market because of cutbacks in shipments by major US companies. (CRS 61)

On 18 January 1980, Japan announces willingness to cooperate with sanctions with exception of Japanese-Iranian petrochemical project at Bandar Khomeini. (CRS 87)

On 22 April 1980, Japan says it will go along with sanctions supported by EC; Japanese cabinet announces sanctions will become effective 2 June 1980. (CRS 87, 115)

Austria

30 December 1979: Tehran Radio reports Austrian ambassador to Iran as saying his country will not cooperate with US economic sanctions against Iran. (CRS 74)

Soviet Union

9 January 1980: Tass says USSR "will not allow the US to impose a decision to apply economic sanctions against Iran." (CRS 81)

On 22 April 1980, USSR signs new trade agreement with Iran that, according to Iranian finance minister, is expected to offset US sanctions. (CRS 163)

Australia

On 15 January 1980, in response to US request, Australia reviews trade relations with Iran. (CRS 85)

On 19 February 1980, Australia sells 450,000 tons of wheat to Iran for delivery in March, July 1980. (CRS 108)

On 21 April 1980, Australia bans all trade with Iran except for food, medicine. (CRS 162)

On 20 May 1980, Australia cancels all contracts, including those signed before 4 November 1979. (CRS 189)

China

30 January 1980: Tehran Radio announces China has agreed to maintain normal economic, commercial relations with Iran, to not cooperate with economic sanctions. (CRS 96)

Poland

On 6 May 1980, Poland signs trade protocol with Iran. (CRS 176)

European Community, other West European countries

On 17 January 1980, Chancellor Helmut Schmidt announces German support for sanctions against Iran. (CRS 87)

On 17 April 1980, Portugal bans all trade with Iran—first US ally to do so. (CRS 158)

On 22 April 1980, EC foreign ministers agree to reduce diplomatic representation in Iran, suspend arms sale, require visas for Iranian travel in Europe, discourage purchase of Iranian oil at prices above OPEC standard of $32.50 per bbl. (Iran is asking $35.50 per bbl). Export embargo is threatened if "decisive progress" is not made by 17 May. (CRS 163)

Sweden says it will not impose sanctions. Denmark, Britain, Norway recall ambassadors from Iran. (CRS 163)

On 28 April 1980, following US military rescue attempt, EC heads of state reaffirm solidarity with US, commitment to sanctions. (CRS 170)

On 13 May 1980, UK House of Commons passes enabling legislation for economic sanctions; Danish Parliament votes to apply sanctions. (CRS 183)

On 18 May 1980, EC issues communiqué stating that, on 22 May 1980, all contracts concluded with Iran since 4 November 1979 will be suspended. (CRS 187)

On 19 May 1980, UK decides against retroactive action on contracts concluded since 4 November 1979; instead it bans all new contracts after 22 May 1980. Other EC countries express dismay at UK's action. (CRS 188)

On 21 May 1980, West German, French, Italian cabinets approve, take necessary legal steps for implementation of EC sanctions. (CRS 190)

Canada

On 23 May 1980, Canada bans exports to Iran, discourages citizens from travel there. (CRS 191)

Economic Impact

Observed Economic Statistics

Iran: trade with United States and OECD countries, 1978–81 (millions of dollars)

	Exports		Imports	
Year	US	Total OECD	US	Total OECD
1978	2,880	18,636	3,684	15,432
1979	2,784	15,084	1,020	5,885
1980	336	10,560	24	7,716
1981	63	6,996	300	8,088

Source: Organization for Economic Cooperation and Development.

Iran: assets subject to US freeze and their disposition (billions of dollars)

Assets held outside US	5.6
of which:	
Claims representing Western loans to Iran	3.7
Escrow account for unresolved claims (nonsyndicated loans of US banks, about $130 million of contested interest)	1.4
Cash returned to Iran	0.5
Assets in US	6.4
of which:	
Holdings in nonbank US companies, on deposit in US commercial banks	3.6
Deposits with NY Federal Reserve Bank, returned to Iran	2.4
On deposit at US Treasury against orders for US defense equipment	0.4
Total	12.0

Source: Carswell 256; Malawer 479.

Calculated Economic Impact (annual cost to target country)

Reduction of Iranian imports from US during 1980–81 by annual average of $858 million from 1979 level; welfare loss calculated at 30 percent of face value of trade.	$257 million
Reduction in Iranian exports to OECD area during 1980–81 by annual average of $6.3 billion from 1979 level; welfare loss calculated at 30 percent of face value of trade.	1,892 million

Estimated annual loss resulting from freeze of about $12 billion of Iranian assets, at 10 percent of face value.	1,200 million
Total	$3,349 million

Relative Magnitudes

Gross indicators of Iranian economy	
Iranian GNP (1979)	$87.4 billion
Iranian population (1979)	37.0 million
Annual effect of sanctions related to gross indicators	
Percentage of GNP	3.8
Per capita	$90.51
Iranian trade with US as percentage of total trade	
Exports (1979)	14
Imports (1979)	12
Ratio of US GNP (1979: $2,418 billion) to Iranian GNP	28

Assessment

Robert A. Carswell

"Assessing the effect of the trade sanctions is difficult, particularly since the results of economic mismanagement in Iran can easily be confused with problems arising from externally caused shortages . . . even though the sanctions largely prevented direct resupply of these critical areas (many units of the armed forces and key installations in the gas and oil sector), Iran apparently was able, by paying exorbitant prices through middlemen, to meet its most critical needs. . . . Hence, the best that can be said now is that the sanctions undoubtedly caused Iran difficulties but probably not insuperable ones." (Carswell 254)

"In sum, the financial sanctions employed against Iran over the hostage issue were effective because of special circumstances that differentiated the situation sharply from other cases where economic sanctions had historically been attempted. And the freeze of Iranian assets not only created negotiating complications but involved both short and long-term costs that cannot yet be fully assessed, as well as risks of a major change in banking practice that could seriously affect the status of the dollar as the world's principal reserve currency. Finally, it must again be emphasized that the degree of leverage the sanctions exerted . . . depended on a high degree of cooperation by other countries." (Carswell 264)

The Economist

"The Europeans, for example, imposed sanctions on Iran mainly to show their solidarity with the United States, rather than in the hope that they would help free the hostages." (*The Economist*, 2 October 1982, 102)

Authors' Summary

Overall assessment

☐ Policy result, scaled from 1 (failed) to 4 (success)   4

☐ Sanctions contribution, scaled from 1 (none) to 4 (significant)   3

☐ Success score (policy result *times* sanctions contribution),
   scaled from 1 (outright failure) to 16 (significant success)   12

Political and economic variables
☐ Companion policies: J (covert), Q (quasi-military), or R (regular military)   Q
☐ International cooperation with sender, scaled from 1 (none) to 4 (significant) 3
☐ International assistance to target: A (if present)   —
☐ Sanctions period (years)   2
☐ Economic health and political stability of target, scaled from
   1 (distressed) to 3 (strong)   1
☐ Presanction relations between sender and target, scaled from
   1 (antagonistic) to 3 (cordial)   3
☐ Type of sanction: X (export), M (import), F (financial)   X,M,F
☐ Cost to sender, scaled from 1 (net gain) to 4 (major loss)   3

Comments
The US objective in this case was specific: the safe return of the hostages. Progress toward this objective was painstakingly slow, yet the desired result was achieved, although at very high economic and political cost. Sanctions, in particular the financial controls, made a modest contribution to the outcome by increasing the cost of traded goods in the Iranian economy and, more importantly, by freezing a substantial share of Iran's financial reserves held in US banks.

Bibliography

Alexander, Yonan, and Allan Nanes, eds. 1980. *The United States and Iran: A Documentary History.* Frederick, MD: University Publications of America.

Carswell, Robert. 1981–82. "Economic Sanctions and the Iran Experience." 60 *Foreign Affairs* (Winter): 247–65.

Congressional Research Service, Library of Congress. 1981. *The Iran Hostage Crisis: A Chronology of Daily Developments.* Prepared for House Committee on Foreign Affairs. 97 Cong., 1 sess. March. Washington.

Malawer, Stuart S. 1981–82. "Rewarding Terrorism: The US–Iranian Hostage Accords." 6 *International Security Review* (Winter): 477–96.

Organization for Economic Cooperation and Development. *Statistics on Foreign Trade, Monthly Bulletin.* Various issues.

Rubin, Barry. 1980. *Paved with Good Intentions.* New York: Oxford University Press.

CASE 80-1

US v. USSR

(1980–81: Afghanistan)

Chronology of Key Events

20 October 1975   US, USSR sign bilateral framework agreement on supply of US grain, leaving tonnages to be negotiated periodically. (Schnittker Associates 1)

3 October 1979   Administration of President Jimmy Carter approves export of 8 million metric tons (mmt) of grain to USSR. (Congressional Research Service [CRS] 2)

26 December 1979   Soviet troops enter Afghanistan, stage coup in which President Hafizullah Amin is killed, establish Babrak Karmal (Afghanistan's ambassador to Czechoslovakia) as president. (Falkenheim 1)

4 January 1980   Carter announces actions against USSR. He stops licenses of high-technology, strategic goods exports to USSR pending review of licensing procedures; embargoes 17 mmt of grain exports that exceed 8 mmt already committed under 1975 agreement; curtails USSR fishing rights in US 200-mile zone from 435,000 metric tons to 75,000 metric tons in 1980, zero thereafter; hints at Olympic boycott; defers cultural-scientific exchanges; delays opening of consular facilities in Kiev, New York; restricts Aeroflot service; requests Senate to defer consideration of second Strategic Arms Limitation Treaty (SALT II); pledges military, other assistance to Pakistan, possibly other countries in area. Central Intelligence Agency (CIA) provides covert assistance to Afghan rebels. (CRS 20–26; Falkenheim 38; *Washington Post*, 28 July 1984, A1)

5 January 1980   Secretary of Agriculture Bob Bergland announces steps to reduce impact of embargo on US farmers: incentives for adding grain to farmer-owned grain reserve; additional purchases by Commodity Credit Corporation (CCC) of up to 4 mmt; paid acreage diversion program in 1980 if supply and demand conditions warrant; additional export promotion funding for CCC; incentives for production of gasohol. (CRS 26)

11 January 1980   Department of Commerce begins review of high-technology exports, suspends issuance of new licenses pending completion of review, suspends previously issued validated licenses for goods not yet shipped, announces denial of eight licenses for goods that could be put to military use (such as seismic data processing equipment), revokes license for export of spare parts for Kama River truck plant (trucks from plant were used in Afghanistan). (CRS 65; Falkenheim 3)

14 January 1980   UN General Assembly resolution, adopted by vote of 104 to 8 (29 abstentions), calls for withdrawal of all foreign troops from Afghanistan, does not name USSR. (United Nations 3)

18 January 1980   Carter restricts 1980 imports of Soviet ammonia, expected to rise from 0.7 mmt to 1.5 mmt, to 1 million short tons, citing potential "market disruption." (CRS 59)

20 January 1980   Carter proposes that summer 1980 Olympics be postponed or transferred from Moscow unless Soviet troops leave Afghanistan in one month. International Olympic Committee opposes moving games. (Falkenheim 3–4)

25 January 1980   In State of the Union address, Carter warns USSR that US will react with force if Soviets approach Persian Gulf, offers to resume US military assistance to Pakistan, authorizes sale of military-related technology to China, proposes draft registration. (*Facts on File* 42)

5 February 1980   Commerce Department announces that exports of phosphate rock, concentrates of phosphoric acids, concentrates of phosphatic fertilizer to USSR will require validated rather than general licenses; no applications for validated licenses will be considered pending interagency review. On 25 February, Secretary of Commerce Philip M. Klutznick announces that ban on exports of phosphates for fertilizer will continue indefinitely. (CRS 53)

20 February 1980   Carter announces US boycott of summer Olympic games. On 28 March administration embargoes all exports intended for Olympics except medical supplies. On 12 April US Olympic Committee votes to boycott Olympics. (CRS 79, 86)

18 March 1980   Commerce Department announces that completed review of high-technology export licensing procedures points to more-restrictive guidelines: "[it] looks like [the new controls] will cover anything that is remotely of possible military or strategic use." Restrictive criteria are applied to computers, software, high-technology defense goods, technology for manufacture of oil and gas equipment, with revised Commodity Control List (CCL) to take effect 25 June. US also adopts "no exceptions" policy vis-á-vis Coordinating Committee for Multilateral Export Controls (COCOM), significant departure since US has previously requested more exceptions than any other member since mid-1970s. (CRS 66)

20 March 1980   US International Trade Commission holds that imports of ammonia from USSR do not cause "market disruption," thereby nullifying Carter's retaliatory quota. (CRS 65)

26 September 1980	Senate votes to block funds for grain embargo. However, similar measure was defeated in House in July. (*New York Times,* 27 September 1980, A29)
24 April 1981 ·	Announcing that "the United States. . . remains opposed to the Soviet occupation of Afghanistan and other aggressive acts around the world and will react strongly to acts of aggression wherever they take place," President Ronald Reagan lifts Carter grain embargo, restrictions on all other agricultural commodities, including fertilizer phosphates. As result, USSR is committed, under old agreement, to purchase 6 mmt to 8 mmt of grain a year. (*Weekly Compilation of Presidential Documents,* 27 April 1981; *New York Times,* 25 April 1981, A1; 18 May 1983, D1)
October 1982	Reagan offers to raise limit on USSR purchases for 1982–83 crop year to 23 mmt, but Moscow ignores offer. (*New York Times,* 21 October 1982, A1; 26 March 1983, D1)
May 1983	In effort to improve image as "reliable supplier," US gives Saudi Arabia unilateral no-embargo pledge on farm exports. (*Washington Post,* 10 May 1983, D7)
August 1983	US, USSR enter five-year agreement providing for Soviet purchases of 9 mmt to 12 mmt of grain annually. As concession to USSR, US agrees not to impose export controls for foreign policy purposes or to use short-supply "escape clause." (*New York Times,* 2 August 1983, D1)
25 July 1984	State Department announces Reagan has approved lifting of ban on Soviet fishing in US waters. Soviets will be allowed "to catch 50,000 tons of fish off Alaska and western coast" of US, far below pre-invasion levels. " 'They still have to accept it,' an official said, but added that the response is expected to be positive since Moscow has been seeking reinstatement of its fishing rights." (*Washington Post,* 26 July 1984, A1)
27 July 1984	Congressional sources reveal that House Appropriations Committee has approved $50 million in new assistance for Afghan rebels as requested by President Reagan. If approved by whole House, Senate, this would bring total funding for rebels in 1984 to $85 million. Annual aid to resistance has averaged $30 million to $35 million since invasion. (*Washington Post,* 28 July 1984, A1; *Wall Street Journal,* 27 July 1984, 1)
15 January 1987	Citing widespread foreign availability, adverse effect on US industry, Commerce Secretary Malcolm Baldrige announces lifting of controls on oil and gas drilling technology, equipment. (See also Case 78–5 US v. USSR [1978–80: Dissident Trials]). (*Washington Post,* 16 January 1987, A1)
April 1988	USSR, US, Afghanistan, Pakistan sign accords in Geneva to end Soviet intervention in Afghanistan. USSR pledges to complete withdrawal of troops by 15 February 1989. (*New York Times,* 25 January 1989, A1)

May 1988	USSR begins to withdraw troops from Afghanistan. Several COCOM members request relaxation of no-exceptions policy imposed in March 1980, final remaining sanction against USSR for invasion. Under Secretary of State Richard H. Armacost says such a move would be "premature" while Soviets are still in Afghanistan. (*New York Times,* 25 January 1989, A1)
19 January 1989	Just before leaving office, Secretary of State George P. Shultz writes Defense Secretary Frank C. Carlucci urging lifting of no-exceptions policy. Although ban was imposed initially for foreign policy reasons, Carlucci, Defense Department support continuation of policy for national security reasons. (*New York Times,* 25 January 1989, A1)
February 1989	Several COCOM members, led by UK, reportedly challenge US position by making formal applications for sale of items covered by no-exceptions policy for first time since invasion. President George Bush's Secretary of State, James A. Baker III, is quoted in *Time* calling for additional Soviet concessions in return for lifting sanction: "Give away something unilaterally without a quid pro quo? . . . . No sir." (*Washington Post,* 7 February 1989, A19)
27 May 1989	In his speech at NATO summit outlining his proposals for conventional, nuclear force reductions in Europe, Bush announces that he is lifting no-exceptions policy. (*Washington Post,* 30 May 1989, A1)

Goals of Sender Country

President Jimmy Carter

In address to nation 4 January 1980: "We must recognize the strategic importance of Afghanistan to stability and peace. A Soviet-occupied Afghanistan threatens both Iran and Pakistan and is a stepping stone to possible control over much of the world's oil supplies." (CRS 20)

Briefing for members of Congress, 8 January 1980: "In my judgment our own nation's security was directly threatened. There is no doubt that the Soviet move into Afghanistan, if done without adverse consequences, would have resulted in the temptation to move again and again until they reached warm water ports or until they acquired control over a major portion of the world's oil supplies." Carter admits he did not expect sanctions to cause USSR to withdraw from Afghanistan, says sanctions were intended primarily "to make the Soviets pay a price for aggression," deter USSR from further aggression. (CRS 20)

Late January 1980: ". . . the exports being curtailed by this action make a significant contribution to the military potential of the Soviet Union that is detrimental to the national security of the United States." (*Weekly Compilation of Presidential Documents,* 28 January 1980, 185).

Under Secretary of State Richard N. Cooper

20 August 1980: "It is, of course, obvious that any interference with trade would involve costs for the exporting country as well as for the importing country. But under the circumstances it was inappropriate to maintain business as usual." (US Senate 46)

Congressional Research Service

April 1981: "The United States acted to inflict economic costs on the Soviet Union in order to reduce the prospects [for the USSR–sponsored regime in Kabul] and to deter Soviet leaders from using the Afghanistan invasion as a prototype for other such extensions of power by inflicting 'punishment.' " (CRS 19)

"The political message of the largely economic sanctions was probably as effective as political-military action and far less risky. . . . Initial statements on the invasion of Afghanistan by President Carter and other members of the administration strongly implied that the administration viewed the Soviets' motivations as expansionistic. Concern that the invasion, if not reacted to, might serve as a pattern for future Third World ventures led the Carter administration to impose the economic sanctions announced on January 4 and elaborated during the months that followed." (CRS 19)

"Like the other sanctions, the grain embargo was not expected to induce a Soviet withdrawal but was intended to inflict damage on the Soviet feed and grain-livestock complex. While administration officials did not specify how much damage they intended to inflict, the president did state that the intent was not to starve Soviet citizens, but to deny them a planned improvement in their diet." (CRS 38)

"Although [the Carter administration] recognized that ready foreign availability reduced the effectiveness [of high-technology controls] . . . without this control the United States would not have as many means of communicating its views to the USSR." (CRS 78)

Peggy L. Falkenheim

"The popular impression is that the sanctions were invoked to persuade the Soviet Union to withdraw its troops from Afghanistan. However, it seems doubtful that this interpretation accurately reflects Carter's main objective . . . . He imposed the sanctions because he felt that forcing Moscow to pay a price for its intervention would deter it from future acts of aggression . . . . Although Carter did not feel that the primary purpose of the sanctions was to get the Soviet troops out of Afghanistan, he felt that the sanctions should remain in effect until the troops were withdrawn . . . ." (Falkenheim 10)

"Although foreign policy considerations may have provided the main impetus for the sanctions, domestic political pressure was also important. In the United States, the invasion of Afghanistan occurred at the beginning of the primary campaign for the 1980 presidential election. Carter's popularity was low, and public opinion polls revealed a lack of confidence in his leadership abilities . . . ." (Falkenheim 11)

"The post-Afghanistan sanctions provided a pretext for the American government to take steps which had been advocated for other reasons. For a number of years before the invasion there had been growing pressure within the US government to impose tighter restrictions on high technology exports to the Soviet Union." (Falkenheim 11)

Response of Target Country

Robert L. Paarlberg

According to Paarlberg: head of Soviet grain purchasing agency went to Buenos Aires, negotiated "an agreement whereby Argentina would supply the Soviet Union, over the next five years, with at least 20 million tons of corn and grain sorghum, and with 2.5 million tons of soybeans." Soviets reportedly offered to pay up to 25 percent above US prices to obtain immediate shipments. (Paarlberg 153)

Soviet news agency Tass

"Even if one cannot rule out the possibility that a tear may roll, unbidden, from the wistful eye of a ruminating cow in Russia as a result of Washington's grain decision, the Soviet people will not shed tears . . . . The fact is that the Soviet Union today is not the poor czarist Russia where a piece of bread was frequently a coveted dream for the masses. Today, the USSR is a mighty industrial power with a developed agriculture." (*New York Times*, 10 January 1980, 18)

Shaheen Ayubi et al.

"Given the political interest of the Soviet leadership in promoting self-reliance and downplaying the significance of sanctions, as well as the plain fact that they did find replacements for most imports of grain outside the United States, the grain embargo became almost a nonevent in Soviet thinking." (Ayubi 30)

V. Malkevich

"It would be useful to recall, as well, that no one has yet succeeded in influencing the home or foreign policy of the USSR by means of economic blackmail, discrimination, or *diktat*. If it ever had any effect, moreover, it has been simply the opposite of the one counted on: tension between countries always forces each of them to harden its position." (Malkevich 15)

Attitude of Other Countries

Grain embargo

Canada, EC, Australia, Argentina (acting in coordination)

Conference of grain exporting nations on 12 January 1980 approves following statement: "There is general agreement among the export representatives here that their governments would not directly or indirectly replace the grain that would have been shipped to the Soviet Union prior to the actions announced by President Carter." In later interpretations, officials of Canada, Australia, EC say statement "was viewed as a commitment not to allow sales to the USSR to exceed 'normal' or 'traditional' levels." (CRS 7)

Subsequently, export levels of sales exceed "normal" levels for previous several years. (CRS 43)

Thus, "during the last months of 1980 Allied support for the continuation of restrictions on grain sales to the Soviet Union appeared to be crumbling." (CRS 47)

Argentina

Saying it has no legal means to control activities of its private traders, Argentina refuses to "participate in economic sanctions" or to "control its sales by destination." Preembargo Argentine grain shipments to USSR average 1.5 mmt annually; sales for 1979–80 reach 7.6 mmt. In July 1980 Argentina signs pact with USSR guaranteeing 4.5 mmt annually for five years. (CRS 37; Falkenheim 6)

Brazil

Brazil increases grain sales to USSR in 1979–80; in 1981, Brazil signs five-year agreement for exchange of Soviet oil for Brazilian soybeans, soya oil, corn. (Falkenheim 6)

Canada

Unlike President Carter, Prime Minister Joe Clark sees sanctions as means of persuading USSR to leave Afghanistan: "We are expecting that our actions and, more particularly, the actions of a number of countries acting together may persuade the Soviet Union to withdraw from Afghanistan. That is the point of the exercise." (*Globe and Mail* [Toronto], 12 January 1980, 1)

In November 1980, Prime Minister Pierre Elliott Trudeau lifts partial embargo imposed by Clark. Partial embargo had limited grain sales to 3.8 mmt during 1979–80 crop year (already higher than sales during three previous years). Timing of Trudeau's decision seems influenced by US–China grain agreement of October 1980, which erodes "traditional" Canadian market; also by Ronald Reagan's election as US president on campaign pledge to lift grain embargo. In December 1980, Canada agrees to sell 4.7 mmt in 1981, removes all quantitative restrictions on future sales to USSR. In May 1981, Canada signs five-year agreement with USSR providing up to 5 mmt annually. (CRS 47; Falkenheim 6–7)

Australia

Australia agrees to limit 1980–81 sales to 1979–80 level of 4.2 mmt (a record) but seeks early talks with Reagan administration on lifting embargo. (CRS 48)

European Community

France seeks to end sanctions on ground that other countries are violating them, but EC agrees to limit 1980–81 sales to previous year's level of 1.7 mmt. (CRS 48)

Olympic boycott

United Kingdom

On 22 January 1980, Prime Minister Margaret Thatcher requests British Olympic Committee (BOC) not to participate in games; in early March Parliament endorses this position; however, on 25 March 1980, BOC votes to attend. (CRS 79–93)

Canada

On 26 January 1980, Prime Minister Clark supports boycott; position is endorsed by Canadian Olympic Committee. (CRS 79–93)

Australia, New Zealand, Italy

Governments of these countries take position similar to that of US, Canada, but as in UK their Olympic committees vote to attend. (Falkenheim 9)

China, Zaire, Saudi Arabia, Egypt, Israel, West Germany, Japan, Norway, Monaco, Liechtenstein

Olympic committees of these countries, at urging of their governments, vote not to attend. (CRS 79–93)

High-technology exports

Western Europe

Beginning in spring 1980, West Germany, other European nations actively explore USSR–Europe gas pipeline project. (See Case 81–3 US v. USSR [1981–82: Poland]).

France

In 1980, Armco (US), Nippon Steel (Japan) are denied permission to use American technology in building steel plant at Novolipetsk; Creusot-Loire (France) then signs contract to build cold rolling mill at same site. (*New York Times*, 15 October 1980, A1)

Japan

In spring 1980, Tokyo successfully persuades Washington to exempt joint Sakhalin oil, gas development project with USSR from sanctions. (Falkenheim 9)

Legal Notes

US Export Administration Act of 1979

"Sec. 3(2)—It is the policy of the United States to use export controls only after full consideration of the impact on the economy of the United States and only to the extent necessary. . . . (B) to restrict the export of goods and technology where necessary to further significantly the foreign policy of the United States or to fulfill its international obligations. . . .

"Sec. 6(a) Authority—(1) In order to carry out the policy set forth in paragraph (2), (3), (7) or (8) of Section 3 of this Act, the President may prohibit or curtail the exportation of any goods, technology, or other information subject to the jurisdiction of the United States or exported by any person subject to the jurisdiction of the United States, to the extent necessary to further significantly the foreign policy of the United States or to fulfill its international obligations."

Economic Impact

Observed Economic Impact

United States: exports to USSR, 1979–81 (billions of dollars)

Year	Total	Agriculture
1979	3.6	3.0
1980	1.5	1.2
1981	2.4	1.7

Source: Schnittker 4.

Soviet Union: grain imports, 1979–82 (millions of metric tons)[a]

Source	1979–80	1980–81	1981–82
US	15.2	8.0	11.0
Argentina	5.1	11.2	12.0
Canada	3.4	6.9	8.5
Australia	4.0	2.9	2.5
EC	0.9	1.1	2.5
Others	1.8	3.9	3.0

Miscellaneous grains			
(all sources)	0.6	0.5	0.5
Total	31.0	34.5	40.0

a. Yearly figures are from July to June.

Source: Schnittker 10.

Effect on Soviet meat production: Agriculture Department estimate of 15.1 mmt produced in 1980 is 600,000 tons below planned goal, 2.6 percent lower than in 1979; this would imply per capita consumption of 57 kilograms v. 58 kilograms in 1979. Agriculture Department estimates Soviet milk production to be 4 percent lower in 1980 than in 1979, in part because of bad weather. (CRS 38; Falkenheim 12)

For year beginning January 1980, US exports of high-technology goods to USSR fall 52 percent compared with same period in 1979 (from $155 million to $74 million). Over same period, total US exports to USSR decline by 67 percent. (CRS 76)

Calculated Economic Impact (annual cost to target country)

Embargo on US grain shipments to USSR in excess of 8 mmt committed by 1975 grain pact:	
Reduction in total Soviet grain imports of 2.5 mmt from levels projected prior to embargo; welfare loss estimated at 30 percent of trade.	$89 million
Additional transshipment costs for grain purchased to compensate for blocked US shipments	23 million
Additional cost of 4.5 mmt of corn, grain sorghum bought from Argentina at 25 percent premium.	99 million
Reduction of 600,000 metric tons in Soviet meat production; welfare loss estimated at 10 percent of value of reduced output, $1,500 per metric ton.	90 million
Ban on US high-technology exports; welfare loss estimated at 30 percent of $80 million reduction in trade.	24 million
Ban on US shipments of 1 mmt of superphosphoric acid (SPA); welfare loss estimated at 50 percent of $400 million projected sales value (US accounts for 90 percent of world production of SPA).	200 million
Total	$525 million

Relative Magnitudes

Gross indicators of USSR economy	
USSR GNP (1979)	$1,375 billion
USSR population (1979)	263 million
Annual effect of sanctions related to gross indicators	
Percentage of GNP	0.04
Per capita	$2.00

USSR trade with US as percentage of total USSR trade	
Exports (1979)	1
Imports (1979)	6
Ratio of US GNP (1979: $2,418 billion) to USSR GNP	2

Assessment

Robert L. Paarlberg

Fall 1980: "However slim its chances of success, the grain embargo must have appeared, last January, as more attractive than the alternative. The alternative was to continue with plans, which had been made the previous October, to sell in 1980 an all-time record 25 million tons of US grain to the Soviet Union. For reasons unrelated to domestic food prices, these sales would have proved at least as embarrassing to the President [Carter], this year, as his ineffectual embargo. Without an embargo of some kind, the President would have found himself presiding over the largest 'Russian grain deal' on record, much larger than Richard Nixon's still remembered sale to the Russians in 1972, the so-called Great Grain Robbery. To important allies abroad, this would have been an inappropriate token of the administration's new policy toward the Soviet Union, so soon after Afghanistan. Likewise, to his political audience at home, these sales would have raised large doubts, at the time, about the President's capacity to make hard decisions. Politically, the only thing worse than announcing a grain embargo two weeks before the Iowa caucuses would have been *not* to announce such an embargo. The President's entire foreign policy would have appeared hostage, in a moment of crisis, to a few Iowa corn growers." (Paarlberg 160)

President Ronald Reagan

30 July 1982: "In the spring of 1981, I lifted the grain embargo imposed by the previous administration because it was not having the desired effect of seriously penalizing the USSR for its brutal invasion and occupation of Afghanistan. . . . [Increased sales by other suppliers] substantially undercut the tremendous sacrifices of our farmers, and I vowed at the time not to impose a grain embargo unilaterally unless it was part of a general cutoff of trade between the US and the Soviet Union. . . . Grain sales have little impact on Soviet military-industrial capability. They absorb hard currency earnings and feed the people of the Soviet Union who are suffering most from the disastrous economic policies of the Soviet Government." (*Department of State Bulletin,* October 1982, 40–41)

Congressional Research Service

"The policy of economic punishment was neither clearly successful in the short run nor likely to become effective in the long run." (CRS 6)

Peggy L. Falkenheim

"The sanctions would have been considered a failure by those who expected them to bring about a withdrawal of Soviet troops from Afghanistan. They would also have disappointed those whose primary aim was to inflict punishment on the Soviet Union in order to deter it from future agression. . . . Even if support for the sanctions had been greater, it is unlikely that they would have been effective. . . ." (Falkenheim 12, 13)

Washington Post

In course of renegotiating grain agreement in 1983, Acting Under Secretary of Agriculture Alan Tracy, speaking in Moscow, "blamed the Carter administration's grain embargo for 'long-term damage to our trade' with Moscow." Principal suppliers to USSR now are Argentina, Canada. US share of Soviet grain import market drops from 74 percent in year before embargo to 19 percent in 1982–83. (*Washington Post*, 26 March 1983, A1; *Journal of Commerce*, 7 March 1983, 3A; *US Export Weekly*, 3 January 1984, 495)

Authors' Summary

Overall assessment

☐ Policy result, scaled from 1 (failed) to 4 (success)   1

☐ Sanctions contribution, scaled from 1 (none) to 4 (significant)   1

☐ Success score (policy result *times* sanctions contribution),
   scaled from 1 (outright failure) to 16 (significant success)   1

Political and economic variables

☐ Companion policies: J (covert), Q (quasi-military), or R (regular military)   J

☐ International cooperation with sender, scaled from 1 (none) to 4 (significant)   3

☐ International assistance to target: A (if present)   —

☐ Sanctions period (years)   1

☐ Economic health and political stability of target, scaled from
   1 (distressed) to 3 (strong)   3

☐ Presanction relations between sender and target, scaled from
   1 (antagonistic) to 3 (cordial)   1

☐ Type of sanction: X (export), M (import), F (financial)   X

☐ Cost to sender, scaled from 1 (net gain) to 4 (major loss)   3

Comments

The grain embargo had no impact on Soviet intervention in Afghanistan, nor did it perceptibly weaken the Soviet military apparatus. It is unknown what effect, if any, economic sanctions had on Soviet calculations with respect to adventures in other parts of the world.

Bibliography

Ayubi, Shaheen, Richard E. Bissell, Nana Amu-Brafih Korsah, and Laurie A. Lerner. 1982. *Economic Sanctions in U.S. Foreign Policy*. Philadelphia Policy Papers. Philadelphia: Foreign Policy Research Institute.

Brougher, Jack. 1980. "U.S.–U.S.S.R. Trade After Afghanistan." *Business America* (7 April): 3–7. Congressional Research Service, Library of Congress. 1981. *An Assessment of the Afghanistan Sanctions: Implications for Trade and Diplomacy in the 1980s*. Prepared for House Committee on Foreign Affairs. 97 Cong., 1 sess. Washington.

Cooper, Richard N. 1987. "Trade Policy as Foreign Policy." *U.S. Trade Policies in a Changing World Economy*, ed. Robert M. Stern. Cambridge, MA: The MIT Press.

Facts on File. 1980.

Falkenheim, Peggy L. 1987. "Post Afghanistan Sanctions." In *The Utility of International Economic Sanctions,* ed. David Leyton-Brown. London: Croom Helm.

Malkevich, V. 1981. *East-West Economic Cooperation and Technological Exchange.* Moscow: Academy of Sciences.

Paarlberg, Robert L. 1980. "Lessons of the Grain Embargo." 59 *Foreign Affairs* (Fall): 144–62.

Schnittker Associates. 1982. *Effects of the 1980 and 1981 Limitations on Grain Exports to the USSR on Business Activity, Jobs, Government Costs, and Farmers.* Report prepared for National Corn Growers Association, 12 February. Washington.

United Nations. 1980. "Resolutions and Decisions Adopted by the General Assembly at its Sixth Emergency Special Session: 10–14 January 1980." Press release GA/6172, 21 January. New York.

US Senate. Committee on Banking, Housing and Urban Affairs. 1980. *Export Restrictions in the USSR.* Statement by Richard N. Cooper. 96 Cong., 2 sess., 20 August. Washington. (Reprinted in 80 *Department of State Bulletin* 2043, October 1980.)

CASE 81-1

US v. Nicaragua

(1981–90: El Salvador War; Destabilize Sandinistas)

Chronology of Key Events

See also Case 77–5 US v. Nicaragua (1977–79: Somoza)

19 July 1979   Sandinista front, with moral, economic support from US, ousts General Anastasio Somoza Debayle as president of Nicaragua. (*Wall Street Journal,* 11 November 1982, 1)

Fall 1979   President Jimmy Carter unfreezes $10.5 million in economic assistance, extends $8.8 million in emergency assistance to Nicaragua, submits $75 million aid package to Congress. However, "For many reasons, there were endless and unfortunate delays, until the Nicaraguans began to feel that the money was being politically held over their heads." (Anderson 168)

17 October 1980   US, Nicaragua finally sign $75 million aid agreement, but only after Carter provides assurances to Congress that Sandinistas are not aiding leftist insurgents in El Salvador. Congress stipulates that money "could be recalled at any time, with immediate payment made in full, including interest, if the United States determined that Nicaragua was indeed engaging in subversion abroad." (Anderson 168, 190)

22 January 1981   President Ronald Reagan freezes aid approved previous year (of which only $15 million has not been transferred), $9.6 million wheat sale, Food for Peace aid. On 1 April Reagan suspends aid indefinitely because of Sandinistas' support of leftist guerrillas in El Salvador. Cancellation of wheat sale reportedly results in flour shortage, rationing in Nicaragua. Sandinista leadership warns that US actions amount to "economic aggression." (*Keesing's* 30975; Anderson 190)

August 1981   Assistant Secretary of State Thomas O. Enders visits Managua, promises US aid, noninterference if Sandinistas terminate support of Salvadoran leftists. (*Newsweek,* 8 November 1982, 48)

December 1981   Reagan administration authorizes $20 million for Central Intelligence Agency (CIA) plan to create 500-man paramilitary force of Nicaraguan rebels in Honduras to cut off Nicaraguan arms, other supplies to El Salvador, indirectly to destabilize Sandinista regime.

In companion action, Argentina agrees to train additional 1,000 men. (*Newsweek*, 8 November 1982, 43, 48)

Late 1981   US vetoes Nicaraguan request for $30 million credit from special operations fund of Inter-American Development Bank (IDB) for fisheries project. (*Washington Post*, 1 July 1983, A1)

April 1982   US Ambassador to Honduras John Negroponte establishes contact with exiled Somoza supporters (Somocistas) living in Honduras; directs actions of 50 CIA personnel, related operatives in Honduras; coordinates military operations with Honduran army. US provides Honduran military with $187 million in 1981–82, proposes $78 million for 1983. (*Newsweek*, 8 November 1982, 43–48; *New York Times*, 4 December 1982, A1; *Washington Post*, 19 January 1983, A10)

21 December 1982   Concerned about administration aims in Nicaragua, Congress passes amendment, offered by Congressman Edward P. Boland (D-MA), prohibiting US from providing "military equipment, military training, or advice or support for military activities for the purposes of overthrowing the government of Nicaragua or provoking a military exchange between Nicaragua and Honduras." Senator Daniel Patrick Moynihan (D-NY): "[it is] difficult to draw the line between harassment activities and a deliberate attempt to destabilize or overthrow a government." (*Washington Post*, 1 January 1983, A10; Mayer 72)

March 1983   Under Secretary of Defense Fred C. Iklé testifies before Congress that USSR has provided $440 million in aid to Nicaragua since Sandinistas took power. Iklé expresses irritation that nearly four times that much, some $1.6 billion, has come from non-Soviet sources, most of them "misguided" European governments. (*Washington Post*, 5 April 1983, A1)

7 April 1983   Leaked National Security Council (NSC) document on US policy in Central America calls for "increasing the pressure on Nicaragua and Cuba to increase for them the costs of intervention." (*New York Times*, 7 April 1983, A16)

Spring 1983   CIA informs Congress that $20 million previously authorized for operation in Honduras is not sufficient, that agency will use another $11 million from its fund for covert operations (which does not require congressional approval). Congress becomes increasingly concerned that administration is violating Boland amendment, despite presidential assurances to contrary. (*New York Times*, 15 April 1983, A1; *Wall Street Journal*, 15 April 1983, 2; *Newsweek*, 11 April 1983, 50)

3 May 1983   House Select Committee on Intelligence votes to cut off all funds in support of covert activity in Nicaragua. Reagan labels vote "partisan" and "irresponsible." Senate Intelligence Committee later approves $19 million in funds for anti-Sandinista rebels ("contras"). (*New York Times,* 7 May 1983, A1; 18 May 1983, A8; *Wall Street Journal,* 5 May 1983, 3)

9 May 1983   US officials reveal that Reagan administration will redistribute most of Nicaragua's sugar export quota among "Central American nations friendly to US." Honduras would receive largest share; El Salvador, Costa Rica also would benefit; total sugar exports from these countries to US would increase by about $14 million. Nicaragua subsequently contests action in GATT (General Agreement on Tariffs and Trade). (*Washington Post,* 10 May 1983, A1; *New York Times,* 11 May 1983, A12; *Journal of Commerce,* 14 March 1984, 9A)

27 May 1983   State, Defense departments release white paper that links Cuba, Nicaragua in efforts to destabilize governments of El Salvador, Honduras, Costa Rica. (*New York Times,* 28 May 1983, A3)

7 June 1983   US closes all six Nicaraguan consulates in US, expels 21 consular officials in retaliation for ouster of three US diplomats from Managua. (*New York Times,* 8 June 1983, A1)

29 June 1983   US vetoes Nicaraguan request for extension of time to complete $18 million rural road financed by IDB loan granted in 1976. By voting against extension, US essentially deprives Nicaragua of remaining $2.2 million that was unspent because of flooding in project area. (*The Economist,* 9 July 1983, 19)

30 June 1983   US Treasury official announces that US will vote against World Bank, IDB loans to Nicaragua until Sandinistas "revitalize the private sector," "improve the efficiency of the public sector." US has power to block loans from IDB's special operations fund but cannot unilaterally block regular loans from World Bank or IDB. In 1982 Nicaragua obtained loans of $16 million, $34 million, respectively, from those two institutions. (*Washington Post,* 1 July 1983, A1)

July 1983   Reagan announces appointment of special bipartisan commission, chaired by Henry A. Kissinger, to suggest long-term US strategy toward Central America. In subsequent days Reagan announces plans for large-scale military exercises involving air, land, sea forces to be held in and off coast of Honduras. Meanwhile, Nicaragua backs off earlier insistence on holding bilateral talks with US, Honduras, indicates willingness to discuss regional problems in regional forum. (*New York Times,* 22 July 1983, A1; *Washington Post,* 26 July 1983, A1)

4 August 1983   US, Nicaraguan officials announce cancellation of $7.5 million loan for rural education appropriated in 1978 but never disbursed. Spokesman in US embassy in Managua, Gilbert Callaway, says Nicaragua never submitted plan showing how money would be spent; "On top of that, Nicaragua never fulfilled certain [unspecified] requirements necessary for the disbursement of the loan." "Education Minister Carlos Tunnerman called the decision 'one more proof of the political and economic blockade imposed on Nicaragua by the United States.' " (*Washington Post*, 5 August 1983, A16)

September 1983   Nicaragua announces it will pay all external debt (some $3.3 billion), compensate foreign owners of nationalized mines. Agreement is reached to pay Amax, parent of one of the nationalized mining companies, for $8.8 million claim. (*Journal of Commerce*, 30 September 1983, 3A)

21 October 1983   Sandinistas propose security accords with US; House votes (227 to 194) to cut off covert assistance to contras. (*Washington Post*, 21 October 1983, A1)

18 November 1983   House yields to Senate; Congress provides $24 million in covert funds for contras, amount estimated to last through June 1984. Congress also places $24 million ceiling on amount that CIA, Defense Department, or any other agency "involved in intelligence activities" can spend out of other funds to support contras. CIA concludes, however, that contras, now numbering 10,000 to 20,000, cannot achieve victory over Sandinista government. Curtin Winsor, Jr., US ambassador to Costa Rica, remarks, "An invasion of Nicaragua is not impossible." (*Washington Post*, 19 November 1983, A21; 25 November 1983, A1; Tower Commission Report 450–51)

Early 1984   Nicaragua's main port at Corinto, two other ports are mined, allegedly with direct CIA assistance. Contras also carry out attacks by air, small boats against ships in Corinto's harbor. French government offers to help Nicaragua clear ports if "one or several friendly European powers" will cooperate. "[T]he attacks on the ports have the potential to devastate Nicaragua's foreign trade." Nicaragua files suit against US in International Court of Justice over mining of harbors. (*Washington Post*, 2 April 1984, A1; 6 April 1984, A1; Mayer 73–74)

13 March 1984   GATT Council unanimously adopts report charging US with violation of GATT obligations in cutting Nicaragua's quota for US sugar imports. Acting deputy US trade representative in Geneva, Warren Lavorel, says US does not oppose panel report, is willing to open talks with Nicaragua. However, US officials refuse to comply with GATT ruling, noting that "in order for the United States to solve the problem of Nicaraguan sugar quotas, the larger political issues between the United States and Nicaragua had to be addressed." (*Journal of Commerce*, 14 March 1984, 9A; *Wall Street Journal*, 9 March 1984, 35; *New York Times*, 14 March 1984, D1)

April 1984   US informs International Court of Justice that it will not accept court's jurisdiction over Nicaraguan suit filed against US role in mining of Nicaragua's harbors. "State Department officials acknowledged that it was the first time since the United States joined the World Court in 1946 that it had taken such an action to block resolution of a specific dispute." (*New York Times*, 10 April 1984, A1)

25 June 1984	Following two House votes opposing additional aid to Nicaraguan rebels, Senate votes 88 to 1 to delete $21 million for contras from emergency spending bill which also includes funds for domestic programs. Administration previously requested additional funds reportedly because CIA had only $100,000 left of $24 million originally appropriated. House Speaker Thomas P. ("Tip") O'Neill, Jr. (D-MA), notes that "The Senate's action should bring to a close US support for the war in Nicaragua." (*New York Times*, 26 June 1984, A1; 27 June 1984, A1)
4 November 1984	Nicaragua holds elections; junta leader Daniel Ortega Saavedra is elected president. US labels elections "a sham" because major opposition parties did not participate. (*Washington Post*, 12 January 1985, A11)
11 October 1984	Congress passes strengthened Boland amendment that prohibits CIA, Defense Department, any other agency involved in intelligence activities from using funds appropriated by Congress for direct or indirect assistance to contras. (Mayer 80; Tower Commission Report 451)
December 1984	Senator David F. Durenberger (R-MN), new chairman of Senate Intelligence Committee, makes known his opposition to renewal of covert aid to contras, proposes that administration find ways to apply overt and legal pressure on Sandinistas. Administration, Congress spend first months of 1985 debating alternative policies, including humanitarian aid for contras, their families, possible trade embargo. (*Washington Post*, 12 January 1985, A11; 28 January 1985, A1; 11 March 1985, A16; 24–25 April 1985, A1)
27 February 1985	In effort to stimulate peace talks with US, other Central American countries, Ortega proposes sending home 100 Cuban military advisers, declares "indefinite moratorium" on acquisition of weapon systems. Moves are dismissed by US as insignificant and containing "a lot of air." Nicaragua acknowledges presence of only 200 Cuban military advisers; US cites 2,000. (*Washington Post*, 28 February 1985, A1; 1 March 1985, A1; 8 March 1985)
7 March 1985	Secretary of State George P. Shultz meets with IDB president, Antonio Ortiz Mena, to express administration's "strong" opposition to $58 million IDB loan to Nicaragua. Shultz says approval of loan would make new US contributions to bank "even more difficult." US is already nearly $1 billion in arrears on pledged IDB contributions because of disputes over management of bank. (*Washington Post*, 8 March 1985, A1)
24 April 1985	US House of Representatives again votes down contra aid. Nicaraguan government repeats pledge to send home 100 Cuban military advisers, announces release of 107 prisoners held in association with insurgency. (*Washington Post*, 24–25 April 1985, A1, A3)

29 April 1985	Ortega meets with Soviet leader Mikhail Gorbachev in Moscow, signs new economic agreement. (*Washington Post*, 30 April 1985, A1)
1 May 1985	Ronald Reagan invokes International Emergency Economic Powers Act to impose sanctions against Nicaragua. Measures include total embargo on trade, prohibition on Nicaraguan-registered ships entering US ports, ban on Nicaraguan air transport services operating in US, notification of US intent to terminate Treaty of Friendship, Commerce, and Navigation. (*Washington Post*, 1 May 1985, A1; *International Trade Reporter*, 8 May 1985, 637)
Mid-June 1985	Reacting primarily to Ortega's Moscow visit, House votes 248 to 184 to provide $27 million in nonmilitary aid to contras over next nine months, to be distributed by agencies other than Defense Department, CIA. Nicaragua denounces vote, says it will end voluntary moratorium on weapons acquisitions. (*Washington Post*, 13 June 1985, A1)
December 1985	Congress renews modified Boland amendment, allowing CIA to provide communications, communications equipment training, "advice" for contras. Chairman of House Committee on Intelligence Lee H. Hamilton writes letter to CIA Director William J. Casey giving his interpretation that such advice does not include logistical advice "upon which military and paramilitary operations depend for their effectiveness." (Tower Commission Report 461, 549)
25 June 1986	Under heavy pressure from administration, House of Representatives approves 18-month, $100 million aid package for contras, allows Boland amendment to lapse in October. (Krauss 564–65; Tower Commission Report 469–70)
Early November 1986	GATT rules that embargo, justified by US under national security exception (Article XXI), is not violation of international trading rules, but is contrary to basic GATT objectives. Panel appointed to review case concludes that US did not properly weigh need to invoke Article XXI "against the more basic need for stable trade regulations. . . ." Reagan extends trade embargo for another year. (*International Trade Reporter*, 12 November 1986, 1368–69; *Facts on File* 999)
Late November 1986	Attorney General Edwin S. Meese, III, discloses that, during period when Congress had barred funding for contras, NSC officials were involved in a scheme to provide funds to contras by diverting profits from secret arms sales to Iran. (*New York Times*, 27 February 1990, A14)
March 1987	House tries to block disbursement of last $40 million from contra aid package passed previous year, but measure is rejected by Senate. (Robinson 591–92)
August 1987	Presidents of five Central American countries sign agreement, based on plan proposed in February by Costa Rican President

Oscar Arias Sánchez, designed to end conflicts in Nicaragua, El Salvador, Guatemala. Agreement calls for cease-fires, amnesties, democratization measures (including freedom of press, right of organization for political oppositions, lifting of states of emergency) to be implemented simultaneously with end to use of territory by, aid to insurgent groups. Administration initially plans to go ahead with request for $270 million in aid for contras, but "back[s] down in face of congressional opposition." Congress approves only nonlethal, "stopgap" funding of $11.3 million to support contras while negotiations toward implementation of Arias plan continue. (Robinson 594–601, 610)

January 1988   Faced with congressional vote on aid to contras on 3 February, Nicaragua suspends its state of siege, agrees for first time to negotiate directly with contras on cease-fire. (Hayes 181)

3 February 1988   House votes down administration's request for $36 million in contra aid, which includes small amount of military aid. "The demoralized contra leadership read the writing on the wall: there would be no bipartisan support for their program; they had best explore accommodation with the Sandinistas." (Hayes 182)

March 1988   Nicaraguan government, contras agree to 60-day cease-fire to take effect 1 April 1988. (*New York Times,* 27 February 1990, A14)

February 1989   Five Central American presidents sign agreement setting specific timetable for democratization in Nicaragua, culminating in holding of elections no later than 25 February 1990. Agreement also calls for disbanding of contras, but their leadership refuses to do so until after elections are held. US argues that repatriation is voluntary process, refuses to pressure contras to disband. (Fauriol 124–26)

April 1989   In return for congressional approval of $50 million in humanitarian support for contras until Nicaragua holds elections, administration agrees not to seek military aid. (Fauriol 125)

25 October 1989   Administration of President George Bush extends 1985 trade embargo against Nicaragua, arguing that El Salvador rebels continue to receive Sandinista military supplies. Bush calls embargo "an essential element of our policy that seeks a democratic outcome in Nicaragua by diplomatic means." (*Washington Post,* 26 October 1989, A34)

9 November 1989   Bush signs $9 million election aid package to assist National Opposition Union (UNO), coalition led by opposition presidential candidate Violeta Chamorro de Barrios, promises to end trade embargo if she defeats Ortega. (*Washington Post,* 9 November 1989, A56)

Early 1990   UNO's campaign emphasizes Nicaragua's economic woes, blaming them on Sandinistas: Francisco Mayorga, chief economic advisor to Chamorro: "More than the war, the economic situation reflects mismanagement." (*Washington Post,* 8 January 1990, A19)

23 February 1990	Amid growing reports that ruling Sandinistas will win elections, Secretary of State James A. Baker III testifies that Nicaragua must show "a substantial period of good behavior" before bilateral relations can improve. (*Washington Post*, 28 February 1990, A17)
25 February 1990	Chamorro easily defeats Ortega with 55 percent of vote, but UNO fails to win enough seats in National Assembly to ensure passage of constitutional changes. Bush hails elections as "clear mandate for peace and democracy." (*New York Times*, 27 February 1990, A1; 28 February 1990, A19; *Wall Street Journal*, 5 March 1990, A1)
13 March 1990	Bush lifts trade embargo, proposes transferring $500 million from US defense budget to Nicaragua, including $300 million in immediate aid, $200 million for the next fiscal year. (*Wall Street Journal*, 14 March 1990, A20)
25 April 1990	US Department of Agriculture reinstates Nicaragua's sugar quota. (*Journal of Commerce*, 26 April 1990, 6A)
25 May 1990	Bush signs bill providing $300 million in aid for Nicaragua. (*Washington Post*, 27 May 1990, A4)

Goals of Sender Country

1982

"While US officials maintain that the primary objective of the operation remains cutting off the supply routes, they also hope that a threatened Sandinista government will bring itself down by further repressing its internal opposition, thereby strengthening the determination of moderate forces to resist." (*Newsweek*, 8 November 1982, 48)

1983

Thomas O. Enders, assistant secretary of state for inter-American affairs, in congressional testimony 12 April: "Since the Somoza government collapsed and the Sandinistas came to power, US policy in Nicaragua has focused on attempting to convince Nicaragua to:
—renounce support for insurgency in neighboring countries;
—abandon its pursuit of dominant military power in Central America; and
—come to terms with its own society through the creation of democratic institutions." (US Senate 1)

1984

In April, allegations of CIA involvement in mining of Nicaragua's ports renew debate over Reagan administration's objectives in Central America. "In an effort to contain the uproar, President Reagan sent the Senate a carefully drafted letter last week asserting that his objectives were to get Nicaragua to 'cease to involve itself in the internal or external affairs of its neighbors' and to draw the Sandinistas into 'meaningful negotiations' for a Central American peace settlement. In his letter, he denied his administration was trying to overthrow or disrupt the Sandinista Government." (*New York Times*, 11 April 1984, A1)

1985

Office of the White House Press Secretary: "The activities of Nicaragua, supported by the Soviet Union and its allies, are incompatible with normal commercial relations. . . It should be understood, however, that the President does not consider the imposition of these sanctions to be a substitute for U.S. assistance to the unified democratic opposition." (Statement on U.S. Economic Sanctions Against Nicaragua, Office of the White House Press Secretary, 1 May 1985)

Summer 1987

Administration endorses proposal by Speaker of the House Jim Wright (D-TX) for settlement of Nicaraguan conflict that emphasizes three main objectives: "no Soviet military base in Nicaragua, no subversion of its neighbors, and full democracy." (Robinson 601)

When Wright plan is rejected in favor of Arias plan, Reagan says, "we have always been willing to talk, we have never been willing to abandon those who were fighting for democracy and freedom." A few months later, however, Reagan criticizes Arias plan, saying it "falls short of the safeguards for democracy and our national security." (Robinson 602)

Response of Target Country

August 1981

Sandinistas ignore offer of US aid in exchange for pledge of nonintervention in El Salvador. (*Newsweek,* 8 November 1982, 48)

December 1981

Nicaraguan Foreign Minister Miguel D'Escoto Brockman denies his country supports El Salvador leftists. (*Newsweek,* 8 November 1982, 48)

August 1982

Nicaraguan Ambassador to US, Francisco Fiallo Navarro, says virtual state of war exists between Honduras, Nicaragua. (*Newsweek,* 8 November 1982, 48)

Spring 1983

Nicaragua twice takes its case before UN Security Council, accusing US of waging war against it. First debate ends without resolution or vote, but majority of delegates are sympathetic to Nicaraguan position. In May, resolution submitted to Security Council is so innocuous that both US, Nicaragua support it. (*Washington Post,* 10 May 1983, A14; *New York Times,* 20 May 1983, A3)

5 April 1983

Spokesman for Nicaraguan embassy in Washington calls proposed US sugar quota reduction "economic attack" intended to "kill the Nicaraguan revolution." On 11 May 1983, quota reduction is criticized by Orlando Solorzano, acting foreign trade minister, as "a hard blow . . . taken for purely political reasons, which goes against all principles of international trade." Nicaragua files GATT complaint against quotas; it is upheld in March 1984. (*Washington Post,* 5 April 1983, A11; *Financial Times* [London], 12 May 1983, 45; *Journal of Commerce,* 14 March 1984, 9A)

April 1984

Nicaragua files suit in International Court of Justice claiming US has participated in mining of harbors in violation of international law. (*New York Times*, 10 April 1984, A1)

May 1985

Sergio Ramírez Mercado, Nicaraguan vice president: "We will become closer to all countries that support this revolution. . . . This includes the Soviet Union." He also states that Nicaragua will file protest before International Court of Justice. Ramírez calls US sanctions "absolutely illegal and arbitrary . . . irrational reprisals. . . . The United States is responding to its inability to destroy the revolution militarily." (*New York Times*, 2 May 1985, A10)

12 May 1985

Ortega commends US support of UN resolution to resume direct talks with Managua, states that Nicaragua will "survive" US embargo with "pluralistic assistance" from "socialist countries, Western Europe, Latin America and the Arab countries." (*Washington Post*, 13 May 1985, A14)

Attitude of Other Countries

Cuba

In 1981–82, Cuba supplies 4,000 civilian specialists, 2,000 military advisers to Nicaragua, acts as channel for military equipment from USSR. (*Newsweek*, 8 November 1982, 49)

Soviet Union

In October 1982, Nicaraguan Interior Minister Tomás Borge Martínez asks USSR for financial assistance, receives $100 million credit for agricultural equipment (Nicaragua already has abundance of unused farm equipment). (*Wall Street Journal*, 11 November 1982, 24)

Failing to meet terms under 1982 accord with Mexico, Nicaragua signs agreement with USSR in which 80 percent to 90 percent of its petroleum needs for 1985 will be met. Mexico had supplied 40 percent to 50 percent of Nicaragua's needs in 1984, but Nicaragua is now over $500 million behind in payments. (*Washington Post*, 21 May 1985, A22)

In September 1988, Gorbachev sends envoy to Nicaragua to inform Ortega that support will henceforth be limited, that Sandinistas should try to reach accommodation with US. In spring of 1989, Gorbachev writes letter to President Bush claiming to have ended arms shipments to Nicaragua in response to American shift from military to diplomatic track. (*Washington Post*, 16 May 1989, A1)

Argentina

"[T]he reliance on Argentina [as a main conduit for initial CIA aid] drew the United States indirectly into support of paramilitary units that seek to overthrow the Sandinistas and include former supporters of General Somoza." (*New York Times*, 4 December 1982, A7)

Following US support of UK in Falklands war in spring 1982, Argentina withdraws its military advisers from Honduras. (*New York Times*, 4 December 1982, A1)

Mexico, Venezuela, Panama, Colombia

These countries form "Contadora Group" that attempts to mediate regional conflict with encouragement of UN Security Council. (*New York Times*, 20 May 1983, A3)

Following US embargo, Nicaragua, Mexico sign trade agreement worth $26 million for 1985. Mexico will provide 730,000 barrels of crude oil as well as raw materials for manufacture of PVC, agricultural chemicals, in exchange for shellfish, frozen meat, products formerly traded between US, Nicaragua. (*Financial Times*, 31 May 1985, 6)

UN Conference on Trade and Development

"It was in large part the American measures against Nicaragua that impelled [UNCTAD] in Belgrade last weekend to denounce, with some anger, intimidation of poor countries by rich." Eighty-one UNCTAD delegates, most from developing countries, vote for motion that "denounced coercive economic measures applied for political reasons;" 18 delegates, most from industrialized states, vote against resolution, seven abstain. (*The Economist*, 9 July 1983, 20; *Washington Post*, 3 July 1983, A25)

Western Europe

France, Spain, West Germany, Netherlands, Sweden extend lines of credit to Nicaragua for purchases of machinery, other goods, despite opposition from US. (*New York Times*, 26 September 1983, A10; *Journal of Commerce*, 30 September 1983, 3A)

At economic summit in Bonn in May 1985, West German Foreign Minister Hans-Dietrich Genscher conveys his government's position that trade, economic sanctions serve no useful purpose. Italian Foreign Minister Giulio Andreotti denounces embargo as "ineffective measure." British Foreign Minister Geoffrey Howe, French Foreign Minister Roland Dumas warn of closer Soviet-Nicaraguan ties. On 15 May, EC announces plans to double aid to Central America including Nicaragua. (*Facts on File* 436; *Washington Post*, 4 May 1985, A16)

November 1985: EC signs five-year cooperation accord with six Central American nations, reaffirming its disagreement with US policy. EC pledges to substantially increase its aid, which has averaged about $33 million annually. (*Washington Post*, 13 November 1985, A28)

June 1989: Nicaragua, hoping to get $250 million in aid, receives commitments for $50 million from Spain, Norway, Sweden, Denmark, Finland. EC members say Nicaragua cannot expect increased aid until after scheduled February elections. Administration later reveals that Baker "burned up the telephone wires" pressuring leaders to condition aid on elections. (*Washington Post*, 5 June 1989, A20; 28 February 1990, A18)

Algeria, Iran, France

These countries purchase Nicaraguan sugar previously sold to US. (*Journal of Commerce*, 30 September 1983, 3A)

Central America

Costa Rica, El Salvador, Guatemala, Honduras quietly refuse to join US economic boycott of Nicaragua. In 1987, they join with Nicaragua to negotiate regional solution to conflicts in their countries. (*New York Times*, 26 September 1983, A10; Robinson)

Canada

Following imposition of embargo, Canada permits Nicaragua to move its Miami-based foreign-trade office to Toronto. US expresses concern that trade office will serve as conduit for goods, thus circumventing embargo. Canadian Foreign Minister Joe Clark states that Canada "doesn't agree" with US embargo, that it has "a perfect right" to sell Nicaragua anything it wants to buy. Canada continues to provide $4 million in economic aid per year. (*Washington Post*, 23 April 1985, A25; 21 May 1985, A22)

China, India

September 1986: China offers Nicaragua $20 million low-interest loan, doubling level of Chinese aid. India also pledges $10 million in assistance. (*Facts on File* 436; *Washington Post*, 15 September 1986, A17)

Economic Impact

Observed Economic Statistics

Nicaragua: trade with United States and total foreign trade, 1980–88 (millions of dollars except where noted)

Year	Total exports	Exports to US	Percent of total	Total imports	Imports from US	Percent of total
1980	414	160	38.6	882	242	27.4
1981	490	138	28.2	804	203	25.2
1982	370	82	22.2	775	148	19.1
1983	429	99	23.1	747	145	19.4
1984	428	63	14.7	665	123	18.5
1985	301	45	15.0	544	46	8.5
1986	301	1	0.3	466	3	0.6
1987	253	1	0.4	494	4	0.8
1988	311	1	0.3	540	7	1.3

Source: International Monetary Fund.

Nicaragua: official development assistance, 1983–88 (millions of dollars)

Year	From EC	From other European countries	From Soviet bloc
1983	46	14.5	52
1984	53	22.4	109
1985	46	20.8	120
1986	72	36.1	201
1987	72	47.4	116
1988	88	80.4	52

Source: Organization for Economic Cooperation and Development.

United States: aid to Nicaragua (millions of dollars)

Fiscal Year	Economic	PL 480 (food)
1977	9.8	0.4
1978	14.6	0.1
1979	18.5	7.0
1980	38.7	18.0
1981	59.9	1.2

Source: Agency for International Development.

From 1979 to 1982, Nicaragua receives $125 million in military equipment, supplies from USSR, $121 million in economic assistance from US. (US Senate 1, 10)

Following Reagan administration's suspension of aid to Nicaragua, cancellation of wheat sale, USSR agrees to deliver 20,000 tons of wheat beginning in May 1981; Bulgaria promises another 10,000 tons. Libya signs agreement for $100 million grant for development of mixed agricultural enterprise; Cuba pledges $64 million in aid for 1981. Nicaragua is said to receive about $500 million in aid annually in early 1980s, including assistance from OPEC ($10 million), loan from Libya ($100 million), aid from various West European countries. (*Keesing's* 30975; *New York Times*, 13 August 1983, A3)

CIA estimates that USSR provided $515 million in military aid, $400 million in economic aid to Nicaragua in 1988. (*Washington Post,* 16 May 1989, A1)

In 1982, Nicaragua earns $15.6 million from sugar sales to US—only 3 percent of Nicaragua's total exports. Sanctions, which take effect in October 1983, reduce Nicaragua's sugar quota from 58,800 short tons to 6,000 short tons. (*New York Times*, 6 April 1983, D9; Bureau of National Affairs, *US Import Weekly,* 11 May 1983, 202)

In June 1983, Nicaragua fails to make repayment of $45 million owed to foreign commercial banks, its first such delay. (*Washington Post,* 1 July 1983, A1)

In August 1983, Mexico makes further oil shipments contingent on Nicaraguan commitment to pay Venezuela $20 million, Mexico some $300 million for oil previously shipped; Venezuela suspended shipments in June. Nicaragua turns to USSR for petroleum needs. (*Wall Street Journal,* 8 June 1983, 30; *New York Times,* 13 August 1983, D3)

In fall 1983, Nicaragua has to cut fuel rations by 10 percent to 30 percent in response to shortages caused by rebel attacks. (*New York Times,* 25 October 1983, A5)

Nicaragua suggests US sanctions cost $354 million in 1983. (Authors' note: We regard this figure as much too high.) Estimates indicate $18 million loss from lower sugar quota, $112.5 million in multilateral loans that US has blocked since 1980. (*Journal of Commerce,* 5 August 1983, 23B)

Before embargo, Nicaragua exports primarily bananas, beef, shellfish, coffee to US; it imports primarily pesticides, fertilizers, feed, agricultural machinery, spare parts. Mexico, Libya, Europe, Canada, Japan now take commodities once shipped to US. (*U.S. News and World Report,* 1 April 1985, 32; *Washington Post,* 30 April 1985, A12)

"The bare figure for Nicaraguan imports from the United States [20 percent of total imports] understates the economic dependence. . . . Most of the country's capital equipment is American-made." However, over time, US exports to Nicaragua of chemical products and spare parts become less important as machinery or whole factories are replaced by Communist-bloc equipment. (*U.S. News and World Report*, 1 April 1985, 32; *Washington Post*, 30 April 1985, A12; *The Economist*, 29 June 1985, 76)

In 1984 Nicaraguan imports from USSR triple as relations with US deteriorate. Nicaragua is now second-largest Latin American importer of Soviet goods after Cuba. USSR is supplying chemical fertilizer, machinery, motor vehicles, other capital goods which used to dominate American shipments. (*New York Times*, 12 May 1985, A5)

Although it has comparatively small external debt ($4.5 billion), Nicaragua is first country to fall six months in arrears to World Bank. Debt service of $6.2 million was paid in April; $15 million will be paid over 1986. (*New York Times*, 17 June 1985)

In November 1986, 18 months after its imposition, Nicaragua's Minister of Foreign Trade Alejandro Martínez Cuenca charges that embargo has cost Nicaraguan economy $108 million. (*Facts on File* 999)

In early 1990, Martínez Cuenca (now planning and budget minister) reveals that current account deficit has been around $500 million for over five years, more than double Nicaragua's exports. Through cutbacks in spending, elimination of most government subsidies, fiscal deficit is reduced in 1989 to 5 percent of GDP from 27 percent in 1988. Total debt is $7.35 billion, $250 million of which is owed to World Bank, IDB. Nicaragua owes $2.5 billion to international commercial banks, $2.7 billion to COMECON bloc, $900 million to other Latin American governments, $400 million to other Central American countries, $300 million to Paris Club governments, $300 million in short-term credits. Negotiations with International Monetary Fund to reschedule debt, enter new agreements have begun. (*Financial Times*, 28 February 1990, 20)

Credits from USSR, Eastern Europe, Nordic countries have financed Nicaragua's current account deficit. Soviet Foreign Ministry official, Yan Burlyai, reports that Moscow provides Nicaragua with $333 million annually in credits, $25 million in free rice, wheat. (*New York Times*, 28 February 1990, A16)

Nicaragua records inflation of 36,000 percent in 1988, while real GDP falls by 8 percent. After 32 devaluations, cordoba is worth 42,000 to the dollar. USSR is reducing unspecified economic support to Nicaragua. (It had been supplying 825,000 tons of petroleum per year on easy credit terms.) Likewise, low-interest East bloc loans for fertilizer, pesticides, farm equipment will not continue. (*Journal of Commerce*, 27 February 1990, A1; *Washington Post*, 8 January 1990, A19)

As of early 1990, Nicaraguan arrears to World Bank total $172 million; arrears to IDB total $118.5 million. (*Financial Times*, 27 February 1990, 6)

Confidential study, prepared in 1989 for Sandinista government by team of international experts, estimates that consumption declined 70 percent in last decade, reports annual per capita income of $300, lowest in Western Hemisphere. Total cumulative cost of war, including disruption of economic activity, is estimated by Sandinistas at $12 billion, with defense spending accounting for up to half of total government expenditures. Former Sandinista Planning Minister Xabier Gorostiaga estimates that, since 1983, 20 percent of total national output has gone to military. (*New York Times*, 26 June 1989, A1; 6 July 1989, A6; *Financial Times*, 27 February 1990, 6)

Calculated Economic Impact (annual cost to target country)

Suspension of US economic aid in 1981; welfare loss valued at 90 percent of average aid levels FY 1979–81.	$35 million
Reduction of 90 percent in US sugar import quota for Nicaragua; welfare loss valued at 40 percent of value of 1981 trade.	6 million
Suspension of US wheat sale, PL 480 food aid; welfare loss valued at 40 percent of trade, aid.	9 million
Reduction in trade due to US embargo; welfare loss estimated as 40 percent of value of average annual trade, 1980–84.	110 million
Reduction in concessional loans from IDB in 1981–83 because of US vetoes; welfare loss estimated at 75 percent of value of loans ($32.2 million) lost during three-year period.	8 million
Offsets Increase in official grants, loans from Soviet bloc countries; welfare gain valued at 70 percent of average annual transfers, 1983–88.	($76 million)
Increased shipments of 30,000 tons of grain from USSR, Bulgaria, valued at 40 percent.	(2 million)
Increase in official development assistance from Western European countries; welfare gain estimated at 70 percent of average annual increase in transfers in 1986–88 as compared to 1983–85 levels.	(45 million)
Total	$45 million

Relative Magnitudes

Gross indicators of Nicaraguan economy	
Nicaraguan GNP (1979)	$1.4 billion
Nicaraguan population (1980)	2.7 million
Annual effect of sanctions related to gross indicators	
Percentage of GNP	3.2
Per capita	$16.67
Nicaraguan trade with US as percentage of total trade	
Exports (1980)	39
Imports (1980)	27
Ratio of US GNP (1979: $2,418 billion) to Nicaraguan GNP	1,727

Assessment

Wall Street Journal
As of early 1983: "President Reagan's economic reprisals have aggravated a sickly economy that has Nicaraguans grumbling about having to wait in lines for scarce gasoline and to carry ration cards for many staples. . . . But while the Reagan administration has succeeded in putting Nicaragua in a pressure cooker, its policies

haven't succeeded in forcing the nation into ending support for revolutionaries in El Salvador or reversing the military buildup that alarms its neighbors. (*Wall Street Journal*, 31 May 1983, 1)

Glennon J. Harrison

Fall 1987: "The unilateral nature of the embargo has reduced [its] effectiveness. . . . The lack of international support for the embargo . . . led to a diversification of [Nicaragua's] trade relations with some of the United States' major trading partners. . . . The contra war, bad weather, and the generally poor economic climate in Nicaragua (and Latin America as a whole) are more important for explaining Nicaragua's economic performance than the U.S. trade embargo." (Harrison 3–5)

New York Times

At time of 1988 cease-fire: "Undoubtedly the relentless United States pressures on Nicaragua were a principal factor in driving its Government to the bargaining table. The military cost was evident, both in blood and treasure. But the economic embargo, which prevents businesses from importing even the most commonplace items from the United States, has also been harshly effective. The prospect of living in eternal hostility with such a powerful neighbor no longer appeals to Mr. Ortega. American cooperation is now more vital to Nicaragua then ever, because with the advent of the Gorbachev era in the Soviet Union, economic aid from Moscow no longer covers even basic needs. Especially keenly felt are limitations on Soviet oil exports." (*New York Times*, 26 March 1988, 1)

Mario Alagria, opposition economist

"I agree that the war and the embargo have had a big effect on the deterioration of the economy, but so has the maladministration of the state resources." (*Washington Post*, 8 January 1990, A19)

Senior administration officials (anonymous)

"The Soviet Union's economic and political pressure on the Sandinista[s] . . . was crucial to ensuring the free elections last February. . . . The Soviets . . . withheld military and economic aid to Managua in response to persistent U.S. pressure and in an effort to remove Central America as an obstacle to improved U.S.–Soviet relations. . . ." (*Washington Post*, 30 May 1990, A22)

Authors' Summary

Overall assessment

☐ Policy result, scaled from 1 (failed) to 4 (success)   4

☐ Sanctions contribution, scaled from 1 (none) to 4 (significant)   2

☐ Success score (policy result *times* sanctions contribution),
  scaled from 1 (outright failure) to 16 (significant success)   8

Political and economic variables

☐ Companion policies: J (covert), Q (quasi-military), or R (regular military)   J,Q

☐ International cooperation with sender, scaled from 1 (none) to 4 (significant)   1

☐ International assistance to target: A (if present)   A

☐ Sanctions period (years)	9
☐ Economic health and political stability of target, scaled from 1 (distressed) to 3 (strong)	2
☐ Presanction relations between sender and target, scaled from 1 (antagonistic) to 3 (cordial)	2
☐ Type of sanction: X (export), M (import), F (financial)	X,M,F
☐ Cost to sender, scaled from 1 (net gain) to 4 (major loss)	3

Comments

In addition to the desire for peace, the state of the Nicaraguan economy was a major factor in the elections that removed the Sandinistas from power in 1990. However, Nicaragua's economic collapse was caused primarily by the cost and disruption of the contra war; US economic sanctions, the effects of which were partially offset by assistance from the Soviet bloc and Western Europe, played only a minor role in the outcome.

Bibliography

Agency for International Development. *Overseas Loans and Grants*. Various issues.

Anderson, Thomas P. 1982. *Politics in Central America*. New York: Praeger.

Fauriol, Georges A. "The Shadow of Latin American Affairs." 69 *Foreign Affairs:* 116–34.

Harrison, Glennon J. 1987. *The U.S. Trade Embargo against Nicaragua after Two-and-a-Half Years*. CRS Report for Congress 87–870E, 30 October. Washington.

International Monetary Fund. *Direction of Trade Statistics*. Various issues.

Keesing's. 1981. Hayes, Margaret Daly. 1989. "The U.S. and Latin America: A Lost Decade?" 68 *Foreign Affairs:* 180–98.

Krauss, Clifford. 1987. "Revolution in Central America." 65 *Foreign Affairs:* 564–81.

Organization for Economic Cooperation and Development. *Geographical Distribution of Financial Flows to Developing Countries*. Various issues.

Robinson, Linda. 1988. "Peace in Central America." 66 *Foreign Affairs:* 591–613.

The Tower Commission Report. 1987. New York: Bantam Books, Inc., and Times Books, Inc.

US Senate Committee on Foreign Relations, Subcommittee on Inter-American Affairs. 1983. *US Policy toward Nicaragua and Central America*. Statement by Assistant Secretary of State Thomas O. Enders. 98 Cong., 1 sess., 12 April. Washington.

CASE 81-2

US v. Poland

(1981–87: Martial Law)

Chronology of Key Events

See also Case 81–3 US v. USSR (1981–82: Poland)

September 1981	Poland's Solidarity trade union holds national convention, calls for free elections; leader Lech Walesa is criticized as too moderate. (Simes 52)
October 1981	General Wojciech Jaruzelski replaces Stanislaw Kania as first secretary of the Central Committee of the Communist Party. (Simes 52)
October– November 1981	Wildcat strikes spread to 28 of 49 provinces; millions of Poles stage one-hour strike 28 October. (Adam 732–33)
2 December 1981	Military crushes cadet strike at firefighters' academy in Warsaw. (Simes 52)
13 December 1981	Martial law is declared in Poland. Solidarity leaders, including Walesa, are subsequently arrested. (*New York Times,* 14 December 1981, A1)
23 December 1981	President Ronald Reagan announces sanctions against Poland: administration cancels US Export-Import Bank credit insurance; suspends Polish airline (LOT) landing rights; suspends Polish fishing rights in US waters; requests allies to restrict sales of high-technology goods to Poland. Reagan says that if Polish authorities will ease repression, US will help rebuild Polish economy. Poland suspends principal, interest payments on debt to foreign governments. (*Wall Street Journal,* 24 December 1981, 1; *Washington Post,* 24 December 1981, A1; *Financial Times* [London], 2 March 1983, 1)
29 December 1981	US extends sanctions to USSR. (*Washington Post,* 30 December 1981, A1)
January– February 1982	US government pays $71 million guaranteed loan owed by Poland rather than declare Poland in default. House of Representatives rejects proposal that would force administration to declare Poland in default. (*New York Times,* 3 February 1982, A1; *Washington Post,* 10 February 1982, A18)

Summer–fall 1982	In early July, Western bankers, Polish officials meet to discuss debt rescheduling. Poland faces $7 billion in principal, $3 billion in interest payments due in 1982, with prospect of no new credits, few hard-currency exports. Western governments, however, led by US, refuse to discuss rescheduling. On 14 September, Western banks agree to allow Poland to postpone payment of two-thirds of $1.1 billion in interest due. Meanwhile, US blocks Polish application to join International Monetary Fund (IMF). (*Financial Times*, 9 July 1982, 18; *New York Times*, 15 September 1982, D1; *Washington Post*, 22 May 1983, A13; 30 September 1983, A30)
8 October 1982	Polish parliament outlaws Solidarity. (*New York Times*, 9 October 1982, A1)
9 October 1982	Reagan announces intention to suspend Poland's most-favored-nation (MFN) status, granted 22 years earlier, citing Poland's failure to increase imports by 7 percent per year as promised upon accession to General Agreement on Tariffs and Trade (GATT). Reagan later submits proposal to Congress for approval. (*New York Times*, 10 October 1982, A1; *Congressional Quarterly*, 16 October 1982, 2693)
Mid-November 1982	Lech Walesa is freed. (*New York Times*, 15 November 1982, A1)
Late November– early December 1982	Rumors circulate that Jaruzelski will lift martial law on first anniversary of its imposition. Reagan says that if regime takes "genuine liberalizing actions," US will respond accordingly. (*Washington Post*, 11 December 1982, A1)
30 December 1982	Jaruzelski suspends some martial law regulations but replaces many of them with new, harsher laws. Western governments accordingly refuse to reschedule debt. West German bank official remarks: "There is a perception among Western governments that Poland has institutionalized martial law. The Poles will have to do something to change this perception before we will get much help from governments." (*Wall Street Journal*, 30 December 1982, 9)
10 January 1983	"Although the internment of political dissidents was formally ended December 30 with the suspension of the basic provisions of martial law, the authorities are still arresting underground Solidarity activists." (*New York Times*, 10 January 1983, A1)
21 January 1983	Poland attempts to change terms of membership in GATT in order to undermine legal arguments offered by US in revocation of MFN status. Poland explores possibility of replacing its 7 percent per year import growth commitment with cap on tariffs, as most other GATT participants have done. (*Wall Street Journal*, 21 January 1983, 26)
May 1983	US Assistant Secretary of State Richard R. Burt explores with US allies in Europe possible ways to lift sanctions gradually, with each step conditioned on reciprocal steps by Polish government. (*Washington Post*, 22 May 1983, A13)

June 1983	Pope John Paul II visits Poland, admonishes leadership, sees Walesa. (*Washington Post*, 24 June 1983, A1)
21 July 1983	Poland ends 19 months of martial law, proclaims partial amnesty for political prisoners. In response, Reagan comments, "We're going to go by deeds, not words." US State Department spokesman elaborates: "In particular we will be focusing on whether the vast majority of political prisoners are being released." (*Washington Post*, 22 July 1983, A1)
29 July 1983	US agrees with Western allies to resume talks with Poland on rescheduling foreign debt. (*Washington Post*, 30 July 1983, A1)
18 August 1983	Poland reaches agreement with several international banks to reschedule 1983 commercial debt service of $1.5 billion in principal, $1.1 billion in interest. Terms provide five-year grace period on principal, new trade credits for 65 percent of 1983 interest due ($715 million). (*Wall Street Journal*, 19 August 1983, 1)
3 November 1983	In response to "very modest improvement in the human rights situation" in Poland, Reagan administration relaxes restrictions on Polish fishing in US waters (with no practical effect until 1984), indicates willingness to discuss debt rescheduling. Poland denounces these "two limited steps" as "illusory." US ban on LOT landing rights, restrictions on high-technology sales, freeze on new credits, denial of MFN status, veto on IMF membership all remain in place. (*New York Times*, 4 November 1983, A3)
5 December 1983	Walesa calls for end to Western sanctions because of pain economic crisis is causing Polish people. He repeats plea for reconciliation between government and people in Nobel Peace Prize acceptance speech delivered for him by colleague in Oslo. (*Washington Post*, 12 December 1983, A21)
20 January 1984	Reagan administration, in response to appeal from Walesa, lifts ban against Polish fishing in US waters, allows chartered LOT flights to US. Administration spokesmen cite Walesa's appeal, "positive developments" in Poland as reasons for actions. (*New York Times*, 20 January 1984, A1; *Washington Post*, 20 January 1984, A16; *Wall Street Journal*, 20 January 1984, 8)
21 July 1984	Polish parliament approves amnesty for almost all prisoners, including 652 political prisoners. US State Department calls freeing of prisoners "positive move." On 25 July, administration officials indicate willingness to lift remaining minor sanctions, with stiffer sanctions to remain in effect until implementation of amnesty can be studied. Polish spokesman Jerzy Urban criticizes reported steps as "comical" and "not serious." Polish leaders are reported to be most interested in having US veto on Polish membership in IMF withdrawn. (*Wall Street Journal*, 20 July 1984, 25; 23 July 1984, 21; 24 July 1984, 38; *Financial Times*, 24 July 1984, 14; *Washington Post*, 25 July 1984, A22; *New York Times*, 25 July 1984, A11)

3 August 1984	Reagan lifts ban on regular LOT flights to US and on scientific, cultural exchanges, pledges to lift other sanctions if there is "further significant movement toward national reconciliation." Reagan says he will "withdraw the US objection" to Poland's application for membership in IMF upon "complete and reasonable" implementation of amnesty decree. "Complete" is defined as meaning release of all 652 political prisoners, including 11 top Solidarity, KOR (Workers' Defense Committee) leaders. So far 518 have been freed, but many prominent members remain in jail. " 'Reasonable' was said to mean that there would not be rearrests or other steps that would undercut the sincerity of the amnesty." Poland identifies sanctions lifted as "less significant" ones, calls for unconditional lifting of all those remaining. (*Washington Post*, 4 August 1984, A1)
December 1984	Final two jailed Solidarity activists are released. US lifts objection to Polish reentry into IMF. (*New York Times*, 15 December 1984, A1)
January 1985	Following approval of Poland's economic and financial plans, 17 Western governments agree to reschedule $10.5 billion of Poland's debt. US officials estimate that $1.4 billion is owed to US. (*Wall Street Journal*, 17 January 1985, 31)
September 1986	As part of broader amnesty, Interior Minister General Czeslaw Kiszczak announces that all remaining political prisoners, 225 by government's count, will be released. (*Facts on File*, 17 October 1986)
January 1987	US Deputy Undersecretary of State John C. Whitehead, highest-ranking US official to go to Poland since 1981, meets with Polish Prime Minister Zbigniew Messner, Jaruzelski to discuss possible withdrawal of remaining sanctions. Polish leaders refuse to normalize relations until remaining sanctions are lifted. Whitehead also meets with Walesa, who encourages US to lift sanctions. At about same time, Pope John Paul II and Jozef Cardinal Glemp, Roman Catholic Primate of Poland, urge US to lift sanctions. (*Facts on File*, 6 February 1987; *New York Times*, 13 February 1987, A7)
19 February 1987	President Reagan restores MFN status, Poland's eligibility for trade credits, commending Polish government for its progress on human rights, national reconciliation. Reagan cautions, however, that "We will be watching to see that further steps are taken toward national reconciliation in Poland, and that the progress made is not reversed." (*New York Times*, 20 February 1987, A1)
7 April 1989	Polish parliament approves new laws amending constitution to create office of president; restoring upper house of parliament, whose members are to be freely elected in June; legalizing Solidarity. Under agreement negotiated with opposition, new legislation allows two-thirds of seats in lower house to be reserved for Communists, their allies. (*New York Times*, 8 April 1989, 1, 4)

17 April 1989   President George Bush proposes package of economic assistance measures to support Poland's reforms, including seeking Generalized System of Preferences status for Poland; authorizing Overseas Private Investment Corporation to operate in Poland; encouraging debt-equity swaps to encourage private investment and participation in "environmental, educational or other humanitarian projects"; willingness to consider significant rescheduling of Poland's Paris Club debt; providing support for World Bank, IMF programs in Poland. (*Washington Post,* 13 April 1989, A45; *Journal of Commerce,* 17 May 1989, 1A)

Goals of Sender Country

23 December 1981

Reagan declares in Christmas address: "I want to state emphatically tonight that, if the outrages in Poland do not cease, we cannot and will not conduct 'business as usual' with the perpetrators and those who aid and abet them. . . . Make no mistake: their crime will cost them dearly in their future dealings with America and free peoples everywhere.
. . . I have urged [Jaruzelski] to free those in arbitrary detention, to lift martial law, and to restore the internationally recognized rights of the Polish people to free speech and association." (*Washington Post,* 24 December 1981, A1)

9 October 1982

Following ban on Solidarity, Reagan declares: "There can only be one path out of the current morass in Poland and that is for the military regime to stand up to its own statements of principle, even in the face of severe outside pressure from the Soviet Union, to lift martial law, release Lech Walesa and his colleagues now languishing in prison, and begin again the search for social peace through the arduous but real process of dialogue and reconciliation with the church and Solidarity." (*New York Times,* 10 October 1982, A16)

22 July 1984

State Department calls amnesty announcement "positive move," but indicates "that it wants Warsaw to take additional actions." Administration official suggests that "The White House also will have to consider the domestic political consequences of any decision regarding sanctions in light of the significant number of Polish-American voters and President Reagan's hard-line conservative constituency." (*Wall Street Journal,* 23 July 1984, 21)

3 August 1984

"A State Department official [unnamed at his request] said the opening of a 'genuine dialogue' with the Polish labor movement would be required for lifting of . . . broader sanctions [such as restoration of official credits and MFN status]. He added that the United States is not asking that the banned union, Solidarity, be reinstated. . . . [W]e face a real opportunity in Eastern Europe, including Poland, to open a new chapter at a time when there is 'an inability on the Soviet part to meet the economic needs' there and 'considerable tension' in Soviet–East European relations." (*Washington Post,* 4 August 1984, A1)

Response of Target Country

January 1982

Zbigniew Karcz, head of foreign department of finance ministry, speaking on Polish debt, suspension of rescheduling negotiations: "I am waiting for the normal situation with Western countries to be restored. Every week we wait is lost. It is not a secret that Poland will suffer most. I have said this many times during the talks in Paris. But Western countries will suffer also." (*New York Times,* 28 January 1982, D3)

3 February 1982

Polish government spokesman Urban: "We are not hiding the fact that sanctions hit us in a touchy spot." He, Agriculture Minister Jerzy Wojtecki declare planned reorientation of national priorities that would make Poland self-sufficient in agriculture, ending dependency on imported US corn for poultry industry. "Polish officials suggested today that the US sanctions were helping to strangle the livestock industry here and starve the country." (*Washington Post,* 4 February 1982, Al)

July 1982

"It is true that [sanctions] pressure was a factor behind General Jaruzelski's moves in early May to free some internees and partially to relax the curfew. But this liberalisation came to a dead halt when it became clear that the Polish people did not feel grateful but merely freer to express their feelings in street protests." (*Financial Times,* 9 July 1982, 18)

June 1983

Vice Premier Janusz Obodowski proposes that Western banks accept eight-year moratorium on principal and interest due on $25 billion debt. (*Washington Post,* 15 June 1983, A21)

12 July 1983

Polish government spokesman Urban states: "At an appropriate moment Poland will present the United States with a bill of the losses suffered by Poland as a result of the unilateral severance of [the 1970 bilateral economic] agreement, and we will demand an appropriate compensation at a proper time." In June 1983 Vice Premier Obodowski states that Western sanctions, particularly those imposed by US, have cost Poland $6 billion, not counting "rather considerable indirect losses." (*Washington Post,* 13 July 1983, A14)

July 1983

After lifting martial law, Jaruzelski states, "There are still governments that cherish illusions toward Poland. Recently they have tried the stick-and-carrot approach. It is ridiculous now. The stick proved too short and the carrot not fresh enough. . . . We are ready to normalize mutual relations, but any conditions are out of the question." (*New York Times,* 22 July 1983, A1)

21 July 1984

In speech to parliament, Jaruzelski "alluded to the period of Solidarity as one of chaos and warned his political opponents that 'anarchy' would never again reign in Poland. . . . [He] spoke disparagingly of the 'imperialist' US and its 'superpower arrogance.'

But he left open a window for improved political and economic relations with Washington and the West, saying: 'Poland doesn't want to be an isolated island.' " (*Wall Street Journal*, 23 July 1984, 21)

24 July 1984
Following reports of planned US response to amnesty, Urban calls American demands "dishonest," accuses Reagan administration of repeatedly "chang[ing] the conditions for ending the sanctions, ignoring developments here [in Poland] and aiming to weaken Poland's place in the world as part of a general anticommunist policy. . . . 'The dishonesty of the demands [is] becoming increasingly clear. The demands are being multiplied and modified and are increasingly unrelated to the situation in Poland. The United States knows that we will not change our political system in answer to its demands, so it doesn't really expect its demands to be fulfilled.' " (*Washington Post*, 25 July 1984, A22)

19 February 1987
Spokesman Miroslav Miernik calls lifting of remaining sanctions "major step," but adds that sanctions inflicted "a lot of damage [that] ought to be made up for." (*New York Times*, 20 February 1987, A1)

Attitude of Other Countries

North Atlantic Treaty Organization
On 11 January 1982, NATO foreign ministers meet in Brussels, condemn violation of human rights in Poland, call for Jaruzelski to take steps outlined by Reagan as conditions for lifting sanctions; they also decide to suspend future commercial credits except for food, delay negotiations on rescheduling Poland's debt to NATO governments, study possible long-term sanctions. (*Washington Post*, 12 January 1982, A1)

European Community
Communiqué from foreign ministers' meeting, 4 January 1982: "Other measures will be considered as the situation in Poland develops, in particular measures concerning credit and economic assistance to Poland, and measures concerning the Communities' commercial policy with regard to the USSR. In addition, the 10 will examine the question of further aid to Poland." (*Wall Street Journal*, 5 January 1982, 2)

On 11 October 1982, following Reagan's suspension of Poland's MFN status: "Irritation was reported from several European capitals yesterday that President Ronald Reagan had once again taken unilateral action without prior consultation with US allies." (*Financial Times*, 12 October 1982, 3)

West Germany
On 5 January 1982, Chancellor Helmut Schmidt, meeting with Reagan, "gave some support to the American moves in the Polish crisis but held out little hope that he would follow the US in imposing economic sanctions against the Soviet Union." (*Wall Street Journal*, 6 January 1982, 1)

Senior (unidentified) West German politician, commenting in September 1983: "The American approach to Poland still emphasizes punishment. Our approach is broader. We are neighbors. We must show the Polish people that we care for them but must also do what we can to prevent the awful day when Soviet tanks move in." (*Washington Post*, 30 September 1983, A30)

United Kingdom

In late February 1982, Prime Minister Margaret Thatcher announces movements of Polish, Soviet diplomats will be restricted, no new financial credits granted to Poland. British official states, "They are not really sanctions as such but a signal to the Polish and Soviet authorities of Allied disapproval. We believe this is just as strong a signal as the US measures." (*Washington Post*, 16 February 1982, A1)

Japan

Japan bans new government-sponsored credits to Poland, suspends negotiations on rescheduling debt, imposes travel restrictions on Polish diplomats. Chief Cabinet Secretary Kiichi Miyazawa says actions are taken because "unity and cooperation among Western countries are of utmost importance in coping with the Polish question." (*Washington Post*, 23 February 1982, A13)

Belgium

Belgium suspends negotiations on rescheduling of Polish debt, suspends scientific, technical accords with Poland. (*Washington Post*, 23 February 1982, A13)

Soviet Union

On 6 January 1982, USSR extends $3.4 billion credit to Poland to cover part of 1981 trade deficit, anticipated 1982 deficit; USSR continues to supply Poles with Soviet energy, raw materials. (*Washington Post*, 7 January 1982, A1)

In late October 1982, Western sources predict Soviet shipments of goods, raw materials to Poland will reach record levels in 1982—18 percent higher than in 1981. Wharton Econometrics report, however, says USSR has reduced aid, exports to Poland (latter by some 10 percent compared to 1981). (*Journal of Commerce*, 28 October 1982, 1A; *Wall Street Journal*, 9 November 1982, 39)

July 1984: "President Konstantin Chernenko seems to have carried on his predecessor's policy of allowing Poland some political as well as economic leeway in sorting out its problems. His despatch of Mr. Nikolai Tikhonov, the Soviet Prime Minister, to the amnesty ceremony said as much." (*Financial Times*, 24 July 1984, 14)

Economic Impact

Observed Economic Statistics

Credit Freeze

Total Polish external debt, end-1981, amounts to $29 billion, of which about $7.4 billion from US, West European, Japanese banks is not guaranteed by Western governments; another $8.5 billion in bank loans is guaranteed by Western governments. Of unguaranteed loans, about $1.2 billion is owed to US banks. In 1982 Poland owes $10 billion in current interest, principal payments to Western banks, governments. (*Washington Post*, 15 January 1982, A1; *New York Times*, 15 January 1982, D1)

"According to Wharton Econometric Forecasting Associates, for every dollar decline in Poland's bank loans [through default], its debt to governments increases by about 90 cents." (*Washington Post*, 30 September 1983, A30)

In early 1982, US denies Poland $740 million credit for purchase of US corn. Chicken accounts for 10 percent of each person's average consumption of 5.5 pounds of meat per month; poultry industry depends heavily on imported feed corn. As of February

1982, Poland is short 3 million to 3.5 million tons of grain, which could lead to loss of 350,000 tons of poultry. However, Western analysts estimate that about one-third of Polish grain shortfall reflects refusal of Polish farmers to sell to government. (*Washington Post*, 4 February 1982, A1)

In early 1982, debate over default rages in Western circles. Arguments in favor of declaring Poland in default on loans:

☐ Default "Would put the financial burden of the Polish economy where it belongs, on the Soviet Union's shoulders"

☐ Resulting drain on Soviet resources would force USSR to reduce military spending, foreign adventurism;

☐ Default would punish Polish martial law government.

Arguments against default declaration:

☐ US taxpayers would have to pick up $2.4 billion tab, including $1.9 billion in government-guaranteed credits, $500 million in tax write-off claims by commercial banks.

☐ Ripple effects of default would cause major lending crisis in Third World; some developing countries might also be forced to default as result.

☐ US would lose all influence over events in Poland.

☐ Default would force Poland deeper into Soviet orbit, discourage future liberalization. (*Wall Street Journal*, 26 February 1982, 34)

MFN Revocation

"While there are varying estimates of how much the US action is costing financially ailing Poland, Mr. Kaczurba said, 'It definitely goes into tens of millions of dollars a year, if it's going to last that long, for direct loss and potential losses.' " (*Wall Street Journal*, 21 January 1983, 26)

About two-thirds of Polish imports into US are manufactured goods that now will be subject to higher tariffs. Current tariffs on textile imports (19 percent of Polish exports to US) range from 5 percent to 40 percent; non–MFN rates are 10 percent to 60 percent. (*New York Times*, 10 October 1982, A1)

White House says Polish exports dropped from $427 million in 1979 to $250 million in 1985, estimates that renewal of MFN status could increase Polish exports from $100 million to $200 million a year. (*New York Times*, 20 February 1987, A1)

Poland: foreign trade, 1981–82 (millions of dollars except where noted)

	Exports			Imports (f.o.b.)		
Partner	1981	1982	1981–82 per-centage change	1981	1982	1981–82 per-centage change
US	329	220	−33	879	142	−84
West Germany	1,097	959	−13	903	736	−18
France	288	306	+6	614	431	−30
UK	396	400	+1	419	331	−21

Total nonsocialist countries	5,446	5,183	−5	5,959	4,020	−33

f.o.b. = free on board
Source: Vanous.

In 1982, Polish exports to USSR grow almost 30 percent over 1981 levels; imports fall more than 1 percent, mostly because of drop in machinery imports. "Net *real* inflow of resources to the Polish economy from the Soviet Union (in terms of 1981 prices) declined from 1,653 million rubles to a mere 270 million rubles." (Vanous 1)

Poland passes 1983 budget that adds $3 billion to overall Western debt; budget reflects plans for new short-term credits, rescheduling of entire $4 billion in principal due in 1983, postponement of repayment of more than $2 billion in interest. (*Wall Street Journal,* 30 December 1982, 9)

Poland estimates cost of sanctions at $12 billion to $13 billion, "a figure based largely on the impact on its economy of the cut off in Western government trade and food credits, but clearly much inflated by a failure to recognise that most of this credit would have dried up for 'economic' not 'political' reasons, anyway." (*Financial Times,* 24 July 1984, 14)

Solidarity adviser Jacek Kuron calls Polish government's estimates of sanctions' cost exaggerated, asserting, "Very simply, in determining the cost of sanctions, the Government is presenting the Americans with a bill for everything that has gone wrong with the economy dating back to the beginning of the collapse, which occurred three years before the sanctions were applied." (*New York Times,* 21 February 1987, A3)

Calculated Economic Impact (annual cost to target country)

Reduction in trade with US; welfare loss calculated at 40 percent of reduced trade flows.	$338 million
Increase in US import duties on Polish manufactured exports; welfare loss reflects estimated average 20 percent ad valorem tariff increase on two-thirds of total 1982 Polish exports to US.	29 million
Suspension of Commodity Credit Corporation (CCC) and Eximbank direct credits and guarantees; welfare loss estimated at 10 percent of value of credit line affected.	77 million
Offsets Interest paid by US government on Poland's CCC loans; welfare gain estimated at 40 percent of deferred payments.	($28 million)
Credits from USSR to cover 1981–82 trade deficits; welfare gain estimated at 5 percent of total transfers.	(170 million)
Total	$246 million

Relative Magnitudes

Gross indicators of Polish economy	
Polish GNP (1981)	$178 billion
Polish population (1981)	36 million
Annual effect of sanctions related to gross indicators	
Percentage of GNP	0.1
Per capita	$6.83
Polish trade with US as percentage of total trade	
Exports (1981)	3
Imports (1981)	5
Ratio of US GNP (1981: $2,938 billion) to Polish GNP	17

Assessment

Journal of Commerce

"The effectiveness of the sanctions depended largely on Comecon [Council for Mutual Economic Assistance] coming to the aid of one of its member states. US policy-makers expected that the Soviet Union, along with the other Eastern bloc nations, would be forced to stretch already limited resources to bail out the crippled Polish economy. These added economic burdens would, in turn, yield political advantages for the United States vis-á-vis the Soviet bloc. . . . Neither the Soviet Union nor the other Comecon countries are subsidizing the Polish economy. In fact, during the last 10 months, Polish exports to the Comecon countries have exceeded imports and its trade deficit with the Soviet Union has substantially decreased. . . . As is evident by these measures [intended to contain the economic crisis within Poland] the American sanctions have merely served to hasten the reintegration of the Polish economy into the Soviet system." (*Journal of Commerce*, 6 December 1982, 1A)

Dimitri K. Simes

"The marginal sanctions adopted by Reagan hardly suffice to influence Polish and Soviet policy concerning an interest as vital as the survival of communism in Poland." (Simes 63)

"Washington's casual use of marginal sanctions, which the West Europeans did not support and never were expected to support, succeeded only in communicating America's sense of frustration and impotence." (Simes 64)

Wall Street Journal

"Polish official sources and Western diplomats believe [Jaruzelski] was willing to take the bold action of freeing 652 political prisoners largely due to his desperate need for western capital to restructure and revive the economy. . . . Those in the US who have supported the sanctions are gloating that their policy is directly responsible for Poland's amnesty program. However, others argue that the policy has only distanced Poland from the West, and that domestic considerations ruled Warsaw's decision." (*Wall Street Journal*, 24 July 1984, 38)

Jan Vanous, Wharton Econometric Forecasting Associates

"I can't imagine the Soviets put them up to this [amnesty]. You can interpret this that the Poles didn't get what they were hoping to get from Moscow. Hence, the only hope they have is money from the West." (*Wall Street Journal,* 24 July 1984, 38)

Solidarity

Communiqué of 29 July 1984, released by Solidarity leaders Wladislaw Frasyniuk (freed under amnesty) and Zbigniew Bujak (then still underground): " 'Polish society, Solidarity militants, the Roman Catholic Church and the West' had pressured the country's Communist government into declaring [the] amnesty. . . . 'This measure, which could have marked an important step in Polish life, is aimed at serving the current interests of power.' . . . Solidarity in an illegal radio broadcast Monday [23 July] said that the government amnesty was a sham aimed at improving the country's international image." (*International Herald Tribune* [Paris], 1 August 1984, 1)

New York Times

"[S]anctions effectively registered American outrage at the grim 1981–82 events— crude Soviet pressures prior to the crackdown, mass detention of popular leaders, dragooning of a resisting European society. Sanctions were a measured response, symbolic and real, chastising the victors and sustaining the victims." (9 February 1987, A18)

"[T]he suggestion that the sanctions failed to achieve their aim is not fully convincing. Few Poles, inside or outside Government, would deny that the sanctions influenced the authorities to release political prisoners, liberalize economic management and ease political procedures." (15 February 1987, IV, 3)

Stanislaw S. Wasowski

"[The sanctions'] impact was a function of four considerations: direct economic damage to Poland's economy; strength of the political signal conveyed to Poland's population and the regime; Poland's ability to adjust to the sanctions by diminishing their incidence and circumventing them; and finally, performance of the Western side at the poker game of politics. The damage was of medium size but became greatly exaggerated by the government of [Poland]; the tactics struck back at them. The political signal conveyed was weakened by the lack of unity between the United States and Western Europe but strengthened by the favorable initial reception of sanctions by the Polish population. The ineptness of the Polish economic leadership and economic structure in adapting to the sanctions increased their significance. In playing the game, the US side adroitly started to ease the sanctions as the situation and the outlook among the Poles changed, the hand was played well and strongly at the beginning but the US game became somewhat limp later on." (Wasowski 181–82)

Authors' Summary

Overall assessment

- ☐ Policy result, scaled from 1 (failed) to 4 (success) — 3
- ☐ Sanctions contribution, scaled from 1 (none) to 4 (significant) — 3
- ☐ Success score (policy result *times* sanctions contribution), scaled from 1 (outright failure) to 16 (significant success) — 9

Political and economic variables

☐ Companion policies: J (covert), Q (quasi-military), or R (regular military) —
☐ International cooperation with sender, scaled from 1 (none) to 4 (significant) 3
☐ International assistance to target: A (if present) A
☐ Sanctions period (years) 6
☐ Economic health and political stability of target, scaled from
   1 (distressed) to 3 (strong) 1
☐ Presanction relations between sender and target, scaled from
   1 (antagonistic) to 3 (cordial) 2
☐ Type of sanction: X (export), M (import), F (financial) X,M,F
☐ Cost to sender, scaled from 1 (net gain) to 4 (major loss) 2

Comments

Although domestic economic and political factors were undoubtedly uppermost in Jaruzelski's mind at all times, the Western sanctions seem to have been a concern as well. The angry reaction by Polish spokesmen, both in November 1983 and in July and August 1984, to the limited steps taken by the Reagan administration in response to liberalizing measures in Poland indicates that lifting the sanctions was one objective of Polish policy. Thus, the sanctions seem to have made a modest contribution to a positive outcome. The 1989 reforms were undertaken after all sanctions had been lifted, were primarily a response to the deteriorating economic situation within the country, and were possible because of more tolerant policies in the Soviet Union under President Mikhail Gorbachev.

Bibliography

Adam, Elaine P. 1982. "Chronology 1981." 60 *Foreign Affairs* 3 (Spring): 719–52.

Simes, Dimitri K. 1982. "Clash over Poland." 46 *Foreign Policy* (Spring): 49–66.

Vanous, Jan. 1983. "Polish Foreign Trade Performance in 1982." Washington: Wharton Econometric Forecasting Associates, 29 April.

Wasowski, Stanislaw S. 1986. "U.S. Sanctions Against Poland." 9 *The Washington Quarterly* (Spring): 167–84.

Woolcock, Stephen. 1982. *Western Policies on East-West Trade*. Chatham House Papers no. 15. London: Royal Institute of International Affairs.

CASE 81-3

US v. USSR

(1981–82: Poland)

Chronology of Key Events

Also see Case 81–2 US v. Poland (1981–84: Martial Law)

12 December 1980	NATO ministers issue communiqué warning Soviets that "Any intervention [in Poland] would fundamentally alter the entire situation. The Allies would be compelled to react in the manner which the gravity of this development would require." (Marantz 131)
24 April 1981	President Ronald Reagan lifts grain embargo imposed by President Jimmy Carter in retaliation for USSR invasion of Afghanistan. (*New York Times*, 25 April 1981, A1)
Late July 1981	At Ottawa summit, Reagan presses European, Japanese leaders for tighter restrictions by Coordinating Committee for Multilateral Export Controls (COCOM). He also urges reconsideration of Yamal pipeline deal in which Western European firms provide pipeline equipment in return for gas deliveries later. Europeans agree to review COCOM but refuse to drop pipeline. (*Journal of Commerce*, 21 January 1982, 2A)
24 July 1981	USSR, West Germany conclude outline agreement for financing pipeline. (*Business Week*, 10 August 1981, 36)
1 October 1981	US extends existing grain agreement for one year, will allow USSR to buy up to 15 million metric tons (mmt) above 8 mmt allowed without consultation under old agreement. (*New York Times*, 2 October 1981, A1)
6 October 1981	Italy announces signing of agreement in principle to buy USSR natural gas, first firm commitment by Western European country. (*New York Times*, 19 October 1981, D8)
20 November 1981	West Germany, USSR sign agreement for delivery of gas, clearing way for pipeline to go forward. (*Washington Post*, 21 November 1981, A1)
13 December 1981	Martial law is declared in Poland; USSR rushes to nail down contracts for pipeline equipment. (*Washington Post*, 14 December 1981, A1)

23 December 1981	Reagan's Christmas address to nation announces sanctions against Poland. (*Washington Post,* 24 December 1981, A1)
29 December 1981	US sanctions imposed on USSR for role in declaration of martial law in Poland are characterized by US Secretary of State Alexander M. Haig, Jr., as "interim step that hardly exhausts the list of potential actions." Actions taken include suspension of Aeroflot flights; suspension of export licenses for high-technology items including oil, gas equipment; closing of Soviet Purchasing Commission office in New York; suspension of negotiations on new long-term grain agreement; suspension of new maritime agreement; allowing technical exchange agreements to lapse (energy, space in May; science, technology in July). (*Washington Post,* 30 December 1981, A1)
11 January 1982	NATO Council condemns Soviet interference in Poland, agrees to restrictions on activities of Soviet, Polish diplomats, reduction of scientific and technical exchanges with USSR. (*Department of State Bulletin,* February 1982, 19)
Early January 1982	US refuses to grant export licenses to General Electric Co. to ship $175 million worth of components for gas compressor turbines to be built for pipeline by Nuovo Pignone of Italy, AEG Telefunken of West Germany, John Brown Engineers, Ltd., of UK. (*New York Times,* 11 January 1982, A1)
23 January 1982	France concludes 25-year contract with USSR for 280 billion cubic feet of gas per year, one-third of France's gas imports. (*Washington Post,* 24 January 1982, A1)
28 January 1982	Italy reaches tentative agreement with USSR on price, volume of gas shipments. (*Wall Street Journal,* 29 January 1982, 33)
Early June 1982	Participants at Versailles economic summit discuss subsidized export credits to USSR. Reagan pressures Western Europe to charge market interest rates on such credits. Final summit communiqué calls for "prudent and diversified economic approach to the Soviet bloc and to take into account a need for 'commercial prudence' in limiting export credits to the Soviet Union and its allies." However, "conflicting statements from US and European officials in the week following the summit indicated that the communiqué did not reflect a consensus on the subject of export credits." (Moyer 81)
18 June 1982	Reportedly in response to reluctance of West European allies, particularly France, to limit export credits to Soviet bloc, US extends ban on sale of oil, gas equipment to foreign subsidiaries of US companies and foreign companies producing equipment under US license, effective 22 June. (*Washington Post,* 19 June 1982, A1)
Late June 1982	"European governments promptly denounced the extraterritorial extension of U.S. regulation as violative of their sovereignty, contrary to international law, inconsistent with the understandings purportedly reached at the Versailles Summit, and insensitive to their commercial interests." (Moyer 81–82)

22 July 1982	France orders French companies to honor their contracts and supply equipment for pipeline despite Reagan's ban. (*Washington Post*, 23 July 1982, A1)
22 July 1982	OECD officials announce agreement on new arrangement for export credits. Included is reclassification of USSR, other Eastern European countries from intermediate to "relatively rich" category, which increases minimum allowable interest rate on credits to USSR from 10.5 percent to a range of 12.15 percent to 12.40 percent. (*Keesing's* 31639)
25 July 1982	Italy announces "signed agreements will be honored" but stops short of ordering its companies to fulfill contracts associated with pipeline. (*Wall Street Journal*, 26 July 1982, 21)
26 July 1982	Belgium postpones signing of contract with USSR for gas. (*Financial Times* [London], 27 July 1982, 4)
28 July 1982	UK announces it will not order British companies to defy US sanctions but that British government will defend firms from US retaliation if they choose to go ahead with pipeline deals. (*Washington Post*, 29 July 1982, A30)
30 July 1982	Reagan announces one-year extension of grain agreement with USSR but refuses to negotiate new long-term agreement because the Soviet Union "should not be afforded the additional security of a new long-term grain agreement as long as repression continues in Poland." (*Department of State Bulletin*, October 1982, 40–41)
2 August 1982	UK reverses policy, orders British companies to fulfill contracts for pipeline equipment. Trade Secretary Lord Cockfield invokes Protection of Trading Interests Act in issuing the order. In preelection speech to National Corn Growers Association, Reagan says Russians can buy as much grain as they want if they pay cash. (*Washington Post*, 3 August 1982, A4, A11)
11 August 1982	House Foreign Affairs Committee votes 22 to 12 to rescind administration's pipeline sanctions. (*Washington Post*, 12 August 1982, A1)
23 August 1982	France orders Dresser-France to deliver 21 pipeline booster compressors already on order. Dresser Industries orders its French subsidiary to comply with French order, files suit in US federal court to block implementation of US penalties for violating sanctions. (*Wall Street Journal*, 26 August 1982, 4; *New York Times*, 24 August 1982, D1)
25 August 1982	West Germany informs its firms that US sanctions are illegal under international law, violate German sovereignty. (*Washington Post*, 26 August 1982, A1)
26 August 1982	Three compressors leave French port of Le Havre bound for USSR. US bans Dresser-France, Creusot-Loire from importing any US goods, services, or technology until further notice. (*Financial Times*, 27 August 1982, 14)

27 August 1982	Senior administration officials say sanctions could be lifted "if other means could be found to keep equivalent economic pressure on Moscow." Goal still is said to be end to repression in Poland; desired means are said to include limiting export credits; tightening technology transfer controls; withholding exports of other oil, gas technology and equipment; canceling second strand of gas pipeline. (*New York Times*, 28 August 1982, A1)
1 September 1982	US Treasury Secretary Donald T. Regan announces sanctions on French firms will be lessened to restrict only imports of US oil, gas equipment. (*New York Times*, 2 September 1982, A1)
6 September 1982	US imposes sanctions on Nuovo Pignone of Italy for shipping three pipeline turbines with US parts to USSR. (*Wall Street Journal*, 7 September 1982, 3)
10 September 1982	US imposes sanctions against John Brown Engineers, Ltd. (*Wall Street Journal*, 10 September 1982, 5)
16 September 1982	European nations say it is US responsibility to resolve dispute caused by its unilateral action. (*Financial Times*, 16 September 1982, 3)
5 October 1982	US imposes sanctions against AEG-Kanis and Mannesmann of Germany for shipping two turbines for pipeline to USSR. AEG-Kanis announces it is not certain it will fulfill rest of its contract for pipeline turbines. (*Washington Post*, 6 October 1982, A20; 7 October 1982, A37)
15 October 1982	Reagan says USSR can buy up to 23 mmt of grain in 1982, guarantees contract sanctity if orders are placed before 30 November; USSR does not oblige. (*Weekly Compilation of Presidential Documents*, 18 October 1982; *Financial Times*, 20 October 1982, 19)
16 October 1982	Administration officials announce they have provided British, French, Italian, West German officials with draft proposal that could lead to lifting of sanctions. (*New York Times*, 17 October 1982, A1)
18 October 1982	Reagan publicly states willingness to consider lifting sanctions. (*Wall Street Journal*, 19 October 1982, 3)
11 November 1982	Leonid Brezhnev, Soviet president and Communist party general secretary, dies. (*New York Times*, 12 November 1982, A1)
13 November 1982	Reagan announces lifting of sanctions, saying US, West European allies have reached "substantial agreement" on overall economic strategy with East. France immediately announces it is not party to agreement. Reagan's announcement pertains only to restrictions on sales of oil, gas equipment, does not affect curbs on airlines or other sanctions imposed on Poland, USSR for martial law in Poland. Main elements of agreement are as follows: not to engage in trade agreements that "contribute to the military or strategic advantage of the USSR," particularly high-technology goods and oil, gas equipment; not to give preferential aid; not to sign new gas

agreements pending completion of study of alternative energy options by allies; to strengthen COCOM controls; to monitor financial relations with view to harmonizing credit policies. (*Congressional Quarterly*, 20 November 1982, 2883; *Department of State Bulletin*, January 1983, 28)

In practice, new policy means that validated export licenses will be required only for oil, gas exploration, production equipment, no longer for oil, gas transmission and refining equipment exported by domestic US companies, their overseas subsidiaries. In addition, all enforcement actions against these subsidiaries are dropped. (*New York Times*, 14 November 1982, A1; Moyer 83–85)

6 January 1983   USSR announces completion of 2,000-mile trunk gas pipeline linking Siberia with Ukraine, expects completion of Siberian–Western European pipeline by end of 1983. (*Journal of Commerce*, 6 January 1983, 1A)

11 January 1983   Reagan announces he will sign legislation "that substantially restricts the power of the president to limit grain sales abroad as an instrument of foreign policy." Under new legislation, restrictions will not affect "agricultural exports covered by contracts calling for delivery within 270 days of an embargo announcement." However, president still will have authority to restrict foreign grain sales in declared national emergencies. (*New York Times*, 12 January 1983, A1)

22 April 1983   Reagan lifts ban on negotiations for long-term grain agreement with Soviet Union; stated reason is "to reaffirm our reliability as a supplier of grain" to USSR. In July 1982, president said ban would continue "until the Soviet Union indicates that it is prepared to permit the process of reconciliation in Poland to go forward and demonstrates this desire with deeds and not just words." On 22 April 1983, Mark Palmer, acting assistant secretary of state for European affairs, states, "It's not linked to the situation in Poland. We continue to be deeply concerned about developments in Poland." US Trade Representative William Brock adds that ban on negotiations "simply had no validity as a tool in that capacity anymore . . . we believe this sanction has made its political point." (*New York Times*, 23 April 1983, A1)

8 May 1983   US, Europe, negotiating in context of International Energy Agency (IEA), agree on pledge to avoid "undue dependence" by Europe on Soviet energy. Agreement falls short of European commitment to abandon planned second strand of USSR–European gas pipeline. (*Wall Street Journal*, 9 May 1983, 37; *Washington Post*, 10 May 1983, A12)

20 August 1983   Following policy battle between Defense Secretary Caspar W. Weinberger on one side, Commerce Secretary Malcolm Baldrige and Secretary of State George P. Shultz on other, Reagan lifts export controls on sale of Caterpillar Tractor pipelayers to USSR. Controls were imposed in July 1978 by Carter, in response to jailing of dissidents Anatoly B. Shcharansky, Aleksandr Ginzburg, and continued by Reagan as part of pipeline embargo. While Commerce Department had approved licenses for sale of 200 pipelayers costing $90 million, USSR diverted its orders to Komatsu of Japan as long as vestigial US export controls remained in place. Lifting all controls is said to represent "a major policy shift by the administration because pipelayers have become the touchstone of East-West trade policy." (*New York Times*, 21 August 1983, A1; *Washington Post*, 20 August 1983, A1)

25 August 1983 US, USSR sign five-year grain agreement, raising minimum annual Soviet purchases from 6 mmt to 9 mmt and containing "no-export-control" clause. (*Washington Post*, 26 August 1983, A19)

January 1984 Fire reportedly destroys imported electronic equipment at pumping station at Urengoy in USSR, largest of 41 such stations on pipeline. Western sources estimate damage could delay Urengoy commissioning six months or more. Soviet sources previously claimed pipeline had been completed months ahead of schedule despite sanctions and that gas shipments to France through it had begun. One Western diplomatic source expresses skepticism that pipeline would be completed before 1985 or even 1986. (*New York Times*, 11 January 1984, A1)

Goals of Sender Country

29 December 1981

President Reagan: "The repression in Poland continues and President Brezhnev has responded in a manner which makes it clear the Soviet Union does not understand the seriousness of our concern and its obligations under the Helsinki Final Act and the UN Charter.

"By our actions we expect to put powerful doubts in the minds of the Soviet and Polish leaders about this continued repression. . . . The whole purpose of our actions is to speak for those who have been silenced and to help those who have been rendered helpless."

Secretary of State Haig: Sanctions are needed because "we just could not go on doing business as usual while freedom is being trampled in Poland." He lists US goals as lifting of martial law in Poland, freeing of Solidarity leaders, opening of dialogue with Solidarity. (*Washington Post*, 30 December 1981, A1)

31 January 1982

"One month after President Reagan announced economic sanctions against the Soviet Union for its 'heavy and direct responsibility for the repression in Poland' the administration is studying new steps that could delay if not block the completion of the largest single East-West project: the $25 billion natural gas pipeline from Western Siberia to Europe." (*Washington Post*, 31 January 1982, A1)

10 February 1982

It is believed that delaying or blocking the pipeline could significantly affect Soviet economy, which needs revenues from gas sales to replace hard currency lost from declines in oil exports as reserves are depleted. Pipeline also has raised concern because of potential leverage it could provide USSR over Western Europe if Soviet Union threatened to cut off gas supplies, or did so. (*New York Times*, 10 February 1982, D1)

18 June 1982

President Reagan, announcing extension of pipeline sanctions to US subsidiaries, licensees abroad: "The objective of the United States in imposing the sanctions has been and continues to be to advance reconciliation in Poland. Since December 30, 1981, little has changed concerning the situation in Poland; there has been no movement that would enable us to undertake positive reciprocal measures." (*Washington Post*, 19 June 1982, A1)

23 July 1982

Assistant Secretary of Commerce for Trade Administration Lawrence J. Brady: "There is little question that if the West exercises its collective will to enforce these sanctions, the entire Soviet bloc will find itself in very difficult straits throughout the rest of the decade." (*Washington Post*, 24 July 1982, A1)

30 July 1982

Under Secretary of State James L. Buckley: "Above all, we seek an end to the repression of the Polish people. The sanctions imposed against the sale of oil and gas equipment increase the internal costs to the Soviet Union of the project and cause an additional strain on already thinly stretched Soviet resources." *Department of State Bulletin*, September 1982, 38)

September 1982

US Trade Representative Brock: "We cannot continue to provide subsidized export credits to the Soviets which they can then use to strengthen their military capacity, further threaten us—because it forces us to respond, and it costs everybody in any number of ways." (*US News & World Report*, 13 September 1982, 27–29)

21 September 1982

Secretary of Defense Weinberger: "In recent weeks the evidence has been mounting that the Soviet Union may be using slave labor" to build pipeline. Weinberger concedes "the evidence is not conclusive" but is "profoundly troubling." He also reiterates administration's other fears: ". . . it is a little hard to see how trade of this kind, that has such an obvious military advantage in providing this much [hard currency earnings] most of which would go into military spending, can do anything but increase the danger to all of us." (*Washington Post*, 22 September 1982, A14)

27 September 1982

Secretary of State Shultz, in New York for opening of UN General Assembly, meets with French, West German representatives but avoids discussion of pipeline sanctions because of divisiveness of issue.

The previous week, "a senior administration official, speaking with reporters on background, [had] warned that unless the allies agree on measures even tougher than the US strategy on the pipeline, President Reagan intends to keep pursuing his current strategy." (*Washington Post*, 28 September 1982, A20)

13 November 1982

Reagan's radio address announcing lifting of sanctions: "The understanding we and our partners have reached and the actions we are taking reflect our mutual determination to overcome differences and strengthen our cohesion. I believe this new agreement is a victory for all the allies. It puts in place a much-needed policy in the economic area to complement our policies in the security area." (*New York Times*, 14 November 1982, A1)

Response of Target Country

19 November 1981

Vladimir Filanovsky, chief of oil and gas industry department of USSR state planning committee: "The USSR has never used its gas supplies as a lever to pressure its partners, nor is it going to. Also, it has always honored scrupulously its commitments." (*Journal of Commerce*, 20 November 1981, 1A)

30 December 1981

Tass: "The Soviet Union is a great power which has never allowed and will never allow anyone to speak to it in the language of blackmail and diktat. . . . [President Reagan is trying] to hurl the world back to the dark times of the cold war." (*Washington Post*, 31 December 1981, A1)

Mid-July 1982

From Soviet journal *Literaturnaya Gazeta*: "The master of the White House wanted to disrupt or slow down the construction of the gas pipeline but he achieved quite an opposite effect: the embargo only piqued the pride of the Soviet people and worked up the workers' enthusiasm. In this sense, Reagan's embargo has boomeranged against him." (*New York Times*, 20 July 1982, D1)

14 November 1982

Tass: The sanctions have failed. "By means of those measures, Washington unsuccessfully tried to frustrate the construction of the Siberian–Western European gas pipeline." (*Washington Post*, 15 November 1982, A15)

16 November 1982

USSR Minister of Foreign Trade Nikolai Patolichev says US–Soviet trade would increase only after Soviets have "regained complete confidence that agreements will not be broken. It is necessary for the US to renounce once and for all the doctrine of using trade as a weapon against our country." (*Financial Times*, 17 November 1982, 1)

Spring 1983

"In order to speed the completion of the export line the Ministry of Gas and Oil Construction seems likely to opt for its own Soviet built compressors rather than wait for the delivery of all the import compressor units ordered from Western European manufacturers." (*Financial Times*, 5 April 1983, 14)

Attitude of Other Countries

North Atlantic Treaty Organization and European Community

30 December 1981: In meetings of EC officials in London and NATO ambassadors in Brussels, allies are reluctant to follow US lead; they "agreed only to continue consultations at a special meeting of their foreign ministers in Brussels Monday." (*Washington Post*, 31 December 1981, A1)

Text of 11 January 1982 NATO Council declaration: "Recognizing that each of the Allies will act in accordance with its own situation and laws, they will examine measures which could involve arrangements regarding imports from the Soviet Union, maritime agreements, air service agreements, the size of Soviet commercial representation and the conditions surrounding export credits." (*Department of State Bulletin*, February 1982, 20)

January 1982: Allies pledge not to "undermine" US–imposed sanctions but do not commit themselves to any specific trade actions. Compliance is uncertain as West Germany goes ahead with sale of turbines for pipeline to USSR despite US ban on US components. (*Washington Post*, 15 January 1982, A1; Moyer 80)

12 August 1982: EC issues formal protest against pipeline sanctions, saying they violate both international, American law. Protest note also states, "The recent US measures provide the Soviets with a strong inducement to enlarge their own manufacturing capacity and to accelerate their own turbine and compressor developments, thus becoming independent of Western sources." (*Washington Post*, 13 August 1982, A12)

September 1982: "The Europeans have opposed the US tactics as interference in their internal affairs, as a contributor to unemployment at a time when their economies are in recession, and as an ineffective and potentially dangerous way to deal with Moscow." (*Washington Post*, 28 September 1982, A20)

November 1982: Sources say November agreement entails little in way of new commitments by allies, "with one apparent exception, an undertaking not to sign or approve new contracts for the purchase of Soviet natural gas while a series of studies are under way. The agreement covers areas where attempts have been made for years to coordinate Western policy." These sources say Europeans made no concessions, and elements announced by Reagan "represented studies rather than concessions to harder trade policies with the Soviet Union." Existing oil glut, they say, makes new gas contracts with Soviets a dead letter in any event. (*New York Times*, 14 November 1982, A1)

"All European sources concur that the 'substantial agreement' is so vague that 'it doesn't mean anything,' in the words of one German official, but most of the Europeans accepted it as a means for Reagan to get off a hook that was causing trouble at home as well as abroad." (*Journal of Commerce*, 29 December 1982, 1A)

Italy

29 December 1981: Prime Minister Giovanni Spadolini says his country is reconsidering participation in the Soviet gas pipeline deal. (*New York Times*, 30 December 1981, A6)

7 July 1982: Spadolini announces that Italy will fulfill its commitment to provide turbines (produced under license from General Electric) for pipeline despite US embargo. (*New York Times*, 8 July 1982, A1)

West Germany

29 December 1981: "Although the West Germans have not ruled out the theoretical possibility of participating in sanctions—they seemed relieved that the Reagan administration's first package of measures involving the Polish military regime was essentially mild—their attitude in the past about the use of such pressures has been both negative and contradictory." (*New York Times*, 30 December 1981, A6)

9 July 1982: Chancellor Helmut Schmidt: "We will stick to the agreements our firms made with the Soviet Union and so will France and Britain. . . . This will create some irritation in our relations with the United States but that will have to be overcome." (*Washington Post*, 10 July 1982, A24)

29 July 1982: Minister of Economics Otto Graf Lambsdorff: "The West Europeans are in agreement: the application of the principle of extraterritoriality in US government decisions is unacceptable to us. It violates our sovereignty. Therefore, we have to reject it . . . we have no differences of opinion on the events in Poland. The declaration of NATO in January 1982 was unanimous. But we do doubt that embargoes are an adequate answer. In my opinion, this applies to both the pipeline and the grain!" (*Washington Post*, 28 July 1982, A21)

Horst Kerlen, vice president of AEG-Kanis: "There is a doubt, a lack of trust, a feeling against the United States, that is the worst thing to come out of this affair. We have to be very cautious now about any new contracts that would bind us so totally to the United States." (*Journal of Commerce*, 29 December 1982, 1A)

United Kingdom

30 June 1982: UK Trade Ministry "issued an order under the Protection of Trading Interests Act of 1980, asserting that the US move was damaging to British trading interests. This enables Britain to take whatever legal steps are available to overturn the embargo." (*Washington Post*, 1 July 1982, A1)

UK Foreign Secretary Francis Pym, on 14 November 1982: "We now have a broad measure of agreement to guide the West's economic approach to the East. More work remains to be done but a good start has been made." (*Washington Post*, 14 November 1982, A9)

France

4 July 1982: "French President François Mitterrand, who feels he was duped by Reagan at the Versailles Summit into believing that such an extension of the pipeline equipment ban—already in force for American firms—would not take place, said publicly last week that Reagan had exhibited 'a grave lack of solidarity with his allies.' " (*Washington Post*, 4 July 1982, F1)

13 November 1982: Mitterrand says sanctions had been directed against allies rather than USSR and no concessions would be connected to their removal. France, however, is expected to accede to agreement later. (*New York Times*, 14 November 1982, A1)

14 November 1982: "It was the joining of the East-West trade agreement and the lifting of the sanctions in the same public announcement that left the French 'very disappointed, very surprised,' the sources said." (*Washington Post*, 15 November 1982, A15)

"True, after dinner at the Quai d'Orsay, Mr. Shultz and French Foreign Minister Claude Cheysson, both dressed in dinner jackets, sipping drinks, and speaking

English—a sign, I suppose of the Frenchman's extraordinary willingness to please—jointly briefed a few reporters. That hardly amounted to a joint statement, much less a formal agreement. . . .

". . . all future efforts to broaden the studies into a general economic strategy will be met by the French with at best delaying tactics—and at worst, with open opposition." (*New York Times*, 4 January 1983, A19)

Legal Notes

West German Minister of Economics Lambsdorff

"The West Europeans are in agreement: the application of the principle of extraterritoriality in US government decisions is unacceptable to us. It violates our sovereignty. Therefore, we have to reject it. This is the unanimous position in Bonn, London, Paris and Rome—despite the content and clauses in civil law contracts between European and US companies. Such private agreements, the concrete content of which still would have to be examined carefully, cannot and must not alter the legal basis of international relations between states. Above all, they must not retroactively block execution of contracts that were concluded between the European companies and the Soviet Union long before the events in Poland." (US Senate 1982b, 10)

Duane D. Morse and Joan S. Powers

"The novel question raised but not resolved in the pipeline controversy is whether the Act [EAA] authorizes the president to impose new restrictions on foreign use of commodities or technical data that have *previously* been exported from the United States and punish foreign nationals who refuse to observe these new restrictions. . . .

"The pipeline controversy marked the first time wholly foreign nationals faced the denial of export privileges for reexporting previously exported commodities or foreign-produced products of previously exported technical data to newly forbidden destinations. . . .

"Recognizing . . . the possibility that trade restrictions may prompt international resentment and retaliatory measures against the United States, Congress has confined the president's delegated power to apply export control restrictions to persons or property 'subject to the jurisdiction of the United States.' The pipeline controversy illustrates quite clearly the dangers of ignoring that limitation. Once goods and technical data have left U.S. shores and reached foreign hands, the United States must relinquish jurisdiction to regulate, at least absent a direct threat to our national security. That international and domestic furor that surrounded the United States' largely unsuccessful attempt to impede construction of the Soviet pipeline provides an important lesson as to the limits of U.S. regulatory power." (Morse 545, 553, 567)

Economic Impact

Observed Economic Statistics

Initial press reports indicate pipeline will be installed at expected capital cost of $10 billion to $15 billion; that total USSR hard currency earnings in 1981 from oil and gas were $17 billion; earnings from new gas flow could be as much as $6.5 billion. (*Washington Post*, 21 November 1981, A1; Hewett 15–18)

However, primarily because of estimates of declining demand, and secondarily because of warnings from US about dependence on Soviet energy, project is scaled back. Under agreements as signed, Soviets are committed to gradually increasing existing gas exports, if demanded by buyers, up to approximately 60 billion cubic meters (BCM) annually. USSR in 1983 is delivering 27 BCM of gas to Europe. "[West Germany] has signed a contract for 10.5 BCM, with an additional 0.7 BCM for West Berlin; France for 8 BCM; Austria for 1.5 BCM, with an option on an additional 1 BCM; and Switzerland for 0.36 BCM. There is a strong indication that Italy will eventually sign for 8 BCM; Belgium, the Netherlands, Spain and Greece may be interested in small volumes at some later date." (Stern 22; also see *The German Tribune* [Hamburg], 8 May 1983, 6)

Contract for new USSR gas has floor price, rising at 3 percent per year in real terms, to reach $5.70 per million BTU in 1990 (1981 dollars), plus base price indexed to oil prices. (*Wall Street Journal*, 15 March 1983, 26)

". . . only some 21 BCM have thus far been firmly contracted. . . . At a level of 21 BCM, Soviet hard currency earnings from Urengoy sales will amount to $3.8 billion per year in 1982 dollars, considerably less than the often quoted sum of $10 billion per year." (Stern 23; also see *New York Times*, 29 July 1983, D1)

"A total of 45,000 people now work on the 7.5 billion roubles (£6.8 billion) export line. So far they have laid over three-quarters of the 4,500km pipeline. The export line is but one of six being laid along the 'energy corridor' from Urengoi. Some 25 billion roubles (£22.7 billion) is being invested during the 1980–85 period on these pipelines which total 20,000 kilometres in length." (*Financial Times*, 5 April 1983, 14)

Imports account for about 30 percent of pipelaying machinery used on export line. Another $3.5 billion has been spent on imported pipe, turbines, ancillary equipment. (*Financial Times*, 5 April 1983, 14)

Under Secretary of State James Buckley: "US firms have lost at least $800 million worth of potential business with the Soviet Union. . . ." Press report cites US, West European, Japanese sources as saying US lost at least $1 billion in contracts related to pipeline. (*Department of State Bulletin*, September 1982, 38; *Journal of Commerce*, 16 September 1982, 1A)

Washington Post estimates loss to US companies, subsidiaries from sanctions at $2.2 billion. Under Secretary of Commerce Lionel H. Olmer says that $2.2 billion estimate covers three-year period, feels most of it could be recouped. (*Washington Post*, 14 November 1982, A1; *New York Times*, 15 November 1982, A10)

Wharton Econometrics estimates that, by importing 1 mmt of grain at cost of $160 million, USSR can free sufficient resources to produce 2.8 mmt of oil, worth $700 million on world market. (*Financial Times*, 20 October 1982, 19)

State Department estimates Soviets lost $122 million in exports of furs, diamonds, caviar, salmon, other products to EC because of their ban on imports of 56 Soviet products. (US House of Representatives 10)

Calculated Economic Impact (annual cost to target country)

Delay in construction of pipeline; welfare loss estimated at 15 percent of value of reduced gas production (assumes either deferred export earnings or diversion of domestic gas supplies to export sales).	$190 million
Increased construction cost of pipeline caused by unavailability of US equipment, technology; welfare loss estimated at 25 percent of value of canceled US purchases ($800 million).	200 million
Suspension of export licenses for oil, gas field equipment, high-technology exports; welfare loss estimated at 60 percent of reduced US exports ($150 million).	90 million
Total	$480 million

Relative Magnitudes

Gross indicators of USSR economy	
USSR GNP (1981)	$1,587 billion
USSR population (1981)	268 million
Annual effect of sanctions related to gross indicators	
Percentage of GNP	negl.
Per capita	$1.79
USSR trade with US as percentage of total trade	
Exports (1981)	0.3
Imports (1981)	3
Ratio of US GNP (1981: $2,958 billion) to USSR GNP	2

Assessment

Homer E. Moyer, Jr., and Linda A. Mabry

"The effects of the pipeline controls on the Soviet Union appear to have been negligible. Even advocates of the controls admitted that the sanctions would only cause approximately a two-year delay in the completion of the project. This projection assumed, of course, that the controls would remain in place. . . . The pipeline controls, in fact, remained in place only five months, and were generally disregarded by foreign subsidiaries of US companies under contract to supply pipeline equipment to the Soviets. As a result, it appears that the sanctions neither thwarted nor appreciably delayed construction of the Yamal pipeline." (Moyer 88–89)

". . . it is not too harsh to characterize the pipeline controls as perhaps the least effective and most costly controls in U.S. history." (Moyer 91)

Congressional Quarterly

"Reagan initially imposed the sanctions in December 1981 as a protest against Soviet pressure on the Communist government of Poland, which had imposed martial law and imprisoned leaders of the independent Solidarity trade union. But as it became increasingly clear that the sanctions were having no effect on Soviet behavior, Reagan shifted their focus to disrupting construction of a 2,600-mile natural gas pipeline from Siberia to Western Europe." (*Congressional Quarterly*, 20 November 1982, 2882)

"The reaction from US allies was less than enthusiastic. Although praising Reagan's decision to lift the sanctions, allied leaders made it clear that they had agreed only to study future limits on trade with the Soviet Union and had not committed themselves in advance to take specific actions." (*Congressional Quarterly*, 20 November 1982, 2883–84)

Paul Marantz

"Moscow was informed that should its troops be sent into Poland, the West would respond with a broad range of economic sanctions. Although little is known about Kremlin decision-making during the Polish crisis, it may well be that Soviet concern about the effect of an invasion on East-West economic relations was one of the factors that caused the Soviet leadership to temporize for so long and ultimately to choose a more indirect and less provocative means of crushing Solidarity." (Marantz 131)

"If anything Moscow was probably sorry to see US Secretary of State George Shultz succeed in negotiating a face-saving compromise that enabled the United States to abandon its ill-fated attempt to stop the pipeline. From the Soviet perspective, the minor economic inconvenience caused by having to shift to European suppliers was far outweighed by the political benefits resulting from the deep cleavage in the Western alliance that was provoked by American attempts to limit the activities of European companies." (Marantz 139)

". . . perhaps we should be thankful that the attempt to apply sanctions against Poland and the Soviet Union was anemic and half-hearted. Had Western nations moved more forcefully, in all likelihood they would have done more damage to their own economies and alliance structure, without in any way loosening the cruel repression that has been inflicted upon the Polish people." (Marantz 144)

"The unwillingness of the Europeans to impose stronger sanctions meant that the Soviet Union was made to pay only a minor economic penalty for its actions in Poland, a penalty which indeed was insufficient to alter Soviet conduct." (Marantz 136)

". . . rather than limit their exports which would directly affect employment in their own industries, they [the Europeans] curtailed imports from the Soviet Union. . . . The truly significant commodities such as oil, natural gas, and raw materials were never even considered for restrictions, and as a result, it was estimated that the measures adopted would affect no more than 1.5 percent of the $10 billion in goods that the nations of the EEC import annually from the Soviet Union." (Marantz 137)

Journal of Commerce

"While the measures may have slowed pipeline progress somewhat, they did not stop the project. They did cost American companies hundreds of millions of dollars. They also showed the world that the United States does not fully respect contracts and is prone to the use of trade sanctions as foreign policy weapons." (*Journal of Commerce*, 9 May 1983, 4A)

Gordon Crovitz

"President Reagan did not adequately emphasize the credits and hard currency issues and instead cited the Soviet role in Poland's martial law as the reason for the sanctions. Although in the end the sanctions were lifted without any firm agreement on future trade, it is doubtful that there would even now be any debate about East-West trade if the United States had not applied its temporary sanctions against the pipeline." (Crovitz 407)

Richard Pipes, former Soviet expert on National Security Council

"It is an open secret that the Reagan Administration is not of one mind on the issue of trade with the Communist bloc. . . . One school of thought, strongly represented in the Departments of Commerce and State, regards embargoes on energy equipment as not only futile but also counterproductive. . . . The other school, forcefully championed by the Department of Defense, views all commerce with the Communist bloc in the context of 'Grand Strategy.' It wishes to deny the Soviet Union the opportunity to earn additional hard currency from energy exports on the grounds that such money would be used to bolster Soviet military capabilities and to make Western Europe dependent on Soviet good-will. Rather than give up on embargoes as unenforceable, we should agree with our Allies on a coordinated policy of economic containment. . . . The Soviet Union is one giant war machine. . . . Thus, Western energy assistance helps the USSR to build up its military and to avoid shifts in budgetary allocations that now favor the military. . . ." (*New York Times*, 21 August 1983, F2)

Under Secretary of State for Economic Affairs Allen W. Wallis

". . . the Soviets completed the pipelaying phase of this project last year [1983], installed a small number of compressor sets, and have transported relatively small amounts of gas over the line. . . . However, we should recall that the Soviets originally planned to complete the project, including both laying the pipe and installing all associated compressor stations, by 1984. We now estimate that this task will not be finished until 1986. We believe that much of this delay can be attributed to our sanctions. Moreover, in evaluating the effectiveness of our sanctions, it is impossible for us to ascertain to what extent the Soviets have been forced to divert resources from other priority projects simply to meet this delayed target for pipeline completion." (US House of Representatives 6)

Authors' Summary

Overall assessment

- [ ] Policy result, scaled from 1 (failed) to 4 (success)　　　　　　　　　1
- [ ] Sanctions contribution, scaled from 1 (none) to 4 (significant)　　　　1
- [ ] Success score (policy result *times* sanctions contribution), scaled from 1 (outright failure) to 16 (significant success)　　　1

Political and economic variables

- [ ] Companion policies: J (covert), Q (quasi-military), or R (regular military)　—
- [ ] International cooperation with sender, scaled from 1 (none) to 4 (significant)　2
- [ ] International assistance to target: A (if present)　　　　　　　　　—
- [ ] Sanctions period (years)　　　　　　　　　　　　　　　　　　　1
- [ ] Economic health and political stability of target, scaled from 1 (distressed) to 3 (strong)　　　　　　　　　　　　　　　　3
- [ ] Presanction relations between sender and target, scaled from 1 (antagonistic) to 3 (cordial)　　　　　　　　　　　　　1

☐ Type of sanction: X (export), M (import), F (financial)   X

☐ Cost to sender, scaled from 1 (net gain) to 4 (major loss)   3

Bibliography

Crovitz, Gordon. 1982. "The Soviet Gas Pipeline: A Bad Idea Made Worse." 5 *World Economy* (December): 407–13.

Drabek, Zdenek. 1983. "The Impact of Technological Differences on East-West Trade." 119 *Weltwirtschaftliches Archiv*.: 630–48.

Hewett, Edward A. 1982. "The Pipeline Connection: Issues for the Alliance." *The Brookings Review* (Fall): 15–20.

Marantz, Paul. 1987. "Economic Sanctions in the Polish Crisis." In *The Utility of International Economic Sanctions*, ed. David Leyton-Brown. London: Croom Helm.

Morse, Duane D., and Joan S. Powers. 1983. "U.S. Export Controls & Foreign Entities: The Unanswered Questions of Pipeline Diplomacy." 23 *Virginia Journal of International Law*: 537–67.

Moyer, Homer E., Jr., and Linda A. Mabry. 1983. "Export Controls as Instruments of Foreign Policy: The History, Legal Issues, and Policy Lessons of Three Recent Cases." 15 *Law and Policy in International Business*: 1–171.

Stern, Jonathan P. 1982. "Specters and Pipe Dreams." 48 *Foreign Policy* (Fall): 21–36.

US House of Representatives. Committee on Foreign Affairs, Subcommittee on Europe and the Middle East. 1984. *Hearings on East-West Economic Issues: Sanctions Policy and the Formulation of International Economic Policy*. Statement by Under Secretary of State for Economic Affairs Allen W. Wallis. 98 Cong., 2 sess., 29 March. Washington.

US Senate. Committee on Foreign Relations, Subcommittee on International Economic Policy. 1982a. *Hearings on Economic Relations with the Soviet Union*. 97 Cong., 2 sess., 30 July, 12–13 August. Washington.

———. 1982b. Statement by Alexander B. Trowbridge, president, National Association of Manufacturers. 13 August. Washington.

CASE 85–1

US v. South Africa

(1985– : Apartheid)

Chronology of Key Events

See also Case 62–2 UN v. South Africa (1962– : Apartheid)

Spring 1981   Administration of President Ronald Reagan announces policy of "constructive engagement" with South Africa; State Department says it "represents above all the reality that there is a limit on the U.S. capacity to use negative pressure to achieve policy results in South Africa." New policy, formulated by Assistant Secretary of State for African Affairs Chester A. Crocker, includes relaxation of diplomatic, economic sanctions imposed under previous administrations, including allowing more South African honorary consuls in US, granting visas to South African rugby team, relaxing controls on nonlethal exports for South African military and police and on restrictions on exports of dual-use military equipment, technology. (*Washington Post,* 23 July 1986, A14; Baker 8–12)

May 1983   Rev. Leon Sullivan, who, following 1976 Soweto riots, proposed series of principles governing treatment of black employees by US corporations operating in South Africa, says principles are "beginning to work . . . but not getting the desired results quickly enough." He calls on US government to make compliance with Sullivan code mandatory, back it up with sanctions, such as tax penalties, loss of government contracts, against recalcitrant firms. (Sullivan)

September 1984   South Africa institutes new constitution under which Prime Minister P. W. Botha moves into even more powerful presidency; constitution establishes separate parliamentary chambers for Indian, "colored" representatives while still excluding blacks. New constitution sparks widespread protests, rioting in black townships, which continue sporadically for next two years. (*The Economist,* 30 March 1985, 27)

21 November 1984   Three prominent black Americans are arrested in front of South African embassy in Washington, thus initiating "Free South Africa Movement." By October 1986, when sanctions legislation is enacted, about 6,000 people have been arrested at embassy, South African consulates around US. (Baker 29; *Washington Post*, 25 July 1985)

12 December 1984 Of approximately 350 US companies operating in South Africa, 119 agree to expansion of Sullivan principles, committing themselves "to press for broad changes in South African society, including the repeal of all apartheid laws and policies." (*New York Times*, 13 December 1984, D1)

Late December 1984–early January 1985 Archbishop Desmond Tutu, on visit to Washington after accepting Nobel Peace Prize in Oslo, criticizes administration's "constructive engagement" policy, says US could end apartheid "tomorrow" by adopting get-tough policy. (*Washington Post*, 24 December 1984, C1; *International Herald Tribune*, 4 January 1985, 1)

7 January 1985 Coalition of six employer groups, claiming to represent 80 percent of South African workers, issues statement calling for significant changes in apartheid system: meaningful political participation for blacks; recognition of right of all groups to ownership of property, employment; universal citizenship; free, independent unions; equal justice; end to forced removal of people. Statement cautions that such changes can be made only in atmosphere of economic growth, thus opposes sanctions, disinvestment. (*Wall Street Journal*, 9 January 1985, 31)

15 April 1985 South Africa announces that it is abolishing Mixed Marriages Act, provisions of Immorality Act prohibiting sexual relations between races. (*Washington Post*, 17 April 1985, A1)

Mid-May 1985 Following imposition of complete trade embargo against Nicaragua, Crocker defends administration's opposition to sanctions against South Africa by arguing that "South Africa's economy is 30 times larger than Nicaragua's and much less vulnerable to the impact of sanctions. . . ." (*Washington Post*, 15 May 1985, A3)

21 May 1985 As part of South African effort to destabilize regime in Angola, South African commandos attempt to blow up oil storage tanks in Angola belonging to Gulf Oil Co. but are intercepted by Angolan soldiers. Incident increases support for sanctions in Congress. US Ambassador to South Africa Herman W. Nickel is recalled for consultations. (*Washington Post*, 10 June 1985, A1)

Summer–fall 1985 Blacks, who account for over half of all retail sales in South Africa, impose boycott on white-owned businesses in eastern Cape region. Some communities retaliate, while others attempt to negotiate with leaders of boycott. In October, one group of white businessmen sends delegation to Pretoria seeking to improve welfare of blacks in their area. (*Washington Post*, 27 July 1985, A1; 7 October 1985, A15)

20 July 1985 In response to ongoing protests, violence in townships, South Africa declares state of emergency in 35 selected areas. (Ovenden 82)

24–26 July 1985	France, protesting state of emergency, recalls its ambassador, bans new investment in or loans to South Africa, offers resolution in UN Security Council calling for voluntary sanctions against South Africa, including bans on new investment, imports of krugerrands, new contracts in nuclear energy sector, exports of computers for use by South African army or police. Resolution also calls for immediate lifting of state of emergency, unconditional release of all detainees, freeing of political prisoners, including African National Congress (ANC) leader Nelson Mandela, jailed since 1964. UK, US veto resolution backed by several African nations calling for mandatory sanctions against South Africa, but abstain on French resolution, allowing it to pass. Reagan administration for first time publicly calls on Botha government to lift state of emergency, release detainees, which now number more than 900. At least 16 blacks have been killed by police since state of emergency was declared, 500 since protests began in September. (*Washington Post,* 25, 26, 27 July 1985, A1; Lipton 19)
31 July 1985	House, Senate conferees agree on compromise bill that would impose sanctions similar to those called for in French UN resolution, would also ban all new bank loans to South African government, which most American banks voluntarily suspended seven years before. Legislation would also make observance of Sullivan principles mandatory for US companies with operations in South Africa employing more than 25 people. Citing economic, not political, reasons, Chase Manhattan Bank confirms that it has decided to stop lending to South Africa, will not renew maturing short-term loans, which reportedly total around $400 million. South Africa recalls its ambassador-designate to US, Herbert Beukes, for consultations; bans public funerals for victims of unrest, political statements at any funeral. (*Washington Post, New York Times,* 1 August 1985, A1; *Wall Street Journal,* 1 August 1985, 21; Ovenden 128)
15 August 1985	In speech expected to include announcement of significant new reforms, Botha takes hard line, saying he has "crossed the Rubicon" on road to reform, but that he will set pace, choose terms. Botha rules out significant political power-sharing, blames "barbaric communist agitators" for disturbances in South Africa. Value of rand drops 20 percent following speech. Botha's speech, in addition to increasing pressure on Reagan administration to take some action, also spurs reassessment of investment policies on part of number of major US colleges, universities. (Baker 32–33; *Washington Post,* 16 August 1985, A1; 23 September 1985, A22; Ovenden 82–83)
27 August 1985	South Africa arrests Rev. Allan Boesak, founder of United Democratic Front (UDF), largest legal anti-apartheid coalition in South Africa, just before he is to lead mass march on prison in which Mandela is being held. Concerns about continuing unrest, political instability in South Africa cause foreign banks to reduce lending, refuse to renew maturing short-term loans, causing plunge in value

of rand to record low 36 US cents. Of South Africa's total foreign debt of $17 billion, $11.5 billion will mature within coming year. South Africa closes foreign-exchange, stock markets until 2 September. (*Washington Post*, 28 August 1985, A1; *Financial Times* [London], 28 August 1985, 1)

28 August 1985 Central Bank Governor Gerhard de Kock leaves for Europe seeking assistance in dealing with financial crisis. Black mineworkers, union announces that it will strike at seven gold mines beginning 1 September. (*New York Times, Washington Post*, 29 August 1985, A1; *Washington Post*, 30 August 1985, A1)

29 August 1985 South Africa's four main business groups call on government to open negotiations with black leaders, asserting that any measures adopted to deal with economic crisis must include political changes to be effective. (*Financial Times*, 30 August 1985, 1)

1 September 1985 South Africa announces temporary "standstill" on repayments of commercial debt principal, including short-term interbank loans, sets up two-tiered exchange system for rand to discourage disinvestment. Finance Minister Barend du Plessis says South Africa will continue to service its debts; total interest on foreign loans is estimated to be no more than 6 percent of annual export earnings; hence meeting interest payments is not expected to be problem. (*Washington Post*, 3 September 1985, A1; 4 September 1985, A26; *Financial Times*, 2 September 1985, 1, 16; 3 September 1985, 1; 4 September 1985, 1)

5 September 1985 Responding to debt repayment moratorium, uncertainty over how it will be resolved, American banks refuse to extend short-term credits for US exports to South Africa. (*Washington Post*, 6 September 1985, A29)

9 September 1985 Reagan imposes limited economic sanctions by executive order in effort to head off embarrassing defeat in Congress, where House-approved compromise legislation has been stalled in Senate by Jesse Helms (R-NC) filibuster. Executive order bans exports of US–manufactured computer hardware, software to agencies that administer or enforce apartheid; exports of nuclear goods, technology; loans to South African government, except for educational, housing, or health facilities open to all races. Order also mandates compliance with Sullivan principles as called for in congressional legislation. Unlike congressional measure, order does not immediately ban importation of krugerrands, instead calling for discussions of possible legal problems of krugerrand ban under General Agreement on Tariffs and Trade (GATT), nor does it mandate additional sanctions if "significant progress" toward ending apartheid is not made in 12 months. (*Washington Post*, 10 September 1985, A1)

10 September 1985 Eleven of 12 EC nations agree on package of limited sanctions, including tighter enforcement of arms embargo, ban on all nuclear, military cooperation with South Africa; UK withholds approval

pending assessment of sanctions' impact. UK also objects to recall of military attachés, "discouraging" of cultural, scientific exchanges. In Basel, Switzerland, central bankers meeting at Bank for International Settlements reportedly refuse to consider request from de Kock to put together official "rescue" package for South Africa. (*Washington Post,* 11 September 1985, A1, A20)

25 September 1985 UK agrees to adopt measures previously approved by other EC ministers, withdraws its defense attachés from British embassy in South Africa. (*Washington Post,* 26 September 1985, A33)

1 October 1985 Following consultations with major trading partners, none of whom object, Reagan imposes ban on import of krugerrands, effective 11 October. (*Washington Post,* 3 October 1985, A27)

20 October 1985 Commonwealth of Nations overcomes UK objections, adopt sanctions package similar to those adopted by US, EC. Commonwealth package also includes ban on government loans to South African government, threatens increased sanctions if progress on dismantling apartheid is not made within six months. Package falls short of Commonwealth's Third World members' call for immediate comprehensive, mandatory sanctions. (*Washington Post,* 21 October 1985, A16; 22 October 1985, A22; Lipton 16)

2 November 1985 South Africa bans all television, radio, photographic news coverage of unrest in the 38 designated emergency areas. "The decree also requires print reporters to obtain permission from local police before entering emergency areas, and authorizes the police to supervise their movements." (*Washington Post,* 3 November 1985, A1)

18 November 1985 One hundred eighty-six American companies operating in South Africa, all signatories of Sullivan principles, send telex to Botha urging him to do something to "lower tensions" in black school system. "It is the first time any group of foreign companies has intervened so directly with the government on a domestic political issue." (*Washington Post,* 19 November 1985, A1)

10 December 1985 Unable to reach mutually acceptable agreement with its creditors, South Africa announces that it is extending freeze on debt repayments until 31 March 1986. (*Washington Post,* 11 December 1985, A32)

31 January 1986 "[A]pparently as a gesture in the direction of the political reforms that the banks had indicated were a precondition for settlement," Botha gives speech announcing that pass laws controlling movement of blacks into "white" areas would be repealed 1 July. (Ovenden 89)

February 1986 Fritz Leutwiler, Swiss banker mediating between South Africa and its foreign creditors, meets with representatives of banks whose loans are caught in standstill "net"; they agree to interim settlement, until 30 June 1987, that includes "an increase of 1% in the interest payable, an immediate principal repayment of 5% on those debts originally maturing before the end of March 1986, a 5% percent principal repayment on the original maturity date of all other debt caught in the 'net'." (Ovenden 89)

4 March 1986   Botha lifts state of emergency. (*Washington Post,* 13 June 1986, A26)

19 May 1986   South African commandos strike alleged ANC "operational centers" in Zimbabwe, Botswana, Zambia. Botha attempts to justify attacks as legitimate response to terrorism, similar to recent US raid on Libya. Reagan administration lodges formal protest, recalls its military attaché from Pretoria, expels South Africa's military representative, but refuses to impose additional economic sanctions. (*Washington Post,* 20 May 1986, A1, A23; 21 May 1986, A1; Baker 42)

12 June 1986   To head off planned protests marking 10th anniversary of Soweto uprising, South Africa declares nationwide state of emergency. More than 1,000 persons are detained on first day of decree. Simultaneously, Eminent Persons Group, appointed by Commonwealth to mediate between South African government and ANC, reports that it has failed, claims that Botha "is not interested in negotiations at this point in time," calls on Western nations to impose widespread sanctions. Reagan administration criticizes South Africa's actions but reiterates its opposition to additional economic sanctions. (*New York Times,* 13 June 1986, A1, A12)

16 June 1986   In commencement address adapted for *New York Times,* Tutu rejects argument that foreign businesses help black cause by staying in South Africa, calls for international economic sanctions: "There is no guarantee that sanctions will topple apartheid, but it is the last nonviolent option left, and it is a risk with a chance. President Reagan's policy of constructive engagement . . . [has] failed dismally." (*New York Times,* 16 June 1986, A19; *Financial Times,* 16 June 1986)

18 June 1986   By voice vote, House approves, sends to Senate legislation imposing trade embargo against South Africa, requiring all US companies with operations there to disinvest within 180 days. US, UK veto UN Security Council resolution that would have imposed limited sanctions against South Africa. World Council of Churches reports that nearly 3,000 persons have been detained in week since state of emergency was declared. (*New York Times,* 19 June 1986, A1)

29 June 1986   Zulu Chief Gatsha Buthelezi denounces House sanctions bill, asserting blacks "want more jobs, not less jobs. They want more investment, not less investment." (*Washington Post,* 30 June 1986)

22 July 1986   In his first major speech devoted to South Africa, Reagan urges Congress, Western Europe to "resist this emotional clamor for punitive sanctions," criticizes state of emergency, but praises Botha regime for "dramatic change" in recent years. Moderate Senate Republicans criticize speech for offering no new initiatives, indicate their support for limited additional sanctions. One journalist writes that speech "seemed deliberately calculated to provoke the worst possible responses from all sides: it gave Pretoria comfort, black South Africa reason to despair, and Congress no choice." (*Washington Post,* 23 July 1986, A1; 28 July 1986, A17; Baker 44)

4 August 1986   Seven representatives of Commonwealth nations, meeting at "minisummit" in London, split over sanctions against South Africa, with Thatcher agreeing only to call for voluntary bans on new investment, promotion of tourism in South Africa. She also pledges not to block possible EC sanctions, including ban on new investment as well as on coal, iron, steel imports to be considered next month. Other six representatives agree to recommend additional immediate measures, including banning new bank loans to private as well as public borrowers, imports of agricultural goods, uranium, coal, iron and steel, air links. Proposed measures would also define reinvestment of retained earnings as new investment, thus bringing it under ban. (*Wall Street Journal,* 5 August 1986, 1; 6 August 1986, 21; *Washington Post, New York Times,* 5 August 1986, A1; Commonwealth Secretariat, app. 3, 3)

4 September 1986   In attempt to head off sanctions legislation, Reagan renews executive order authorizing limited sanctions for another year. A week later, Congress approves compromise sanctions legislation, anyway. (Baker 44–45)

16 September 1986   EC votes to ban imports of iron, steel, gold coins, new investment in South Africa; investment ban does not extend to reinvestment of retained earnings. Ban on coal imports, most significant of proposed sanctions, is blocked by West German, Portuguese opposition. (*Washington Post,* 17 September 1986, A1; Lipton 29)

17 September 1986   Coca-Cola Co., one of largest, most visible US companies remaining in South Africa, announces it will sell its operations there to multiracial group of investors as "statement of our opposition to apartheid." Company executives deny move was motivated by planned boycott of its products announced a week earlier by Southern Christian Leadership Conference. (*Washington Post,* 18 September 1986, A1)

19 September 1986   Following EC's lead, Japan bans imports of iron and steel, but not iron ore or coal. (*Washington Post,* 20 September 1986, A16)

26 September 1986   Reagan vetoes sanctions bill. California Governor George Deukmejian signs legislation requiring state to divest $11 billion in South African–related investments. (*New York Times,* 27 September 1986, A1)

2 October 1986   Senate overrides Reagan's veto of sanctions bill by vote of 78 to 21, following House vote to override earlier in week (313 to 83). Though falling well short of House-proposed sanctions, Comprehensive Anti-Apartheid Act (CAAA) substantially expands upon existing sanctions: it bans all loans to, new investment in South Africa (ban does not extend to letters of credit, loan rescheduling,

reinvestment of retained profits); bans imports of iron and steel, coal, uranium, textiles, agricultural products, goods produced by government-controlled firms (parastatals), except for strategic materials for the US military; transfers South Africa's sugar quota to Philippines; bans export of petroleum and products, weapons and munitions; severs air links; prohibits US banks from accepting South African government deposits (worth $329 million in March); prohibits government agencies from cooperation with South African military, promoting trade or tourism in South Africa. In addition, Act authorizes $40 million in aid for disadvantaged South Africans, $4 million a year in scholarship funds for victims of apartheid; calls on ANC to suspend "terrorist activities"; threatens to impose additional sanctions if "substantial progress" toward dismantling apartheid is not made within a year of enactment. Act also restricts US military assistance to countries that do not join UN arms embargo, provides for sanctions against countries that "benefit from or take commercial advantage of" limitations imposed on US business. CAAA also sets five conditions for lifting of sanctions (see *Goals of Sender Country*). (*Washington Post*, 3 October 1986, A1, A16; *New York Times*, 3 October 1986, A1; Hayes 2; Baker 44–45, app. D; Lipton 18, app. 6)

Fall 1986   "Flood" of companies announce withdrawal from South Africa (see *Observed Economic Statistics*). Anti-apartheid activitists, however, criticize licensing, other arrangements that allow parent companies to continue selling, servicing their products in South Africa. Barclays Bank, until recently largest British investor in South Africa, becomes first British firm to pull out, announcing that it will sell its 40 percent share in South Africa's second largest commercial bank, worth estimated $250 million. Student groups have been pressuring Barclays to withdraw; its share of student loan market has fallen to 17 percent from 28 percent in 1981. Barclays sells its interest for only $8.10 a share, far below market price of $14.58. (*Washington Post, New York Times,* 22 October 1986, A1; *Wall Street Journal,* 22 October 1986, 3; *Wall Street Journal,* 24 October 1986, 2; *Washington Post,* 25 November 1986, A1, A17; *The Economist,* 29 November 1986, 65; *Business Week,* 8 December 1986, 54)

9 December 1986   Rev. Sullivan announces that he will mount major divestment campaign, call for total economic embargo in June if significant progress in South Africa is not made by then. Sullivan says he has already received pledges of cooperation from pension funds, university and other investment funds with more than $60 billion in assets. (*Washington Post,* 10 December 1986, G1)

January 1987   Five major anti-apartheid groups issue guidelines for local governments with divestment laws on how to tighten them so as to prohibit types of licensing, franchise agreements signed by most US companies when pulling out of South Africa. Groups identify Kodak, which, when it withdrew in November, also prohibited its branches worldwide from selling its products to South Africa, as only company thus far to meet their criteria for severing all ties when disinvesting. Reagan administration grants exception to sanctions for South African uranium imported for reprocessing on behalf of third countries (e.g., Japan). (*Washington Post*, 20 November 1986, A1; *New York Times*, 9 February 1987, D1; Lipton 53, 65)

24 March 1987   With interim agreement due to expire in June, South Africa reaches three-year agreement with foreign creditor banks on rescheduling its debt. Under agreement, South Africa will continue to service all its debt, will continue to make principal payments on official debt (which were never frozen) as originally scheduled, and, by June 1990, will repay 13 percent of total principal of debt in standstill net. Agreement also contains two "exit" options, one that allows banks to convert "short-term claims frozen inside the net into repayable long-term debt," another that allows creditors to use claims to purchase equities in South Africa. News of agreement is interpreted in South Africa as indicating "a major shift in the perceptions and attitudes towards South Africa of some of the world's biggest and most influential banks" and as "taking the sting out of the most damaging sanction yet." (*Financial Times*, 25 March 1987, 1; Ovenden 91–93)

3 June 1987   Rev. Sullivan calls on 127 US companies that are signatories to his code to pull out of South Africa, urges Congress to penalize other countries replacing US business, urges administration to break diplomatic relations, impose complete economic embargo against South Africa until it ends apartheid. (*Washington Post*, 4 June 1987, E1)

9 August 1987   National Union of Mineworkers begins three-week strike, longest legal strike in South African history. (Baker 94)

October 1987   In report to Congress required by CAAA, Reagan says that sanctions have not contributed to achieving Act's goals, that he will not recommend additional sanctions. (Ovenden xiv; Baker 84)

December 1987   Congressman Charles B. Rangel (D-NY) successfully adds amendment to FY 1988 Deficit Reduction Finance Bill that denies foreign tax credits to US firms operating in South Africa. (Ovenden 51; Baker 62)

February–March 1988   South Africa "bans" all major nonwhite opposition groups, prohibits political activity by trade unions. Variety of new sanctions bills are introduced in Congress. (*Washington Post*, 23 March 1988, A1; *International Trade Reporter*, 30 March 1988, 473)

May 1988   US importers of strategic minerals increase purchases, stockpile to guard against possible retaliatory actions by South Africa if Congress passes tough sanctions bill. South Africa continues to reject retaliatory export embargoes, saying that it is opposed to sanctions, boycotts in principle. (*Washington Post*, 6 May 1988, A1)

11 August 1988   House, 244 to 132, approves sanctions legislation that would end all trade with South Africa except for imports of strategic minerals; require complete disinvestment; end military and intelligence cooperation; deny federal oil, gas, coal leases to international oil companies with investments in South Africa (primarily Royal Dutch–Shell, British Petroleum); prohibit US–owned or US–registered ships from transporting oil to South Africa; require retaliation against other countries undercutting US sanctions. Legislation does not come to vote in Senate, dies at end of session. (*Washington Post,* 12 August 1988, A1)

Early 1989   Newly elected President George Bush adopts more conciliatory attitude toward ANC, other black opponents to Botha regime. Within first six months of his administration he meets with Albertina Sisulu, wife of imprisoned ANC leader Walter Sisulu and co-president of banned UDF, Rev. Boesak, Archbishop Tutu. (*Financial Times,* 20 June 1989, 20; *Washington Post,* 19 July 1989, A16)

11 January 1989   Rev. Boesak credits sanctions with role in inducing South Africa to sign UN accord providing for withdrawal of Cuban troops in Angola, independence for Namibia. In calling for additional sanctions, Boesak says, "The pressure of sanctions forced them [South African government] to the negotiating table. If that is true for Namibia and Angola, it must also be true for South Africa." (*Washington Post,* 12 January 1989, A30)

26 April 1989   Mobil, largest remaining American employer in South Africa, cites Rangel amendment, which may have cost it $5 million in 1988, as one reason for its planned withdrawal from South Africa. Mobil reportedly will sell its assets there, said to be worth $400 million, for around $150 million. In June, Goodyear also cites Rangel amendment as one factor in its decision to withdraw. (*New York Times,* 27 April 1989, D1; 8 June 1989, D5; *Wall Street Journal,* 27 April 1989, A3)

Late May 1989   Central Bank Governor De Kock warns that economic stagnation threatens country if political reforms are not taken to head off additional sanctions, induce lifting of existing ones. (*Washington Post,* 2 June 1989, A28; *New York Times,* 4 June 1989, section 4, 2)

1 June 1989   Tutu, three other prominent church leaders urge international banks to exert financial pressure on South Africa to dismantle apartheid by refusing to reschedule its debts, refusing to extend trade credits. (*Washington Post,* 2 June 1989, A28)

July 1989   Mandela, still prisoner, meets with Botha in president's office in Cape Town. US General Accounting Office (GAO) releases report noting that failure to identify products associated with parastatals has inhibited enforcement of ban on imports from South African government agencies, state-owned companies identified by State Department. In particular, US Customs Service was generally unaware that gold bullion should fall under parastatal ban because mining companies sell gold to South Africa Reserve Bank, which then markets it internationally. Although US imports of gold bullion from South Africa fell to zero in 1987–88 from their 1986 level of $79 million, US imports of gold bullion from UK, Switzerland between January 1987, March 1989, were $175 million, $164 million, respectively. (*Washington Post,* 13 July 1989, A1; GAO 3)

Early August 1989	Bush refuses to meet with National Party leader F.W. de Klerk. Black activists in South Africa step up civil disobedience campaign in advance of September elections. (*Financial Times,* 1 August 1989, 4; 7 August 1989, 10; *Washington Post,* 8 August 1989, A18)
8 August 1989	Commonwealth foreign ministers meeting in Canberra, Australia, propose package of financial sanctions to be considered by Commonwealth heads of government at meeting in October. Measures recommended include official lobbying of banks to impose tough conditions on South Africa when its debt is rescheduled next year; tightened restrictions on new lending to South Africa; imposition of tougher terms for trade financing. (*Financial Times,* 9 August 1989, 1)
14 August 1989	Botha, who suffered mild stroke in January, resigns abruptly. In his resignation speech, he takes hard line against ANC, harshly criticizes expected successor de Klerk. (*Washington Post,* 15 August 1989, A12)
August–September 1989	Congress considers defining CAAA ban on new loans to include rescheduling of old ones. Treasury officials testify against such changes, arguing that they would encourage South Africa to default, which would help government rather than anti-apartheid cause. British anti-apartheid coalition launches campaign to pressure three British banks not to reschedule South Africa's debt; group also calls for tighter enforcement of existing oil, arms embargoes, as well as additional trade, financial sanctions. (*International Trade Reporter,* 9 August 1989, 1049; *Financial Times,* 2 September 1989, 3)
5–6 September 1989	Black opposition groups call for general strike to protest exclusion from elections. Acting President de Klerk, campaigning on platform of reform, negotiations, is elected to five-year term; his National Party wins majority in parliament, although by slimmest margin since party was founded. Seats are lost nearly equally to newly formed liberal Democratic Party, Conservative Party; de Klerk interprets results as mandate for pursuing his reformist platform. (*Financial Times,* 8 September 1989, 6)
13 September 1989	Largest legal protest march since 1959, involving over 20,000 people, takes place peacefully in Cape Town. (*Washington Post,* 14 September 1989, A1)
28 September 1989	Johannesburg lifts racial restrictions on public buses, swimming pools, recreation areas. (*Washington Post,* 29 September 1989, A1)
2–3 October 1989	President Bush sends annual CAAA report to Congress in which he concludes that sanctions "have not to date been successful," declines to impose additional measures. Testifying on report, Assistant Secretary of State for African Affairs Herman J. Cohen is a bit

more optimistic, saying that "sanctions have played a role in stimulating new thinking within the white power structure of South Africa." Cohen says administration would like to see some normalization of political life in South Africa, such as releasing political prisoners, unbanning political organizations, by end of year; he adds that administration would consider imposing additional sanctions if actions toward ending apartheid are not taken in next parliamentary session, to be held from February to June 1990. (*Washington Post,* 4 October 1989, A8)

15 October 1989   De Klerk announces Walter Sisulu, six colleagues will be released from prison on 15 October, phoned Margaret Thatcher directly to inform her. Move is "clearly [timed] in order to strengthen the anti-sanctions posture of. . . Thatcher" in advance of Commonwealth heads of state meeting beginning 11 October. (*Financial Times,* 12 October 1989, 15; *Washington Post,* 16 October 1989, A1)

18 October 1989   Preempting anti-apartheid activists' efforts to increase financial pressure, South Africa concludes three-and-a-half-year rescheduling agreement with its creditors several months before current agreement is due to expire. It is estimated that, with no new capital forthcoming, South Africa might be able to grow at rate of 3 percent to 4 percent per year, but with capital outflows called for in agreement, it will probably be able to manage no more than 2 percent a year. Anti-apartheid groups criticize banks for easing pressure on South Africa. (*Washington Post,* 19 October 1989, A45; 20 October 1989, A37; *Financial Times,* 20 October 1989, 4, 18)

22 October 1989   Commonwealth meeting ends with Britain isolated on issue of sanctions against South Africa. Although leaders at summit issue joint communiqué agreeing to maintain existing sanctions, threatening to impose additional measures if progress in dismantling apartheid is not made in six months, Thatcher undercuts joint statement by issuing her own that is critical of sanctions, calls for "positive and constructive steps" rather than "tightening [of] sanctions and the imposition of new punitive measures. . . ." (*Financial Times,* 23 October 1989, 2; *Washington Post,* 25 October 1989, A38)

16 November 1989   De Klerk orders immediate opening of whites-only beaches to blacks, announces his intention to repeal Separate Amenities Act, which enforces system of "petty" apartheid measures (much of which has already eroded), as soon as possible after parliament convenes in February. (*Washington Post,* 17 November 1989, A1)

24 January 1990   Assistant Secretary of State Cohen meets with de Klerk, tells him that, if conditions set out in CAAA are met, "the administration will immediately consult with Congress with a view toward suspending or modifying sanctions." (*Washington Post,* 25 January 1990, A29)

2 February 1990   In speech opening parliament, de Klerk promises to release Mandela as soon as possible; suspends death penalty; unbans ANC, Pan Africanist Congress, South African Communist Party, 33 other opposition organizations; releases some political prisoners, although not those imprisoned for violent offenses (Human Rights Commission in South Africa estimates that only one-fourth of 2,500 convicted political prisoners serving sentences will be eligible for release); repeals parts of Emergency Regulations, but does not lift state of emergency completely; lifts all restriction orders on individuals; limits duration of detentions under Emergency Regulations. (*Washington Post, New York Times,* 3 February 1990, A1)

11 February 1990 Mandela is released without conditions, asks international community to keep pressure on South Africa: "To lift sanctions now would be to run the risk of aborting the process toward ending apartheid." Bush telephones Mandela, invites him to visit White House. Bush says he spoke two days earlier with de Klerk, invited him to visit as well. (*New York Times,* 12 February 1990, A1, A17; *Washington Post,* 12 February 1990, A1)

12 February 1990 Thatcher calls for meeting of EC foreign ministers to consider community-wide lifting of voluntary sanctions. Bush says US sanctions cannot be lifted until South Africa has met conditions outlined in CAAA. (*Financial Times,* 13 February 1990, 1; *New York Times,* 13 February 1990, A17)

15 February 1990 Twenty thousand whites march through Pretoria in protest against de Klerk's release of Mandela, legalization of ANC. (*Washington Post,* 16 February 1990, A25)

20 February 1990 Thatcher unilaterally lifts ban on new investment in South Africa after 11 other EC foreign ministers decide only to "re-engag[e] South Africa in cultural and scientific cooperation." (*Financial Times,* 21 February 1990, 1)

22 March 1990 Secretary of State James A. Baker III meets with de Klerk in Cape Town, in highest-level meeting between the two countries in more than a decade. Mandela, other black leaders criticize meeting as premature. (*Washington Post,* 23 March 1990, A15)

31 March 1990 ANC postpones preliminary talks with government after police shoot, kill at least seven protestors in peaceful demonstration in township outside Johannesburg. Similar incidents occur throughout spring, including one in which police shoot to death five teen-age boys who left school to watch protest march. (*Washington Post,* 2 April 1990, A13; 17 June 1990, A1)

17 April 1990 De Klerk rejects majority rule as "unacceptable" to whites: "We believe that majority rule is not suitable for a country like South Africa because it will lead to the domination and even the suppression of minorities." (*Washington Post,* 18 April 1990, A1)

19 April 1990 In speech to parliament, de Klerk announces that, while government will go ahead with plans to scrap Separate Amenities Act, it will delay for at least a year consideration of main "pillars" of apartheid: Group Areas Act, Land Acts, Race Classification Act. He also noted that those laws may not be fully repealed, but may be replaced with substitute legislation. (*Washington Post*, 20 April 1990, A20)

2 May 1990   South African government, ANC hold first formal talks; talks are to pave the way for substantive negotiations on political reform by resolving remaining obstacles, including release of all political prisoners, lifting of state of emergency, general amnesty for all political exiles, end to ANC's armed struggle. (*Washington Post*, 3 May 1990, A1)

8 May 1990   De Klerk begins 16-day trip to EC. Netherlands says it would welcome de Klerk visit later in year, Portugal pledges to support lifting of sanctions at upcoming meeting of EC foreign ministers. Other EC leaders praise de Klerk's reforms but refuse to discuss lifting of sanctions. (*Financial Times*, 9 May 1990, 6; 16 May 1990, 24)

4 June 1990   Mandela begins 6-week, 13-nation tour, including several days in US, during which he says sanctions will be "uppermost in all the discussions." (*Washington Post*, 5 June 1990, A20)

7 June 1990   De Klerk announces that state of emergency will not be renewed when it expires 8 June, except in Natal, where interfactional violence between ANC, Zulu Chief Buthelezi's Inkatha organization has killed 3,500 people in last three years. De Klerk also says 48 blacks detained under state of emergency will be released as gesture of goodwill; however, between 350 and 3,500 political prisoners remain in custody. (*Washington Post*, 8 June 1990, A1; 19 June 1990, A1)

25–26 June 1990   Mandela meets with Bush at White House, addresses Congress, urges both to keep sanctions in place. EC leaders reject Thatcher's suggestion of immediate lifting of some sanctions, but say they would consider "gradual relaxation" of sanctions "when there is further clear evidence that the process of change already initiated continues." In South Africa, right-wing leaders call for early elections, claiming that de Klerk has no mandate for his reforms. (*Washington Post*, 26 June 1990, A1; 27 June 1990, A23; *Financial Times*, 27 June 1990, 1)

16 July 1990   UN Secretary General Javier Pérez de Cuéllar announces that fact-finding mission he sent to South Africa in June has determined that South Africa has completely lifted ban on ANC, other political parties, movements, but that it has not "released all political prisoners, withdrawn all troops from black townships, ended rule by emergency decree and other repressive legislation, or completely halted political trials and executions." (*New York Times*, 17 July 1990, A6)

August–September 1990   Violence in Natal escalates, spreads to Soweto, other Johannesburg townships. After 500 people are killed in 12-day period, South African government declares areas of greatest violence to be "unrest areas," imposes restrictions, grants police powers similar to those under state of emergency. ANC criticizes move, charges police are siding with Inkatha against ANC, trying to promote tribal strife, weaken ANC in negotiations. In September, Inkatha attacks workers' hostel, with support from police and army units, killing at least 34 persons, wounding many more. Claiming that white extremists are fanning violence to undermine negotiations, Mandela says ANC may have to resume its armed struggle if killing does not stop soon. (*Washington Post,* 25 August 1990, A6; 5 September 1990, A21; 12 September 1990, A16)

23–25 September 1990 De Klerk becomes first South African head of state to visit Washington in 45 years. Following meeting at White House, Bush praises de Klerk as "a courageous leader who had put his country on an 'irreversible' course toward dismantling apartheid." Administration officials say South Africa has met two of CAAA's five conditions—lifting ban on political parties, agreeing to enter good-faith negotiations with black opposition—and Bush says he would ask Congress to lift or modify sanctions if two more conditions— lifting state of emergency in Natal, freeing all political prisoners— are met. (CAAA gives president discretion to lift some or all sanctions if four of five conditions outlined in the act are met, fifth being repeal of the two main pillars of apartheid: Group Areas Act, Population Registration Act.) Meeting with members of Congress, de Klerk says he wants to move to American-style democracy based on principle of one man, one vote, although combined with guarantees to protect white minority. (*New York Times,* 25 September 1990, A1; 26 September 1990, A3)

15 October 1990 Repeal of Separate Amenities Act becomes effective. However, officials in many small towns, villages say they will use Group Areas Act (which bars blacks from residing in white areas), other municipal regulations to continue barring blacks from using public libraries, swimming pools, other public facilities. For example, farming town of Bethal says it will require nonresidents (i.e. blacks) to pay prohibitively expensive membership fee to use public library. (*Financial Times,* 15 October 1990, 24)

18 October 1990 Saying level of violence is now only sporadic, de Klerk lifts state of emergency in Natal; 27 black townships around Johannesburg remain "unrest areas." (*Washington Post,* 19 October 1990, A25)

Goals of Sender Country

Reagan administration: first term

Assistant Secretary of State for African Affairs Chester A. Crocker, in April 1981 meeting with South African officials, stresses that "top U.S. priority [in southern Africa] is to stop Soviet encroachment," states that "our objective is to increase South African government confidence." (Baker 8–10, 107–08)

Crocker concentrates on settlement of disputes in Angola, Namibia, believing that "Regional security would diminish white South Africans' siege mentality, produced by their country's isolation in the region, and increase their willingness to embark on a program of serious reform. Based on this premise, external pressures, such as public criticism and sanctions, would be counterproductive, exacerbate white fears, and increase government intransigence." (Baker 9–10)

Reagan administration: second term

Opposing House-passed legislation banning imports from, investment in South Africa, "[Secretary of State George P.] Shultz, who in the past criticized economic sanctions as 'light-switch diplomacy' which is turned on and off ineffectively, said pressures against South Africa should be adjusted gradually like a rheostat, or light dimmer." (*Washington Post,* 21 June 1986, A18)

Reagan, in announcing September 1985 sanctions: "Yes, we in America, because of what we are and what we stand for, have influence to do good. We also have immense potential to make things worse. Before taking fateful steps, we must ponder the key question: Are we helping to change the system? Or are we punishing the blacks whom we seek to help? American policy through several administrations has been to use our influence and our leverage against apartheid, not against innocent people who are the victims of apartheid." (*Washington Post,* 10 September 1985, A12)

Congress

Section 311 of Comprehensive Anti-Apartheid Act of 1986 provides for termination of sanctions if South African government takes following steps:

"(1) releases all persons persecuted for their political beliefs or detained unduly without trial and Nelson Mandela from prison;

(2) repeals the state of emergency. . . and releases all detainees held under such state of emergency;

(3) unbans democratic political parties and permits the free exercise by South Africans of all races of the right to form political parties, express political opinions, and otherwise participate in the political process;

(4) repeals the Group Areas Act and the Population Registration Act and institutes no other measures with the same purposes; and

(5) agrees to enter into good faith negotiations with truly representative members of the black majority without preconditions."

Section 311 also provides for modification of any sanctions if president determines that South Africa has taken "three of the four actions listed in paragraphs (2) through (5)" and "made substantial progress toward dismantling the system of apartheid and establishing a nonracial democracy." (Lipton 145)

Howard Wolpe (D-MI), Chairman of House Foreign Affairs Subcommittee on Africa: "Sanctions aren't a quick fix for apartheid. There is a long, protracted struggle in process, and [sanctions] are part of a pattern of developments that will shorten this time frame and accelerate the onset of negotiations." (*Wall Street Journal,* 21 September 1987, 24)

US state and local governments

"The [1980s] trend towards government sanctions has often been preceded—and in many cases exceeded—by measures adopted by state and local legislatures. . . ." (See *Observed Economic Statistics*; Lipton 23–24)

Response of Target Country

". . . the South Africans pursued a number of strategies designed to heighten their ability to withstand potential American pressures: (1) establishment of intense economic ties in other directions, as with Taiwan and Israel; (2) the pursuit of technological self-sufficiency; (3) maximizing the value of exports and capitalizing on good fortune like the skyrocketing price of gold in 1979–80; and (4) pointing out to the US and others the collateral damage that sanctions would wreak on nearby black states in southern Africa." (Bissell 93)

South Africa's tools for countering sanctions include import substitution (partly through technology licensing); "sanctions busting" (transshipment, false labeling); adjustments in macroeconomic policies (exchange controls, dual exchange rate system). (Lewis 75)

"South Africa's destabilization policy, as its military and other punitive pressures against its neighbors came to be known, steadily escalated in the 1980s. . . . Just as constructive engagement was being launched, therefore, Pretoria was stepping up its aggressive attacks against its neighbors." (Baker 14)

President P.W. Botha

In his first major policy statement after declaring first state of emergency: "We have never given in to outside demands and we are not going to do so. South Africa's problems will be solved by South Africans and not by foreigners. We are not going to be deterred from doing what we think best, nor will we be forced into doing what we don't want to do." (*Washington Post*, 16 August 1985, A1)

On 1 August 1986, following approval of sanctions package by Senate Foreign Relations Committee, South Africa implements licensing system for imports from Zimbabwe, expands application of financial rand to unlisted companies and most foreign purchases of property (see description of dual exchange rate system for rand under *Observed Economic Statistics*). (*Financial Times*, 2 August 1986, 1)

Following Reagan's imposition of sanctions, Botha states: "Whatever the intention, the effect is punitive. It is a negative step. Cooperation should not be based on coercion. Such actions diminish the ability of the United States to influence events in southern Africa." (*Washington Post*, 10 September 1985, A12)

Deputy Foreign Minister Louis Nel

Releasing brochure intended to influence Senate vote on sanctions in September 1985: "Let us be frank; our neighboring states will suffer before we do. Those measures will have an impact on the whole of southern Africa, and South Africa will be better able to absorb them than its neighbors. The choice is between sanctions on the one hand and political, social and economic progress on the other." (*Washington Post*, 6 September 1985, A1)

Foreign Minister Roelof Botha

During fall 1986 congressional debate on overturning Reagan's veto of CAAA, Botha calls Senators Charles E. Grassley (R-IA), Edward Zorinsky (D-NE) threatening to retaliate against sanctions by cutting off grain purchases from US. Both senators nevertheless vote to override. (*Washington Post, New York Times*, 3 October 1986, A1)

Archbishop Desmond Tutu

Reacting to Reagan's imposition of limited sanctions: "I'm not impressed. He is merely trying to save himself from the humiliation of a veto override. . . . The South African government is laughing all the way to the bank. They know it's not even a flea bite. . . . [Reagan] has really been saying blacks are expendable. He sits around in equanimity because the fatalities are black fatalities. I said [last week in a television interview] he was a crypto-racist. I think I should say now he is a racist pure and simple. . . . Get rid of constructive engagement, apply to South Africa the policies you apply to Nicaragua, and voila, apartheid will end." (*Washington Post*, 10 September 1985, A1)

Private sector

Anticipating possible freeze of bank accounts in US, most South Africans move their deposits offshore, primarily to Switzerland, which already "handles most of South Africa's gold transactions" according to spokesman for major US bank. (*Journal of Commerce*, 28 July 1986, 3A)

Following congressional imposition of sanctions, spokesman for Anglo American Corp. (South African conglomerate) says, "Business which has been pressing for fundamental reforms will have less leverage. Energies will be spent on finding loopholes instead of pressing for changes." (*Wall Street Journal*, 7 October 1986, 37)

President F.W. de Klerk

In February 1990, following Mandela's release: "[Rhodesia] waited too long before engaging in fundamental negotiation and dialogue . . . we are determined not to repeat that mistake." (*Financial Times*, 12 February 1990, 18)

Attitude of Other Countries

European Community

"All EC members subscribe to the EC sanctions package of September 1986. . . . The Thatcher government opposes further economic sanctions, and only reluctantly agreed to participate in the recent Commonwealth and EC measures, having whittled away the compulsory elements of these as far as possible. The Kohl administration in West Germany and the Portuguese government share Mrs Thatcher's reluctance to impose further sanctions. But all three governments have gradually shifted their position, probably mainly in response to developments in the USA. The policy of France used to lag behind that of the UK and USA. . . . Then, in July 1985, [France] unexpectedly took a number of initiatives on South Africa. . . . However, France continued to supply nuclear exports and maintenance for Koeberg [French-supplied commercial nuclear power project in South Africa], in accordance with its 1979 contract for the nuclear plant." (Lipton 18–19)

Scandinavian countries

In October 1985, foreign ministers of Nordic Council (representing Denmark, Finland, Iceland, Norway, Sweden) approve "Nordic Program of Action against South Africa" calling for mandatory UN sanctions and, in the meantime, unilateral restrictions on investment, loans, certain goods (e.g., arms, oil, computers, krugerrands). In early 1986, Denmark bans imports of coal from South Africa; a few months later, it becomes "the first European country to ban all trade in goods and services (with the exception of imports of raw phosphate, vermiculite and tanning extracts)." In early 1985, Sweden closes loopholes in earlier sanctions, tightens restrictions on investment in South Africa.

In 1987, both Sweden, Norway impose nearly comprehensive trade, investment bans against South Africa, with limited exceptions for some raw materials. Norway's ban includes shipping of North Sea oil; measure is strongly opposed by Norwegian shipping industry. Scandinavian countries are among leading donors to so-called front-line states (Angola, Botswana, Lesotho, Malawi, Mozambique, Swaziland, Tanzania, Zambia, Zimbabwe). (*Financial Times,* 21 February 1985, 2; Lipton 19, app. 7)

Commonwealth of Nations
"African and Asian countries have used the Commonwealth as a particular source of pressure on South Africa. . . . Commonwealth pressures also contributed to the UK's gradual ending of its defence links with South Africa. . . . Over the last decade, Canada, Australia and New Zealand have gradually shifted to support for sanctions against South Africa, leaving the UK increasingly isolated within the Commonwealth. . . . Elsewhere in the Commonwealth, India was the first country to sever trade (and all other) relations with South Africa in 1964, and has since had no official relations or commerce. Among the African countries, Nigeria has taken a lead in calling for economic sanctions, and has taken punitive action against some transnational companies involved in South Africa." (Lipton 16, 20)

Australia
Responding to Botha's defiant August 1985 speech rejecting fundamental reform of apartheid system, Australia decides to close its trade office in Johannesburg, ban direct investment in Australia by South African government or its agencies, ban import of krugerrands, end export assistance for Australian firms trading with South Africa. In addition, Australia asks banks, financial institutions to voluntarily cease lending to South Africa, bans export of petroleum products, computers, other products of potential use to South African police or army. Defending "apparent mildness" of actions, Foreign Affairs Minister Bill Hayden says, "The important thing is not to use up all your shots in one volley." (*Washington Post,* 20 August 1985, A10; *Financial Times,* 20 August 1985, 1)

Japan
In summer 1986, Japan bans export of computers to South Africa, discourages import of gold coins from South Africa. Following adoption of additional sanctions by US, EC in fall, Japan bans imports of iron and steel, restricts travel and tourism to and from South Africa. (*Financial Times,* 16 June 1986, 2; Lipton 23)

Hong Kong
In November 1986, Hong Kong bans import of krugerrands, new contracts for iron and steel. (Lipton 23)

Southern African Development Coordination Conference
This organization of front-line states estimates that South African "aggression" and "destabilization" have cost its neighbors $10 billion since 1980, including $1.6 billion in direct war damages. Conference Executive Secretary Simba Makoni says, "Sanctions are a road not to a peaceful change but a less violent change." He also says that South Africa's neighbors realize that economic sanctions will hurt them as well, but that they are willing to bear that cost "because there is no other alternative." (*Washington Post,* 20 November 1985, A24)

In 1989, UN study estimates cost to SADCC members of South African aggression and destabilization to have been $11 billion in 1988, $62 billion cumulatively in decade. (United Nations 6)

South Africa: foreign trade, 1982–88[a] (millions of dollars)

Year	World[b] As reported by South Africa	As reported by partners	US	Japan	Germany	Italy	UK	Nordics
Imports from								
1982	17,026	12,345	2,368	1,652	2,536	545	2,090	344
1983	14,544	11,071	2,129	1,741	1,946	470	1,676	353
1984	14,963	12,084	2,265	1,837	2,343	520	1,612	432
1985	10,338	7,869	1,205	1,029	1,690	330	1,300	283
1986	11,417	8,538	1,158	1,368	1,941	352	1,247	206
1987	14,126	10,739	1,281	1,882	2,548	456	1,557	128
1988	17,333	13,236	1,690	2,047	3,332	501	1,911	22
Exports to								
1982	17,647	13,049	2,048	1,870	1,269	1,593	1,313	308
1983	18,612	11,174	2,099	1,618	1,078	1,288	1,167	237
1984	17,377	12,410	2,577	1,635	1,049	1,708	979	234
1985	16,405	13,154	2,180	1,878	1,085	1,845	1,262	253
1986	19,718	14,671	2,476	2,266	1,376	1,916	1,218	148
1987	21,603	13,362	1,399	2,455	1,248	1,788	1,073	34
1988	25,847	15,852	1,589	1,955	1,727	2,163	1,434	27

a. Except as indicated, trade flows are as reported by partner country.

b. World export figures are c.i.f. (cost plus insurance and freight), because partner-country imports are reported in that manner.

c. Denmark, Finland, Norway, Sweden.

Source: International Monetary Fund.

South Africa: selected exports, 1982–88 (millions of dollars)

	To US		To other OECD	
Year	Coal	Iron and steel	Coal	Iron and steel
1982	22	292	1,146	451
1983	30	259	914	410
1984	27	329	1,060	538
1985	43	294	1,275	647
1986	52	330	1,111	765
1987	—	151	873	772
1988	—	212	n.a.	n.a.

— = negligible.

n.a. = not available.

Source: Organization for Economic Cooperation and Development.

South Africa: net capital flows, 1980–87[a] (millions of dollars)

Year	Long-term	Short-term
1980	−897	−465
1981	162	1,797
1982	2,353	803
1983	−260	969
1984	1,845	295
1985	−621	1,373
1986	−1,294	−1,266
1987	−833	−509

a. Negative numbers represent capital outflows.

Source: International Monetary Fund.

Following his release, front-line states endorse Mandela's call for continuation of international sanctions until de Klerk's reforms are "irreversible," criticize Thatcher's decision to lift new investment ban. (*Washington Post,* 1 March 1990, A30)

In 1983, Zimbabwean Prime Minister Robert Mugabe criticizes Reagan administration policy of "constructive engagement," saying it has encouraged South Africa "to become more aggressive" toward neighboring black-ruled nations. Zambian President Kenneth Kaunda earlier called on West to pressure South Africa, asking, "Why action in [Poland] and no action in [South Africa]?" (*Washington Post,* 2 April 1983, A16; 19 August 1983, A14)

Writing in *Foreign Affairs,* Mugabe concedes that "It became clear that some frontline states are not able to impose sanctions because their economies are tied into the South African economy like Siamese twins. . . . Although unable to do so themselves they urge those who can—especially the big powers—to adopt sanctions." Zimbabwe has also taken lead in trying to reduce dependence of front-line states on South Africa for transport routes. "At present, 60 per cent of the external trade of the neighbouring countries is said to go to, from or via South Africa." (*Washington Post,* 11 February 1988, A37; Hayes 79)

Economic Impact

Observed Economic Statistics

South African real GDP grows a *total* of 4.7 percent from 1981 to 1987; nonagricultural employment is stagnant, population grows by 2.5 percent annually during same period, leading to 10 percent drop in per capita income. (Lewis 27–28)

Greater part of increase in foreign direct investment in South Africa since 1950 has been reinvested earnings; since 1956, remittances of profits, dividends have substantially exceeded new capital inflows. "For the past 20–30 years, South Africa has financed virtually all its growth from domestic investment." Declining productivity of investment has more impact on growth than does level of investment, whether domestic or foreign. (Lewis 66–71)

Despite decrease in lending to public sector from about $500 million in 1979 to $200 million in 1985, US bank lending to nonbank private sector in South Africa doubles to over $1 billion, while lending to South African banks increases fivefold to more than $3 billion in 1984. By 1985, short-term debt is 40 percent of total South African liabilities to foreigners. (*Financial Times*, 18 February 1985, 10; *New York Times*, 29 April 1985, D8; Lewis 65; Lipton 60)

Finance Minister Barend du Plessis estimates in 1985 that shortfall in foreign investment capital has reduced annual growth rate from possible 5.5 percent to 3.5 percent "in recent years." (*Washington Post*, 1 September 1985, A30)

Financial Crisis

American banks reportedly withdraw $1 billion in first half of 1985. "It was their refusal to extend new credit, primarily on political grounds, that touched off the short-term debt crisis [in August]. British banks, which are owed more than a quarter of the $12 billion debt falling due in the next 12 months, are also unwilling to make new loans. . . . [However, an] official at Commerzbank, West Germany's third largest bank, said the situation was not threatening. 'South Africa has been and will continue to service its foreign debt. There's no question of default, but there's no talk of fresh loans. The problem is in refinancing existing credit.' " (*Washington Post*, 1 September 1985, A1)

At end of August, rand falls from 54 cents to 34 cents before South Africa closes exchange. "It is widely acknowledged that the collapse of the rand . . . was not justified by the economic fundamentals . . . politics intervened in the dual form of domestic unrest and the threat of economic sanctions which between them precipitated the currency crisis." (*Financial Times*, 29 August 1985, 10; 30 August 1985, 10)

September 1985 debt repayment moratorium affects $13.6 billion in debt "inside the net." South Africa continues regular repayments on the 40 percent of its debt that is "outside the net," including "public bonds, debts guaranteed by governments and outstanding debts to international financial institutions (mainly the IMF)." Pending rescheduling agreement, South Africa unilaterally sets interest rate for servicing of debt inside net at ¼ percent over London interbank offer rate (LIBOR). "In nominating a ¼% loading over LIBOR, the South African government was effectively conceding to lenders some compensation for the moratorium." (Ovenden 85)

Financial rand, reintroduced during liquidity crisis in August–September 1985, trades at discount relative to commercial rand, must be used for investments in South Africa by nonresidents; capital imported by immigrants; proceeds from sale of South African securities, other equities if repatriated abroad; investments abroad by South

African residents (these transactions must first be approved by authorities); capital exports by emigrants. Other transactions, goods trade, payments of investment income, royalties, use commercial rand. In period 1985–88, financial rand trades at average discount to commercial rand of 40 percent. Because financial, commercial rand accounts must be kept separate, dual exchange rate, primarily intended to discourage disinvestment, also limits impact on balance of payments of any disinvestment that occurs. (Ovenden 113)

GAO estimates that $10.8 billion flowed out of South Africa from January 1985 through June 1989, including $3.7 billion in loan repayments to banks, $7.1 billion in other debt repayments, capital flight. GAO report also notes that most US banks appear to have stopped providing even short-term trade credits to South Africa; reasons cited include "the absence of Export-Import Bank guarantees, the combined economic and political risks in South Africa, the increase in laws at the state and local level in the United States directing government business and pension plan investments away from companies and banks dealing with South Africa, and the growth in public sensitivity on the apartheid issue." (GAO 12, 17)

"Direct American investment in South Africa is estimated by the State Department at $2.3 billion down from the $2.8 billion calculated by the South African Institute of Race Relations for 1982. Other estimates put overall American investment, including loans and gold stocks, at $14 billion." (New York Times, 28 October 1984, 18).

"Of the approximately 350–400 US companies with direct investments in South Africa in January 1984, the IRRC (Investor Responsibility Research Center) estimated that seven withdrew in 1984 and 39 in 1985. During 1986 the pace quickened: 40 left and 13 announced their intention of leaving, including some of the biggest—Eastman Kodak, Coca-Cola, Exxon, General Motors and IBM. By June 1987 a further 39 had left or announced their intention of leaving, including Ford Motor Co, Citicorp and ITT." By mid-1988, only 136 US companies remain in South Africa. (Lipton 64; Baker 59)

"[G]reat majority of disinvestment sales have occurred at prices below both the capital value of the assets and the quoted stock exchange price of the companies' shares. Mobil, for instance, is believed to have sold its four South African subsidiaries to Trek . . . for half the book value of the assets. Anglo-American . . . acquired another 18% of the shares in Samcor, the vehicle-assembly business that was previously owned by the Ford Motor Company, for what Ford described as a 'nominal' sum." (Ovenden 153)

"Bell & Howell was so anxious to get out that in April it sold the entire subsidiary—with an estimated book value of $5 million—to a South American conglomerate for $1." (Washington Post, 17 November 1986, A1)

"While the disinvestment program has mostly benefited white-owned businesses, which have often acquired assets at fire-sale prices, few businessmen believe it is in the long-term interests of the country. They regret losing the guaranteed access to know-how that a multinational connection brings, and they fear the loss of positive U.S. involvement in the economy. And . . . large amounts of investment capital are absorbed in buy-outs instead of being applied to new investment." (Journal of Commerce, 27 February 1989, 1A)

"[B]ecause of exchange controls, the selling of equity stakes in South African subsidiaries [does not have consequences as serious as the drying up of new loans]. Barclays, for example, has to repatriate the proceeds of its sale of Barnat . . . through the financial rand. This means that it has to find other foreign investors to purchase the rands from it. But the sale also ends the outflow of fairly generous dividends from

Barnat in South Africa to a foreign owner. Dividends can be paid at the higher commercial rand rate. . . . As a result, the Barclay's disinvestment may even have a favourable effect on South Africa's balance of payments." (*Financial Times*, 6 August 1987, 16)

Wisconsin (1978), Nebraska (1980), Connecticut (1980) adopt legislation calling for divestment of shares held by public institutions in US companies with investments in South Africa. In the mid-1980s, Maryland, Massachusetts, Michigan, cities of Philadelphia, Washington, Boston, New York pass laws forbidding investment of municipal or state funds in companies operating in South Africa. In 1986, California announces it will gradually divest itself of holdings in companies with ties to South Africa; decision affects about $10 billion in investments. By end of 1988, 23 states, 19 counties, 79 cities adopt various economic measures to distance themselves from South Africa. (Chettle 106–08; *New York Times*, 28 October 1984, A18; *Los Angeles Times*, 25 December 1984, A1; Lipton 23–24; Baker 61)

"Assuming that, in the absence of politics, money might have flowed into the country at the rate it did before 1985, economists at Trust Bank, a South African commercial bank, calculate that South Africa has forgone some R32 billion ($14 billion) in loans and direct investment over the past five years. They add to that an estimated R8 billion of exports lost as a result of trade sanctions (most notably on coal, iron and steel, and fruit), bringing the total amount of foreign exchange lost to R40 billion." (*The Economist*, 10 February 1990, 69)

Trade Sanctions

South African government estimates that of $8.1 billion in goods imported by manufacturing sector in 1985, less than $2 billion could be replaced "economically" by domestic production. (*New York Times*, 6 October 1986, D5)

"Protectionist lobbies within the USA—coal, textiles and agriculture (including tobacco, until it was realised that the USA is a net exporter to South Africa)—were active in shaping the items selected for the 1986 CAA Act. Clearly, the selection of items worldwide reflects these interests and pressures and not simply their possible effectiveness in inflicting costs on the South African government, while avoiding costs which hit the victims of apartheid. Coal, iron and steel, sugar, wine and fruit are labour intensive industries, heavily geared to export production." (Lipton 52)

Import bans on South African coal by Denmark, France in 1985 led to "desperate price cutting by the South African mines, so that by April 1986 South African coal was selling for substantially less than its competitors." (Lipton 46)

South African Chamber of Mines says embargoes imposed by Denmark, France, "reluctance by other countries" to buy South African coal have cut expected 1986 exports by 17 percent, threatening 40,000 jobs in mining industry. To maintain exports, South Africa has also had to sell its coal at 10 percent discount below world price of $25 to $26 per metric ton for that grade of coal. (*Washington Post*, 25 July 1986, A27)

It is estimated in March 1989 that "almost 8% of South Africa's current gold production was, at the then price, being produced at a loss. . . . A further reduction in the world price to say a band between US$330 and $360 would mean that" 22 of 43 mines would be operating at a loss and "could only continue to maintain production with a further, drastic, devaluation of the Rand." (Ovenden 173)

"The international trade in Kruggerrands [sic], which by the early 1980s absorbed about 100 tonnes of South African gold, has been virtually eliminated by the international embargo." (Ovenden 175)

It is estimated that krugerrand ban cost South Africa only about 3 percent of value of gold exports, as loss is limited to value of coin's premium over value of gold it contains. Anglo-American owns 29 percent of corporation manufacturing American Gold Eagle, gold coin created to replace krugerrand. (Hayes 30; Lipton 47)

Only "distinctive" South African exports—gold, strategic minerals—have been nearly untouched by sanctions. "Beyond these products, shifts of international markets could have been expected to absorb the relatively small amounts of South African exports [affected by sanctions] with relatively low price discounts." Major exception has been coal, which is easily traceable, reportedly resulting in reduced shipments, relatively steep price discounting. "It is difficult to read any significant effect of the trade sanctions at the aggregate economic level, even though in certain cases trade clearly had decreased, apparently in direct response to sanctions. Examples include the total volume and value of coal exports and the level of trade in specific commodities between South Africa and the United States." (Lewis 105–06)

Because CAAA does not clearly define when a product is South African, administration interpretations of law allow products shipped from South Africa under varying circumstances to legally enter US. For example, tuna shipped from Cape Town is allowed as long as it is caught in international waters by non–South African fishermen; lobster tails caught by South African fishermen in South African waters are allowed if they are processed on non-South African-flagged vessel; fabricated iron and steel of various types, including 11 million tons for suspension bridge in Houston, are permitted because those shapes were not banned by EC (interpretation based on legislative history of CAAA). Also, narrow definition of petroleum products allows certain petroleum-based products to continue being shipped to South Africa despite ban on exports of petroleum and products. (*Journal of Commerce*, 15 May 1990, 1A)

"On trade, there has been little effect [of sanctions]. . . . Disinvestment has an intense psychological impact on white South Africa. . . . Its economic effect, at least in the short run, has been exaggerated. . . . Sanctions in finance seem to have had the greatest real impact. They were imposed in 1985 not by governments but by international banks, mainly because lenders had come to regard South Africa as a poor credit risk." (*The Economist*, 14 October 1989, 45)

Economist Stephen Lewis estimates that oil embargo, other trade sanctions impose cost on South Africa of $2 billion a year, primarily in terms-of-trade effects. He predicts that end of sanctions, political and economic reforms in South Africa might also result in increase in capital flows of $2 billion to $3 billion per year. His estimate does not include economic effects of distortions from import substitution, government policies designed to counteract effects of sanctions (e.g., promotion of oil-from-coal plants, indigenous arms production). (*Washington Post*, 18 February 1990, B1; Lewis 114, 147)

Authors' note: Effects of oil, arms embargoes have been calculated in Case 62–2 *UN v. South Africa*. Since present case focuses on sanctions imposed by US since 1985, those estimates have not been repeated here.

Calculated Economic Impact (annual cost to target country)

Impact of US sanctions on imports from South Africa (excluding coal, see below); welfare loss estimated at 30 percent of reduction in trade from average annual value in 1982–85.	$210 million
Impact of US, French, Nordic, Commonwealth ban on South African coal imports; welfare loss estimated at 40 percent (because of significant discounting) of reduction in trade from average annual value in 1982–85.	103 million
Impact of krugerrand ban; welfare loss estimated at 3 percent of value of gold used in coins (calculated as 100 metric tons at 1982–84 average annual price of $386 per ounce).	41 million
Reduction in access to international capital due to federal, state, local government measures; welfare loss calculated at 10 percent of average annual net outflows, 1985–87.	196 million
Total	$550 million

Relative Magnitudes

Gross indicators of South African economy	
South African GNP (1984)	$70 billion
South African population (1984)	32 million
Annual effect of sanctions related to gross indicators	
Percentage of GNP	0.8
Per capita	$17.19
South African trade with US as percentage of total trade	
Exports (1984)	8
Imports (1984)	16
Ratio of US GNP (1984: $3,775 billion) to South African GNP	54

Assessment

Journal of Commerce

"The sanctions passed by Congress have scarcely put a dent in the volume of trade between the United States and South Africa. . . . Why did the sanctions turn out to be a paper tiger? First, the law was compromised from the start by the vague language in which it was cast. And, second, neither the Reagan nor the Bush administration aggressively enforced it." (*Journal of Commerce*, 15 May 1990, 1A)

Financial Times

"It is clear from everything [Mandela] has done since he was released from prison . . . that he regards international pressure on the South African Government as the principal weapon available to the ANC. Without it, Mr. Mandela would probably still be a prisoner and militant black nationalist organisations would still be illegal. . . . From the black point of view, the overthrow of apartheid has come to depend more than ever on a single factor: the desire of white South Africans to rejoin the world community and see both economic sanctions and constant expressions of opprobrium brought to an end." (*Financial Times,* 18 April 1990, 20)

Helen Suzman, member of South African Progressive Federal Party

"Many far-reaching noncosmetic changes took place before the U.S. Anti-Apartheid Act of October 1986 was passed, such as legal recognition of black trade unions and the repeal of the laws that severely restricted the mobility of South Africans. The main impetus to reform has been the escalating black resistance in South Africa to apartheid . . . the growing impossibility of implementing apartheid laws in the teeth of the irresistible tide of urbanization, and the astronomical cost of administering a system designed to maintain racial segregation in a country where de facto economic integration has been proceeding apace." (*Washington Post,* 27 June 1990, A19)

Stephen R. Lewis, Jr.

"It is not entirely clear how the economic costs of apartheid and international pressure have affected the nature and pace of political change in South Africa. It is clear, however, that economic pressures have played a major role in forcing the South African government to change its policies on a wide range of issues from labor reform to the release of political prisoners; and that in the absence of fundamental political change, the prospects for economic growth in South Africa are bleak." (Lewis 167)

Keith Ovenden and Tony Cole

"Of all the many measures that have been proposed, and in some cases implemented over the years to bring about the abolition of apartheid, the financial sanction that has been in place since August 1985 has undoubtedly placed more pressure on the regime than any other. . . . South Africa is being excluded from the world stock of savings not because bankers and financiers are ideologically united in their detestation of apartheid . . . but because most of them now see South Africa as a bad risk. . . . Many commercial banks in the Western world, with some notable exceptions in Europe, have also been profoundly influenced by public opinion. The threat of the loss of substantial domestic business as a consequence of engaging in South African lending has been an important deterrent. So too, though more latterly, has been government intervention. . . . The effect of this combination of forces is to ensure that the financial sanction is almost ideal, because although in some cases backed up by governments, it is by and large a sanction that market forces work to encourage." (Ovenden 187, 189–90)

Authors' Summary

Overall assessment

☐ Policy result, scaled from 1 (failed) to 4 (success)　　2

☐ Sanctions contribution, scaled from 1 (none) to 4 (significant)　　3

☐ Success score (policy result *times* sanctions contribution),
　scaled from 1 (outright failure) to 16 (significant success)　　6

Political and economic variables

☐ Companion policies: J (covert), Q (quasi-military), or R (regular military)　　—

☐ International cooperation with sender, scaled from 1 (none) to 4 (significant)　　4

☐ International assistance to target: A (if present)　　—

☐ Sanctions period (years)	5+
☐ Economic health and political stability of target, scaled from 1 (distressed) to 3 (strong)	2
☐ Presanction relations between sender and target, scaled from 1 (antagonistic) to 3 (cordial)	2
☐ Type of sanction: X (export), M (import), F (financial)	X,M,F
☐ Cost to sender, scaled from 1 (net gain) to 4 (major loss)	2

Comments

Since taking office, de Klerk has fulfilled some of the conditions specified in the CAAA for the lifting of sanctions: releasing Mandela, unbanning the ANC and other political groups, and lifting the state emergency. However, an unknown number of political prisoners remain in detention, and de Klerk has refused even to consider repealing major apartheid laws (including the Group Areas Act and the Population Registration Act) until at least 1991. The inability to resolve these issues, exacerbated by continuing interfactional violence among blacks and increasing white vigilantism, has prevented the two sides from beginning substantive negotiations on a political solution in South Africa. Thus, we conclude that the outcome is still uncertain, although we believe that the sanctions have contributed modestly to the steps taken by de Klerk in the first six months of 1990.

Bibliography

Baker, Pauline H. 1989. *The United States and South Africa: The Reagan Years*. South Africa UPDATE Series. New York: Ford Foundation–Foreign Policy Association.

Commonwealth Secretariat. 1989. *Independent Expert Study on the Evaluation of the Application and Impact of Sanctions*. Final Report to the Commonwealth Committee of Foreign Ministers on Southern Africa (Hanlon Report). London, April.

General Accounting Office. 1990. *South Africa: Relationship with Western Financial Institutions*. GAO/NSIAD-90–189. Washington, June.

Hayes, J.P. 1987. *Economic Effects of Sanctions on Southern Africa*. Thames Essay No. 53. London: Trade Policy Research Centre.

International Monetary Fund. 1988. *Balance of Payments Statistics Yearbook*. Washington.

International Monetary Fund. *Direction of Trade Statistics*, various issues. Washington.

Lewis, Stephen R., Jr. 1990. *The Economics of Apartheid*. New York: Council on Foreign Relations Press.

Lipton, Merle. 1988. *Sanctions and South Africa: The Dynamics of Economic Isolation*. Economist Intelligence Unit Special Report No. 1119. London: The Economist Publications Ltd.

Organization for Economic Cooperation and Development. *Foreign Trade by Commodities*, various issues. Paris.

Ovenden, Keith, and Tony Cole. 1989. *Apartheid and International Finance: A Program for Change*. Ringwood, Victoria, Australia: Penguin Books.

Sullivan, Leon H. 1983. "It's Time to Step Up the Pressure on South Africa." *Washington Post*, 10 May, A19.

United Nations Economic Commission for Africa. 1989. *South African Destabilization: The Economic Cost of Frontline Resistance to Apartheid*. New York, October.

CASE 87–1

US v. Panama

(1987–90: Destabilize Noriega)

Chronology of Key Events

1983	Chief of Military Intelligence Manuel Antonio Noriega takes over command of Panamanian Defense Forces (PDF). US chooses to ignore evidence of Noriega's involvement with drug smuggling, other illegal activities because Central Intelligence Agency (CIA) argues that he is "too valuable an intelligence source to alienate." (Millett 50–51; Sullivan 5)
3 April 1987	US Senate recommends suspending aid to Panama under Anti-Drug Abuse Act of 1986, which requires that sanctions be imposed against countries found not to be "fully cooperating" in war against drugs. (*Keesing's* 35192)
Early June 1987	After being forced to resign, PDF Chief of Staff Colonel Roberto Díaz Herrera publicly charges Noriega with corruption. Incident triggers three days of protests by opposition, leading President Eric Arturo Delvalle to declare national state of emergency. (*Keesing's* 35189–92)
26–29 June 1987	US Senate passes resolution calling for restoration of constitutional guarantees in Panama, investigation into allegations of illicit activities by "high ranking" Panamanians. Resolution sparks anti-American sentiment in Panama, culminating in protest that damages US embassy. (Sullivan 13; Dinges 269)
July 1987	Following allegations that Noriega supporters paid embassy protestors $20 each, Reagan administration accuses it of "dereliction of responsibility," suspends economic, military aid. (*Keesing's* 35189, 35296; *Facts on File* 560; Sullivan 13; Dinges 269)
29–30 July 1987	Panama pays $106,000 for damages to US embassy. State Department spokesman announces that aid suspension is being reviewed; a few days later, US says it has no plans to resume aid. (*Facts on File* 560; US House of Representatives 1989b, Attachment I)
7 October 1987	Nine US servicemen are arrested in Panama, questioned for 11 hours; US claims action is part of continuing campaign of harassment against Americans. (*Facts on File* 854)

| Late 1987 | Panamanian government extends landing rights to Soviet airline Aeroflot, whose first flight lands on 26 November; Panama reportedly seeks $200 million in emergency aid from Libya. (*Facts on File* 1000) |

| 22 December 1987 | President Ronald Reagan signs omnibus spending bill prohibiting all economic, military aid to Panama until president reports that democratically elected government has been established. Legislation also suspends Panama's sugar quota, requires US delegates to vote against new loans to Panama from international financial institutions. (*Facts on File* 950) |

| 5 February 1988 | With concurrence of administration officials in Washington, Noriega is indicted by Florida federal grand juries on charges of drug smuggling, money laundering, racketeering. "[I]t would have been nearly impossible to make a political argument for reversing the judicial process so near its completion. It was an election year; Congress was united and ready to pounce on any signs of softness toward Noriega. . . ." (Dinges 294) |

| 25–26 February 1988 | Delvalle attempts to dismiss Noriega as commander-in-chief of PDF; instead Delvalle is dismissed by Noriega-dominated National Assembly. Delvalle goes into hiding, declares that any financial assistance "to the illegitimate government of General Noriega will not be recognized by the constitutional government of Panama," calls for trade embargo. Vice President Manuel Solís Palma is appointed acting president. (*Washington Post*, 29 February 1988, A12) |

| 1 March 1988 | President Reagan "decertifies" Panama under Anti-Drug Abuse Act; move is purely symbolic given sanctions already mandated by Congress in December. White House Spokesman Marlin Fitzwater notes that while trade sanctions "have not been very successful in the past in other cases, we certainly have them under consideration." (*Washington Post*, 1 March 1988, A1; 2 March 1988, A17) |

| Early March 1988 | Opposition-led general strike largely succeeds in shutting down Panama City. (*Washington Post, New York Times*, 2, 3, 4 March 1988, A1) |

| 2 March 1988 | New York judge at request of Delvalle's lawyers issues injunction barring withdrawal of $10 million in Panamanian assets from Republic National Bank in New York. Acting Secretary of State John C. Whitehead signs official certification recognizing Delvalle as legitimate president of Panama, Ambassador Juan B. Sosa as his representative in US (see *Legal Notes*). Certification supports Sosa's requests to five US banks holding some $50 million in Panamanian assets not to release funds to representatives of Noriega government. Delvalle requests that all fees, taxes owed Panamanian government be placed in escrow. Consular offices in New York, West Germany, UK, Italy, which collect fees for registering ships in |

Panama, agree to comply with request. (*Washington Post, New York Times*, 3 March 1988, A1; *Financial Times* [London], 3 March 1988, 4)

3 March 1988
Freezing of Panamanian assets in US banks forces Banco Nacional de Panama (BNP) to suspend delivery of cash to commercial banks, causing most to close. Senator Alfonse M. D'Amato (R-NY), several Senate colleagues criticize slow pace of administration policy, introduce legislation to impose trade, currency, air-travel ban on Panama. (*Washington Post*, 4 March 1988, A17)

4 March 1988
Government of Panama orders all banks to close "until the supply of dollar bills can be regularized"; move forces many businesses just reopened after general strike to close again because of lack of cash (Panama uses US dollar as currency for most transactions). US initiates six weeks of military exercises that it says are conducted annually to train troops in defense of Panama Canal. (*New York Times*, 5 March 1988, A1; 9 March 1988, A16)

7 March 1988
New York judge extends restraining order preventing transfer of Panamanian assets to its national bank for 10 days. In Panama, elderly pensioners protest lack of funds to cash their bimonthly pension checks. Government reportedly is able to cover only $2 million of $7 million in checks issued to 60,000 people. Some Panamanians call for US military intervention to get rid of Noriega; one says, "The United States government put this man in power. It's time they take him down." (*Washington Post, New York Times, Financial Times*, 8 March 1988)

8 March 1988
Miami judge freezes Panamanian assets in Florida banks. (*Washington Post*, 9 March 1988, A16; *Financial Times*, 9 March 1988, 24)

9–10 March 1988
Roman Catholic Church intervenes for first time, calls on military-dominated government to allow civilian rule. Noriega pays his officers at least part of their salaries in cash. BNP says banks may open for limited operations, acceptance of deposits, interbank operations; none do. Panama fails to pay $21 million bond payment owed Japanese investors, but investors opt not to declare Panama in default. Government is unable to meet payment schedule on $421 million in commercial debt rolled over in 1987; banks refuse to negotiate another rollover agreement. (*Financial Times*, 11 March 1988, 4; *New York Times*, 10 March 1988; *Washington Post*, 10 March 1988, A43; 11 March 1988, A21; Sullivan 37)

11 March 1988
Reagan administration announces additional sanctions against Noriega regime: it places all US payments to Panama in escrow, including upcoming $6.5 million payment due under canal treaties; suspends special trade benefits under Generalized System of Preferences (GSP), Caribbean Basin Initiative (CBI); orders US Customs Service to more closely scrutinize persons, shipments going to and from Panama. Petroterminales de Panama, joint venture between US company (Northville Industries), Panamanian government that operates pipeline carrying Alaskan oil across Isthmus of

Panama, agrees to place payments due Panamanian government, estimated at $70 million to $95 million per year, in escrow. Panamanian Treasury announces that payment of wages for civil servants will be delayed. Barter becomes important means of exchange. (*New York Times*, 12 March 1988, A1; *Washington Post*, 13 March 1988, A1; Sullivan 36)

15–16 March 1988	Protests, strikes by unpaid public employees intensify. Coup attempt by head of national police in Panama fails. Through selective promotions, expulsions, Noriega consolidates his power base in PDF. (*Washington Post*, 16, 17 March 1988, A1; 22 March 1988, A1)
17–18 March 1988	Oil pipeline across Panama is shut down because of power blackout at pumping station. Public services disrupted by strikes (including electricity, water, hospitals, port facilities) are placed under direct military control; most services are at least partially restored, pipeline is reopened. (*New York Times*, 18 March 1988, A9)
18 March 1988	Two State Department officials meet face to face with Noriega to discuss terms under which he would agree to step down, go into exile if US agrees not to extradite him. (*Washington Post*, 19 March 1988, A1)
21 March 1988	Opposition proclaims general strike despite declaration of "state of urgency." Noriega reportedly is unsuccessful in getting offsetting economic assistance from Cuba, Nicaragua, or Libya; creation of new Panamanian currency to replace dollar is debated. (*Financial Times*, 14 March 1988, 1; *New York Times*, 21 March 1988, A1)
22 March 1988	Defector from Panamanian Air Force, Major Augusto Villalaz, says that he was sent to Cuba 14 March to pick up $50 million to be provided by Libya, but that money never materialized. (*Washington Post*, 23 March 1988, A1)
25 March 1988	Delvalle signs decree extending deadline for payment of income taxes from 31 March to 30 April, requiring that tax payments be placed in Federal Reserve escrow account. He warns that taxes paid to BNP or other accounts controlled by Noriega will not be credited. Noriega is reportedly unable to pay defense forces. (*Washington Post*, 26 March 1988; *New York Times*, 28 March 1988, A1; *International Trade Reporter*, 30 March 1988, 476; Lombard 326)
29 March 1988	In Caracas, Venezuela, 22 Latin American, Caribbean nations urge US to lift its sanctions. (*Washington Post*, 30 March 1988, A1; *International Trade Reporter*, 30 March 1988, 476)
30 March 1988	Panama's banking commission orders all banks to reopen, renew check-clearing operations, although with some limitations. Noriega reportedly collects some $3 million in cash from quarterly tax payments of US corporations operating in Panama. Representatives of Texaco, Eastern Airlines say State Department officials did not advise them against making the payments. (*Washington Post, New York Times*, 31 March 1988, A1; *International Trade Reporter*, 30 March 1988, 476)

31 March 1988	Panama declares early Easter holiday to avoid cashing checks issued to pensioners. More businesses open; general strike gradually collapses. Reagan administration asks US corporations to voluntarily place tax payments due Panama in escrow account in US, assures them that they will receive foreign tax credits for monies so placed. Associated Press reports that Noriega has received $19 million in quarterly tax revenues, $5.5 million of which is from US companies. Senate approves by 92-to-1 margin resolution calling on president to invoke International Emergency Economic Powers Act (IEEPA), take all possible measures against Panama. (*Washington Post*, 1 April 1988, A17)
1 April 1988	Reagan administration announces that it will send 1,300 more troops to Panama to protect US citizens, keep canal open. (*Washington Post*, 2 April 1988, A1)
3 April 1988	Fearing anti-American backlash, Delvalle opposes any additional sanctions against Panama. Consensus emerges among opposition in Panama that economic measures "are not working and will not achieve their goal without causing irreparable damage to Panama's economy. . . ." (*New York Times*, 4 April 1988, A7; *Washington Post*, 6 April 1988, A27, A34)
8 April 1988	President Reagan invokes IEEPA, freezes all Panamanian government assets in US, prohibits all US payments to Noriega government. In Panama, US forces conduct exercise simulating attempted takeover of canal. (*Washington Post*, 9 April 1988, A1, A15; *New York Times*, 9 April 1988, A1; *Investor's Daily*, 11 April 1988, 1)
13 April 1988	US Marines in Canal Zone are involved in firefight with unidentified intruders. (*Washington Post*, 14 April 1988, A1)
24 April 1988	Panama's electric company cuts off power to about 45 apartments, housing 110 people, for refusal to pay bills in compliance with US sanctions. (*Washington Post*, 25 April 1988, A17)
28 April 1988	Reagan administration reportedly reaches tentative agreement with Noriega under which he would step down but not necessarily leave Panama. Noriega arrests several members of opposition, accusing them of being involved in "subversive plan" of "urban violence." (*Washington Post*, 29 April 1988, A1; *New York Times*, 29 April 1988, A1, A11; *Financial Times*, 29 April 1988, 8)
9 May 1988	Banks open for nearly normal operations, although withdrawals are limited to 25 percent of checking account balances, with maximum withdrawal of $1,000. (*Washington Post*, 4 May 1988, A30; Sullivan 29)
25 May 1988	Noriega suddenly rejects latest US proposal; Secretary of State George P. Shultz announces that all offers have been withdrawn, no further negotiations are contemplated. (*Washington Post*, 26 May 1988, A1)

31 May 1988	Treasury issues regulations allowing some exemptions to general policy of restricting payments to Panamanian government. Exemptions include payments for postal services, telecommunications fees, utilities, sales taxes, travel-related fees. (*International Trade Reporter*, 6 July 1988, 995)
23 June 1988	Administration decides, for "humanitarian reasons," to pay $4.5 million to Panamanian government to cover social security taxes for canal's Panamanian employees. It also adds exception to regulations allowing US corporations in Panama to do same. (Sullivan 35; US House of Representatives 1989b, 27; *International Trade Reporter*, 6 July 1988, 995)
July 1988	Reagan approves covert action plan to promote opposition political activity intended to discredit Noriega. Also, over objections of Defense Department, CIA, Reagan signs order "authorizing the CIA to foment a coup against Noriega by dissident military officers." Senate Intelligence Committee, concerned that Noriega might be killed in coup attempt, thus reopening issue of CIA involvement in assassinations, blocks implementation of plan. (*Washington Post*, 28 July 1988, A1; *New York Times*, 24 April 1989, A1; *US News & World Report*, 1 May 1989, 40–41)
22 August 1988	Treasury amends sanctions regulations a second time, permitting "payment of import duties and other fees that U.S. businesses complained were impeding their Panamanian operations." Still prohibited are "payment of 'income taxes, rental fees, or direct taxes and fees (e.g., export taxes and fees).'" (*International Trade Reporter*, 24 August 1988, 1196)
Summer–Fall 1988	Reagan administration shifts to low-key approach on Panama, reportedly to avoid damaging Vice President George Bush's presidential campaign. (*New York Times*, 28 October 1988, B6)
3 January 1989	Treasury issues final regulations allowing companies to place taxes owed Panama in their own reserve accounts rather than having to place them in special account at Federal Reserve. Representative Sam Gejdenson (D-CT) charges that federal account contains only about $4 million rather than approximately $70 million that should be in it. (*International Trade Reporter*, 4 January 1989, 26)
6 February 1989	President Bush signs intelligence finding authorizing CIA to provide $10 million in assistance to opposition in Panama. Opposition leaders later "vehemently" deny ever receiving any such funds. (*New York Times*, 24 April 1989, A1; *US News & World Report*, 1 May 1989, 40–41; *Washington Post*, 11 October 1989, A1)
27 March 1989	Chairman of Panama Canal Commission William R. Gianelli charges that increasing harassment of canal employees threatens continued effective operation of canal. (*Washington Post*, 28 March 1989, A14)
5 April 1989	Panamanian authorities arrest American businessman Kurt Muse, seize $350,000 worth of radio, communications equipment, which

was used to make clandestine radio broadcasts as part of US–financed covert operation to support opposition in upcoming election campaign. (*Washington Post,* 29 April 1989, A1)

6 April 1989
Bush determines that "national emergency" still exists, extends sanctions for another year. Canal commission head Gianelli resigns, claiming that "U.S. sanctions against Panama jeopardized operation of the canal." (*Journal of Commerce,* 7, 10 April 1989)

23 April 1989
Washington Post reports that Libyan leader Moammar Gadhafi provided $24 million in cash sometime in April 1988 to help Noriega survive sanctions. "The CIA reported that 'Noriega [had] run through his Libyan money' by late September. . . ." (*Washington Post,* 23 April 1989, C1)

7–8 May 1989
Panama holds presidential elections. Former President Jimmy Carter, in Panama as election observer, charges government with widespread fraud, manipulation of vote count; church-sponsored straw poll conducted immediately after vote found opposition presidential candidate Guillermo Endara leading with 74.2 percent of vote. (*Washington Post,* 9 May 1989, A1)

10 May 1989
Noriega's paramilitary force, the "Dignity Battalion," brutally breaks up opposition demonstration protesting election fraud; government nullifies election results. (*Washington Post,* 11, 12 May 1989, A1)

11 May 1989
Bush sends brigade of combat troops (1,881 soldiers) to Panama, prepares to evacuate American civilians. In addition, Ambassador Arthur H. Davis is recalled; most of embassy staff, government employees, their families are moved to military bases; US businessmen are "encouraged" to move their families out of country; State Department issues warning to US citizens against traveling to Panama or getting off ships while transiting canal. "There are an estimated 51,300 Americans in Panama, including 21,000 business people and retirees. About 200 US firms operate there." (*Washington Post,* 12 May 1989, A1)

17 May 1989
Organization of American States (OAS) adopts resolution condemning "abuses by" Noriega, decides to send delegation to Panama to "seek a formula for transferring power from the Noriega regime to a new government." (*New York Times,* 18 May 1989, A8)

3 July 1989
International Monetary Fund (IMF) declares Panama ineligible for new borrowing because of its arrears of $162 million. (*Financial Times,* 4 July 1989, 2; *New York Times,* 5 July 1989, D1)

26 July 1989
The five American members of Panama Canal Commission approve previously announced 9.8 percent toll hike to cover growing operating deficit. "The deficit was largely spawned by spiraling costs, such as a $600,000 monthly expense for busing the canal's 8,500 employees" to work (busing was begun in response to official harassment of canal employees, including refusal to issue them automobile licenses—see "Response of Target Country"). In Wash-

ington, General Accounting Office Assistant Comptroller General Frank C. Conahan testifies that exemptions have halved monetary impact of sanctions, that there is evidence of evasion of sanctions by US subsidiaries operating in Panama. (*Journal of Commerce,* 27 July 1989, 1A; *International Trade Reporter,* 2 August 1989, 1028)

23 August 1989	OAS mediators report that they have failed in their attempt to bring about peaceful transfer of power from Noriega to democratically elected regime by 1 September, when term of Acting President Solís Palma expires. OAS team criticizes recent US military maneuvers in Panama as "inopportune" and having "negative effect" on their efforts, also criticizes "violations of human, civil and political rights" by Noriega regime. (*New York Times,* 24 August 1989, A2)
31 August–1 September 1989	Panamanian Council of State dissolves National Assembly, announces that interim government headed by Francisco Rodríguez, close friend of Noriega's, will take over when Solís Palma's term ends on 1 September. Since Delvalle's term also would have ended 1 September, Ambassador Sosa officially closes Panamanian embassy in Washington, turns it over to State Department until such time as legitimate government takes power in Panama. Bush formally cuts US diplomatic ties with Panama, predicts that other nations will join US in imposing sanctions. (*Washington Post,* 1 September 1989, A20; *Financial Times,* 2 September 1989, 1)
4 September 1989	Relying on implementing regulations for Cuban embargo, Bush administration names 120 Panamanian firms, individuals "associated with" Noriega as "specially designated nationals of Cuba." Regulations forbid US companies or agencies to do business with persons or firms on list, just as they do for such persons actually residing in Cuba. (*Washington Post,* 5 September 1989, A15)
2 October 1989	Opposition coalition urges people to delay paying taxes, utility bills, and to boycott state-run lottery in order to increase economic pressure on Noriega. (*Washington Post,* 2 October 1989, A19; 3 October 1989, A21)
Early October 1989	Second coup attempt against Noriega fails. Noriega cracks down on opposition, arrests Endara, begins restructuring PDF with replacements for those involved in coup coming "from Gen. Noriega's inner circle, [which will] narrow his power base, [but] will also strengthen his grip on the PDF." Incident generates intense criticism of Bush administration for its failure to take advantage of opportunity to remove Noriega from office. (*Financial Times,* 7 October 1989, 13; 12 October 1989, 3; *Washington Post,* 9 October 1989, A1; *New York Times,* 9 October 1989, A7)
10 October 1989	Interim government issues decree intended to cut costs, punish those involved in or sympathetic with attempted coup. Measure, retroactive to 1 September, makes work stoppages, slowdowns, other acts of opposition to government punishable by dismissal, is used to lay off estimated 20 percent of public-sector work force.

Other austerity measures include "a moratorium on all public sector pay increases, bonuses, or hiring of new personnel. . . ." (*Financial Times*, 12 October 1989, 3)

11 October 1989   Report written by rebel officer reveals that coup leader Major Moises Giroldi told Noriega that he " 'had to go' because Panama was on the verge of economic ruin and the [PDF] had low morale. . . that Panamanians were going hungry, there were no jobs and rank-and-file soldiers in the PDF were unhappy." (*Washington Post*, 12 October 1989, A35)

16 November 1989   *Los Angeles Times* reports that President Bush has signed presidential finding allowing CIA to spend up to $3 million to recruit Panamanian military officers, exiles to overthrow Noriega. (*Washington Post*, 17 November 1989, A1)

30 November 1989   Bush bans Panamanian-flag vessels from entering US ports after 31 January. Panamanian registry "brings a direct annual income of $30m to the Panamanian Treasury and a further $50m in fees charged by agencies, lawyers, and company representations in Panama for the purposes of registering ships of foreign-based companies." Several countries with open registries, including Singapore, Liberia, Hong Kong, Netherlands Antilles, reduce registration fees and required paperwork to attract ships transferring out of Panamanian registry. One observer predicts that "the US Administration's actions may have a domestic cost approaching the revenues lost to the Noriega regime." (*Washington Post*, 1 December 1989, A11; *Financial Times*, 14 December 1989, 12; *Journal of Commerce*, 21 December 1989, 8B; 6)

15 December 1989   National Assembly of Representatives, appointed by Noriega, declares country is "in a state of war" with US as result of economic sanctions, names Noriega "chief of government," granting him sweeping powers "while the aggression lasts." (*Washington Post*, 16 December 1989, A21)

16 December 1989   US military officer is shot, fatally wounded by members of PDF at checkpoint in Panama City. Another officer and his wife, who were stopped earlier and observed incident, are detained for four hours; officer is allegedly beaten, his wife harassed. (*Washington Post*, 18 December 1989, A20)

20 December 1989   At 1 a.m., just after Endara has been informed of US plans and is sworn in as president, US troops invade Panama, capturing major PDF military installations, destroying Noriega's headquarters; Noriega escapes. In announcing invasion and installation of Endara government, Bush also declares that all economic sanctions will be lifted immediately. Canal is shut down for 24 hours, first time in its history that it has been shut down for any reason other than landslides or strikes. (*Washington Post*, 20 December 1989, A1)

21 December 1989   Fighting dies down to scattered gunfire. Widespread looting breaks out in Panama City, Colon; merchants decry failure of US troops to

take action against looters. Insurance companies refuse to cover looting, other damages because they fall under wartime exclusion. (*Journal of Commerce,* 28 December 1989, 1A; 29 December 1989, 1A)

24 December 1989   Noriega appears at residence of papal nuncio, Pope's representative in Panama, requests asylum. US officials say that Noriega is an international criminal not deserving of political asylum, demand that he be turned over to US authorities. Ten days later, Noriega surrenders to US officials, is flown to Miami to face drug smuggling, money laundering charges. (Dinges 308–10)

25 January 1990   Bush announces plans for $1 billion relief package for Panama. First part of package involves lifting of remaining sanctions, restoring Panama's eligibility for Export-Import Bank loans, Overseas Private Investment Corporation insurance and guarantee programs, sugar quota, GSP and CBI benefits. Bush administration expects to approve programs in these areas worth $500 million. Second, administration proposes to submit request to Congress for $500 million special appropriation, most of which will go to balance of payments support, to help Panama reduce arrearages on its debt, and to establish public investment projects to increase employment, domestic demand. In addition, Agency for International Development will provide $42 million in emergency humanitarian aid to rebuild housing destroyed in invasion, restore damaged infrastructure, provide loans to victims of widespread looting. (*New York Times,* 26 January 1990, A1; *Washington Post,* 26 January 1990, A8; US House of Representatives 1990, 4–6)

1 February 1990   Treasury Department issues final regulations unblocking Panama's assets in US, authorizing payments to new government. About $170 million in assets have been released so far. (*International Trade Reporter,* 7 February 1990, 201)

13 February 1990   White House Press Secretary Marlin Fitzwater announces that last of US invasion forces have been withdrawn from Panama. (*Washington Post,* 14 February 1990, A22)

14 February 1990   President Bush signs 1990 Urgent Assistance for Democracy in Panama Act, providing $42 million in emergency aid for Panama, restoring its eligibility for GSP, CBI benefits, Export-Import Bank, OPIC programs. (*Washington Post,* 8 February 1990; *New York Times,* 8 February 1990, A8; *International Trade Reporter,* 7 February 1990, 192; 21 February 1990, 253)

25 May 1990   Bush signs aid appropriation for Panama passed by Congress, which has trimmed it by $80 million to $420 million. (*Washington Post,* 27 May 1990, A4)

Goals of Sender Country

Section 570 of FY 1988 Foreign Assistance Appropriation Act

Congress sets four conditions for resumption of aid to Panama:

☐ Civilian control of PDF (or substantial progress toward that end)

☐ Impartial Government of Panama investigation of illegal activities of members of PDF

☐ Agreement with opposition on conditions for free and fair elections

☐ Restoration of freedom of press, other constitutional guarantees suspended under state of emergency declared by Delvalle in June 1987. (Congressional Research Service 1988, 158)

Frank C. Conahan, assistant comptroller general

"U.S. national security interests in Panama have traditionally centered on the security and effective operation of the Panama Canal and on U.S. military base rights in Panamanian territory. Over the last several years, however, Panama's role in international drug trafficking has become an important aspect of overall U.S. national security concerns. . . . By February 1988, the indictment of General Noriega on drug trafficking and racketeering charges led U.S. objectives to become specifically identified with removing General Noriega from power." (US House of Representatives 1989b, 1–2)

In order "to minimize the impact of sanctions on the U.S. business community and thereby allow it to operate in Panama," Reagan and Bush administrations ultimately allow 46 exceptions to regulations for various types of payments, including utilities, social security, import duty fees. (US House of Representatives 1989b, 12)

Senior administration officials (anonymous)

These officials say US is seeking to destabilize Noriega by "foster[ing] discontent in the P.D.F." (*New York Times*, 6 April 1988, A6)

By August 1989: "Our position is Noriega should leave office. We want a democratic transition. The United States is not insisting that Noriega leave Panama. Our position is he should leave power. Everything after that is up to the Panamanians; it ceases to be our business." (*New York Times*, 16 August 1989, A9)

Response of Target Country

Roman Catholic Church

Panama's Roman Catholic bishops issue statement declaring, "As a Church and as Panamanians, we reject U.S. sanctions because they violate national sovereignty. We believe that because of the dependent nature of our economy, any political pressure is a threat to our people's lives." (Sullivan 40)

Minister of Commerce and Industries Mario Rognoni

In summer of 1988, Rognoni expresses opinion that Panama can survive indefinitely with sanctions: "All you're doing is impoverishing the nation. We might live like Biafrans someday, but we'll still be alive." (Sullivan 42)

Noriega government

Noriega exploits Reagan administration fears of leftist influence in Panama by seeking offsetting economic assistance from Soviet Union, Cuba, Libya. Noriega also exploits fears within PDF that "attacks on him are attacks on the institution as a whole. . . . Noriega has craftily used this impression to undercut opposition within [his party] and the military, fostering the fear that those within these institutions who assist U.S. pressures against him will only be promoting their own political demise." (Millett 53, 55, 61)

Harassment of canal employees, others complying with sanctions includes refusing to issue new automobile license plates to applicants unable to prove that they have paid their taxes. In some cases, vehicles or even bank accounts are seized. One response by canal authorities is to bus some employees to and from work, at cost of $13,000 per day. (*Washington Post*, 28 March 1989, A14)

May 1988: Government issues order requiring US firms to pay employees their gross wages, out of which they should then pay income taxes directly to government. (US House of Representatives 1989b, 18)

June 1988: Panama's Finance Minister issues order "to get U.S. firms not to negotiate Panamanian government-issued checks, and to consider the value of those checks as tax payments. Some U.S. firms reportedly [buy] such checks at less than face value and, by not cashing them, could claim the face value as tax payment." Market for unused tax credits issued to firms involved in nontraditional exports also springs up. (US House of Representatives 1989b, 14)

Fall 1989: Noriega approves "Economic Battle Plan" under which US truckers can take advantage of reciprocity clauses in two treaties governing use of Pan-American highway. This would allow US truckers to register in Panama, operate in US without paying interstate highway taxes, obtain insurance rates that are, on average, half those charged by US firms. About 200 trucks are estimated to be licensed in Panama as of September. Panamanian license plates bear slogan, "Panama 2000—Total Sovereignty." (*Financial Times*, 8 September 1989, 4)

Attitudes of Other Countries

Latin America

Early April 1988: Although mildly supportive of US efforts to get rid of Noriega, most Latin American countries increasingly resent unilateral US intervention in Panamanian affairs, lack of consultation with other nations in region. (*New York Times*, 6 April 1988, A6)

Following Noriega's nullification of elections: Most Latin American nations, with exception of Nicaragua, Cuba, condemn action but caution US against military intervention. Venezuela calls for special meeting of OAS to discuss Panama. Other Latin American countries issue statements condemning Noriega's action. Mexico recalls its ambassador for consultations, departs from its traditional policy of nonintervention, issuing statement "blasting Noriega for his unsavory 'moral and ethical reputation.' " (*Washington Post*, 16 May 1989, A16)

As 1 September end of Solís Palma's term approaches, Colombia, Venezuela, Brazil, Argentina, Uruguay, Peru call their ambassadors home for consultations. (*Washington Post*, 1 September 1989, A20)

After invasion, OAS votes 20 to 1 to censure US. Peru temporarily suspends cooperation with US anti-drug efforts in Huallaga Valley; Peruvian President Alan García initially says he will not attend 15 February drug summit in Colombia as long as there are US troops in Panama, but changes his mind after Bush announces that troops will be withdrawn before end of February. (*Washington Post*, 23 December 1989, A7; *Financial Times*, 7 February 1990, 5)

European Community

European Community, as well as governments of West Germany, Spain, UK, condemn nullification of elections. Although 10 nations, including Soviet Union, China, several Latin American nations, vote in favor of UN Security Council resolution condemning US invasion of Panama, vetoes by US, UK, France (which was critical of invasion) block its adoption. (*Washington Post*, 24 December 1989, A16)

Nicaragua

Nicaragua offers to send troops to help PDF defend itself if US troops intervene with force. (*Washington Post*, 12 May 1989, A1)

Washington Post reports that Nicaraguan army has sent "several planeloads" of weapons supplied by Soviet bloc, including AK-47 rifles, ammunition, grenade launchers, light artillery, to Noriega to help him prepare for possible US military attack. Nicaraguan officials reportedly believe that attack on Panama might set stage for similar attack on Nicaragua. (*Washington Post*, 9 June 1989, A1)

Legal Notes

Initial legal basis for freezing Panamanian assets in US banks is section 25(b) of Federal Reserve Act, passed in 1941 to allow seizure of central bank assets of countries overrun by German or Japanese forces during World War II. "Under the law, the Secretary of State certifies what the United States recognizes as the legal government of a foreign country and instructs the banking system as to what authority has control over the funds." (*New York Times*, 8 March 1988, A3; *Washington Post*, 23 March 1988, A22; Lombard 325)

Economic Impact

Observed Economic Statistics

United States: economic and military assistance to Panama, 1980–87
(millions of dollars)[a]

| | US bilateral | | | | Multilateral [b] | | | |
| | Economic | | | | | | | |
Year	Loans	Grants	Military	Total	World Bank	IDB	Other[c]	Total
1980	0.0	2.0	0.3	2.3	58.0	91.4	0.5	149.9
1981	6.4	4.2	0.4	11.0	45.5	28.5	0.5	74.5
1982	8.1	4.9	5.4	18.4	24.4	99.0	3.5	126.9

1983	3.8	3.6	5.5	12.9	85.0	52.0	0.7	137.7
1984	5.0	7.0	13.5	25.5	74.2	8.4	0.0	82.6
1985	7.9	66.6	10.6	85.1	51.0	48.7	37.7	137.4
1986	7.5	25.9	8.2	41.6	0.0	16.2	23.5	39.7
1987	0.0	12.1	3.5	15.6	100.0	102.1	0.0	202.1

IDB = Inter-American Development Bank.

a. By US fiscal year.

b. Data are loan commitments, not disbursements. Most of 1987 loans have been withheld because of debt arrearages.

c. International Finance Corporation and United Nations.

Source: Agency for International Development.

In 1986, US payments to Panama related to its military presence, running of canal total $532 million, more than 10 percent of Panamanian GNP. Of that, payments from canal revenues, as agreed to in treaties, are about $80 million per year, including fixed annuity of $10 million per year, about another $10 million for public services provided by Panama, and between $50 million and $60 million as Panama's share of toll receipts. Salary payments for canal's Panamanian employees (about $6 million per month) are unaffected by sanctions. (*Financial Times,* 27 January 1988, 4; *New York Times,* 22 February 1988, D8; 7 March 1988, A1; Sullivan 35)

It is estimated that US agencies, primarily US Army Southern Command, Canal Commission, spend nearly $900 million annually on goods and services in Panama. (*Washington Post,* 5 September 1989, A15)

There are about 150,000 civil servants in Panama, a quarter of total work force, plus 15,000 in military, with total monthly payroll of $66 million. Economy is dependent on financial, other services, including activities of the Canal and Colon Free Trade Zone, for estimated 80 percent of GDP. (*Washington Post,* 6 April 1988, A34; *Financial Times,* 25 April 1988; Sullivan 22; US House of Representatives 1990, 3)

At end of May 1989, *The Economist* reports that, according to banking sources, "government salaries were paid last week with help from a Libyan grant of $50m; the Libyans are also offering a credit line of $100m in oil supplies, though there are doubts whether Colonel Qaddafi will really deliver." (*The Economist,* 27 May 1989, 42)

Growth in 1987 is stagnant; according to one source, strikes and protests of June 1987 "severely damaged" economy even before sanctions were imposed. Average personal income is estimated to have fallen from $2,340 in 1987 to $1,840 a year later. By early 1989: "Most construction has stopped, the government is desperately short of real money to pay its own employees, and the banking system is theoretically paralysed. Panama's GDP went down by some 20% last year." Construction sector, which employed 34,000 in 1986, is the most devastated by lack of capital for investment. Economic activity in that sector is estimated to have declined 95 percent by June 1988. (*The Economist,* 15 April 1989, 43–44; 14 October 1989, 46; Millett 46; Sullivan 24–25, 30–31)

IMF estimates that Panama's economy shrank 16 percent in 1988 and was stagnant in 1989. Unemployment has increased from 14 percent to 25 percent. (*Wall Street Journal,* 4 January 1990, A7; *Washington Post,* 25 January 1990, A1; US House of Representatives 1990, 3–4)

After assets freeze, BNP chairman tells bankers that liquid cash resources are only $17 million, down from $300 million at beginning of 1987. Following Reagan's invocation of IEEPA, one foreign banker in Panama estimates that as many as 60 of 130 offshore banks in Panama have "quietly shut down or [have] made the decision to do so as soon as they can transfer their assets." (*New York Times,* 8 February 1988, A8; 5 March 1988, A1; *Financial Times,* 7 March 1988, 4; *Washington Post,* 9 March 1988, A16; *Wall Street Journal,* 7 April 1988; *Washington Post,* 10 April 1988, A1; Sullivan 32)

Unnamed US official notes that Noriega is getting cash into country in various ways, including continued agricultural exports, as well as access to drug-related money in Colombia, elsewhere. One "well-placed U.S. source" estimates that "the amount of cash in Panama City has ballooned to between $3 billion and $4 billion in recent months, as much as 10 times the U.S. government's official estimates of $300 million to $400 million." Following invasion, bankers in Panama estimate that offshore deposits dropped from about $38 billion to $12 billion over past two years as result of economic, political crisis. (*Washington Post,* 27 January 1989, A1; *Wall Street Journal,* 4 Janury 1990, A7)

Panamanian government responds to liquidity squeeze by issuing salary checks in denominations of $20, $30, $100, "persuad[ing] businesses to treat them as cash." Although checks are usually sold or traded at discount (averaging 30 percent in summer of 1988), "buyers, including many businesses, can then use the checks at full face value to pay taxes and utilities to the government." (Sullivan 29–30)

In 1987, Panama has largest per capita foreign debt in world, including $1.9 billion in long-term debt owed to foreign commercial banks, $1.8 billion owed to official creditors, $1.7 billion in short-term debt (with population of approximately 2.3 million). It has received no new money from commercial banks since 1985. (Sullivan 37; *New York Times,* 8 February 1988, A8; *Financial Times,* 3 March 1988, 4; World Bank, 178)

In early 1988, World Bank cancels $50 million portion of structural adjustment loan to Panama because of its failure to meet conditions; Bank suspends disbursements on other loans, including one for $51 million, because of arrears of $11 million. (*New York Times,* 8 February 1988, A8; *Financial Times,* 3 March 1988, 4; *Washington Post,* 29 January 1989, A28; Sullivan 37)

By early 1990, Panama's arrears to international financial institutions total $540 million; to commercial banks, $433 million. Assistant Secretary of the Treasury for International Affairs Charles H. Dallara testifies in favor of administration proposal to provide $130 million to Panama as part of multilateral effort to help reduce its arrears so it can become eligible for new funds. (US House of Representatives 1990, 4–5)

Panama: foreign trade, 1980–88 (millions of dollars except where noted)[a]

	Exports (f.o.b.)			Imports (c.i.f.)		
Year	Total	To US	US share (percentages)	Total	From US	US share (percentages)
1980	360	173	48	1,449	489	34
1981	328	167	51	1,540	536	35
1982	375	129	34	1,569	549	35
1983	321	161	50	1,412	456	32
1984	276	153	55	1,423	451	32

1985	335	193	57	1,392	438	31
1986	350	225	64	1,229	448	36
1987	340	225	66	1,306	449	34
1988	281	143	51	795	300	38

a. Does not include Colon Free Trade Zone.
Sources: International Monetary Fund; Contraloría General de la República.

Panamanian imports from US consist primarily of chemicals, machinery and vehicles, petroleum, other manufactured goods. Panama exports primarily bananas, shrimp, sugar, refined petroleum. Although Panama is eligible for GSP, CBI benefits, refined petroleum is not an eligible product; imports of bananas, coffee, shrimp are duty-free in any case. Only apparel exports would be significantly affected. In first half of 1988, Panama's previously preferential exports to US drop to $19 million, compared with $49 million in same period of 1987, a decline of 61 percent. Overall, exports to US decline 17 percent. (Sullivan 34)

Panama's initial sugar quota allocation for 1988 was 30,537 metric tons. Estimated value, based on average US import price in 1988 of 22 cents per pound, is $15 million. Panama was able to sell only $6 million worth of sugar on world market in 1988 at average price two-thirds of that received in 1987. (*New York Times,* 13 September 1989, A5; IMF, *International Financial Statistics*)

General Accounting Office (GAO) estimates that as result of sanctions, declining economy, Panamanian government revenues were nearly $480 million less in 1988 than the approximately $1.1 billion in 1987. GAO attributes 26 percent ($125 million) to direct effects of sanctions. It also cites estimates by State Department that up to 40 percent of decline in economy is due to direct, indirect effects of sanctions. GAO further estimates that direct payments of $650 million would be needed before Panama would be able to generate new investment from international financial institutions. (US House of Representatives 1989b, 17–22; *International Trade Reporter,* 2 August 1989, 1028)

As of 20 December 1989, when sanctions are lifted, GAO reports $375 million in frozen assets: $188 million in US government escrow accounts; $31.7 million in frozen Panamanian government assets in US banks; $9.5 million in corporate tax payments in escrow accounts; $145.7 million in corporations' own bank accounts or carried as liabilities on their books. (*Washington Post,* 28 December 1989, A28)

Only 12 ships cancel Panamanian registry before US sanction is lifted in late December 1989, although 560 ships have begun cancellation procedures (out of total of 12,149 ships flying Panamanian flag). (*Financial Times,* 12 January 1990, 5)

Calculated Economic Impact (annual cost to target country)

From financial sanctions:	
Reduction in US economic, military aid; welfare loss estimated at 90 percent of transfers in 1987.	$14 million
Freezing of Panamanian government assets in US banks; welfare loss estimated at 100 percent of face value.	32 million

US government withholding of payments owed Panamanian government; welfare loss estimated at 100 percent of average annual value of such payments.	103 million
US corporations' withholding of taxes, fees owed Panamanian government; welfare loss estimated at 50 percent of value of funds placed in escrow or carried as liabilities on companies' own books.	78 million
From trade sanctions: Suspension of sugar quota; welfare estimated at 100 percent of estimated value of sugar sales lost.	9 million
Suspension of GSP, CBI trade benefits; welfare loss estimated at 40 percent of value of exports lost (assumed to be two-thirds of eligible exports in 1987).	26 million
Indirect effect of sanctions: Welfare loss estimated at 10 percent of overall decline in output of goods, services (based on IMF estimate of 16 percent decline in output in 1988, State Department estimate attributing 40 percent of decline to direct, indirect effects of sanctions).	85 million
Offsets Increase in grants from Libya; welfare gain estimated at 75 percent of average annual value of Libyan assistance.	($28 million)
Total	$319 million

Relative Magnitudes

Gross indicators of Panamanian economy	
Panamanian GNP (1987)	$5.3 billion
Panamanian population (1987)	2.3 million
Annual effect of sanctions related to gross indicators	
Percentage of GNP	6.0
Per capita	$138.70
Panamanian trade with US as percentage of total trade	
Exports (1987)	66
Imports (1987)	34
Ratio of US GNP (1987: $4,527 billion) to Panamanian GNP	854

Assessment

Mark P. Sullivan

As of January 1989: "The sanctions . . . have not yet achieved the objective of bringing about a return to civilian democratic rule. Both the economy and the government have shown considerable resiliency, and the regime has received moral and financial support from Latin American and other U.S. allies. Panama's opposition appears to be somewhat divided over the use of sanctions, and the PDF's loyalty to Noriega has not been broken." (Sullivan i)

Representative Sam Gejdenson (D-CT)

"There are two contradictory and therefore unattainable goals for the economic sanctions. We wanted to get Noriega out, but we did not want to hurt US businesses, the people of Panama, or the Panamanian economy. In other words, we wanted to have our cake and eat it too. And, since the Administration was not fully committed to either goal, we failed to accomplish either one. We still have Noriega and we have severely damaged both U.S. and Panamanian businesses and the economy of Panama." (US House of Representatives 1989a, 1)

Former Ambassador to Panama Ambler Moss

"If the U.S. had sat back and done nothing, he [Noriega] might not have made it through 1988 . . . but increasing external pressure has only given him additional excuses for repression, and a scapegoat for his own mismanagement." (*Wall Street Journal*, 18 October 1989, A1)

John Dinges

"The sanctions soon proved a blunt instrument that barely touched Noriega's military and civilian power base. The main sufferers were the U.S.–owned companies, the pro–U.S. Panamanian businessmen who were the backbone of the opposition to Noriega, and the Panamanian middle class." (Dinges 300)

"[T]he decision to force Noriega from power was not the result of any considered policy drafted by experts measuring the costs, benefits and alternatives. In fact, the Reagan and Bush administrations seemed to improvise as they went along, reacting to events in Panama and adapting to a building furor of antidrug sentiment in the United States. That incoherence of strategy is why they failed for so long to neutralize the Panamanian leader. . . . The administration remained deeply divided until well into 1988 over what to do about Noriega. Until Bush authorized the invasion, the administration was never a leader, never a shaper of events." (Dinges 313)

Authors' Summary

Overall assessment

- ☐ Policy result, scaled from 1 (failed) to 4 (success)   4
- ☐ Sanctions contribution, scaled from 1 (none) to 4 (significant)   1
- ☐ Success score (policy result *times* sanctions contribution), scaled from 1 (outright failure) to 16 (significant success)   4

Political and economic variables

- ☐ Companion policies: J (covert), Q (quasi-military), or R (regular military)   J,Q,R
- ☐ International cooperation with sender, scaled from 1 (none) to 4 (significant)   1
- ☐ International assistance to target: A (if present)   A
- ☐ Sanctions period (years)   3
- ☐ Economic health and political stability of target, scaled from 1 (distressed) to 3 (strong)   2

☐ Presanction relations between sender and target, scaled from
  1 (antagonistic) to 3 (cordial)   3
☐ Type of sanction: X (export), M (import), F (financial)   M,F
☐ Cost to sender, scaled from 1 (net gain) to 4 (major loss)   3

Comments

No other case in this study has been scored a success (4) in which sanctions either contributed nothing or worsened the situation (1). Despite Panama's unique economic dependence on the US (due both to the canal and its use of the dollar as its currency), the Panamanian government found numerous creative methods for surviving the liquidity crisis provoked by the sanctions. Although the economic sanctions severely disrupted the economy, after two years and two coup attempts, Noriega appeared no closer than ever to stepping down, and it took direct military intervention to remove him from power. The only contribution of the sanctions was, perhaps, to improve the reception American troops got in Panama, because the invasion was accepted as a last resort after economic pressure had failed.

Bibliography

Agency for International Development. 1983, 1987. *US Overseas Loans and Grants*. Washington.

Congressional Research Service, Library of Congress. 1988. *U.S. Economic Sanctions Imposed against Specific Foreign Countries, 1979 to the Present*. CRS Report for Congress no. 88–612 F (revised), 9 September. Washington.

Contraloría General de la República. *Panamá en Cifras*, various issues. Panama City.

Dinges, John. 1990. *Our Man in Panama*. New York: Random House.

Facts on File. 1987.

Harrison, Glennon J. 1988. *Panama: Trade, Finance, and Proposed Economic Sanctions*. CRS Report for Congress, No. 88–188 E, 7 March. Washington.

International Monetary Fund. *Direction of Trade Statistics*, various issues. Washington.

Keesing's Contemporary Archives. 1987.

Lombard, Joseph C. 1989. "The Survival of Noriega: Lessons from the U.S. Sanctions against Panama." 26 *Stanford Journal of International Law* no. 1 (Fall): 315–69.

Millett, Richard. 1988. "Looking Beyond Noriega." 71 *Foreign Policy* (Summer): 46–63.

Sullivan, Mark P. 1988. *U.S. Sanctions and the State of the Panamanian Economy*. CRS Report for Congress no. 88–578 F, 22 August. Washington.

US House of Representatives. Committee on Foreign Affairs, Subcommittee on International Economic Policy and Trade and Subcommittee on Western Hemisphere Affairs. 1989a. Statement by Representative Sam Gejdenson. 101 Cong., 1 sess., 26 July. Washington.

US House of Representatives. Committee on Foreign Affairs, Subcommittee on International Economic Policy and Trade and Subcommittee on Western Hemisphere Affairs. 1989b. *GAO Review of Economic Sanctions Imposed Against Panama*. Statement by Frank C. Conahan. 101 Cong., 1 sess., 26 July.

US House of Representatives, Committee on Foreign Affairs. 1990. Statement by Assistant Secretary of the Treasury Charles H. Dallara. 101 Cong., 2 sess., 6 February. Washington.

World Bank. 1990. *World Debt Tables 1989–90*. Washington.

CASE 89–2

US v. China

(1989–   : Tiananmen Square Massacre)

Chronology of Key Events

December 1986   Students begin pro-democracy protests, which spread from provinces to Beijing. (*Facts on File* 955–56)

January 1987   Chinese leader Deng Xiaoping denounces protests; Hu Yaobang, regarded as Deng's likely successor, champion of political, economic reform, accepts responsibility for protests, is replaced as General Secretary of Communist Party by Zhao Ziyang. Deng also criticizes leading intellectuals, including astrophysicist Fang Lizhi, who is stripped of university vice presidency, denounced for his espousal of complete "Westernization" of China, support for student unrest. (*Facts on File* 9–10; *New York Times*, 25 February 1987, A10)

April 1989   Death of Hu Yaobang sparks new pro-democracy protests; 10,000 students rally in Tiananmen Square in Beijing, 1,000 in Shanghai on 16 April. Following week, about 100,000 demonstrate in Tiananmen Square for political reforms. On 24 April, students begin boycotting classes in Beijing. Supported by almost 500,000 onlookers, more than 100,000 people march through Beijing on 27 April for over 12 hours in largest demonstration since death of Zhou Enlai in April 1976. (*Facts on File* 298)

15–18 May 1989   Visit by Soviet President Mikhail Gorbachev to China, first Sino-Soviet summit in 30 years, is upstaged by more than 1 million demonstrators in Tiananmen Square. Protesters call for democratic reforms, resignation of Deng, other leaders. (*Facts on File* 353)

20 May 1989   Premier Li Peng declares martial law, orders protestors to clear Tiananmen Square; protestors ignore order, remain in square. More than 1 million people show their support for demonstrators by erecting roadblocks, barricades to deter military intervention. (*Facts on File* 369)

25 May 1989   Li Peng stations 200,000 troops in outskirts of Beijing, appearing to have won power struggle with Zhao Ziyang, who opposed decision to involve army. (*Facts on File* 369, 396)

29 May 1989	Protestors construct 33-foot-tall statue resembling Statue of Liberty, name it "Goddess of Democracy." (*Facts on File* 396)
3–5 June 1989	Army disperses protestors, killing hundreds, perhaps thousands of people in Tiananmen Square. Clashes between army units in Beijing fuel speculation of leadership rift. Fang Lizhi takes refuge in US embassy. (*New York Times*, 4 June 1989, A1; 6 June 1989, A1; *Washington Post*, 4 June 1989, A1)
5 June 1989	President George Bush suspends all arms sales to, military contacts with China. Action reportedly affects $600 million in government-to-government contracts, perhaps another $100 million in commercial sales, including more than 300 items on munitions control list, three communications satellites, navigational equipment on Boeing 757–200 jets. In addition, Bush offers to extend visas of Chinese students in US, orders review of existing bilateral arrangements. (*Washington Post*, 6 June 1989, A18; 2 July 1989, A1; *Business Week*, 19 June 1989, 29)
6 June 1989	House, Senate pass concurrent resolutions urging president to condition applications for Overseas Private Investment Corporation (OPIC) and Export-Import Bank (Eximbank) loans, relaxation of export controls on improvement in "deteriorating condition" of human rights in China; president is also urged to consult with Western allies on "whether multilateral sanctions are necessary to demonstrate abhorrence of the repressive actions" of Chinese authorities. (*International Trade Reporter*, 14 June 1989, 776)
9 June 1989	Bush administration reaffirms decision taken 31 May to extend waiver of Jackson-Vanik amendment that allows China to continue to receive most-favored-nation (MFN) tariff treatment. In Beijing speech, Deng congratulates army for suppressing "counterrevolutionary rebellion" led by "a rebellious clique and a large quantity of the dregs of society . . . that wanted to overthrow our state and the party." (*New York Times*, 30 June 1989, A6; *International Trade Reporter*, 14 June 1989, 776)
20 June 1989	Seeking to deter Congress from pushing for harsher sanctions, Bush suspends all high-level government exchanges with China, including planned July visit by Commerce Secretary Robert A. Mosbacher, announces intention to seek delays in new loans for China from international financial institutions. Japan suspends negotiations with China on five-year, 810-billion-yen aid program ($5.5 billion at current exchange rate) due to begin in April 1990. (*New York Times*, 21 June 1989, A1; *Financial Times* [London], 21 June 1989, 1)
21 June 1989	Despite appeals for clemency by Western governments, Chinese authorities execute three men for setting fire to train during demonstrations in Shanghai earlier in month. Xinhua (official Chinese news agency) confirms next day that 27 people have been

executed for crimes related to protests. (*Washington Post,* 22 June 1989, A1; *New York Times,* 22 June 1989, A1; *Financial Times,* 23 June 1989, 4)

23 June 1989 Congressman Tom Lantos (D-CA) introduces bill to remove China's MFN trade status. (*New York Times,* 23 June 1989, A5)

24 June 1989 China's communist party purges Zhao Ziyang for his support of student protests. Jiang Zemin, proponent of Deng's policy of economic but not political reform, replaces Zhao as general secretary. Actions culminate week in which top editors of *People's Daily* are replaced by hardliners, arrest warrants issued for influential writers, scholars, economists. (*Washington Post,* 26 June 1989, A1)

26 June 1989 World Bank announces that it will defer consideration of about $780 million in new loans to China, but will continue to disburse funds under existing commitments. (*Financial Times,* 27 June 1989, 1)

27 June 1989 European leaders condemn Chinese repression, suspend high-level contacts, postpone new economic cooperation projects, ban arms sales and military cooperation, postpone examination of new requests for credit insurance as well as loans from World Bank. (*Financial Times,* 28 June 1989, 2; *Washington Post,* 28 June 1989, A18)

29 June 1989 House of Representatives votes 418 to 0 in favor of amendment to foreign aid bill that codifies Bush's earlier sanctions, suspends new investment guarantees and previously authorized funds for US trade development, bans exports of crime-control and "gray-area" nuclear equipment, calls for negotiations in COCOM (Consultative Group and Coordinating Committee for Multilateral Export Controls) to suspend recent reforms of technology transfer rules for China. President is authorized to lift sanctions if China makes progress on political reforms, or if he deems it in national interest to do so. (*Washington Post,* 30 June 1989, A1; *New York Times,* 30 June 1989, A1; *Wall Street Journal,* 30 June 1989, A14)

Early July 1989 National Security Adviser Brent Scowcroft and Deputy Secretary of State Lawrence S. Eagleburger secretly visit Beijing "to personally underscore US shock and concern about the violence in Tiananmen Square," and because "the President felt this face-to-face mission . . . was necessary to show the sense of purpose and direction of the U.S. government." Trip is not revealed publicly until 18 December 1989. (*New York Times,* 19 December 1989, A1)

5 July 1989 GATT (General Agreement on Tariffs and Trade) officials announce that meetings to negotiate China's reentry are being postponed indefinitely because "in the present circumstances the working party was unlikely to be able to make any progress." (*Financial Times,* 6 July 1989, 6)

7 July 1989 US amends sanctions to allow sale of three Boeing jets previously banned because of their Honeywell navigation systems, shipment of a fourth plane scheduled for June delivery. In addition,

Honeywell is allowed to repair defective systems on similar planes already bought by China. US officials argue that "the decision is in keeping with the President's intent not to disrupt nonmilitary commercial trade," reflects effort to encourage China to show leniency for pro-democracy protestors. However, crackdown on pro-democracy movement continues; about 10,000 "hooligans" and "counterrevolutionaries" reportedly have been arrested since June uprising. (*New York Times,* 8 July 1989, A1; *Washington Post,* 8 July 1989, A1; 10 July 1989, A17)

13 July 1989   William F. Ryan, acting Eximbank chairman, testifies that "[n]ew applications for medium and long-term financing support [for China] will not receive final consideration unless it is clear that the U.S. supplier will lose the business in the absence of an Exim financing offer." (US House of Representatives 2)

14 July 1989   Senate, by 81-to-10 margin, approves amendment incorporating China sanctions approved earlier by House, as well as calling for postponement of Eximbank loans, opposition to loans to China by international financial institutions, review of all bilateral trade agreements—including whether to continue MFN status. (*Washington Post,* 15 July 1989, A1)

15 July 1989   Leaders of Group of Seven (G-7) major industrial countries, meeting at economic summit in Paris, announce that "to express our deep sense of condemnation" each has suspended high-level contacts, bilateral arms trade with China; in addition, they agree "that, in view of current economic uncertainties, the examination of new loans by the World Bank [should] be postponed." Actions are taken in hopes that China will "create conditions which will avoid their isolation and provide for a return to cooperation based upon the resumption of movement toward political and economic reform and openness." (*New York Times,* 16 July 1989, A17)

21 July 1989   *People's Daily* editorial warns that Hong Kong will only remain capitalist after 1997 if its residents stop supporting pro-democracy movement. (*Journal of Commerce,* 24 July 1989, 4A)

31 July 1989   Secretary of State James A. Baker III meets with Chinese Foreign Minister Qian Qichen during international conference in Paris on future of Cambodia. (*Washington Post,* 1 August 1989, A1)

31 July 1989   Chinese officials concede that only 383 of 1,168 foreign business offices in Beijing have resumed normal operations since June protests. (*Journal of Commerce,* 1 August 1989, 4A)

17 August 1989   Japan announces it will soon resume, on selective basis, existing economic aid projects frozen after 4 June crackdown. (*New York Times,* 18 August 1989, A9)

31 August 1989   United Nations human rights panel resolution cites concern about recent events in China, "their consequences in the field of human rights." (*Washington Post,* 1 September 1989, A21)

Mid-September 1989	US holds low-level talks in Washington with Chinese trade delegation on prospects for resumption of negotiations on GATT accession. (*Washington Post,* 6 September 1989, A11)
28 October 1989	Former President Richard M. Nixon begins four-day visit to Beijing, reportedly carries message to senior Chinese leaders from Bush. (*Facts on File* 845)
November 1989	China's Central Committee reportedly issues 39-point document calling for increased state planning, new restrictions on private enterprises. (*Financial Times,* 14 December 1989, 16)
19–20 November 1989	House, Senate pass legislation sponsored by Congresswoman Nancy Pelosi (D-CA) waiving requirement that Chinese students holding J-1 visas return home for two years upon completion of their studies in US. Chinese government threatens to cancel Fulbright scholarship program as well as other educational, cultural exchanges if bill becomes law. (*Washington Post,* 23 November 1989, A56; *New York Times,* 24 November 1989, A9)
30 November 1989	Bush vetoes Pelosi bill, promises to issue executive order to same effect. (*New York Times,* 1 December 1989, A24)
9–10 December 1989	In surprise visit to Beijing, Scowcroft, Eagleburger meet with Deng Xiaoping, other Chinese leaders. Agenda reportedly covers bilateral differences over human rights, exports of Chinese M-9 missiles, Cambodia, recent US–USSR summit talks in Malta. (*Washington Post,* 11 December 1989, A1, A25; 12 December 1989, A1, A20; 8 February 1990, A17)
12 December 1989	GATT working party considering Chinese accession to GATT reconvenes in Geneva. (Reuters, 7 December 1989)
13 December 1989	UK Export Credit Guarantee Department announces it will soon relax suspension of export credit guarantees for China. (*Financial Times,* 14 December 1989, 16)
15 December 1989	China devalues its currency by 21 percent, from 3.71 to 4.71 yuan to dollar, in attempt to reverse its increasing trade deficit; however, new official rate is still overvalued compared to black market rate (between 5 and 6 yuan per dollar). (*New York Times,* 16 December 1989, 39)
18–19 December 1989	EC Council meeting in Strasbourg, France, agrees to lift ban on official export credit financing for China. Consortium of 67 Japanese banks announces plans to activate $2 billion line of credit originally arranged with China in 1979, renegotiated in 1985, but never drawn on. On 16 January 1990, Bank of China announces intent to borrow $500 million to be used only for export finance. (*Wall Street Journal,* 19 December 1989, A16; *Financial Times,* 11 January 1990, 4; 17 January 1990, 4)
19 December 1989	Declaring both actions in US national interest, Bush waives controls on exports of three US–made satellites to China, waives restrictions included in International Development and Finance Act of 1989 on

new Eximbank financing commitments. He emphasizes that Eximbank decision does not return its position in China to normal, but continues policy adopted in June of approving commitments only "where project decisions are imminent." (*Wall Street Journal*, 20 December 1989, 16)

9 January 1990   Bush administration announces that, except for earthquake reconstruction, other basic human needs, it will continue to oppose new World Bank loans for China because of unraveling of economic reforms as well as political, human rights considerations. (*Washington Post*, 10 January 1990, A12)

10 January 1990   China lifts martial law. However, army units in Beijing reportedly are reassigned to police. (*Washington Post*, 11 January 1990, A1; *New York Times*, 15 February 1990, A3)

24–25 January 1990   House, by vote of 390 to 25, overrides presidential veto of Pelosi bill, but Senate override fails by vote of 62 to 37. (*Washington Post*, 25 January 1990, A1; 26 January 1990, A1, A14)

2 February 1990   Citing national security considerations, Bush invokes Exon-Florio provision of 1988 trade act to order CATIC, Chinese state-owned corporation, to divest its recent acquisition of Mamco Manufacturing of Seattle, reportedly because of concern that Chinese firm could use Mamco to acquire sensitive jet fighter engine technology. US Eximbank approves $9.75 million loan to China National Offshore Oil Corporation after bank officials determine that purchase of US engineering services for gasfield project depends on such financing. (*Washington Post*, 3 February 1990, A1; *New York Times*, 6 February 1990, D1)

3 February 1990   In report to be released 21 February, State Department charges China with pervasive, severe violations of human rights, citing *inter alia* massacre at Tiananmen Square, "still continuing" crackdown on dissidents. (*New York Times*, 4 February 1990, 26)

6 February 1990   Italy resumes official export credit guarantees for three shipments to China worth about $40 million. China announces that its graduates will be required to work for five years, pass political litmus test before becoming eligible for overseas study. Cumulative effect of restrictions on foreign study issued since June "is to put study abroad out of reach for many Chinese who are not yet locked into the [political] system." (*Financial Times*, 7 February 1990, 6; *Washington Post*, 7 February 1990, A1)

8 February 1990   US Eximbank approves $23 million financing package for Shanghai subway, again stating that "contracts won by American companies would have been jeopardized." World Bank approves $30 million loan for earthquake relief in China, but at US request defers vote on $60 million agricultural development loan. (*Journal of Commerce*, 9 February 1990, 4A; *New York Times*, 9 February 1990, A3)

16 February 1990	Bush signs State Department authorization bill with congressional amendments codifying his earlier sanctions against China, including postponement of Eximbank financing, suspension of OPIC and Trade and Development Program projects, ban on export licenses for military items. Legislation provides for review of bilateral agreements, including MFN trade status, if situation in China worsens. Bush invokes national-interest waiver to avoid imposing additional sanctions. (*New York Times*, 31 January 1990, A8; by communication, US Congress)
27 February 1990	World Bank approves $60 million loan for agricultural development in China; US votes for loan because it deals with "basic human needs," notes that other loans to China will be judged on that criterion. (*Washington Post*, 28 February 1990, A4)
March 1990	Bush admits that "there hasn't been much give" by Chinese leaders in loosening internal repression in response to administration overtures. China reportedly resumes missile sales to Middle Eastern nations to raise badly needed hard currency, despite assurances given Scowcroft in December. European diplomat in Beijing questions whether "the Chinese feel that the relationship with the U.S. is so bad that they can take the risk of selling these missiles." Six bills are introduced in Congress to suspend MFN treatment for China. Foreign Minister Qian Qichen warns that loss of MFN would cause "major retrogression" in bilateral relations. (*New York Times*, 11 March 1990, 1; 29 March 1990, A11; *Washington Post*, 29 March 1990, A1)
9 April 1990	Japanese Finance Minister Ryutaro Hashimoto calls for resumption of five-year, 810-billion-yen development loan to China if it meets "a few conditions," including restoration of human rights. (*Financial Times*, 10 April 1990, 10; *Journal of Commerce*, 5 June 1990, 4A)
Early May 1990	China releases 211 prisoners arrested in previous year's protests. "[D]iplomats and Chinese intellectuals say the move seems aimed at improving China's image abroad and, in particular, derailing U.S. lawmakers' efforts to take away China's most-favored-nation trade status." The American Chamber of Commerce in Hong Kong mounts campaign in opposition to MFN revocation, arguing that it could reduce by half their $8.5 billion in reexports of Chinese-made goods. The US–China Business Council also lobbies for renewal of China's MFN status. (*Wall Street Journal*, 11 May 1990, A10; *Far Eastern Economic Review*, 3 May 1990, 42)
24 May 1990	Bush renews China's MFN status, arguing that "by maintaining our involvement with China we will continue to promote the reforms for which the victims of Tiananmen gave their lives." Bush also praises China's lifting of martial law in Tibet, restoration of US consular access in that region. Asia Watch report, however, says human rights abuses are continuing in Tibet, that martial law was lifted because "the level of repression is secure enough as to no

longer require a conspicuous military role in suppressing dissent." (*Washington Post*, 25 May 1990, A1; 29 May 1990, A18)

29 May 1990   Despite opposition from human rights groups, Chinese students abroad, World Bank approves $300 million loan for reforestation project in China, arguing that it serves "basic human needs" by providing "jobs, fuel and housing material for low-income farmers." At US insistence, Bank delays consideration of $150 million loan for transportation project. (*Washington Post*, 30 May 1990, A17; *Financial Times*, 30 May 1990, 20)

25 June 1990   China allows dissident Fang Lizhi, his wife to emigrate to UK, citing signs of repentance by couple, Fang's reported health problems. Move is thought aimed at influencing discussions on easing sanctions against China at upcoming G-7 economic summit in Houston. (*Washington Post*, 26 June 1990, A1; *The Economist*, 30 June 1990, 33–34)

7–11 July 1990 Just before opening of economic summit, Bush meets with Japanese Prime Minister Toshiki Kaifu, says he will not oppose Japanese plans to gradually resume "humanitarian" lending to China. At summit meeting, Japan also pushes for easing of other sanctions, but with French President François Mitterrand, Canadian Prime Minister Brian Mulroney opposed, G-7 leaders agree only to "explore" resuming World Bank lending for other than "humanitarian" purposes. Following Kaifu's public statement that suspended five-year loan program will go forward after summit, Chairman of Federation of Bankers' Association of Japan Taizo Hashida says Japanese commercial banks will look "positively" on resumption of lending to China. It is expected that ¥120 billion in project loans will be approved by March 1991. (*Washington Post*, 8 July 1990, A1; 11 July 1990, A4; *New York Times*, 11 July 1990, A5, 19 July 1990, A12; *Financial Times*, 11 July 1990, 21; *Wall Street Journal*, 12 July 1990, A8)

Goals of Sender Country

President George Bush

At 6 June press conference: "The United States cannot condone the violent attacks and cannot ignore the consequences for our relationship with China." Bush calls for "a reasoned, careful action, that takes into account both our long-term interests and recognition of a complex internal situation in China . . . that will encourage the further development and deepening of the positive elements of [the US–China] relationship and the process of democratization. . . . I don't want to see a total break in this relationship. . . . I want to see us stay involved and continue to work for restraint and for human rights and for democracy." (*Washington Post*, 6 June 1989, A18)

White House statement notes that curb on high-level government contacts issued on 20 June "is being taken in response to the wave of violence and reprisals by the Chinese authorities against those who have called for democracy." (*New York Times*, 21 June 1989, A1)

Secretary of State James A. Baker III

In speech before Asia Society in New York: "[W]e and the rest of the world must not let our revulsion at this repression blind us to the pressures for reform. . . . The hasty dismantling of a constructive US–Chinese relationship built up so carefully over two decades would serve neither our interests nor those of the Chinese people." (State Department press release, 26 June 1989, 5)

National Security Adviser Brent Scowcroft

In Beijing toast on 9 December, acknowledged that there were "profound areas of disagreement . . . on the events at Tiananmen" but hoped that his trip would "bring new impetus and vigor into our bilateral relationship . . . [and] reduce the negative influence of irritants in the relationship." (*International Trade Reporter*, 13 December 1989, 1616)

US Congress

Provision in House sanctions bill, passed 29 June, conditions "resumption of normal diplomatic and military relations between the U.S. and the People's Republic of China . . . on the Chinese Government's halting of executions of pro-democracy movement supporters, releasing those imprisoned for their political beliefs and increasing respect for internationally recognized human rights." (*New York Times*, 30 June 1989, A7)

Response of Target Country

Chinese government statement after US arms embargo charges that US "has flagrantly made unwarranted charges against China over a matter that is purely China's internal affair and has taken unilateral actions to the detriment of bilateral relations." (*New York Times*, 8 June 1989, A12)

Front-page editorial in official *People's Daily:* "Some people in the American Congress who hate China and the socialist system. . . just want to poke their noses into the internal affairs of China out of their anti-Communist class instinct, dishing up one sanction after another to put pressure on China, in a vain attempt to subjugate China." (*New York Times*, 7 July 1989, A3)

People's Daily editorial calls 1989 economic summit declaration "gross interference in China's internal affairs," argues that "with the interdependence of the global economy ever increasing, the nearsighted practice of keeping China away from the world community may not only undermine world peace and stability, but hurt the interests of Western countries as well." (*Washington Post*, 17 July 1989, A20)

China reopens high-level trade contacts with India for first time in three decades to help offset Western sanctions and in hopes of obtaining technology for use in agriculture, services, public administration. (*Financial Times*, 3 August 1989, 3)

Deng Xiaoping in September 1989: "China is not afraid of sanctions, which will rebound on those imposing them in the long run." (*Washington Post*, 20 September 1989, A29)

Foreign Minister Qian Qichen, in 2 October 1989 speech to Council on Foreign Relations in New York: ". . . the current difficulties in Sino-U.S. relations have arisen not because China has done anything to damage the U.S. interests, but because the United States has applied sanctions against China . . . it is entirely China's internal affairs as to what policy and move it should adopt in handling its purely domestic matters." (*Washington Post,* 3 October 1989, A9)

Deng Xiaoping, after Scowcroft's visit: ". . . in spite of the disputes and the differences between us, after all, Sino-U.S. relations have to be improved. That is something that is necessary for world peace and stability." (*Washington Post,* 11 December 1989, A25)

Chinese foreign ministry spokesman, after House veto override vote in January 1990: "We express great indignation and strongly condemn this hegemonistic act of the U.S. House of Representatives. Should the U.S. Senate also adopt such a bill, it would do serious harm to Sino-U.S. relations and further impair the cultural and educational exchanges between the two countries." (*Washington Post,* 26 January 1990, A14)

Attitude of Other Countries

Japan

Immediately after 4 June massacre, Japan freezes economic, cultural missions to China as well as discussions of five-year aid program due to start in April 1990. Senior officials sidestep talk of sanctions, noting that "we would like to respond by condemning China. But because of our special relationship, the fact that we are blamed for so much, we just cannot risk becoming another scapegoat." (*New York Times,* 7 June 1989, A10)

Senior officials urge cautious response to Chinese developments to avoid isolating China, stirring its "xenophobic" tendencies. Senior foreign ministry official adds, "Sanctions by definition mean punishment. But even if you want to punish the Chinese, you don't get the results which you wish. We don't think sanctions are an appropriate response for the Western democracies to make." (*New York Times,* 22 June 1989, A1)

Tadashi Ikeda, deputy director general in Ministry of Foreign Affairs: ". . . the exercise of military force against Chinese students and ordinary citizens cannot be condoned from a human rights position." He adds that "because of these new circumstances, Japan's relationship with China is constrained for the time being," although he expresses hope that China does not "walk down the path of isolation." (*Journal of Commerce,* 19 July 1989, 13A)

European Community

Declaration of EC Council on 27 June 1989: "The European Council . . . strongly condemns the brutal repression taking place in China. It expresses its dismay at the pursuit of executions in spite of all the appeals of the international community. It solemnly requests the Chinese authorities to stop the executions and to put an end to the repressive actions against those who legitimately claim their democratic rights." EC agrees to ban arms sales, postpone new official export finance, economic development projects. (*Financial Times,* 28 June 1989, A2)

United Kingdom

Expressing "revulsion and outrage" at events in China, Prime Minister Margaret Thatcher bans arms sales to China, postpones number of governmental exchanges, but cautions that EC sanctions could have negative implications for Hong Kong. (*Washington Post,* 7 June 1989, A16; *Financial Times,* 23 June 1989, 4)

Other EC countries

West Germany suspends provisions of export credit guarantees for China, freezes about DM 500 million in bilateral development aid. Italy, Belgium suspend grants, loans. (*Financial Times*, 30 June 1989, 6; Congressional Research Service [CRS] 4)

Canada

On 30 June 1989, Canada withdraws indefinitely its participation in Three Gorges hydroelectric project, cancels three other development projects worth C$11 million over five years, freezes four projects worth C$53.8 million. (*International Trade Reporter*, 5 July 1989, 858)

Australia

On 13 July, Australia suspends all ministerial contacts with China, bars new financing of development projects, noting that "[i]t is imperative that Australia responds strongly to, and signals its abhorrence of, the human rights violations which have occurred." (*Journal of Commerce*, 14 July 1989, 4A)

Economic Impact

Observed Economic Statistics

As of end of June 1989, World Bank has $4.7 billion in loans to China in pipeline, of which $2.9 billion has yet to be disbursed. International Development Agency (Bank's soft-loan window) has $3 billion in commitments to China, of which $1.5 billion has not yet been disbursed. China also has $336 million in loans pending from Asian Development Bank. (*Financial Times*, 30 June 1989, 6; *Wall Street Journal*, 21 June 1989, A2)

In fiscal year 1988, China is largest beneficiary of Eximbank financing, receiving five loans worth $190 million. At end of FY 1988, Eximbank has $277 million in credits outstanding to China, as well as four preliminary commitments totaling $115 million for which funds have been approved if US firms win contracts. In addition, decisions are pending on preliminary commitments for $395 million in loans to China. (*Financial Times*, 30 June 1989, 6; *Journal of Commerce*, 7 February 1990, 2A; 9 February 1990, 4A; CRS 18, 27)

In fiscal 1988, US Trade and Development Program supported 29 projects in China with total value of $6.7 million. (CRS 19)

Of $600 million in US arms sales to China in 1989, about $502 million is for project, still in developmental phase, to modernize F-8 fighter planes. China continues to pay for project under US Foreign Military Sales program after sanctions are imposed. However, on 15 May 1990, China cancels deal, citing projected cost overruns. Other major arms purchases include $28.5 million for technology, assistance to build artillery ammunition plant (already shipped); $62.5 million for four artillery-locating radar sets (two already shipped, two due in 1990); $8.2 million contract for torpedoes, ready for shipment. (*New York Times*, 6 June 1989, A1; *Washington Post*, 28 August 1989, A16; 12 December 1989, A20; 16 May 1990, A14)

In 1988, US approves $85 million in commercial arms sales to China. Average commercial arms deliveries to China in 1986–88 are $40 million. Defense Department estimates that about $130 million in commercial military sales are scheduled for delivery in fiscal 1989–90, that conclusion of $110 million in new Foreign Military Sales agreements could be at risk for fiscal 1989–90. (*New York Times*, 6 June 1989, A1; CRS 20–21)

Cumulative value of French, British, West German, Italian arms deliveries to China in 1983–87 is $400 million. Other major arms exporters to China in recent years have been USSR, Israel. (Arms Control and Disarmament Agency 112)

China's debt more than doubles from just above $20 billion in 1986 to $46.9 billion in 1989; debt is owed about equally to commercial banks, international institutions, foreign governments. (*Journal of Commerce*, 21 June 1989, 7A)

World Bank estimates that foreign investment applications in China declined by 75 percent after June 1989, that access to medium-, long-term borrowing on world markets has been "essentially closed off." (*Washington Post*, 29 June 1990, A1)

According to Minister of Foreign Economic Relations and Trade Zheng Tuobing in October 1989, about $10 billion in loans to China has been suspended since 4 June, no new official borrowing is under negotiation. (*Financial Times*, 27 October 1989, 26)

After 4 June repression, China has difficulty borrowing in foreign markets. In Japan, where Chinese state companies have floated ¥410 billion in yen-denominated bonds, Japanese firms refrain from making markets in Chinese bonds until political situation clarifies. (*Wall Street Journal*, 22 June 1989, A11)

Chinese borrowers face higher margins on international loans, with interest costs ranging from ½ to ¾ percentage point above London interbank offer rate (LIBOR) compared with ⅛ to ¼ percentage point earlier in year. (*Far Eastern Economic Review*, 2 November 1989, 48)

In January 1990, China says it will draw on extant $2 billion credit line from Japanese bank consortium to borrow $500 million, with repayment over 10 years in two tranches: at LIBOR plus ¼ percent for first six years, and LIBOR plus ⅜ percent for last four years. (*Financial Times*, 17 January 1990, 4; 31 January 1990, 5)

China's Ministry of Foreign Economic Relations and Trade says sanctions "caused foreign loan agreements to drop by 51 percent to $4.8 billion." (*New York Times*, 23 January 1990, D8)

Chinese trade deficit rises to $6.6 billion in 1989 from $3.1 billion in 1988. In first quarter of 1990, however, China posts $1.6 billion trade surplus as imports drop 20.2 percent, exports rise 13.4 percent from same period in 1989. (*Financial Times*, 12 April 1990, 4)

Ministry of Foreign Economic Relations and Trade reports that value of China's high-technology imports dropped to $2.9 billion, or by 18 percent, in 1989. (*New York Times*, 23 January 1990, D8)

Central Intelligence Agency (CIA) report estimates that China's industrial output grew by 11 percent in 1989, half its 1988 rate of growth, while inflation remained at 30 percent in urban areas, 19 percent overall. (*Financial Times*, 9 August 1989, 4)

China's State Statistical Bureau reports GNP grew by 4 percent in 1989, down from 11 percent in 1988. (*IMF Morning Press*, 25 January 1990, citing *Reuters*)

China runs cumulative fiscal deficit of 57 billion yuan for decade 1979–89, 7.8 billion yuan in 1988, forcing imposition of controls on state spending, domestic credit (to curb inflation running at 25.5 percent in first half of 1989). In addition, Bank of China President Wang Deyan reports that hard-currency shortage will force stricter controls on foreign-exchange credits, imports. (Associated Press–Dow Jones, 9 August 1989)

In 1988, tourism brings in $2.2 billion in hard currency, or about 2 percent to 3 percent of total foreign-exchange income; reduced tourism due to pro-democracy unrest, martial law could lead to loss of about $1 billion in 1989. (*Wall Street Journal*, 31 July 1989, A1)

Calculated Economic Impact

Suspension of official US arms sales to China; welfare loss estimated at 30 percent of value of suspended shipments that were ready for delivery.	$12 million
Suspension of US commercial arms sales; welfare loss estimated at 30 percent of reduced transfers (from average annual levels in 1986–88).	12 million
Suspension of EC arms sales; welfare loss estimated at 30 percent of reduced transfers (from average annual sales in 1983–87).	24 million
Suspension of $780 million in World Bank loans; annual welfare loss estimated at 25 percent of face value of loans.	195 million
Postponement for average of six months of official export credits, other official finance by US, Japan, Canada, EC[a]; welfare loss estimated at 10 percent of face value of reduced transfers due to sanctions (calculated as 50 percent of 1988 value of gross bilateral disbursements, on grounds that some assistance started trickling back within six months, some projects were canceled for purely business reasons).	79 million
Total	$322 million

a. Includes official EC finance, as well as official finance of member countries that imposed sanctions individually (Belgium, Italy, West Germany).

Relative Magnitudes

Gross indicators of Chinese economy	
Chinese GNP (1988)	$373.3 billion[a]
Chinese population (1988)	1,096 million
Annual effect of sanctions related to gross indicators	
Percentage of GNP	0.1
Per capita	$0.29
Chinese trade with US as percentage of total trade	
Exports (1988)	7
Imports (1988)	12
Ratio of US GNP (1988: $4,881 billion) to Chinese GNP	13

a. Estimate by Chinese State Statistics Bureau.

Assessment

Henry Kissinger

". . . China remains too important for America's national security to risk the relationship on the emotions of the moment. . . . Sooner or later, the punitive sanctions will fail, if only because the Chinese government cannot undo its past actions, and geopolitical realities will dictate a rapprochement between the United States and China." (*Washington Post*, 1 August 1989, A21)

Charles Krauthammer

"Deng has made it clear that politics takes precedence over economics. He knew full well what repression would cost in terms of economic development. For the sake of power, the ultimate Marxist-Leninist value, he decided to pay it." (*Washington Post*, 23 June 1989, A27)

A. Doak Barnett

"The resolution of the present conflict within the Chinese leadership will ultimately be determined by forces within China, not by what any outside power does. . . . Nevertheless, the signal that this action represents is worth sending, to both hardliners and moderates in China." (*Washington Post*, 5 July 1989, A16)

The Economist

"Government sanctions would not work. Spouting anti-foreigner rhetoric last heard during the cultural revolution, a determinedly xenophobic regime is unlikely to pay much heed to official reprimands from abroad. And anyway the world's words would not be matched by its deeds, not for long anyway." (*The Economist*, 17 June 1989, 16)

William F. Ryan

"The ability to cause changes in Chinese government behavior, even by multilateral export credit sanctions, can be seriously questioned on economic grounds. Chinese foreign exchange reserves are quite large, roughly $19 billion. Also, even before recent events, China had adopted a policy of retrenchment that was expected to reduce import demand and foreign borrowing. Depending on China's willingness to pay market interest rates and Western bank willingness to resume new term lending to China, the Chinese could continue to import some items most desired from the West using commercial credits." (US House of Representatives 8)

Roderick MacFarquhar

"Whatever they [the Chinese] planned to do as reciprocity for the two Scowcroft missions in order to show that they did feel some gratitude for Bush had to take second place to the very real consideration of [a threat to their power] as witnessed by events in Eastern Europe." (*Washington Post*, 7 March 1990, A30)

Authors' Summary

Overall assessment

☐ Policy result, scaled from 1 (failed) to 4 (success)   1

☐ Sanctions contribution, scaled from 1 (none) to 4 (significant)   1

☐ Success score (policy result *times* sanctions contribution),
    scaled from 1 (outright failure) to 16 (significant success)   1

Political and economic variables

- ☐ Companion policies: J (covert), Q (quasi-military), or R (regular military) —
- ☐ International cooperation with sender, scaled from 1 (none) to 4 (significant) 3
- ☐ International assistance to target: A (if present) —
- ☐ Sanctions period (years) 1+
- ☐ Economic health and political stability of target, scaled from
  1 (distressed) to 3 (strong) 3
- ☐ Presanction relations between sender and target, scaled from
  1 (antagonistic) to 3 (cordial) 3
- ☐ Type of sanction: X (export), M (import), F (financial) X,F
- ☐ Cost to sender, scaled from 1 (net gain) to 4 (major loss) 2

Bibliography

Arms Control and Disarmament Agency. 1989. *World Military Expenditures and Arms Transfers 1988.* Washington.

Congressional Research Service, Library of Congress. 1989. "China Sanctions: Some Possible Effects." CRS Report for Congress no. 89–424E, 24 July 1989. Washington.

Facts on File, 1986, 1987, 1989.

US House of Representatives. Committee on Foreign Affairs, Subcommittees on Asian and Pacific Affairs, Human Rights and International Organizations, and International Economic Policy and Trade. 1989. Statement by William F. Ryan. 101 Cong., 1 sess., 13 July.

CASE 90–1

US and UN v. Iraq

(1990–   : Invasion of Kuwait)

Chronology of Key Events

17 July 1990   Iraqi President Saddam Hussein denounces Persian Gulf oil-producing countries that exceed their OPEC (Organization of Petroleum-Exporting Countries) quotas. (*Wall Street Journal*, 3 August 1990, A4)

18 July 1990   Iraqi Foreign Minister Tariq Aziz accuses Kuwait of stealing Iraqi oil from disputed Rumaila oil field, claims Kuwait has built military posts on Iraqi land. United Arab Emirates (UAE) says it will cut production to quota level. (*Wall Street Journal*, 3 August 1990, A4)

24–25 July 1990   Iraq deploys thousands of troops on Kuwaiti border, but Arab diplomats say Iraq has given Egypt assurances it will not attack Kuwait. US warships in area are put on alert. (*Wall Street Journal*, 3 August 1990, A4)

27 July 1990   OPEC refuses Iraqi demand to raise oil price to $25 per barrel, decides to raise cartel's reference price to $21 per barrel by end of year. (*Financial Times* [London], 28 July 1990, 1)

1 August 1990   Saudi-mediated talks between Iraq, Kuwait at Jeddah, Saudi Arabia, collapse when Kuwait refuses Iraq's demands, which include reduction in Kuwaiti oil production, compensation of $2.5 billion for oil produced in disputed territory, forgiveness of about $20 billion in debts accumulated during war with Iran, control of Bubiyan and Warba islands giving Iraq direct access to Persian Gulf. (*Financial Times*, 2 August 1990, 1; *Wall Street Journal*, 3 August 1990, A4)

2 August 1990   Iraq invades Kuwait. Invoking International Emergency Economic Powers Act, President George Bush freezes Iraqi, Kuwaiti assets, bans all trade and financial relations with Iraq. Donations of medical supplies, food for humanitarian purposes are exempt from trade embargo. Iraq freezes payment of US portion of its foreign debt, some $2.24 billion. UK, France freeze billions of dollars in Kuwaiti assets. USSR suspends all deliveries of military equipment to Iraq. UN Security Council Resolution 660 condemns invasion, demands immediate, unconditional withdrawal of Iraqi forces from Kuwait. (*Washington Post*, 3 August 1990, A25; Office of the White

House Press Secretary, 2 August 1990; *New York Times,* 3 August 1990, A9)

3 August 1990   Movement of Iraqi troops toward Saudi Arabian border prompts Bush to warn that "integrity of Saudi Arabia" is vital US concern. US, USSR issue joint statement in Moscow condemning Iraq, ". . . calling upon the rest of the international community to join with us in an international cutoff of all arms supplies to Iraq." With Jordan, Palestine Liberation Organization (PLO) abstaining, Libya not present, Arab League issues declaration denouncing invasion, calling for immediate troop withdrawal. Gulf Cooperation Council also condemns attack. West Germany, Belgium, Netherlands, Luxembourg, Norway freeze Kuwaiti assets. Iraq says it will withdraw troops from Kuwait within two days. (*Washington Post,* 4 August 1990, A1; 5 August 1990, A21)

4 August 1990   European Community imposes broad sanctions against Iraq, calls for "immediate and unconditional withdrawal of Iraqi forces" from Kuwait. Measures include embargo on oil imports from Iraq, Kuwait; freeze on Iraqi assets in member countries; ban on sale of arms, military equipment to Iraq; suspension of all military, technical, scientific cooperation with Iraq; suspension of Iraq's preferred trade status with Community. (*Washington Post,* 5 August 1990, A21; *New York Times,* 5 August 1990, A1)

5 August 1990   Japan embargoes oil imports from Iraq, Kuwait, halts all exports to the two states, freezes economic aid to Iraq. China joins arms embargo against Iraq. Bush administration allows Iraqi, Kuwaiti oil shipped before invasion to unload, but requires any payment due to be placed in escrow. (*Washington Post,* 6 August 1990, A13; *New York Times,* 6 August 1990, A1; *Wall Street Journal,* 6 August 1990, A9)

6 August 1990   With Cuba, Yemen abstaining, UN Security Council approves Resolution 661 imposing comprehensive trade, financial sanctions against Iraq, occupied Kuwait. Medical supplies, humanitarian food shipments are excluded from embargo. With no buyers, Iraq closes one pipeline through Turkey, decreases flow through another, reducing its oil exports by at least 40 percent. Several hundred Westerners, including 28 US nationals, are detained in Kuwait, taken to Iraqi capital of Baghdad. Hussein threatens unspecified retaliation if Saudi Arabia increases oil production to help West or shuts down Iraqi pipelines that cross Saudi desert. (UN Security Council Resolution 661, 6 August 1990; *New York Times,* 7 August 1990, A1; *Washington Post,* 7 August 1990, A1; 8 August 1990, A18)

7 August 1990   Bush orders US military aircraft, troops to Saudi Arabia to defend it against Iraqi attack. British, Soviet, French ships join US naval forces already in Gulf area. Turkey freezes Iraqi, Kuwaiti assets, halts transshipment of Iraqi oil. Iraq cuts flow of oil through its other main pipeline, to Saudi Arabia's Red Sea port of Yanbu, by 75

percent. (*Washington Post*, 8 August 1990, A12; *Financial Times*, 8 August 1990, 1; *New York Times*, 8 August 1990, A1)

8 August 1990   Iraq announces annexation of Kuwait. Hussein claims that "comprehensive and eternal merger" redresses "one of the most egregious criminal acts of colonialism." (*Washington Post*, 9 August 1990, A1; *IMF Morning Press*, 9 August 1990)

9 August 1990   UN Security Council resolution 662 declares Iraqi annexation of Kuwait "has no legal validity and is null and void." King Hussein of Jordan says he does not recognize merger, will comply with UN economic sanctions. Iraq seals its borders, barring departure of all foreigners except diplomatic personnel. About 2,500 Americans are trapped in Kuwait, another 500 in Iraq. Iraq's ambassador in Athens says Iraq will use chemical weapons if attacked. (UN Security Council Resolution 662, 9 August 1990; *Washington Post*, 9 August 1990, A1)

10 August 1990   Hussein calls for holy war, urging "Moslem masses" to rise up against US forces in Saudi Arabia, pro-Western Arab leaders, whom he accuses of blaspheming Islam. At emergency summit in Cairo, Arab leaders vote 12 to 3 to send troops to Saudi Arabia to help defend against possible invasion by Iraqi forces. Libya, PLO join Iraq in opposing resolution; Yemen abstains. Jordan votes to approve resolution "with reservations." Iraq orders foreign governments to close their embassies in Kuwait City, move diplomatic functions to Baghdad by 24 August 1990. Canada, France, Australia send ships to Gulf area. (*New York Times*, 11 August 1990, A1; *Washington Post*, 11 August 1990, A1; 12 August 1990, A22)

11 August 1990   Several thousand Egyptian troops arrive in Saudi Arabia. Morocco, Syria promise to send similar number to join Arab effort. British man is shot dead while trying to flee across Kuwaiti border into Saudi Arabia. (*New York Times*, 12 August 1990, A1; *Washington Post*, 13 August 1990, A1)

12 August 1990   Following formal Kuwaiti request under Article 51 of UN Charter, which permits any state under attack to seek collective help in its self-defense, Bush administration adopts policy of "interdiction," including use of force to stop ships attempting to circumvent UN embargo. Hussein says he would withdraw from Kuwait as part of settlement of "all issues of occupation" including Israeli withdrawal from West Bank, Gaza Strip, Syrian pullout from Lebanon. Hussein also proposes pan-Arab force under UN auspices to replace US troops deployed in Saudi Arabia. Hussein asks Iraqis to reduce meat consumption by half, buy less rice, bread, clothes. (*Washington Post*, 13 August 1990, A1; 23 August 1990, A41; *New York Times*, 13 August 1990, A8)

13 August 1990   USSR, France, Canada criticize Bush administration's unilateral policy of interdiction. Bush administration insists sanctions apply to everything except medical supplies; White House spokesman Marlin Fitzwater insists, "it's clearly far too early to consider any foodstuffs as being in a humanitarian need category." Saudi Arabia turns away Iraqi tanker hoping to load oil at Iraq's trans-Arabia pipeline at Muajjizz; two or three other ships are unable to land Iraqi-bound cargoes. Pakistan agrees to send troops to join multinational force defending Saudi Arabia. (*Washington Post,* 14 August 1990, A1; *New York Times,* 14 August 1990, A1; *Wall Street Journal,* 14 August 1990, A7)

14 August 1990   Bush offers financial assistance to Jordan in return for compliance with UN sanctions, warns that US ships will blockade Jordanian port of Aqaba to prevent transshipment of Iraqi commerce. (*Washington Post,* 15 August 1990, A1; *New York Times,* 15 August 1990, A1)

15 August 1990   Hussein offers peace proposal to Iran that includes resolution of dispute over Shatt al-Arab waterway on Iranian terms, release of all Iranian prisoners of war, withdrawal of Iraqi troops from Iranian territory. (*Washington Post,* 16 August 1990, A1; *Financial Times,* 16 August 1990, 1)

16 August 1990   King Hussein tells Bush that Jordan will enforce UN sanctions, close Red Sea port of Aqaba to goods bound for Iraq. Despite Iraq's peace offer, Iranian President Ali Akbar Hashemi Rafsanjani reiterates his demand that Iraq withdraw from Kuwait. (*Washington Post,* 17 August 1990, A1)

18 August 1990   Declaring the US–led naval blockade "an act of war," Iraqi government says that foreign nationals, some of whom are being held at military, strategic civilian sites as "shields" against US–led attack, will suffer along with Iraqis from any food, medicine shortages. UN Security Council votes 15 to 0 to demand that Iraq release all detained foreigners. Saudi Arabia calls for OPEC meeting to discuss increasing output but says it will boost oil production by 2 million barrels a day with or without OPEC approval. US Navy fires warning shots across bow of two Iraqi oil tankers. (*Washington Post,* 19 August 1990, A1; *New York Times,* 19 August 1990, A1; 27 August 1990, A9)

19 August 1990   US, UK reject offer from Hussein to release Westerners if US troops withdraw from Saudi Arabia and trade embargo is lifted. UAE, Bahrain allow deployment of Arab, "friendly" (including US) forces on its territory. Following reports that French nationals have been "displaced" from their hotels to unknown locations, France authorizes its ships in Persian Gulf to use force if necessary to ensure compliance with UN sanctions. (*Washington Post,* 20 August 1990, A1; *New York Times,* 20 August 1990, A1; *Financial Times,* 20 August 1990, 3)

20 August 1990   Reacting to Hussein's offer, Bush for first time describes detained Americans as hostages. Iran says it will abide by UN sanctions despite peace initiative from Iraq. Yemen, which abstained from UN vote on sanctions, agrees to abide by embargo. West German government concludes that its constitution prohibits it from send-

ing troops to Persian Gulf. (*Washington Post*, 21 August 1990, A1; *IMF Morning Press*, 21 August 1990)

21 August 1990   Nine-member Western European Union decides to expand, coordinate naval enforcement in Persian Gulf. Total of 32 naval vessels, including 8 French, 3 British warships, have been mobilized by European countries; Italy, Belgium, Netherlands, Spain pledge to send ships to enforce embargo. (*New York Times*, 22 August 1990, A1; *Financial Times*, 22 August 1990, 2; *Washington Post*, 22 August 1990, A1)

22 August 1990   Bush orders activation of about 40,000 military reserves. Following consultations on requests from Jordan, Bulgaria, UN Security Council approves aid for Jordan; no decision is made on Bulgaria. Japan pledges economic aid to Egypt, will consider requests from other countries injured by enforcement of UN sanctions; Turkey, Jordan are likely to be eligible. With 120,000 refugees already on its territory, Jordan unsuccessfully attempts to close its border to foreigners still fleeing Iraq, Kuwait. There are reports from Baghdad of panic buying of some commodities, severe shortage of cooking oil, soap, sugar. (*Washington Post*, 23 August 1990, A1; *New York Times*, 23 August 1990, A14; *Wall Street Journal*, 23 August 1990, A3)

23 August 1990   As deadline for closing embassies in Kuwait nears, US, most other Western embassies reduce staffs to minimum, vow to remain open. (*Washington Post*, 24 August 1990, A1)

24 August 1990   Iraqi troops surround US embassy in Kuwait, those of other nations defying Iraq's order to close. (*Washington Post*, 25 August 1990, A1)

25 August 1990   UN Security Council approves resolution authorizing countries "deploying maritime forces to the area [to] use such measures commensurate to the specific circumstances as may be necessary . . . to halt all inward and outward maritime shipping." Iraq cuts power to US, Japanese, Italian, British embassies, cuts power, water to East German mission. Israel pledges to block exports of Palestinian fruits, vegetables, other items shipped through Jordan to Iraq. (*Washington Post*, 26 August 1990, A24; *New York Times*, 27 August 1990, A8)

27 August 1990   US expels 36 Iraqi embassy personnel, places travel restrictions on remaining officials. Iraq orders its commercial ships to comply with interdiction in Persian Gulf. Israeli report claims Yemen has been airlifting food, other supplies to Iraq, that Jordan has continued military cooperation with Iraq. (*Washington Post*, 28 August 1990, A1)

28 August 1990   Iraq declares Kuwait to be its 19th province, renames its capital Kadhima, its pre–WWI name. Eventually, disputed Rumaila oil field, Bubiyan and Warba islands are incorporated into Iraq's Basra province, rest of Kuwait remains separate province. Hussein says all foreign women, children will be free to leave Iraq, Kuwait. Bush administration proposes to sell $6 billion to $8 billion worth of military equipment to Saudi Arabia. (*Washington Post,* 29 August 1990, A1; 2 October 1990, A15)

29 August 1990 OPEC ratifies increase in production to offset loss from embargo. Bush proposes Economic Action Plan under which wealthy US allies will share cost of US deployment in Gulf, help those countries adversely affected by enforcement of embargo. Plan could total $23 billion in donor aid in first year. Japan pledges $1 billion in food, water, medical supplies for forces in Gulf. Turkey rejects Iraqi request to allow shipments of "medicine and food for children," saying it will continue to enforce embargo. (*Washington Post,* 30 August 1990, A1; 1 September 1990, A20)

31 August 1990 Bush reportedly will seek congressional approval to forgive Egypt's $7.1 billion military debt to US in recognition of its support during Persian Gulf crisis. Administration sends envoy to tell Jordan it cannot expect financial aid unless it publicly states support for embargo and halts shipments, including food, to Iraq. (*Washington Post,* 1 September 1990, A1)

1 September 1990 UN Secretary General Javier Pérez de Cuéllar ends two days of inconclusive talks with Aziz in Amman, Jordan. Over 550 American, European, Japanese women, children are allowed to leave Iraq. (*Washington Post,* 2 September 1990, A1; *New York Times,* 2 September 1990, A1)

2 September 1990 Iraq limits consumer purchases of basic foods, calling measure "rationalization of consumption" rather than rationing. Libya says it will not obey UN embargo on food shipments to Iraq. (*Washington Post,* 3 September 1990, A1; *New York Times,* 3 September 1990, A1)

5 September 1990 West Germany says it will not contribute funds to Bush's "burden sharing" plan but will supply planes, ships to transport US troops to region. (*Washington Post,* 6 September 1990, A1)

6 September 1990 Saudi Arabia pledges multibillion dollar package for economic support fund, including in-kind contributions of fuel, transportation, supplies to support American deployment in Gulf, funds for front-line states of Egypt, Jordan, Turkey. India decides to send medical supplies to Iraq; China, Iran are reportedly considering sending food, medical supplies to Iraq; Tunisia, Yugoslavia, Romania say they want to send food, medical supplies to their citizens in Kuwait. (*Washington Post,* 7 September 1990, A1; *New York Times,* 7 September 1990, A1; *Financial Times,* 7 September 1990, 7)

9 September 1990 Bush, Soviet President Mikhail Gorbachev meet in Helsinki, Finland, issue joint declaration condemning invasion, stating that both countries will take unspecified further steps if sanctions fail to force Iraqi withdrawal. Statement says that any humanitarian exemptions of food from UN embargo "must be strictly monitored by appropriate international agencies" rather than by individual countries. (*Washington Post,* 10 September 1990, A19)

9 September 1990	Iran, Iraq resume diplomatic ties. Hussein offers free oil to any Third World nation that can collect it; he says this will not violate embargo since oil is free. Saudi Arabia, Kuwait, UAE expand their aid packages to $12 billion through end of 1990, with half going to support US military effort, half to offset cost of sanctions to Egypt, Jordan, Turkey. (*Washington Post,* 11 September 1990, A1)
13 September 1990	Japan contributes additional $1 billion for multinational forces in Persian Gulf, $2 billion in economic assistance for Egypt, Turkey, Jordan. (*Washington Post,* 14 September 1990, A1)
14 September 1990	UN Security Council imposes strict controls on humanitarian food aid to Iraq, Kuwait, says shipments must be channeled through UN or other international agencies. Vote follows Iraq's decision to deny food to hundreds of thousands of Asians in Iraq, Kuwait. Indian vessel is allowed to transport food to Kuwait, where estimated 140,000 Indians are stranded. UK commits ground forces to Saudi Arabia: 6,000 troops, 120 tanks; Syria pledges to send additional troops; Canada, Italy each pledge squadron of jet fighters. Iraqi soldiers storm French, Canadian, Australian, Belgian embassies in Kuwait City, taking four French hostages. (*Washington Post,* 15 September 1990, A1; *Financial Times,* 17 September 1990, 2)
15 September 1990	France condemns violation of embassies, decides to send 4,000 ground troops backed by tanks, combat aircraft to Saudi Arabia. (*Washington Post,* 16 September 1990, A1)
16 September 1990	Egypt announces it will send 15,000 more troops to Saudi Arabia. Bush's Economic Action Plan has so far produced approximately $20 billion in economic, military aid commitments: $10 billion to $12 billion from Saudi Arabia, other Gulf states, including $5 billion from exiled Kuwaiti government; $4 billion from Japan; $2 billion from European Community; over $1.8 billion from West Germany. (*Financial Times,* 17 September 1990, 2)
17 September 1990	Saudi Arabia, USSR reestablish diplomatic ties after 52-year break. (*Washington Post,* 18 September 1990, A1)
23 September 1990	Hussein threatens to attack Saudi oil fields, other Arab countries, Israel if Iraq is "strangled" by economic embargo. (*New York Times,* 24 September 1990, A1)
24 September 1990	South Korea will provide $220 million over two years to international efforts in Gulf: $70 million in materials and services, $50 million in cash, $100 million in aid, supplies to front-line states. (*Financial Times,* 25 September 1990, 2)
25 September 1990	With only Cuba opposed, UN Security Council imposes air embargo against Iraq, cutting off all air traffic to and from Iraq, Kuwait. UN members are to prevent Iraq-bound flights from taking off from their territory, using their airspace. Flights carrying food "in humanitarian circumstances" are excluded from embargo. Resolution does not allow planes to be shot down, allows countries

to detain Iraqi ships which violate embargo, provides for imposition of trade sanctions on any country that breaks embargo. (*New York Times*, 26 September 1990, A1)

7–8 October 1990   Egyptian, Syrian commanders of troops in Saudi Arabia reiterate that their troops are there solely for defense of Saudi Arabia, will not engage in any offensive operation. President Rafsanjani warns that Iran would be "absolutely opposed" to settlement in which Kuwait cedes control of Bubiyan and Warba islands to Iraq, saying Iran "would act within our means to stop it." (*Washington Post*, 9 October 1990, A12)

17–18 October 1990   Secretary of State James A. Baker III, Gorbachev's special envoy Yevgeny Primakov say (on consecutive days) that Hussein must not profit from aggression, thus rejecting rumors that agreement would be reached whereby Iraq would withdraw from rest of Kuwait in return for port islands, Rumaila oil field. (*Washington Post*, 19 October 1990, A28)

Goals of Sender Countries

United States

President George Bush: "The United States strongly condemns the Iraqi military invasion of Kuwait and calls for the immediate and unconditional withdrawal of all Iraqi forces. . . . We deplore this blatant use of military aggression and violation of the U.N. Charter." (White House press release, 1 August 1990)

"Our action in the gulf is not about religion, greed or cultural differences . . . [at stake is] access to energy resources that are key, not just to the functioning of this country, but to the entire world. Our jobs, our way of life, our own freedom and the freedom of friendly countries around the world would all suffer if control of the world's greatest oil reserves fell into the hands of that one man—Saddam Hussein." (*Washington Post*, 16 August 1990, A31)

State Department Spokeswoman Margaret Tutwiler outlines US objectives as follows: immediate, unconditional withdrawal of all Iraqi forces from Kuwait; restoration to power of a legitimate Kuwait government; ensuring safety of all Americans in area; ensuring freedom of navigation in Persian Gulf, free flow of oil from region. (*Washington Post*, 7 August 1990, A15)

United Nations

UN Security Council Resolution 661 condemns Iraq's invasion of Kuwait, demands that Iraq withdraw its forces, prohibits UN members from recognizing any provisional Kuwaiti government established by Iraq. (*New York Times*, 7 August 1990, A1)

Soviet Union

Foreign Ministry spokesman Yuri Gremitskikh: "The Soviet Union believes that no contentious issues, no matter how complicated, justify the use of force. Such events totally contradict the interests of Arab states, create new additional obstacles to the settlement of conflicts in the Middle East and run counter to the positive tendencies of improvement in international life." (By communication from Soviet embassy in Washington)

United Kingdom

Foreign Secretary William Waldegrave: "If there is evidence of sanctions busting, the Navy will take the necessary steps. It is obvious that the economic weapon, which is the principal weapon being used by the world community to restore the independence of Kuwait . . . should work." (*Financial Times*, 14 August 1990, 1)

Other Western European countries

"[There is] a growing dichotomy between what from here appears to be the predominant view in Washington that force is inevitable and perhaps even desirable to rid the world of the menace of Saddam Hussein and the European view that the crisis may be manageable diplomatically and that a military confrontation could wreak profound damage." (*Washington Post*, 26 August 1990, A21)

Response of Target Country

Iraqi Ministry of Labor and Social Affairs

"America and its allies have gone beyond an economic boycott which in essence means only a non-exchange of goods. They embarked on the implementation of an economic blockade by force of arms against Iraq, including food and medicines, and this is an act of war under world norms and international law." (*Washington Post*, 19 August 1990, A31)

Foreign Minister Tariq Aziz

"If the American leaders think this is a vacation like they had in Panama and Grenada, then it is going to be a bloody conflict and America will lose and America will be humiliated." (*Washington Post*, 22 August 1990, A24)

President Saddam Hussein

"We would not allow whoever it is to strangle the people of Iraq without strangling him in return. If we feel the Iraqi people are choking and someone is dealing them a bloody blow, we will strangle all the perpetrators . . . all oil installations will be incapacitated." (*Washington Post*, 24 September 1990, A1)

Attitude of Other Countries

Iran

Foreign Minister Ali Akbar Velayati: "We cannot accept any change in Kuwaiti borders, neither in land nor in water." (*Washington Post*, 8 August 1990, A1)

Jordan

Crown Prince Hassan: "Jordan respects the UN mandate . . . but [sanctions] would bring our economy to a standstill. . . . Clearly in terms of implementing sanctions we just don't turn off the switch in our dealings with Iraq and Kuwait. . . . Jordan will suffer enormously when it applies sanctions." (*Washington Post*, 15 August 1990, C12; *New York Times*, 15 August 1990, A19)

Legal Notes

Excerpts from UN Security Council Resolution 661, 6 August 1990

"[A]ll states shall prevent the import into their territories of all commodities and products originating in Iraq or Kuwait . . . any activities by their nationals or in their

territories which could promote or are calculated to promote the export or transshipment of any commodities or products from Iraq or Kuwait . . . the sale or supply, by
their nationals or from their territories or using their flag vessels any commodities or
products, including weapons or any other military equipment whether or not originating in their territories but not including supplies intended strictly for medical purposes,
and, in humanitarian circumstances, foodstuffs, to any person or body for the purposes
of any business carried on in or operated from Iraq or Kuwait, and any activities by their
nationals or in their territories which promote or are calculated to promote such sale,
or supply or use of such commodities or products." All investment in Iraq, Kuwait is
banned, including all payments, transfers. UN members are prohibited from recognizing any provisional government established by Iraq. UN Secretary General is to report
on compliance with sanctions, establish committee to monitor enforcement of embargo.
(*New York Times,* 7 August 1990, A9)

Economic Impact

Observed Economic Statistics

Iraq: foreign trade, 1982–88 (millions of dollars)

Year	Total imports from:			Food imports from:	
	World	OECD	US	OECD	US
1982	19,497	14,861	846	1,100	130
1983	9,326	6,532	512	909	336
1984	8,967	6,376	664	1,476	503
1985	9,555	6,728	427	1,037	288
1986	7,897	5,629	527	797	292
1987	6,656	4,369	684	1,099	460
1988	9,256	6,156[a]	1,156	n.a.	689

Year	Total exports to:			Petroleum exports to:	
	World	OECD	US	OECD	US
1982	10,589	6,046	42	5,947	35
1983	8,623	4,915	61	4,813	57
1984	9,867	5,486	129	5,332	124
1985	11,117	7,333	491	7,172	485
1986	8,110	5,308	473	5,156	467
1987	10,019	6,689	526	6,473	513
1988	9,970	6,876[a]	1,605	n.a.	1,472

n.a. = not available.

a. At annualized rate.

Source: International Monetary Fund; Organization for Economic Cooperation and
Development.

Kuwait has approximately $100 billion in foreign assets, investments worldwide. Kuwaiti commercial investments, estimated at $50 billion, earned $8.8 billion in 1989 compared with $7.7 billion from shipments of oil. (*Financial Times*, 3 August 1990, 4; 10 August 1990, 4)

US Commerce Department official estimates that half of Kuwaiti foreign investment is in US, 20 percent in UK, 30 percent elsewhere in Western Europe, Japan. (*New York Times*, 3 August 1990, A9)

Iraq's foreign debt is estimated to be between $50 billion and $70 billion, its annual shortfall in hard currency is estimated at $7 billion. Iraq's foreign assets are thought to be negligible. Kuwait estimates that Iraq seized $300 million to $400 million in gold, $10 million to $15 million in foreign currencies in invasion. Much of this money will probably be channeled into sanctions-busting campaign rather than used to pay off debts. (*Washington Post*, 19 August 1990, H1; *Financial Times*, 28 August 1990, 2; Economic Intelligence Unit 35; Commerce Department 5)

Kuwait has fourth largest petroleum reserves in world, produces 1.6 million barrels a day. Following absorption of Kuwait, Iraq stands to double its control of oil reserves to 194 billion barrels, second only to Saudi Arabia with 255 billion barrels. Iraqi, Kuwaiti production together is about 4.5 million barrels a day. Oil accounts for over 90 percent of Iraq's exports; annualized estimate of potential revenue from exports, based on second-quarter 1990 export volumes, prices (average $14.32 per barrel), is $13.2 billion. (*New York Times*, 3 August 1990, A8; 4 August 1990, A5; Rogers 4)

In 1989, oil from Iraq, Kuwait accounted for about 11 percent of total EC imports; Denmark is especially dependent, importing 54 percent of its oil from the two countries. Japan imports 12 percent of its oil from Iraq, Kuwait, is owed about $5 billion by Iraq. (*Washington Post*, 5 August 1990, A24; *Wall Street Journal*, 6 August 1990, A1)

Perhaps 75 percent of shortfall in oil supplies from Iraq, Kuwait could be replaced in short run from other sources: Saudi Arabia increases its oil production by 1.5 million to 2 million barrels per day; Venezuela increases production by 350,000 barrels per day immediately, promises additional 150,000 by year-end; UAE increases production by 500,000 barrels per day. USSR is unable to increase production immediately. To offset Japan's loss of 440,000 barrels per day, Iran will increase its sales to Japan from 280,000 to up to 700,000 barrels per day. Brazil has negotiated to buy 100,000 barrels of oil a day from Iran. (US Department of Commerce 19; *New York Times*, 15 August 1990, D3; 27 August 1990, D10; *Wall Street Journal*, 17 August 1990, A3; 27 August 1990, A3; *IMF Morning Press*, 17 August 1990; *Financial Times*, 24 August 1990, 3)

Saudi Arabia stands to earn extra $11 billion in 1990, additional $33 billion in 1991 from increased oil output, higher prices. (*Washington Post*, 26 August 1990, A25; *IMF Morning Press*, 22 August 1990)

USSR expects to gain $1 billion a year for every $1 a barrel increase in price of oil. USSR produces 12 million barrels per day, exports 20 percent; half goes to Western countries, half to Eastern Europe. China, Mexico, Indonesia, Romania will also gain economically from increased oil prices. (*New York Times*, 10 August 1990, D1; *Washington Post*, 12 August 1990, H7; 19 August 1990, H5)

"About 21 percent of Iraq's total area of 444,400 square kilometers is arable. Up to 70 percent of this arable land is under cultivation, with 44 percent of this area irrigated and the remainder dependent on rainfall and flooding. One-third of Iraq's work force is engaged in agriculture and related activities. Barley, rice and dates are grown in the south and wheat is grown in the north. Milk, sheep and goat meat, poultry and fish are principal products for domestic consumption." (*Financial Times*, 21 August 1990, 3)

US Department of Agriculture calculates that Iraq imports about 60 percent of its food in good harvest years, about 70 percent in bad. Following 1990 summer and fall harvests, Iraq should have four-month supply of wheat, rice, seven-month supply of barley, one-and-a-half-month supply of corn at normal rates of consumption. (*New York Times*, 20 August 1990, A1; *Washington Post*, 27 August 1990, A8; *Wall Street Journal*, 28 August 1990, A12)

US agricultural shipments to Iraq totaled about $1 billion, or 2.5 percent of US farm commodity exports, in 1989, when Iraq was 12th-largest purchaser of US agricultural products overall and largest importer of US rice (taking 14 percent of US rice exports). US share of total Iraqi agricultural commodity imports rose from about 20 percent in 1986 to approximately 40 percent in 1988. (*Journal of Commerce*, 9 August 1990, 6A; *New York Times*, 9 August 1990, D19; *Washington Post*, 23 August 1990, A41; US Department of Agriculture, by communication with authors; US Department of Commerce 14)

Iraq has received about $5 billion in US food subsidies since 1983, $2.5 billion in export loan guarantees since 1988, $141 million in direct export subsidies since 1985. Guarantees were suspended in 1990, all other aid has been cut by embargo. (*Wall Street Journal*, 10 August 1990, A1)

Turkey's trade with Iraq is $2 billion a year, about 3 percent of Turkey's GNP. Turkey will lose about $400 million in revenues from closure of oil pipeline. Iraq owes Turkey $800 million, supplies it with 60 percent of its oil needs. (*Washington Post*, 10 August 1990, A30; 16 August 1990, A31)

Jordan's trade with Iraq is $900 million a year, about 25 percent of Jordan's annual output. Jordan sends 40 percent of its exports to Iraq, imports 90 percent of its oil from Iraq, much of it in lieu of payments on longstanding Iraqi debt. Jordan says it will lose $2 billion a year in implementing embargo, including $200 million in exports, mostly food, to Iraq, $200 million in fees for goods passing through Jordan, over $300 million in workers' remittances. Jordan expects to lose about $190 million in aid from Iraq, Kuwait; Iraq will probably discontinue about $295 million in debt repayment to Jordan. President Hosni Mubarak says Egypt, with foreign debt of $50 billion, could lose $2 billion a year from combined loss of remittances from Egyptian contract workers, reduced tolls on Suez Canal, decline in tourism. (*New York Times*, 15 August 1990, A19; *Washington Post*, 16 August 1990, A31; 23 August 1990, A40; *Wall Street Journal*, 24 August 1990, A12)

Pakistan's balance of payments deficit is expected to increase by $1.1 billion because of increases in oil prices, loss of workers' remittances, costs of enforcing embargo ($600 million in increased oil imports; $300 million in lost remittances). (*IMF Morning Press*, 17 September 1990)

Iraq owes $16.5 million to Hungary, estimated $1 billion to Bulgaria. Poland will lose $1 billion in arms sales, construction contracts, $500 million in exports still awaiting payment. Brazil may have to pay an extra $1.6 billion for oil in 1990, drawing on foreign currency reserves needed to service its $115 billion in foreign debt. (*Washington Post*, 19 August 1990, H5; 20 August 1990, A19; *Financial Times*, 9 August 1990, 3; *New York Times*, 27 August 1990, D10)

Iraq: agricultural trade and consumption, 1987–89ᵃ

Commodity	Major suppliers (percent of total Iraqi imports)						Thousands of metric tons		Imports as percentage of consumption
	US	EC	Australia	Thailand	Brazil	Canada	Imports	Consumption	
Soybean Meal	96.0				3.0		250	250	100.0
Vegetable oils	27.0	4.0					302	318	95.0
Sugar	20.0	13.0					588	630	93.3
Corn	97.0			2.0	40.0		644	725	88.8
Wheat	31.0		40.0			26.0	3,225	3,939	81.9
Rice	92.0			8.0			571	698	81.8
Beef		61.0			32.0		94	139	67.6
Barley	44.0	12.0				43.0	296	1,243	23.8
Poultry	80.0	4.0			14.0		32	306	10.3

ᵃData are averages for the three years.

Source: US Department of Agriculture.

India's current account deficit is estimated to widen by $2 billion in fiscal 1990–91: $1.2 billion of this is due to increased oil prices, $300 million to additional shipping costs plus fall in remittances from 240,000 Indian workers in Iraq, Kuwait. (*Financial Times*, 31 August 1990, 6)

Funds committed to Economic Action Plan (billions of dollars)

Donor	Funds
Saudi Arabia (for Operation Desert Shield)[a]	$ 6.0
Kuwait	5.0
United Arab Emirates	1.0
Total Arab aid	$12.0
Japan	
Aid to front-line states	$ 2.0
Immediate loans	0.6
Operation Desert Shield[b]	2.0
Total Japanese aid	$ 4.6
South Korea	
Aid to front-line states	$ 0.1
Operation Desert Shield	
Cash	0.05
Materials and services	0.07
Total South Korean aid	$ 0.22
European Community	
Pledged aid	$ 2.0
Germany	
Operation Desert Shield[c]	$ 2.0
Total Commitments	$20.8

a. Includes in-kind donations of fuel, water, transportation.

b. For transportation, desert equipment, medical teams, chartered aircraft.

c. For 60 armored vehicles equipped for chemical, biological warfare, plus training.

Source: Washington Post, 23 September 1990, A30.

Calculated Economic Impact (annual cost to target country)

Boycott of Iraqi oil; welfare loss estimated at 90 percent of value of lost oil sales (based on 1990 second-quarter export volume, July OPEC price of $21 per barrel).	$17.4 billion
Embargo on exports to Iraq; welfare loss estimated at 50 percent of lost shipments (based on value of 1988 Iraqi imports).	4.6 billion
Freeze of Iraqi foreign assets; welfare loss estimated at 10 percent of face value of assets frozen.	negl.

Offsets

Assets seized from Kuwaiti central bank; welfare gain estimated at 100 percent of face value of gold and cash seized.	(0.4 billion)
Total	$21.6 billion

Note: Value of Kuwaiti overseas assets, oil exports is not included in these calculations since sanctions were imposed before Hussein could plunder those assets, hence were not Iraq's to lose.

Relative Magnitudes

Gross indicators of Iraqi economy	
Iraqi GDP (1988)	$45 billion
Iraqi population (1988)	17.2 million
Annual effect of sanctions related to gross indicators	
Percentage of GNP	48.0
Per capita	$1,255.81
Iraqi trade with UN[a] as percentage of total trade	
Exports (1988)	100
Imports (1988)	100
Ratio of UN GNP (1988: $10,877 billion[b]) to Iraqi GNP	242

a. Although some members have questioned whether food is included in UN embargo, every UN member has said it would comply with sanctions. Those countries suspected of helping Iraq circumvent embargo—Jordan, Yemen, Libya, possibly Iran—account for minimal portion of Iraq's preinvasion trade. With naval blockade in place to enforce sanctions, we expect any leakage to be minimal.
b. Combined GNP of member countries of Organization for Economic Cooperation and Development is used as proxy.

Assessment

G. Henry M. Schuler, Center for Strategic and International Studies
"It takes a long time for economic sanctions to take hold. . . . The question is who feels the pain first, who flinches or blinks first. I am not sure it will be Iraq. We are feeling the pain already. I'll bet Iraqis are still dancing in the street." (*Washington Post*, 8 August 1990, A12)

Unnamed Bush administration official
"The belief is that the world has changed considerably. We don't have the cold war situation where it was difficult to enforce sanctions because of ideological competition and huge divisions in the world. This time, we've got the Soviet Union on board and virtually everyone else as well. . . . You can shut off the gulf and you've got them locked in on the Mediterranean side. . . . This time we're dealing with a single-source economy based on oil sales that is on its knees because of the war and can be hurt very easily." (*New York Times*, 9 August 1990, A14; *Washington Post*, 9 August 1990, A1)

Former Iraqi Army Colonel Selim Fakhri
"It's more important to stop the oil from getting out than to stop food from getting in. . . . You don't want to be seen starving Iraq, but you want to make sure Saddam doesn't have the money to pay for food." (*Washington Post*, 23 August 1990, A41)

Authors' Summary

Overall assessment

☐ Policy result, scaled from 1 (failed) to 4 (success)   unknown

☐ Sanctions contribution, scaled from 1 (none) to 4 (significant)   unknown

☐ Success score (policy result *times* sanctions contribution), scaled from 1 (outright failure) to 16 (significant success)   unknown

Political and economic variables

☐ Companion policies: J (covert), Q (quasi-military), or R (regular military)   Q

☐ International cooperation with sender, scaled from 1 (none) to 4 (significant)   4

☐ International assistance to target: A (if present)   —

☐ Sanctions period (years)   1+

☐ Economic health and political stability of target, scaled from 1 (distressed) to 3 (strong)   2

☐ Presanction relations between sender and target, scaled from 1 (antagonistic) to 3 (cordial)   2

☐ Type of sanction: X (export), M (import), F (financial)   X,M,F

☐ Cost to sender, scaled from 1 (net gain) to 4 (major loss)   4

Comments

Although the outcome of this case was still unclear as this book went to press, the authors are relatively optimistic that sanctions will contribute to a positive outcome—the withdrawal of Iraqi troops from Kuwait, the release of all hostages, and the restoration of a credible, independent government in Kuwait—but not the complete defeat of Saddam Hussein.

Bibliography

Economic Intelligence Unit. 1990. *EIU Country Profile 1989–90: Iraq.* London: The Economist Publications.

International Monetary Fund. 1989. *Direction of Trade Statistics Yearbook.* Washington.

Organization for Economic Cooperation and Development. *Foreign Trade by Commodity.* Various issues.

Rogers, Scott. 1990. "Invasion of Kuwait: Iraq's Potential Gains and Losses." *World Markets Bulletin,* 18 September.

US Department of Commerce. 1989. *Foreign Economic Trends and Their Implications for the United States: Iraq.* FET 89–98. September. Washington.

OTHER PUBLICATIONS FROM THE INSTITUTE

October 1990

POLICY ANALYSES IN INTERNATIONAL ECONOMICS

1 The Lending Policies of the International Monetary Fund
John Williamson/*August 1982*
$8.00   0-88132-000-5   72 pp

2 "Reciprocity": A New Approach to World Trade Policy?
William R. Cline/*September 1982*
$8.00   0-88132-001-3   41 pp

3 Trade Policy in the 1980s
C. Fred Bergsten and William R. Cline/*November 1982*
(Out of print)   0-88132-002-1   84 pp
Partially reproduced in the book *Trade Policy in the 1980s.*

4 International Debt and the Stability of the World Economy
William R. Cline/*September 1983*
$10.00   0-88132-010-2   134 pp

5 The Exchange Rate System
John Williamson/*September 1983, 2nd ed. rev. June 1985*
(Out of stock)   0-88132-034-X   61 pp

6 Economic Sanctions in Support of Foreign Policy Goals
Gary Clyde Hufbauer and Jeffrey J. Schott/*October 1983*
$10.00   0-88132-014-5   109 pp

7 A New SDR Allocation?
John Williamson/*March 1984*
$10.00   0-88132-028-5   61 pp

8 An International Standard for Monetary Stabilization
Ronald I. McKinnon/*March 1984*
$10.00   0-88132-018-8   108 pp

9 The Yen/Dollar Agreement: Liberalizing Japanese Capital Markets
Jeffrey A. Frankel/*December 1984*
$10.00   0-88132-035-8   86 pp

Subsidies in International Trade
Gary Clyde Hufbauer and Joanna Shelton Erb/*1984*
$35.00 (cloth only)   0-88132-004-8   299 pp

International Debt: Systemic Risk and Policy Response
William R. Cline/*1984*
$30.00 (cloth only)   0-88132-015-3   336 pp

Trade Protection in the United States: 31 Case Studies
Gary Clyde Hufbauer, Diane E. Berliner, and Kimberly Ann Elliott/*1986*
$25.00   0-88132-040-4   371 pp

Toward Renewed Economic Growth in Latin America
Bela Balassa, Gerardo M. Bueno, Pedro-Pablo Kuczynski, and
Mario Henrique Simonsen/*1986*
$15.00   0-88132-045-5   205 pp

American Trade Politics: System Under Stress
I. M. Destler/*1986*
$30.00 (cloth)   0-88132-058-7   380 pp
$18.00 (paper)   0-88132-057-9   380 pp

The Future of World Trade in Textiles and Apparel
William R. Cline/*1987, rev. ed. June 1990*
$20.00   0-88132-110-9   344 pp

Capital Flight and Third World Debt
Donald R. Lessard and John Williamson, editors/*1987*
(Out of stock)   0-88132-053-6   270 pp

The Canada–United States Free Trade Agreement: The Global Impact
Jeffrey J. Schott and Murray G. Smith, editors/*1988*
$13.95   0-88132-073-0   211 pp

Managing the Dollar: From the Plaza to the Louvre
Yoichi Funabashi/*1988, 2nd ed. rev. 1989*
$19.95   0-88132-097-8   307 pp

World Agricultural Trade: Building a Consensus
William M. Miner and Dale E. Hathaway, editors/*1988*
$16.95   0-88132-071-3   226 pp

Japan in the World Economy
Bela Balassa and Marcus Noland/*1988*
$19.95   0-88132-041-2   306 pp

America in the World Economy: A Strategy for the 1990s
C. Fred Bergsten/*1988*

$29.95 (cloth)	0-88132-089-7	235 pp
$13.95 (paper)	0-88132-082-X	235 pp

United States External Adjustment and the World Economy
William R. Cline/*May 1989*

$25.00	0-88132-048-X	392 pp

Free Trade Areas and U.S. Trade Policy
Jeffrey J. Schott, editor/*May 1989*

$19.95	0-88132-094-3	400 pp

Dollar Politics: Exchange Rate Policymaking in the United States
I. M. Destler and C. Randall Henning/*September 1989*

$11.95	0-88132-079-X	192 pp

Foreign Direct Investment in the United States
Edward M. Graham and Paul R. Krugman/*December 1989*

$11.95	0-88132-074-9	161 pp

Latin American Adjustment: How Much Has Happened?
John Williamson, editor/*April 1990*

$34.95	0-88132-125-7	480 pp

Completing the Uruguay Round: A Results-Oriented Approach to the GATT Trade Negotiations
Jeffrey J. Schott, editor/*September 1990*

$19.95	0-88132-130-3	256 pp

SPECIAL REPORTS

1 **Promoting World Recovery: A Statement on Global Economic Strategy**
by Twenty-six Economists from Fourteen Countries/*December 1982*

(Out of print)	0-88132-013-7	45 pp

2 **Prospects for Adjustment in Argentina, Brazil, and Mexico: Responding to the Debt Crisis**
John Williamson, editor/*June 1983*

(Out of print)	0-88132-016-1	71 pp

3 **Inflation and Indexation: Argentina, Brazil, and Israel**
John Williamson, editor/*March 1985*

(Out of print)	0-88132-037-4	191 pp

FORTHCOMING

Deficits and the Dollar Revisited: Retrospect and Prospect
Stephen Marris

International Adjustment and Finance: Lessons of 1985-1990
C. Fred Bergsten, editor

Has the Adjustment Process Worked?
Paul R. Krugman

The United States as a Debtor Country
C. Fred Bergsten and Shafiqul Islam

Equilibrium Exchange Rates: An Update
John Williamson

Managed and Mismanaged Trade: Policy Lessons for the 1990s
Laura D'Andrea Tyson

International Monetary Policymaking in the United States, Germany, and Japan
C. Randall Henning

The United States and Japan in the 1990s
C. Fred Bergsten, I. M. Destler, and Marcus Noland

The Outlook for World Commodity Prices
Philip K. Verleger, Jr.

The Future of the World Trading System
John Whalley

Export Disincentives and US Trade Policy
J. David Richardson

Reciprocity and Retaliation: An Evaluation of Aggressive Trade Policies
Thomas O. Bayard

The Effects of Foreign-Exchange Intervention
Jeffrey A. Frankel

Third World Debt: A Reappraisal
William R. Cline

The New Tripolar World Economy: Toward Collective Leadership
C. Fred Bergsten and C. Randall Henning

Trade Liberalization and International Institutions: What More Could Be Done?
Jeffrey J. Schott